THE
Cornerstone
ANTHOLOGY

THE
Cornerstone
ANTHOLOGY

Alvin Granowsky
Eden Force Eskin
John Dawkins

GLOBE BOOK COMPANY
Englewood Cliffs, N.J.

Alvin Granowsky, author of reading and literature textbooks, is the co-author of Globe's *Career Reading Skills.* He was a teacher of English in New York State junior and senior high schools and served as Director of Reading/Language Arts in the public schools of Greensboro, North Carolina, and Dallas, Texas.

Dr. Granowsky received his B.A. in English Literature from Colgate University, his M.A.T. in English Education from Harvard University, and his Ed.D. in Reading and Curriculum and Instruction from the University of Pennsylvania.

Eden Force Eskin, author and editor of language arts and social studies materials, has served as managing editor of a school dictionary and has been a contributing editor to dictionaries for all levels. In addition, she has contributed articles to reference books on subjects that include vocabulary development, English usage and style, and research and reference skills. She received her B.A. in English and American Literature from Brandeis University.

John Dawkins, author of reading and language arts textbooks, is the co-author of Globe's *Career Reading Skills.* He also writes professional articles on language structure and the teaching of reading and English. He has done extensive graduate work in linguistics and literature at the University of Chicago, where he received his A.M. degree in English Literature.

Dorothy Smith, consulting author, formerly taught English and language arts in the Dallas Independent School District, Dallas, Texas.

Consultants

Jonathan Swift, Director, School of Global Education, Livonia Public Schools, Livonia, Michigan, and past Chair, Secondary Section, National Council of Teachers of English

Stephanie Whitworth, Reading Consultant, Fulton County Schools, Atlanta, Georgia

Alyce Taylor, Curriculum Coordinator, Washoe County School District, Reno, Nevada

Cover: Anne Ricigliano
Cover photo: © Joe Viesti, Viesti Associates, Inc.

ISBN: 0-83590-057-6

Printed in the United States of America. 10 9 8 7 6 5 4 3 2

 Globe Book Company
A Division of Simon & Schuster
Englewood Cliffs, New Jersey

CONTENTS

UNIT 1: AMERICAN EXPERIENCE

UNIT 2: SEARCHING FOR YOURSELF

UNIT 3: MONSTERS AND MYSTERIES

UNIT 4: TRYING HARDER

UNIT 5: GREAT IDEAS

SKILL DEVELOPMENT

INTRODUCTION

Welcome to a new world of literature and reading. Sit back, relax, and get ready to enjoy the selections in every unit.

You will meet many new people in these pages. Some of them are authors. Others are characters in stories, plays, myths, legends, or poems. By getting to know these people through their statements and actions, you may also learn about yourself. In addition, you will experience the world of ideas and literature, of which these people are a part.

This book is divided into five units. Each unit looks at an important theme in literature and life.

As you read, you will learn new words. Words that may be unfamiliar to you are defined at the bottom of the page on which they appear. The words in **bold type** are most important. They are reviewed and appear in a helpful glossary at the back of the book.

While you read, and after you read, take the time to respond and react. The questions in "All Things Considered" will help you check your understanding. Then, in "Thinking It Through," you will have a chance to say, "This is the way I see it, and here is why."

Poetry is approached differently, as it should be. Each poem is followed by questions that help you appreciate the poem.

Lessons on literature, reading, and thinking follow the selections. New terms are defined and made clear by examples. As you learn, you will be encouraged to apply your new knowledge. A short composition activity wraps up each selection.

As you come to the end of each unit, you will find opportunities to review and extend your experiences with literature. Participate by "Speaking Up" and "Writing Your Own" description or story.

We welcome you with excitement to the world of reading and literature in *The Cornerstone Anthology.*

UNIT 1

AMERICAN EXPERIENCE

What is America to me,
A name, map, the flag I see,
A certain word, "Democracy,"
What is America to me?

from "The House I Live In"
by Lewis Allan and Earl Robinson

What is America to you? It is probably many different things. It may be the people who have sacrificed to make it strong. It may be the landscape where you live. It may be the history that belongs to each new generation.

In this unit, you will see America through the eyes of many people—an immigrant, a slave, a pioneer, a farmer, and others. As you read their stories, think about what America meant to each of them and, more important, what America means to you.

MAMA AND PAPA

by Kathryn Forbes

▶ People who came to America from other countries often tried to become "American." To some, being American meant being modern. To others it meant getting to know many different kinds of people. But few people would have tried to be modern in the way Mama does in this chapter from a well-loved book, *I Remember Mama*.

The years that Christine and I spent at Lowell High were good years, for they all flew by so quickly. Our hair, by some miracle, had turned a passable golden color, and we discovered that we had nice complexions and attractive teeth. Clothes and school activities became interesting subjects, and boys were fun to know.

I was finally asked to join the Mummers' Club at school. I wrote plays—most of them tragic—which I insisted upon producing. Christine headed the debating team and the honor society, and Nels was in his fourth year of premedical studies at the university across the bay.

Our Baby Kaaren had become a solemn, lovable treasure of six, and sturdy Dagmar spent her days in collecting stray dogs and cats and her nights in caring for them.

Little by little, the foreignness had disappeared almost entirely from our family life. Only on special occasions did Mama make the *lutefisk* or *fladbröd,* and she and Papa seldom spoke Norwegian anymore. They had learned to play cards and went often to neighborhood card parties or to shows.

But the Steiner Street house remained home in every sense of the word. We never even thought of it as a "boardinghouse," be-

- passable (PAS uh bul) **good enough**
- honor society (ON ur suh SY uh tee) **group of excellent students**
- **solemn** (SOL um) **very serious, not cheerful**
- *lutefisk* (LOOT fish) **Norwegian fishballs with sauce**
- *fladbröd* (FLAD brood) **Norwegian bread pudding**

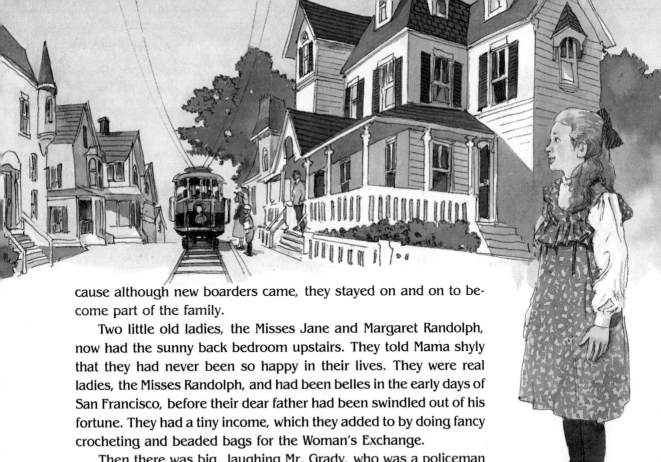

cause although new boarders came, they stayed on and on to become part of the family.

Two little old ladies, the Misses Jane and Margaret Randolph, now had the sunny back bedroom upstairs. They told Mama shyly that they had never been so happy in their lives. They were real ladies, the Misses Randolph, and had been belles in the early days of San Francisco, before their dear father had been swindled out of his fortune. They had a tiny income, which they added to by doing fancy crocheting and beaded bags for the Woman's Exchange.

Then there was big, laughing Mr. Grady, who was a policeman and a widower. He had a fascinating Irish brogue, and every payday he brought Miss Margaret and Miss Jane a box of fancy peppermints from the Pig 'n Whistle. He never learned that the gentle ladies could not stand the flavor of peppermint, and we young ones never told, because we were the final and grateful consumers.

Papa enclosed the huge basement room in beaverboard, cut windows, and laid a smooth pine floor. Mr. Lewis and Mr. Clark and the Stanton brothers had a great time helping him paint it. Mrs. Sam Stanton made cushions for the benches Papa built along the wall, and the Misses Randolph sewed fancy shades for all the lamps.

Professor Jannough was able to get an old practice piano, and Mr. Grady contributed his big old-fashioned phonograph.

- boarder (BOR dur) person who pays to live and eat in someone else's home
- belle (BELL) attractive, popular girl
- **swindle** (SWIN dul) cheat
- brogue (BROHG) Irish accent

3

Nearly every evening the folks would congregate there to visit. They would listen to the phonograph or have the professor play for them, or beg Mrs. Jannough to sing her Polish lullabies.

There, too, Christine and Nels and I brought our friends and gave our parties. We considered ourselves blessed above all the other young folk we knew, who had to entertain in small apartments or flats.

The newest addition to our group was Mr. Johnny Kenmore and his frail and lovely wife. Mr. Kenmore was that exciting thing, an aviator, and every Sunday he took people for airplane rides over the marina. Whenever he flew, Mrs. Kenmore would come out into the kitchen and sit with Mama until the telephone rang and Mr. Kenmore said he was on his way home.

Papa loved to talk of flying and of airplanes, and to hear Mr. Kenmore tell of his many adventures. Papa's eyes would sparkle and shine and he would shake his head in admiration.

"What a wonderful thing," he would marvel. "To fly. To *fly!*"

"It's a great feeling," Mr. Kenmore agreed.

"To fly," Papa said. "High up. Like a bird."

"I'll take you up sometime," Mr. Kenmore offered carelessly one evening. "Any time you say."

Papa sat up eagerly, and I heard Mama catch her breath.

I guess Papa heard her, too, because he sat back in his chair, and after a while he said, "N-n-no, no, I guess not."

"Oh, come on," Mr. Kenmore coaxed, "you'd love it."

"Would be wonderful," Papa said wistfully. "Just once—to fly."

He looked at Mama again, but her face was bent over her sewing. So Papa said, "Thank you for your offer, Mr. Kenmore, but no. Better, perhaps, that I stay on the ground."

Mr. Kenmore started to speak again, but Mrs. Kenmore stood up quickly and her usually quiet voice was shrill. "Stop urging, Johnny," she cried, *"please."*

So nothing more was said about flying, and Papa didn't mention it again. But I could see that Mama was worried about something. Every once in a while she stole quick little glances at Papa's face, trying, perhaps, to read his thoughts.

- aviator (AY vee ay tur) **person who pilots an airplane**
- **shrill** (SHRILL) **high, sharp sound**

One day as I helped her hang out the clothes, she looked up at the sky and said: "This flying, I do not understand it. It is a frightening thing."

When I didn't answer, she continued, as if she were thinking out loud, "To want to go so high. So far away."

Mama never served meals to the boarders on Sunday. That was the family's day. One Sunday, Papa and Nels had gone over to the bay to watch the fishermen. Aunt Sigrid and Uncle Peter had taken Dagmar and Kaaren to the park. Christine and I went down to the library to catch up on our homework.

But by five o'clock we had all returned and gathered in the kitchen to wonder why Mama wasn't home preparing our dinner for us.

Just as Papa had decided to telephone Aunt Jenny's to ask if Mama were there, we heard her quick step in the hall. She came into the kitchen in a rush, her cheeks pink and her eyes glowing.

"Papa," she said, "Papa, you must go flying. You must go with Mr. Kenmore next Sunday."

I had never seen Papa look more surprised. "You mean," he said, "that you would not mind?"

"So badly have you wanted to go," Mama said. "And you are right. It is wonderful."

"But how—"

"Oh," Mama said, "I go up today to see if it safe. Is all right now for you to go."

And Mama could not understand why Papa and the rest of us laughed until we cried.

ALL THINGS CONSIDERED _____

1. Christine and Nels are the storyteller's (a) niece and nephew. (b) sister and brother. (c) classmates.
2. Nels is (a) studying to be a doctor. (b) a fisherman. (c) working in the family business.
3. The family in the story is trying to (a) keep all its Norwegian customs. (b) copy the way the boarders behave. (c) be more American.
4. All of the following are boarders *except* (a) Miss Jane Randolph. (b) Aunt Jenny. (c) Mr. Grady.
5. When Papa fixes up the basement, (a) the boarders help him. (b) the children object. (c) Mama does all the sewing work.
6. The family finds Mr. Johnny Kenmore exciting because he (a) reads interesting books. (b) plays cards well. (c) flies an airplane.
7. The first person in the family who wants to fly in an airplane is (a) Mama. (b) Christine. (c) Papa.
8. At first, Mama (a) tries to talk the family into letting her fly. (b) enjoys taking flying lessons. (c) does not want Papa to fly.
9. On Sunday, the family is surprised because (a) Mama is not home to make dinner. (b) the boarders decided not to eat at home. (c) Nels and Papa went fishing.
10. Mama comes home all excited because (a) she watched Mr. Kenmore fly an airplane. (b) she found out that Papa had gone up in an airplane. (c) she has flown in an airplane.

THINKING IT THROUGH _____

1. The people living in the house on Steiner Street are not all related to each other. (a) Find at least two things in the story that show they get along well with one another. (b) How do you know that the boarders in the house come from different backgrounds?
2. Like many people who come to America, the family in the story is trying to take advantage of the opportunities America offers. (a) How do Christine, Nels, and the storyteller each try to succeed in school? (b) How does the family try to help the children reach their goals? (c) Do you think that families still help each other get ahead today? If so, how?
3. (a) What kind of a person do you think Mama is? (b) Does she actually tell Papa what she does not want him to do? (c) Why do you think she does something that she is afraid to let Papa do?

Literary Skills

Character, Plot, Setting, and Theme

There are several important things to think about in most good stories. They are character, plot, setting, and theme.

The **characters** are *who* is in a story. Usually the characters are people, such as Mama and Papa in the story you just read. Sometimes characters may be animals, space creatures, or even things.

The **setting** is *where* and *when* a story takes place. For example, "Mama and Papa" takes place in the Steiner Street House. The story occurs during the years when Christine and the speaker are of high school age.

The **plot** is *what happens* in a story. As you read, you find out what the characters do and what happens to them. In "Mama and Papa," the plot centers on Papa's wish to fly.

The **theme** is the most important idea of a story. Is there one important idea or theme in "Mama and Papa"?

Here are some sentences from "Mama and Papa." Decide whether each sentence describes a character, a setting, or a plot. To help you figure it out, ask "who?" "where?" "when?" and "what happens?"

1. "Christine headed the debating team and the honor society."
2. "But the Steiner Street house remained home in every sense."
3. "So nothing more was said about flying, and Papa didn't mention it again. But I could see that Mama was worried about something."

Composition

Follow your teacher's instructions before completing *one* of these writing assignments.

1. If you lived in the Steiner Street house, which person do you think would be your closest friend? In two or three sentences, explain why you would choose this person.
2. The author describes the basement of the Steiner Street house as a happy place. Choose one place that you like. Write a paragraph about it. Tell why you enjoy spending time there.

THE FIRST DAY

by George and Helen Papashvily

▶ Imagine that you are about to land in a new country. You do not have money, friends, or a job. It could be scary. Or it could be an adventure, too.

At five in the morning the engine stopped, and after 37 days the boat was quiet.

We were in America.

I got up and stepped over the other men and looked out the porthole. Water and fog. We were anchoring off an island. I dressed and went on deck.

Now began my troubles. What to do? This was a Greek boat and I was steerage, so of course by the time we were halfway out I had spent all my landing money for extra food.

Hassan, the Turk, one of the six who slept in the cabin with me, came up the ladder.

"I told you so," he said as soon as he saw me. "Now we are in America and you have no money to land. They send you home. No money, no going ashore. What a disgrace. In your position, frankly, I would kill myself."

Hassan had been satisfied to starve on black olives and salt cheese all the way from Gibraltar. He begrudged every piece of lamb I bribed away from the first-cabin steward.

- steerage (STEER ij) least expensive way to travel in a ship
- **begrudge** (bi GRUJ) feel angry at something another person has

8

We went down the gangplank into the big room. Passengers with pictures in their hands were rushing around to match them to a relative. Before their tables the inspectors were busy with long lines of people.

The visitors' door opened and a fellow with a big pile of caps, striped blue and white cotton caps with visors and a top button, came in. He went first to an old man with a fur hat near the window, then to a Russian in the line. At last he came to me.

"Look," he said in Russian, "look at your hat. You want to be a greenhorn all your life? A fur hat! Do you expect to see anybody in the U. S. A. still with a fur hat? The inspector, the doctor, the captain—are they wearing fur hats? Certainly not."

I didn't say anything.

"Look," he said. "I'm sorry for you. I was a greenhorn once myself. I wouldn't want to see anybody make my mistakes. Look, I have caps. See, from such rich striped materials. Like railroad engineers wear, and house painters, and coal miners." He spun one around on his finger. "Don't be afraid. It's a cap in real American style. With this cap on your head, they couldn't tell you from a citizen. I'm positively guaranteeing. And I'm trading you this cap even for your old fur hat.

Trading even. You don't have to give me one penny."

Now it is true I bought my fur hat new for the trip. It was a fine skin, a silver lamb, and in Georgia it would have lasted me a lifetime. Still—

"I'll tell you," the cap man said. "So you can remember all your life you made money the first hour you were in America, I give you a cap and a dollar besides. Done?"

- gangplank (GANG plangk) **movable board for going on or off a ship**
- visor (VY zur) **front part of a cap that shades the eyes from sun**
- greenhorn (GREEN horn) **person who is new in a country**
- guarantee (gar un TEE) **promise that something is true**
- Georgia (JOR juh) **section of the Soviet Union**

I took off my fur hat and put on his cap. It was small and sat well up on my head, but then in America one dresses like an American and it is a satisfaction always to be in the best style. So I got my first dollar.

Ysaacs, a Syrian, sat on the bench and smoked brown paper cigarettes and watched all through the bargain. He was from our cabin, too. He knew I was worried about the money to show the examiners. But now, as soon as the cap man went on to the next customer, Ysaacs explained a way to get me by the examiners—a good way.

Such a very good way, in fact, that when the inspector looked over my passport and entry permit I was ready.

"Do you have friends meeting you?" he asked me. "Do you have money to support yourself?"

I pulled out a round fat roll of green American money—tens, twenties—a nice thick pile with a rubber band around.

"Okay," he said. "Go ahead." He stamped my papers.

I got my baggage and took the money roll back again to Ysaac's friend, Arapouleopolus, the moneylender, so he could rent it over again to another man. One dollar was all he charged to use it for each landing. Really a bargain.

On the outer platform I met Zurabeg, who had been down in steerage, too. But Zurabeg was no greenhorn coming for the first time. Zurabeg was an American citizen with papers to prove it, and a friend of Buffalo Bill besides. This Zurabeg first came to America 20 years before as a trick show rider. Later he was boss cook on the road with Buffalo Bill.

"Can't land?" he asked me.

"No, I can land," I said, "but I have no money to pay the little boat to carry me to shore."

"Listen, donkey-head," Zurabeg said, "this is America. The carrying boat is free. It belongs to my government. They take us for nothing. Come on."

So we got to the shore.

And there—the streets, the people, the noise! The faces flashing by—and by again.

We walked a few blocks through this before I remembered my landing cards and passport. I took them out and tore them into little pieces and threw them all in an ash can. "They can't prove I'm not a citizen, now," I said. "What we do next?"

"We get jobs," Zurabeg told me. "I show you."

We went to an employment agency. Conveniently, the man spoke Russian. He gave Zurabeg a ticket right away to start in a Russian restaurant as first cook.

"Now, your friend? What can you do?" he asked me.

"I," I said, "am a worker in decorative leathers, particularly specializing in the ornamenting of whip handles according to the traditional designs."

- conveniently (kun VEEN yunt lee) **making it easy**
- traditional (truh DISH uh nul) **according to customs passed on from parents to children**

10

"My goodness!" the man said. "This is the U. S. A. No horses. Automobiles. What else can you do?"

Fortunately my father was a man of great foresight and I have two trades. His idea was that in the days when a man starves with one, by the other he may eat.

"I am also," I said, "a swordmaker. Short blades or long."

"A whip maker—a swordmaker. You better take him along for a dishwasher," he said to Zurabeg. "They can always use another dishwasher."

The restaurant was on a side street and the lady-owner spoke kindly. "I remember you from the tearoom," she said to Zurabeg. "I congratulate myself on getting you. You are excellent on the *piroshkis,* isn't it?"

"On everything, Madame," Zurabeg said grandly. "On everything. Buffalo Bill, an old friend of mine, has eaten thirty of my *piroshkis* at a meal. My friend"—he waved toward me—"will be a dishwasher."

I made a bow.

The kitchen was small and hot and fat—like inside of a pig's stomach. Zurabeg unpacked his knives, put on his cap, and, at home at once, started to dice celery.

"You can wash these," the owner said to me. "At four we have party."

It was a trayful of glasses. And such glasses—thin bubbles that would hardly hold a sip—set on stems. The first one snapped in my hand, the second dissolved, the third to tenth I got washed, the eleventh was already cracked, the twelfth rang once on the pan edge and was silent.

Perhaps I might be there yet, but just as I carried the first trayful to the service slot, the restaurant cat ran between my feet.

When I got all the glass swept up, I told Zurabeg, "Now, we have to eat. It's noon. I watch the customers eat. It makes me hungry. Prepare lamb and some cucumbers, and we enjoy our first meal for good luck in the New World."

"This is a restaurant with very strict organization," Zurabeg said. "We get to eat when the customers go, and you get what the customers leave. Try again with the glasses and remember my reputation. Please."

I found a quart of sour cream and went into the back alley and ate that and some bread and a jar of caviar, which was very salty—packed for export, no doubt.

The owner found me. I stood up. "Please," she said, "please go on. Eat sour cream. But after, could you go away? Far away? With no hard feelings. The glasses—the caviar—it's expensive

- *piroshki* (pi rush KEE) meat dumpling
- **reputation** (rep yuh TAY shun) idea that most people have of a person
- caviar (KAV ee ahr) tiny eggs of certain fish, usually very expensive

11

for me—and at the same time I don't want to make your friend mad. I need a good cook. If you could just go away? Quietly? Just disappear, so to speak? I give you five dollars."

"I didn't do anything," I said, "so you don't have to pay me. All in all, a restaurant probably isn't my fate. You can tell Zurabeg afterward."

She brought my cap and a paper bag. I walked for hours. I couldn't even be sure it was the same day. I tried some English on a few men that passed.

"What watch?" I said. But they pushed by me so I knew I had it wrong.

I tried another man. "How many clock?" He showed me on his wrist. Four-thirty.

A wonderful place. Rapidly, if one applies oneself, one speaks the English.

I came to a park and went in and found a place under a tree and took off my shoes and lay down. I looked in the bag the owner gave me. A bologna sandwich and a nickel—to begin in America with.

What to do? While I decided, I slept.

A policeman was waking me up. He spoke. I shook my head I can't understand. Then with motions, with gestures (really he was as good as puppets I saw once), he showed me to lie on the grass is forbidden. But one is welcome to the seats instead. All free seats in this park. No charge for anybody. What a country!

But I was puzzled. There were iron armrests every two feet along the benches. How could I distribute myself under them? I tried one leg. Then the other. But when I was under, how could I turn around? Then, whatever way I got in, my chin was always caught by the hoop. While I thought this over, I walked and bought peanuts for my nickel and fed the squirrels.

Lights began to come on in the towers around the park. It was almost dark. I found a sandy patch under a rock and went to sleep. I was tired from America and I slept some hours. It must have been almost midnight when the light flashed in my face. I sat up. It was from the headlight of a touring car choking along on the road below me. While I watched, the engine coughed and died. A man got out. For more than an hour he knocked with tools and opened the hood and closed it again.

Then I slid down the bank. In the war there were airplanes. Of course cars are much the same except, naturally, for the wings. I showed him with my hands and feet and head, like the policeman: "Give me the tools and let me try." He handed them over and sat down on the bench.

I checked the spark plugs and the distributor, the timer, and the coils. I looked at the fuel line, at the ignition, at the gas. In between, I cranked. I cranked until I cranked my heart out onto the ground. Still the car wouldn't move.

- **gesture** (JESS chur) motion, hand signal
- **touring car** (TOO ring KAHR) old car with a top that folds down and a crank to start it moving
- **distributor** (dis TRIB yoo tur) part of a car's engine

12

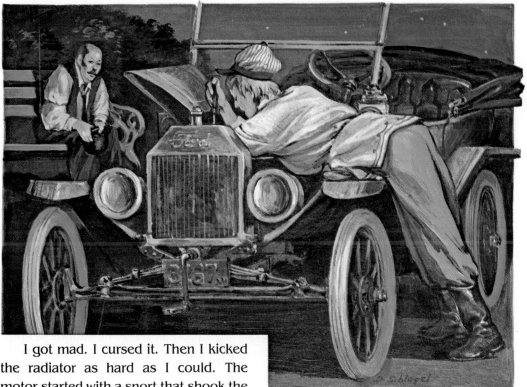

I got mad. I cursed it. Then I kicked the radiator as hard as I could. The motor started with a snort that shook the car like a leaf.

The man came running up. He was laughing and he shook my hands and talked to me and asked questions. But the policeman's method didn't work. Signs weren't enough. I remembered my dictionary—English-Russian, Russian-English—it went both ways. I took it from my blouse pocket and showed the man. Holding it under the headlights, he thumbed through.

"Work?" he found in English.

I looked at the Russian word beside it and shook my head.

"Home?" he turned to that.

"No," again.

I took the dictionary. "Boat. Today."

"Come home"—he showed me the words—"with me"—he pointed to himself. "Eat. Sleep. Job." It took him quite a time between words. "Job. Tomorrow."

"Automobiles?" I said. We have the same word in Georgian.

"Automobiles!" He was pleased we found one word together.

We got in his car, and he took me through miles and miles of streets with houses on both sides of every one of them until we came to his own. We went in and we ate and we drank and ate and drank again. For that, fortunately, you need no words.

Then his wife showed me a room and I went to bed. As I fell asleep, I thought to myself: Well, now, I have lived one whole day in America and—just like they say—America is a country where anything, anything at all can happen.

And in 20 years—about this—I never changed my mind.

13

ALL THINGS CONSIDERED ───────────────

1. The story begins (a) on a boat. (b) in Greece. (c) in a hotel.
2. The storyteller trades his hat for a cap because (a) he wants to keep his head warm. (b) an old man tells him that he cannot land without it. (c) he wants to look like an American.
3. In order to prove to the inspector that he has enough money, the storyteller (a) shows his dollar bill. (b) mentions a job that is waiting for him. (c) rents a roll of money from a moneylender.
4. The first person who helps him find work is (a) a Russian American named Zurabeg. (b) a Syrian named Ysaacs. (c) the man driving the car.
5. Zurabeg used to work for (a) an employment agency. (b) Buffalo Bill. (c) an automobile repair shop.
6. The storyteller was trained to be (a) a leather worker and a swordmaker. (b) an engineer and an automobile mechanic. (c) a waiter and a cook.
7. He loses his first job because he (a) refuses to wash dishes. (b) cannot speak English. (c) breaks glasses and eats caviar.
8. In the park, the policeman (a) tells him that he cannot sleep on the grass. (b) arrests him for making noise. (c) explains that he can't eat in the park.
9. He believes that he knows something about cars because (a) he used to own one. (b) cars are not too different from airplanes. (c) he used to work in a car repair shop.
10. As thanks for his help, the car owner (a) finds him a hotel room and a job. (b) pays him for his work. (c) takes him home and promises him a job.

THINKING IT THROUGH ───────────────

1. (a) Do you think that the storyteller made a good deal in exchanging his hat for the cap? (b) What part of the deal proved to be important to him? (c) Why was it important for him to look like an American?
2. The storyteller has been trained in two trades. Why is he willing to work as a dishwasher?
3. Because the storyteller cannot speak English, he has to find other ways to "talk" to people. (a) Describe two ways he manages to "talk" to people who do not speak his language. (b) Why does he need to "talk"?
4. How difficult would it be for you to land in a new country with no money and no friends? (a) Discuss some of the skills you would need to get along. (b) What kind of attitude would help you the most? (c) Does the storyteller have the skills and attitude you described?

Literary Skills

Understanding Characters

Writers use several different ways to describe the characters in a story. One way is to *state something directly,* as in the following description of Zurabeg:

Zurabeg was an American citizen with papers to prove it, and a friend of Buffalo Bill besides. This Zurabeg first came to America 20 years before as a trick show rider. Later he was boss cook on the road with Buffalo Bill.

What kind of picture does that description give you of Zurabeg?

Another way writers describe a character is through *spoken words.*

When the restaurant owner fires him, the storyteller says, "I didn't do anything, so you don't have to pay me. All in all, a restaurant probably isn't my fate."

What did you learn about the storyteller from what he says?

Another important way to learn about a character is by noticing how the character *behaves.*

You learn a lot about the storyteller by the way he behaves. For example, he tries to help the man fix his car even though he is tired and cold and without a place to sleep. From that you learn that the storyteller is kind and generous.

Composition

Follow your teacher's instructions before completing *one* of these writing assignments.

1. The storyteller does not describe himself, yet you know something about him. Write four sentences about the character who is telling the story. Use things you learned in the story to help you.
2. How would you feel if you found yourself in a strange country where you did not speak the language and did not know anybody? Write a paragraph telling some of the problems you might have and how you would handle them.

15

▶ This poem tells of two different ways people are Americans.
There are really two different speakers. See if you can tell
where the speaker changes.

I AM AN AMERICAN

by Elias Lieberman

I am an American.
My father belongs to the Sons of the Revolution;
My mother, to the Colonial Dames.
One of my ancestors pitched tea overboard in Boston Harbor;
Another stood his ground with Warren;
Another hungered with Washington at Valley Forge.
My forefathers were Americans in the making:
They spoke in her council halls;
They died on her battle-fields;
They commanded her troop-ships;
They cleared her forests.
Dawns reddened and paled.
Staunch hearts of mine beat fast at each new star
In the nation's flag.
Keen eyes of mine foresaw her greater glory:
The sweep of her seas,
The plenty of her plains,
The man-hives in her billion-wired cities.
Every drop of blood in me holds a heritage of patriotism.
I am proud of my past.
I am an AMERICAN.

I am an American.
My father was an atom of dust,
My mother a straw in the wind,
To His Serene Majesty.

- **Warren** general at the Battle of Bunker Hill
- **staunch** (STAWNCH) steady and true
- **heritage** (HEH ri tij) things we inherit from our ancestors
- **atom** (AT um) tiny bit
- **serene** (suh REEN) very calm; "Serene Majesty" is a title used by some kings, queens, emperors, and empresses.
- **Siberia** (sy BEER ee uh) cold northern part of the Soviet Union, used as a place of punishment

One of my ancestors died in the mines of Siberia;
Another was crippled for life by twenty blows of the knout.
Another was killed defending his home during the massacres.
The history of my ancestors is a trail of blood
To the palace-gate of the Great White Czar.
But then the dream came—
The dream of America.
In the light of the Liberty torch
The atom of dust became a man
And the straw in the wind became a woman
For the first time.
"See," said my father, pointing to the flag that fluttered near,
"That flag of stars and stripes is yours;
It is the emblem of the promised land.
It means, my son, the hope of humanity.
Live for it—die for it!"
Under the open sky of my new country I swore to do so;
And every drop of blood in me will keep that vow.
I am proud of my future.
I am an AMERICAN.

WAYS OF KNOWING* _____

1. (a) Who is the first speaker? How long have the ancestors been Americans? (b) Who is the second speaker? How long have the ancestors been Americans?
2. What is meant by "the man-hives in her billion-wired cities"?
3. How has the second American's life been changed by America?
4. What does the poet mean by "an atom of dust" and "a straw in the wind"?
5. (a) Why is the first American proud of the past? (b) Why is the second proud of the future? (c) How have wars made America important to each?
6. Do you know someone who has come to America from another country? If so, describe how that person feels about America. Think about the likes and dislikes a newcomer may have.

- knout (NOWT) leather whip used in Russia
- **humanity** (hyoo MAN i tee) all people

*"A poem is a way of knowing"—John Hall Wheelock

▶ In 278 B.C., a great statue was built in the harbor of the Greek city of Rhodes. The statue was called the "Colossus of Rhodes." It was one of the great wonders of the world.

Emma Lazarus wrote a poem for a modern statue. Her poem can be found at the base of the Statue of Liberty in New York harbor.

from THE NEW COLOSSUS

by Emma Lazarus

"Give me your tired, your poor,
Your huddled masses yearning to breathe free,
The wretched refuse of your teeming shore.
Send these, the homeless, tempest-tossed to me—
I lift my lamp beside the golden door!"

WAYS OF KNOWING

1. (a) Who is speaking in this poem? (b) To whom is she speaking?
2. What is "the golden door"?
3. (a) What is "the new Colossus"? (b) Why do you think the poet used that name?

- **wretched** (RECH id) very unhappy, miserable
- refuse (REFF yoos) **things thrown away**
- **teeming** (TEEM ing) crowded and moving
- tempest (TEM pust) **big storm**

18

Oral Interpretation

Oral interpretation means reading aloud with expression. It is an important reading skill. When you read aloud, you may have to ask yourself: What would be the best way to read this?

First, make sure you are able to pronounce all the words and know their meanings. A dictionary can help you with any words you might not know. The vocabulary lists at the bottom of this book's pages will also be a helpful guide to pronunciation and meaning.

Once you are sure of the words, think about what kind of person would be saying them. Think about which words are most important. Then plan how you would say each part.

Choose one of the sections in "I Am an American" or the selection from "The New Colossus." Practice reading aloud in a place where you can be alone. Then read aloud to a family member or a classmate. Did the message of the poem make sense to the listener?

Composition

Follow your teacher's instructions before completing *one* of these writing assignments.

1. Choose four famous Americans about whom you know something. Write a sentence about each person to tell how that person became an American. Do not use the person's name in your sentences so your classmates can try to guess who you are describing. Read each sentence aloud in class.

2. It is often said that there were seven great wonders of the ancient world. What would you consider a great wonder of our world? Choose one thing and write a paragraph telling why you think it should be considered a wonder of our modern world.

VOCABULARY AND SKILL REVIEW _____

Before completing the exercises that follow, you may wish to review the **boldfaced** words on the bottom of pages 2–18.

I. On a separate sheet of paper, write the *italicized* term that best fills the blank in each sentence. Each term should be used only once.

atom	*shrill*	*begrudge*	*gesture*	*humanity*
reputation	*solemn*	*swindle*	*teeming*	*wretched*

1. The dog seems to _____ any attention given to the cat.
2. The thief tried to _____ the couple out of their money.
3. When you don't know a word in another language, a hand _____ often helps.
4. The ballpark was _____ with excited fans.
5. The scientist hoped that her discovery would be of use to all _____ .
6. The baby cried when she heard the sharp, _____ sound.
7. Martin felt _____ after learning that he had failed the test.
8. The witness took a _____ oath before the judge to tell the truth.
9. The ant picked up a small _____ of food, and climbed into the anthill.
10. He has a _____ for honesty and loyalty.

II. The following poem is by Edgar Lee Masters, a poet born in Garnett, Kansas, in 1869. The poem comes from his best-known book of poetry, *Spoon River Anthology*. In *Spoon River Anthology,* Masters invented the make-believe town of Spoon River in the Midwest. Each poem tells about one person, now dead, who was supposed to live in that make-believe town.

   Read the poem and then answer the questions on a separate sheet of paper.

HAMILTON GREENE

by Edgar Lee Masters

I was the only child of Frances Harris of Virginia
And Thomas Greene of Kentucky,
Of valiant and honorable blood both.
To them I owe all that I became,
Judge, member of Congress, leader in the State.
From my mother I inherited
Vivacity, fancy, language;
From my father will, judgment, logic.
All honor to them
For what service I was to the people!

1. Who is the speaker of the poem? Is it the poet or Hamilton Greene?
2. Which of the several ways you learned to describe character on page 15 does this poem use? To help you decide, listen to the speaker. Is the speaker describing himself or is someone describing him?
3. (a) Name one quality that Hamilton Greene owes to his mother. (b) Name one quality he owes to his father.
4. Find the line in the poem that tells why Hamilton Greene thought it was important for him to be a judge, a member of Congress, and a leader in the State. Copy the line on your paper.

- valiant (VAL yunt) **brave**
- honorable (ON uhr uh bul) **deserving honor and respect**
- vivacity (vi VAS i tee) **liveliness, spirit**
- logic (LOJ ik) **clear thinking, good reasoning**

THE
BACKGROUND

A **biography** is a story written about the life of a real person. The person may be alive or dead. Biographies may be very short, or they may be as long as a whole book. There even have been biographies that are several books long.

To write a biography, a writer must get correct information on the person whose life story is being told. Some biographies are about someone the writer actually knew. Others are based on information the writer found in libraries, old newspapers and magazines, or government records. Sometimes talking to friends and relatives of the person gives the writer a more complete picture.

There is a special kind of biography called an autobiography. An **autobiography** is a biography of the writer's own life.

Langston Hughes (1902-1967)

If you wanted to find an American writer who wrote almost every kind of work possible, you would not have to look much further than Langston Hughes. He wrote poems, stories, novels, biographies, an autobiography, plays, children's stories, words for songs, newspaper and magazine articles, and even ideas for movies. His works have been translated into almost every major language. Hughes's writing is known for its jazz rhythms, a sense of humor, and a concern for black people.

He was born in Joplin, Missouri, but his family moved several times. He graduated from high school in Cleveland, Ohio. Like many other American writers, he traveled and did many kinds of work before he settled down to write full time. In 1921, his poem "The Negro Speaks of Rivers" was published. That helped him get a scholarship to Lincoln University in Pennsylvania. After graduation, he settled in Harlem, a section of New York City.

At the time, Harlem was a great center of writing, music, and art. Langston Hughes became one of the most important Americans in this exciting time for the arts. In addition to his own work, he put together collections of works by and about other black people. The story "Harriet Tubman, Liberator" is from a book of his biographies of great black people.

HARRIET TUBMAN, LIBERATOR

by Langston Hughes

▶ How could a woman who was born a slave become one of the most important figures in the war against slavery? How many readers would have the courage of this woman?

Some forty years before Abraham Lincoln signed the Emancipation Proclamation, Harriet Tubman was born on the eastern shore of Maryland, a slave, the property of the Broadas Plantation. One of 11 brothers and sisters, she was a homely child, moody and willful as well. Harriet was not cut out at all for slavery.

When Harriet was nine or ten years old, she was ordered into the Big House to assist the servants there. On her very first day, her mistress whipped her four times. Soon the white lady grew impatient with the seemingly stupid girl so she sent her to work in the fields. This Harriet liked better than washing pots, emptying garbage, and making kitchen fires. Even a slave out under the sky could look up at the sun and sometimes listen to birds singing in the bright air. But in her early teens a cruel thing happened to Harriet. From the slavemaster's point of view, it was her own fault.

One evening about dusk a slave boy wandered away from the corn husking to which he had been assigned and went down the road to a country store. An overseer pursued him, intending to whip him for leaving the place without permission. When he grabbed the boy in the store, the youth resisted. The white man then called upon other slaves standing about to help him. No one moved to do so. Then the boy started to run and the

- liberator (LIB uh ray tur) **person who sets others free**
- Emancipation Proclamation (ih man sih PAY shun prock luh MAY shun) **the announcement of freedom for slaves in the South, made by President Lincoln on January 1, 1863**
- moody (MOO dee) **having many changes of feelings or mood**
- willful (WIL ful) **wanting things one's own way**
- seemingly (SEEM ing lee) **the way things appear to be**
- overseer (OH vur see ur) **person in charge of slaves on a plantation**
- **pursue** (pur SOO) **chase, follow after**

24

overseer called to Harriet who was standing in the door to stop him. Harriet did not stop him nor did she move out of the door so that the overseer could get by. This made the white man so angry that he picked up an iron weight used on the scales and threw it at Harriet. The weight struck her in the head, making a deep gash and knocking her unconscious in the doorway. As she lay there bleeding, everyone thought she was dead, and she did not come to her senses again for days.

Tossing and turning on the floor of her mother's cabin, talking strange talk, Harriet caused the others in the family to conclude that she might be insane for life. Indeed, when she finally recovered, her master believed her to be half-crazy. Harriet did nothing to change his opinion—but she was not crazy. From the blow on her head there did result, though, an unusual condition. From that time on, all her life, Harriet could not prevent herself at times from unexpectedly blacking out, suddenly falling asleep no matter where she was. Then, after a spell, just as suddenly, she would come to herself again. And the deep dent that the iron weight made in her head remained until her death.

When Harriet grew to be a young woman she determined to escape from slavery. She had never learned to read or write, she had never seen a map, and she had no idea where the North—that place of freedom—was. But, nevertheless, she made up her mind to find it. Meanwhile, she had married. She urged her husband to come North with her but he refused. She also asked some of her brothers and sisters if they would go with her. Only two of them, Henry and Robert agreed, but at the last moment, they turned back. But with company or without, Harriet had made up her mind to risk the dangerous trek to freedom.

Before dawn one morning the young slave girl gathered her necessities into a bundle and started out. For fear that her mother and others would be greatly worried upon finding her missing, perhaps even thinking that slave-catchers had kidnapped her to sell into the Deep South, Harriet wanted in some way to tell them good-bye. But to do this was dangerous, both to them and to herself. So instead, in the early evening of the night she planned to leave, Harriet walked slowly through the slave quarters singing. She knew that all the slaves would understand her song—if not then, soon:

When dat old chariot comes,
I's gwine to leave you.
I's bound for de Promised Land.
Friends, I's gwine to leave you.
Farewell! Oh, farewell!
I's sorry friends to leave you.
Farewell! Oh, farewell!
But I'll meet you in de mornin'
On de other side of Jordan. . . .
Farewell! Oh, farewell!

- **determine** (di TUR min) decide, make up one's mind
- trek (TREK) journey, difficult trip

That night Harriet stole away across the dark fields and through the woods, guided only by the North Star, heading for freedom. When she reached the Choptank River, she trudged hour after hour upstream, for by walking in water bloodhounds trained to scent runaways could not trail her. Eventually she found a sheltering place with kindly Quakers whom she knew to be friendly to escaping slaves. There she was rested and fed and given directions for crossing into Delaware. Finally Harriet reached Philadelphia where she found work, and was no longer anybody's slave. But to Harriet, the North was not heaven so long as her friends and kinfolks remained in the slave country. Almost immediately she began to make plans to go back South to lead others along the hazardous road to freedom. In the years to come, it was as a liberator of slaves that Harriet Tubman became famous. She became one of the most successful conductors in the Underground Railroad, noted for her courage and her cunning. At one time a reward of $40,000 was offered for her capture.

• cunning (KUN ing) cleverness; sly, clever behavior

The *Underground Railroad* was a widespread system of aiding escaped slaves that the Quakers and other friends of freedom had established. Such friends set up way stations along several routes from South to North at which runaways could be sure of assistance. Along these routes slaves were hidden in barns, corncribs, attics, cellars, sometimes even churches. They were provided with hot food, warm clothing, perhaps a little money, and information as to where to find the next friendly family. Passwords, or the correct number of raps on a door in the night, were given. Above all from such friends came the knowledge that not all whites were out to harass and endanger those who sought escape from bondage.

It was dangerous, and eventually illegal, for whites to engage in such activities. But it was doubly dangerous for a Negro to do so, and especially for an escaped slave such as Harriet Tubman. But Harriet did not let fear stand in her way. Most former slaves, once having escaped, never ventured back into slave territory again. But Harriet returned to the South more than 19 times, and each time she brought back with her to the North a band of fugitives. None were ever captured. As a conductor on the Underground Railroad she once said, "I never run my train off de track, and I never lost a passenger." It is estimated that she brought more than 300 slaves to freedom in the ten years between 1850 and 1860.

To earn money, Harriet worked between trips as a servant or hotel maid in Pennsylvania and New Jersey. After the cruel Fugitive Slave Law was passed in 1850, which permitted escaped slaves (and even free Negroes falsely charged as slaves) to be seized in the North and sent back in chains to the South, Harriet had to accumulate enough money to buy train tickets for her fugitives all the way through the Free States to Canada. In Canada slave catchers did not operate. But from Maryland to the Canadian border was almost 500 miles—a long journey for a man or a woman with nothing. Her tales of adventure are beyond anything in fiction. . . . The slaves called her Moses.

Numerous examples of Harriet Tubman's heroism have been recorded. One example is in Troy, New York. There, one day in 1869 while on her way to an anti-slavery meeting in New England, she heard that a runaway slave named

- harass (huh RAS) **give trouble to; bother a lot**
- **bondage** (BON dij) **slavery**
- venture (VEN chur) **dare going; take a risk of going**
- fugitive (FYOO jih tiv) **runaway, one who escapes**
- Moses (MOH zuz) **in the Old Testament, Moses led his people out of slavery in Egypt into the promised land**

27

Charles Nalle was that very afternoon in federal court for return to slavery. Immediately Harriet sprang into action, organized a rescue party of free Negroes and whites and arranged to have a boat ready to take Nalle across the river to Albany as soon as he could be kidnapped from the court. She had no difficulty in getting followers for this daring attempt. The abolitionists believed that whether a rescue attempt failed or not, it got headlines in all the papers, served to keep antislavery sentiment alive, and was worth a hundred speeches.

By pretending to be a crippled old woman of no importance, Harriet hobbled into the courtroom to watch and wait for the proper moment to give a signal to the crowd outside. When they prepared to move the prisoner, Harriet seized the astonished slave and the crowd in the street immediately gathered about them. Harriet and Nalle made for the river but officers overtook them. A battle went on for hours between officers and abolitionists that day and both Harriet and Nalle were injured in the struggle. But finally the police were bested and the boat with the fugitive started for Albany. There, another battle with the authorities took place but eventually Nalle got away. That night he was safely hidden in a wagon bound for Canada. But Harriet Tubman had to go into hiding, for the next day her name made headlines throughout the nation. She had taken a prisoner away from government marshals.

Most of Harriet's rescues from slavery, however, were made without the help of crowds. They began in slave territory itself and were therefore full of danger. One of these dangers was betrayal. All who went North with her were, of course, sworn to secrecy but some grew weak and weary on the way. Frightened, cold and tired, they wanted to turn back. Once back on the plantation they could be beaten until they disclosed all they knew and the names of the other runaways as well as their leader. This Harriet could not permit. For weak-kneed freedom seekers she had a remedy. That remedy was a pistol that she carried in the folds of her dress. And weary ones who wanted to turn back were faced with this pistol and advised that they would either go on or be shot. They always found the strength to go on. In this way no one who started out for freedom with Harriet Tubman ever failed to become free. Her bands of runaways were never betrayed.

- Abolitionist (ab uh LISH un ist) **person working to put an end to slavery**
- **sentiment** (SEN tuh munt) **feeling, emotion**
- best (BEST) **defeat, win out over**

28

Because of her qualities as a leader, when the slave problem split the nation and the war between the North and South broke out, Harriet Tubman went into the service of the Union Army. She became the only woman in American military history ever to plan and conduct an armed expedition against enemy forces.

Harriet Tubman lived for a half-century after the Emancipation Proclamation was signed by President Lincoln and those for whom she cared so greatly were freed. Eventually the government granted her a very small pension of $20 a month. And from the book, *Harriet, the Moses of Her People,* which Sarah H. Bradford wrote, came a little money. But, ever generous to a fault, Harriet Tubman died poor at the age of nearly a hundred. Poor but remembered—for the whole city of Auburn, New York, where she died, went into mourning. And quite appropriately, her last rites as a soldier of liberation, were military. At her funeral the local post of the army presented the colors.

One of the most beautiful of tributes ever paid her came, however, from that other great fighter for the freedom of the slave, Frederick Douglass. In a letter to her years before she died, he wrote:

"The difference between us is very marked. Most that I have done and suffered in the service of our cause has been in public and I have received much encouragement at every step of the way. You, on the other hand, have labored in a private way. I have wrought in the day— you in the night. I have had the applause of the crowd and the satisfaction that comes of being approved by the multitude, while the most that you have done has been witnessed by a few trembling, scared, and footsore bondsmen and women whom you have led out of the house of bondage and whose heartfelt, *God bless you,* has been your only reward. The midnight sky and the silent stars have been the witnesses of your devotion to freedom and of your heroism."

- appropriately (uh PROHP ree ut lee) **fitting the purpose, properly**
- last rites **one of the last ceremonies performed for a dead or dying person**
- colors (KUL urz) **a nation's flag**
- tribute (TRIB yoot) **words of praise**
- marked (MAHRKT) **noticeable, easy to see**
- wrought (RAWT) **worked, made**
- multitude (MUL ti tood) **crowds of people**
- **heartfelt** (HAHRT felt) **sincere, honest**

ALL THINGS CONSIDERED _____

1. Harriet Tubman was born (a) before the Civil War. (b) during the Civil War. (c) after the Civil War.
2. One of the ways Harriet Tubman delivered "secret messages" to her friends and family was by (a) writing on moss. (b) using the army mail. (c) singing songs.
3. She managed to reach freedom (a) without help from anyone. (b) with some help from other slaves. (c) with some help from kindly Quakers.
4. The Underground Railroad was (a) a system of way stations where runaway slaves could hide and be helped. (b) a special railroad system that took slaves to Canada. (c) a train that took slaves back to their masters.
5. In a ten-year period Harriet Tubman (a) helped more than 300 slaves escape. (b) wrote many letters about the evils of slavery. (c) helped 19 families escape.
6. The law that made it necessary for slaves to escape to Canada was the (a) Emancipation Proclamation. (b) Fugitive Slave Law. (c) Anti-Abolitionist Law.
7. Harriet Tubman helped Charles Nalle escape by (a) pretending to be a crippled old woman. (b) hiding in a wagon outside the federal court. (c) taking a government marshal prisoner.
8. Harriet Tubman would not allow escaping slaves to return to their plantations because (a) the Underground Railroad would lose money. (b) a returned slave might make others decide not to escape. (c) a slave who returned might be forced to tell the names of other runaways as well as their leaders.
9. Harriet Tubman helped the Union Army by (a) serving as a general. (b) planning actions against the enemy. (c) acting as a pilot of a gunboat.
10. Harriet Tubman died (a) before the Civil War ended. (b) in a battle during the Civil War. (c) about 50 years after the Civil War.

THINKING IT THROUGH _____

1. Why is Harriet Tubman's life a good story for a biography? Tell which events in her life are the most exciting.
2. Name one person today who you think might have the courage of Harriet Tubman. What reasons might people have for *not* taking some of the risks she took?
3. (a) Why did some people call her the "Moses of her people"? (b) What is similar about what Moses did and what Harriet Tubman did? Look back at page 27 for information about Moses.

Literary Skills

Understanding Characters

On page 15, you learned three ways authors help you understand a character. One way is by describing the character directly. Another way is through the speeches and the thoughts of the character. A third way is by bringing the characters to life through their actions.

There is an additional way an author helps you understand a character. That way is by telling you what *others* say about the character. From the statements of others, you can *infer*, or suppose certain things about the character. Langston Hughes was able to find things that others said about Harriet Tubman. For example, a New England minister called her, "the greatest heroine of the age."

1. In a letter on page 29, Frederick Douglass describes how he feels about Harriet Tubman. Find three things he says about her. Write them on a separate sheet of paper.

2. Now, write five words that *you* would use to describe Harriet Tubman.

Composition

Follow your teacher's instructions before completing *one* of these writing assignments.

1. Think of three people about whom you might like to read or write a biography. Write a sentence about each person. In that sentence, name the person and tell one reason other people might find the person's life interesting.

2. The time in which Harriet Tubman lived helped her choose what she would do. What if she lived today? What important work would she do? Write a paragraph that begins, "If Harriet Tubman lived today. . ."

HARRIET TUBMAN

by Eloise Greenfield

▶ A poet can sometimes use very few words to get an idea across. What idea do you get from this poem?

Harriet Tubman didn't take no stuff
Wasn't scared of nothing neither
Didn't come in this world to be no slave
And wasn't going to stay one either

"Farewell!" she sang to her friends one night
She was mighty sad to leave 'em
But she ran away that dark, hot night
Ran looking for her freedom

She ran to the woods and she ran through the woods
With the slave catchers right behind her
And she kept on going till she got to the North
Where those mean men couldn't find her

Nineteen times she went back South
To get three hundred others
She ran for her freedom nineteen times
To save Black sisters and brothers
Harriet Tubman didn't take no stuff
Wasn't scared of nothing neither
Didn't come in this world to be no slave
And didn't stay one either

    And didn't stay one either

WAYS OF KNOWING

1. (a) What does the poet mean by "Harriet Tubman didn't take no stuff"? (b) Eloise Greenfield goes on to tell some ways she "didn't take no stuff." What are two of the ways?
2. Some facts in this poem can also be found in the Langston Hughes biography of Harriet Tubman. Find at least two facts in the poem that are also in the biography you read.
3. How is the poem different from the biography of Harriet Tubman? How is it similar?
4. (a) Do you think the speaker admires Harriet Tubman? (b) What parts of the poem make you think the way you do?
5. Look at the first four lines and the last five lines of the poem. (a) Which lines are the same? (b) Which are different?

32

WESTERN WAGONS

by Rosemary and Stephen Vincent Benét

▶ The pioneers who opened up America's West had many difficulties as well as joys. As you read the poem, think about the different hopes and problems the pioneers had.

They went with axe and rifle
    when the trail was still to blaze,
They went with wife and children
    in the prairie schooner days,
With banjo and with frying pan—
    Susanna, don't you cry!
For I'm off to California
    to get rich out there or die!

We've broken land and cleared it,
    but we're tired of where we are,
They say that wild Nebraska
    is a better place by far.
There's gold in far Wyoming,
    there's black earth in Ioway,
So pack up the kids and blankets,
    for we're moving out today.

The cowards never started
    and the weak died on the road,
And all across the continent
    the endless campfires glowed.
We'd taken land and settled—
    but a traveler passes by—
And we're going West tomorrow—
    Lordy, never ask us why!

We're going West tomorrow,
    where the promises can't fail.
O'er the hills in legions, boys,
    and crowd the dusty trail!
We shall starve and freeze and suffer.
    We shall die, and tame the lands.
But we're going West tomorrow
    with our fortune in our hands.

WAYS OF KNOWING

1. (a) What did the pioneers hope to find in California? (b) in Wyoming? (c) in Iowa? (d) Do you think most of the people who went west did or did not find what they hoped to find?

2. (a) How do you think the poets feel about the pioneers—do they admire them or think they are foolish? (b) Find some places in the poem that show what the poets feel about the pioneers.

3. (a) According to the poem, what did the pioneers face that made them need courage? (b) What do the poets say happened to the cowards and the weak people?

4. (a) Do you think there are any "trails to blaze" today? (b) If so, what are the trails? If not, why not?

5. The poets use rhymes in some lines, but not in others. (a) In each verse of the poem, which lines rhyme with each other? (Use numbers to give your answer.) (b) How does the rhyme make the poem seem like a song?

THE
BACKGROUND

A **legend** starts out with ordinary people or things. Often, the main character in a legend is a person who really did exist. But then the characters and events are described in a way that is exaggerated. The truth is stretched, and unbelievable events are mixed with real happenings.

Legends often grow around famous people. Because others admire them, details are added to the truth to make the famous person even more amazing. As the story is passed along, the extra details grow in number, and the events in the story become larger than life.

DAVY CROCKETT, FRONTIER FIGHTER

retold by Adrien Stoutenburg

▶ Davy Crockett was born in Tennessee in 1786. He was known for his sense of humor, so he probably would get a good laugh out of this legend about him. As you read, see if you can spot details that could be real as well as things that you feel are definitely made up.

The state of Tennessee wasn't born too many years before Davy Crockett was. In a way, Tennessee and Davy grew up together, and they both grew fast. Davy never became quite as tall as the Great Smoky Mountains, but by the time he was eight years old, he had a good start. All the Crockett family were on the large side. They had to be. Clearing out the wilderness by the Nolachucky River, where Davy first saw the sunrise, took grit and gumption. Davy had plenty of that, and more.

When people wanted to push posts down into the Nolachucky's bed to make supports for a bridge, they called Davy to jump on the posts. Davy would leap from one post to another, pushing them down with his bare feet. He had to be careful not to jump on a single post more than once or it might disappear into the river bottom.

He was a handy boy with an ax, too. There was wonderful timber in Tennessee. Many of the trees were so thick that the settlers couldn't cut them down. They had to tie chains around them and let the trees choke themselves to death. Davy could chop down the biggest sycamores or gum trees with the dull side of his ax blade.

As for hunting, Davy was the terror of the forest. The wild animals who were smart would crawl off and hide in their holes, pulling in their shadows after them, when they saw Davy coming with his rifle. At other times, when Davy wasn't hunting, the animals liked to spend the time of day with him and even talk a little. Davy always did know how to talk to animals.

One of the most special things about Davy was his grin. He could grin from ear to ear, and since his ears were rather far apart, this made for a sizable grin. He inherited his grin from his father, who, it was said, could grin in the teeth of a blizzard and change it into a rainbow. Davy didn't know how powerful his own grin was, until one day he grinned at a raccoon sitting in a tree. The raccoon tumbled to the ground, dead right down to its striped tail.

From then on, Davy did most of his raccoon hunting that way. One night, he was out hunting with his hound dog Rattler. It was a clear, crisp night, with the moon spangling the trees and the wild pea vines, and the frogs croaking in a way that sounded like

- grit (GRIT) **courage, brave stubbornness**
- gumption (GUMP shun) **bold courage, energy**
- spangling (SPANG ling) **causing to sparkle or glitter**

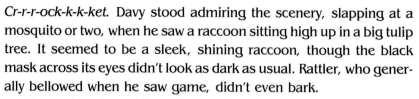

Cr-r-r-ock-k-k-ket. Davy stood admiring the scenery, slapping at a mosquito or two, when he saw a raccoon sitting high up in a big tulip tree. It seemed to be a sleek, shining raccoon, though the black mask across its eyes didn't look as dark as usual. Rattler, who generally bellowed when he saw game, didn't even bark.

Davy grinned up at the creature. He grinned for several minutes, but the raccoon stayed where it was.

"Maybe he can't see me clearly enough," Davy said to Rattler, who had gone to sleep. Davy moved where the moonlight was brighter. He set himself to grinning again, looking straight up at the raccoon. The raccoon didn't even twitch a whisker.

Davy began to get a little mad. Also, his grin-muscles were growing tired.

"You fool raccoon!" Davy yelled and shook his fist. "Don't you know you're supposed to fall dead when I grin at you? . . . If I have to stand here much longer grinning at you, I'll spoil, unless somebody covers me up with salt." . . . Davy was mad enough to spit nails, but curious, too, about the kind of raccoon that could be so stupid it didn't fall dead when it was supposed to. He went back for his ax. The raccoon was still in the tree when Davy returned. Since the tree was rather large, about ten-feet thick, he had to hit it twice with the sharp side of the ax.

The tree crashed down. Davy ran to it. Rattler woke up and ran beside him. Davy searched and Rattler sniffed. There was no sign of the raccoon. But there was something on a top branch that *looked* like a sleek, shining raccoon.

Davy stared at it, feeling foolish. He had been wasting his time grinning at a large knot on the tree branch. The knot was as bare of bark as a hound's tooth, for Davy had grinned the bark completely off the knot and off all one side of the tree. . . .

The time came for Davy to get married; so he did. He found a girl called Polly Finley Thunder Whirlwind, who was just the right-size wife for him, being about half as tall as the Northern Lights and twice as good at dancing. Polly had a good-sized grin, too, and she could laugh the mud chinks out of a log cabin. She laughed so hard dancing with Davy one winter that the cabin was full of holes. The wind naturally poked all its fingers through the holes until everyone nearly froze. They were all too busy shivering to have time for any-

---

• chink (CHINGK) **mud or material used to close up cracks**

thing else. Davy brought home a half-bald wolf to lie in front of the coldest blast and do the shivering for the whole family, which by then included several children.

Davy brought home another pet, a big, good-natured bear. Davy had gotten caught in an earthquake crack and couldn't get free. A bear passed by, and Davy hung on to him until the bear pulled him out of the crack. Davy was so thankful, he hugged the bear. The bear hugged Davy back and almost hugged him to death. Davy named the bear Death-Hug and told him that the next time either of them felt affectionate, it would be safer if they just shook hands. . . .

Around 1812 the War of 1812 began, and Davy went to fight the English and their allies, the Creek Indians. General Andrew Jackson was the leader of the American Army. Jackson was as full of dynamite as Davy, so they got along fine.

Davy and Andy Jackson beat the Indians so badly there wasn't much left except their war paint. Then Davy went down to New Orleans with Jackson and fought the British redcoats until the redcoats turned pale gray.

When there wasn't any fighting left to do, Davy went home to his spring planting. With him, he took another pet he had picked up in the southern swamp country, a slithering, good-natured, grinning alligator called Old Mississippi.

Davy never lost his own grin in all that time. It was his grin that made him decide to go into politics. In those days, just like today, the politician with the biggest grin was apt to win. Davy went into the woods and practiced making speeches to his animal friends.

The animals figured life would be safer for them if Davy were elected to the state legislature and had to spend his time making laws instead of hunting. So they cheered and paraded, barking and howling. It sounded to Davy as if they were saying, "VOTE FOR CROCKETT." It sounded that way to his neighbors, too, so they went along with the animals and elected Davy to the Tennessee legislature.

Davy put on his foxskin cap, dusted off his fringed buckskin jacket, and set out for Nashville. He rode Death-Hug part of the way and Old Mississippi the rest. Some of the other politicians snickered

- slithering (SLIH thur ing) to slide or slip along
- legislature (LEJ is lay chur) lawmakers, group of people who make laws

when they saw him, but Davy paid no attention. All his life he had lived by his motto—*Be sure you're right, then go ahead.* That's what he did then. The Tennessee settlers liked what he did so well that they finally elected him to Congress and sent him to Washington.

Andrew Jackson was president by then. When he saw Davy, he wrapped his arms around him so hard, Davy felt as if Death-Hug had grabbed him. Davy hugged Andy right back. It seemed they might crush each other to death, but when they both got blue in the face, they let go. . . .

Around that time, Davy moved his family to Tennessee's western border. The soil there was richer than a multimillionaire. Davy didn't bother to plant seeds in the regular way; he loaded his shotgun with the seeds and shot them into the ground. Pumpkin vines grew so fast that the pumpkins were worn out from being dragged across the soil. A man had to be a fast runner even to pick one.

Things went along fine, until the time of the Big Freeze. The winter started out cold and grew colder. By January, it was so cold that smoke froze in fireplace chimneys. Davy's hair froze so stiff he didn't dare comb it, for fear it would crack. One morning, daybreak froze solid. When that happened, it became so cold that people didn't even dare think about it, because their thoughts froze right inside their heads.

Davy told his wife Polly, "I reckon I better amble around the country and see what . . . the trouble is."

He put on a foxskin cap and several coonskin caps on over it. He piled on a half-dozen jackets and several pairs of bearskin mittens. He put on so many socks that he had to stand on his head between times to rest his feet. When he left, he took a homemade bear trap with him. Davy walked all day, going toward Cloud Mountain. To keep from freezing to death, he had to shinny up and down a tree all night.

In the morning, he saw what the trouble was. The machinery that kept the earth turning had frozen. The gears and wheels couldn't move, and the sun had been caught between two blocks of ice under the wheels. The sun had worked so hard to get loose that it had frozen in its own icy sweat.

Davy set the bear trap and caught an exceptionally fat bear. He took the bear and held him up over the earth's frozen machinery. Then Davy squeezed the bear until slippery, hot bear oil ran down over the wheels and gears. Next, he greased the sun's face until the oil melted the ice.

"Get moving!" Davy ordered and gave one of the wheels a kick with his heel.

There was a creak, which changed to a whir as the earth began to turn again. The sun rolled over and flipped free. As it circled past, Davy lit his pipe from its trailing sparks. Then he stuck an especially bright piece of sunrise in his pocket and started for home. . . .

- amble (AM bul) to walk slowly and easily
- **shinny** (SHIN ee) climb using the hands and legs
- gear (GEER) a wheel with teeth that connects to other wheels with teeth to make machines work
- whir (WUR) to make a buzzing or humming sound while moving quickly

Most of the people were grateful to Davy for breaking the cold snap, but some began saying Davy wasted his time in Congress dancing, parading, and telling tall tales. When voting time came again, enough people voted against Davy for him to lose the election.

"Well, sir!" said Davy, feeling hot around his collar. "From now on, the people of Tennessee will get no help from me! Anyhow, the state's getting too crowded. I'm moving to Texas!" . . .

Texas in those days was a part of Mexico. Davy and many of the other American settlers didn't like taking orders from the Mexican government. So Davy and his friends decided to make their own laws. When Santa Anna, the president of Mexico, heard this, he ordered his army to go northward and beat the tar out of the rebel Americans.

According to some people, Davy killed enough buffalo to feed the whole Texas army. He roasted the meat by racing along behind the flames of a prairie fire. Also, they say, he talked so many of the animals over to the American side, including wildcats, snakes, wolves, and mountain lions, that he scared the Mexican soldiers out of their boots.

The people who write history books say that Davy died fighting the Mexicans in San Antonio, Texas, at a fort called the Alamo. No one has ever said whether Death-Hug and Old Mississippi were with him. The chances are that they were and fought beside him to the end, since they have never been seen since.

One thing is certain. The sun comes up in Texas and in Tennessee every day, summer or winter. And the earth keeps turning smoothly, the way it's supposed to. If it ever does get frozen fast again, Davy Crockett may come along to squeeze some bear oil over the works and give the wheels a kick to start everything humming once more.

ALL THINGS CONSIDERED ⸺

1. Davy Crockett drove in the posts for a bridge by (a) using the dull end of an ax. (b) chaining trees to the river bottom. (c) jumping on them with his bare feet.
2. Davy's grin could (a) kill a raccoon. (b) melt the frozen earth. (c) tame a rattlesnake.
3. He couldn't kill the raccoon in the tree because (a) it was not really a raccoon. (b) his dog started to bark. (c) he couldn't grin anymore.
4. One of the things Davy liked about his wife, Polly, was that she was good at (a) hunting. (b) dancing. (c) chopping down trees.
5. Death-Hug was the name of (a) Davy's worst enemy. (b) a pet bear. (c) a tame wolf.
6. Davy Crockett fought in (a) the American Revolution. (b) the War of 1812. (c) the Civil War.
7. Davy's pets included (a) a frog and a rattlesnake. (b) a deer and a fox. (c) a bear and an alligator.
8. The first office he was elected to was (a) the state legislature. (b) Congress. (c) governor.
9. Davy planted his garden by (a) throwing seeds on the top of the soil. (b) shooting seeds into the ground. (c) placing seeds near the weeds.
10. The Big Freeze happened because (a) a comet had blocked the sun. (b) Davy's shadow had blocked the sun. (c) the machinery that kept the earth turning had frozen.

THINKING IT THROUGH ⸺

1. Would the story be as interesting if it did not add impossible details? Tell why or why not.
2. What part of the story do you think is the most fun? Why?
3. Look through the story again. See if you can find at least three details that you might also find in a biography.

Vocabulary and Sentence Meaning

Exaggeration

Authors very often use exaggeration in humorous writing. **Exaggeration** is the art of talking about something so that it seems bigger than it really is. It allows the author to make a point while it gives the reader a chance to laugh at the unbelievable.

The story says, "Davy could chop down the biggest sycamores or gum trees with the dull side of his ax blade." The reader gets the idea that Davy was good at chopping trees. At the same time, the reader does not actually have to believe the part about the dull side of his ax blade.

Look through the story again to find at least three other examples of exaggeration. For each example you find, on a separate sheet of paper write (a) the point that the writer is making, and (b) the exaggerated part that the reader does not actually have to believe.

Composition

Follow your teacher's instructions before completing *one* of these writing assignments.

1. Think of a famous person you know something about. Write three sentences describing this person in ordinary language. Then rewrite each sentence as an exaggeration. For example, your ordinary sentence could be, "He was very thin." Your exaggeration could be, "He was so thin he could slip through a keyhole."

2. Write a short paragraph about Davy's wife, Polly. Make the paragraph full of exaggerations. Along with your own ideas, you can use ideas from the story you just read.

Native Americans have put into poetry many ideas and feelings about their culture. The first poem comes from the Sia Indians. The second comes from the Inuit, or Eskimo.

A LESSON IN SHARING

A lame man asked Kaluarsuk to move in with him
and be his hunting mate.
This lame man wasn't able to walk
but he was good at paddling a kayak
so Kaluarsuk teamed up with him
and during the caribou season they shared the meat.

But when winter came, Kaluarsuk figured
that the lame one was not good for much
when it came to hunting at the breathing holes.
He couldn't get there over the ice with his bad legs, could he?
So when Kaluarsuk went out and caught seal
he did not share any with his lame buddy at home
and never gave him a bite to eat.

Two brothers next door saw the poor cripple dying of hunger
and took pity on him
and brought him into their house
telling their wives to feed him dried salmon to revive him.
And when the lame man was no longer weak from hunger
they took him with them to the breathing holes
by driving him there on a sled
and he turned out to be a good shot with a harpoon.
In fact he caught seals right away
which he shared with his old sharing partner,
Kaluarsuk, who had come along.

Kaluarsuk who had caught nothing himself that day
took his share of seal
and said, "How good to have hunting companion."
The two brothers spoke right up:
"You like having hunting mates now?
Then why didn't you think of your hunting mate
when you were the one catching seals!"

- caribou (KAH ri boo) **a kind of large reindeer**
- breathing holes **places in the ice where water animals come up to get air**
- revive (ri VYV) **to bring back to health or life**

LET OUR CHILDREN LIVE AND BE HAPPY

Let our children live and be happy.
Send us the good south winds.
Send us your breath over the lakes that
our great world may be made beautiful
and our people may live.
There, far off, my Sun Father arises,
ascends the ladder, comes forth from his place.
May all complete the road of life, may all
grow old.
May the children inhale more of the sacred
breath of life.
May all my children have corn that they
may complete the road of life.
Here sit down; here remain; we give you
our best thoughts.
Hasten over the meal road; we are jealous
of you.
We inhale the sacred breath through our
prayer plumes.

WAYS OF KNOWING

1. What is the most important idea of "Let Our Children Live and Be Happy"? Do you think that it is a universal idea—one that people all over the world share?

2. Three lines in "Let Our Children Live and Be Happy" begin with "May." How do those lines help get across the idea of the poem?

3. "A Lesson in Sharing" gets its message across with a story. What is the basic story?

4. (a) Would the poem "A Lesson in Sharing" be the same without the last words of the two brothers? (b) Would there be any difference in how the reader understood what was happening? (c) Who is that message really for?

5. Has anyone in your life ever acted like Kaluarsuk? If so, explain.

- **ascend** (uh SEND) go up, rise
- **plume** (PLOOM) large feather, used in some Indian ceremonies

PRAIRIE FIRE

by Laura Ingalls Wilder

▶ As America grew, its people moved west. Families, like the Ingalls family, moved onto the prairie, forcing many Native Americans to leave. The new families faced many dangers and had few neighbors nearby. When trouble came, they had to act quickly.

One day Mary and Laura were helping Ma get dinner. Baby Carrie was playing on the floor in the sunshine, and suddenly the sunshine was gone.

"I do believe it is going to storm," Ma said, looking out of the window. Laura looked, too, and great black clouds were billowing up in the south, across the sun.

Pet and Patty, the horses, were coming running from the field, Pa holding to the heavy plow and bounding in long leaps behind it.

"Prairie fire!" he shouted. "Get the tub full of water! Put sacks in it! Hurry!"

Ma ran to the well, Laura ran to tug the tub to it. Pa tied Pet to the house. He brought the cow and calf from the picket-line and shut them in the stable. Ma was pulling up buckets of water as fast as she could. Laura ran to get the sacks that Pa had flung out of the stable.

Pa was plowing, shouting at Pet and Patty to make them hurry. The sky was black now, the air was as dark as if the sun had set. Pa plowed a long furrow west of the house and south of the house, and back again east of the house. Rabbits came bounding past him as if he wasn't there.

Pet and Patty came galloping, the plow and Pa bounding behind them. Pa tied them to the north corner of the house. The tub was full of water. Laura helped Ma push the sacks under the water to soak them.

- billow (BIL oh) **rise in waves, swell up**
- bound (BOWND) **jump, leap**
- picket-line (PIK it LYN) **rope attached to a thick stick in the ground, used for keeping animals from wandering**
- furrow (FUR oh) **long, narrow, trench that a plow makes in the earth**

"I couldn't plow but one furrow; there isn't time," Pa said. "Hurry, Caroline. That fire's coming faster than a horse can run."

A big rabbit bounded right over the tub while Pa and Ma were lifting it. Ma told Laura to stay at the house. Pa and Ma ran staggering to the furrow with the tub.

Laura stayed close to the house. She could see the red fire coming under the billows of smoke. More rabbits went leaping by. They paid no attention to Jack, the dog, and he didn't think about them. He stared at the red undersides of the rolling smoke and shivered and whined while he crowded close to Laura.

The wind was rising and wildly screaming. Thousands of birds flew before the fire, thousands of rabbits were running.

Pa was going along the furrow, setting fire to the grass on the other side of it. Ma followed with a wet sack, beating at the flames that tried to cross the furrow. The whole prairie was hopping with rabbits. Snakes rippled across the yard. Prairie hens ran silently, their necks outstretched and their wings spread. Birds screamed in the screaming wind.

Pa's little fire was all round the house now, and he helped Ma fight it with the wet sacks. The fire blew wildly, snatching at the dry grass inside the furrow. Pa and Ma thrashed at it with the sacks, when it got across the furrow they stamped it with their feet. They ran back and forth in the smoke, fighting that fire.

The prairie fire was roaring now, roaring louder and louder in the screaming wind. Great flames came roaring, flaring and twisting high. Twists of flame broke loose and came down on the wind to blaze up in the grasses far ahead of the roaring wall of fire. A red light came from the rolling black clouds of smoke overhead.

• staggering (STAG ur ing) **walking in an unsteady way**

Mary and Laura stood against the house and held hands and trembled. Baby Carrie was in the house. Laura wanted to do something, but inside her head was a roaring and whirling like the fire. Her middle shook, and tears poured out of her stinging eyes. Her eyes and her nose and her throat stung with smoke.

Jack howled. Pet and Patty were jerking at the ropes and squealing horribly. The orange, yellow, terrible flames were coming faster than horses can run, and their quivering light danced over everything.

Pa's little fire had made a burned black strip. The little fire went backing slowly away against the wind. It went slowly crawling to meet the racing furious big fire. And suddenly the big fire swallowed the little one.

The wind rose to a high, crackling, rushing shriek, flames climbed into the crackling air. Fire was all around the house.

Then it was over. The fire went roaring past and away.

Pa and Ma were beating out little fires here and there in the yard. When they were all out, Ma came to the house to wash her hands and face. She was all streaked with smoke and sweat, and she was trembling.

She said there was nothing to worry about. "The back-fire saved us," she said, "and all's well that ends well."

The air smelled scorched. And to the very edge of the sky, the prairie was burned naked and black. Threads of smoke rose from it. Ashes blew on the wind. Everything felt different and miserable. But Pa and Ma were cheerful because the fire was gone and it had not done any harm.

Pa said that the fire had not missed them far, but a miss is as good as a mile. He asked Ma, "If it had come while I was in Independence, what would you have done?"

"We would have gone to the creek with the birds and the rabbits, of course," Ma said.

All the wild things on the prairie had known what to do. They ran and flew and hopped and crawled as fast as they could go, to the water that would keep them safe from fire. Only the little soft striped gophers had gone down deep into their holes, and they were the

- back-fire (BAK fire) **fire started to stop an approaching fire by burning out all the grass and other things that can burn**

first to come up and look around at the bare, smoking prairie.

Then out of the creek bottoms the birds came flying over it, and a rabbit cautiously hopped and looked. It was a long, long time before the snakes crawled out of the bottoms and the prairie hens came walking.

The fire had gone out among the bluffs. It had never reached the creek bottoms or the Indian camps.

That night Mr. Edwards and Mr. Scott came to see Pa. They were worried because they thought that perhaps the Indians had started that fire on purpose to burn out the white settlers.

Pa didn't believe it. He said the Indians had always burned the prairie to make green grass grow more quickly and traveling easier. Their ponies couldn't gallop through the thick, tall, dead grass. Now the ground was clear. And he was glad of it, because plowing would be easier.

Pa said he figured that Indians would be as peaceable as anybody else if they were let alone. On the other hand, they had been moved west so many times that naturally they hated white folks. With soldiers at Fort Gibson and Fort Dodge, Pa didn't believe these Indians would make any trouble.

"As to why they are congregating in these camps, Scott, I can tell you that," he said. "They're getting ready for their big spring buffalo hunt."

He said there were half a dozen tribes down in those camps. Usually the tribes were fighting each other, but every spring they made peace and all came together for the big hunt.

"They're sworn to peace among themselves," he said, "and they're thinking about hunting the buffalo. So it's not likely they'll start on the warpath against us. They'll have their talks and their feasts, and then one day they'll a hit the trail after the buffalo herds. The buffalo will be working their way north pretty soon, following the green grass. By George! I'd like to go on a hunt like that, myself. It must be a sight to see."

"Well, maybe you're right about it, Ingalls," Mr. Scott said, slowly. "Anyway, I'll be glad to tell Mrs. Scott what you say."

- cautiously (KAW shus lee) **carefully, trying to avoid danger**
- **bluff** (BLUF) **cliff; high, steep land**
- **congregate** (KON gruh gayt) **gather together, meet**

ALL THINGS CONSIDERED ────────────────

1. The first sign the family has of the prairie fire is (a) black clouds and a dark sky. (b) the smell of burning grass. (c) a red light against the sky.

2. Pa plows a furrow to (a) keep the horses from getting too nervous. (b) let the creek water run into it. (c) separate the prairie fire from their home.

3. All the animals run (a) toward the fire. (b) into the stable. (c) toward the creek.

4. Pa sets fire to the grass on the other side of the furrow (a) by mistake. (b) to burn the grass before the prairie fire gets there. (c) to force all the snakes and other animals to run away.

5. Ma uses the wet sacks to (a) carry water to put out the fire. (b) wrap around the farm animals. (c) beat out the fire that crosses the furrow.

6. A back-fire is a fire (a) people set to put out a bigger fire. (b) that changes its direction. (c) moving against the wind.

7. If Pa had not been there, (a) Ma would have fought the fire the same way. (b) Ma would have taken the children and farm animals to the creek. (c) the family would have died.

8. The Native Americans were known to set fires to (a) make the grass grow and traveling easier. (b) help the farmers who settled nearby. (c) warn neighbors of trouble.

9. One good thing the fire did was to (a) clear the land for plowing. (b) get rid of the wild animals. (c) make the settlers and Indians friendlier.

10. Pa said that the Native Americans were (a) about to leave. (b) making a camp. (c) preparing for a buffalo hunt.

THINKING IT THROUGH ────────────────

1. The family moved onto the prairie only a year before. How do you think they knew what to do when the fire started?

2. Fires are dangerous in many places. (a) What kinds of fires are most dangerous? (b) How do people fight the fires? (c) Do you know of fires today that are fought with back-fires? If so, where?

3. (a) How does the family work together to fight the fire? (b) Do you think one person could have fought it as well? Explain. (c) Could the family have fought the fire without the horses? Why or why not?

4. (a) How do you think the wild animals knew there was a fire? (b) How did they know what to do? (c) Why did Papa have to tie up the horses and cows?

Vocabulary and Sentence Meaning ———

Synonyms

Words that mean the same thing or almost the same thing are called **synonyms.** Writers use synonyms to keep their language more interesting.

This story uses many synonyms. For example, the writer uses the words *bound* and *leap.* They mean almost the same thing. If the writer had used only one of these words in all the places that both are found, it would have been overused.

Below are some other words found in "Prairie Fire." In the same story, try to find a synonym for each word. On a separate sheet of paper, write the word, the synonym you found for it. Then write the page number and first two words of the sentence where you found each one.

1. tug
2. gallop
3. tremble
4. thrash
5. burn
6. naked

Composition ———

Follow your teacher's instructions before completing *one* of these writing assignments.

1. Choose any paragraph in the story that has at least four sentences. Rewrite that paragraph by changing four words, using a synonym for each one.
2. Think about something you do every day. How would you have to change your life if you were part of a family that had just moved onto a prairie in the days when this story took place? Write a paragraph that tells how you and your family would have to do things differently. Think about getting food or clothing, learning, getting together with friends, or entertaining yourself.

Mark Twain (1835-1910)

If everything had gone as he had planned, America might never have known one of its greatest writers. After working as a printer for several years, the young man set out to seek his fortune in Brazil. Instead, he landed in New Orleans and learned how to be a Mississippi riverboat pilot. As a pilot he earned a good salary. Then the Civil War interrupted travel on the river.

It was on the river that the man who was born with the name Samuel Langhorne Clemens first heard the cry, "mark twain." This river expression meant that the boat was in safe water for sailing.

In 1861, his older brother Orion Clemens was named Secretary of the Nevada Territory. Samuel joined him in a trip west. The brothers expected to get rich by mining.

During the journey, Samuel started to write newspaper articles about their experiences. People enjoyed reading them, and he began to write more articles and stories. After a while, he took the name Mark Twain, the name by which the world knows him today.

Mark Twain's first books were travel books. They told of his trips across the country and to other lands. His books showed people places they had never seen. His descriptions had lots of interesting detail in addition to good humor. Humor and good descriptions became two important parts of Twain's writing.

Today, Twain's two best-known books are *The Adventures of Tom Sawyer* and *Adventures of Huckleberry Finn.* Both stories take place in a town very much like Hannibal, Missouri, where the writer grew up.

THE PONY EXPRESS

by Mark Twain

▶ The Pony Express was a way of moving mail fast by horseback between St. Joseph, Missouri, and Sacramento, California. Pony Express service began April 3, 1860, and lasted a little more than a year. It ended in October 1861. The new telegraph lines that crossed the country could carry news and information much faster.

Mark Twain and his brother crossed the country by stagecoach in 1861. The stagecoach carried travelers and regular mail. Twain saw a Pony Express rider and wrote about the sight in his book *Roughing It*.

In a little while, all interest was taken up in stretching our necks and watching for the "pony-rider." This was the speedy messenger who carried letters nineteen hundred miles in eight days! Think of that for horse and human flesh and blood to do!

The pony-rider was usually a little bit of a man, full of spirit and endurance. It didn't matter what time of the day or night his turn came. It didn't matter whether it was winter or summer, raining, snowing, hailing, or sleeting. It didn't matter whether he had a level, straight road or a crazy trail over mountains. It didn't matter whether it led through peaceful regions or regions with many dangers. He must be always ready to leap into the saddle and be off like the wind!

• endurance (en DOO rins) **patience; power to last and keep on going**

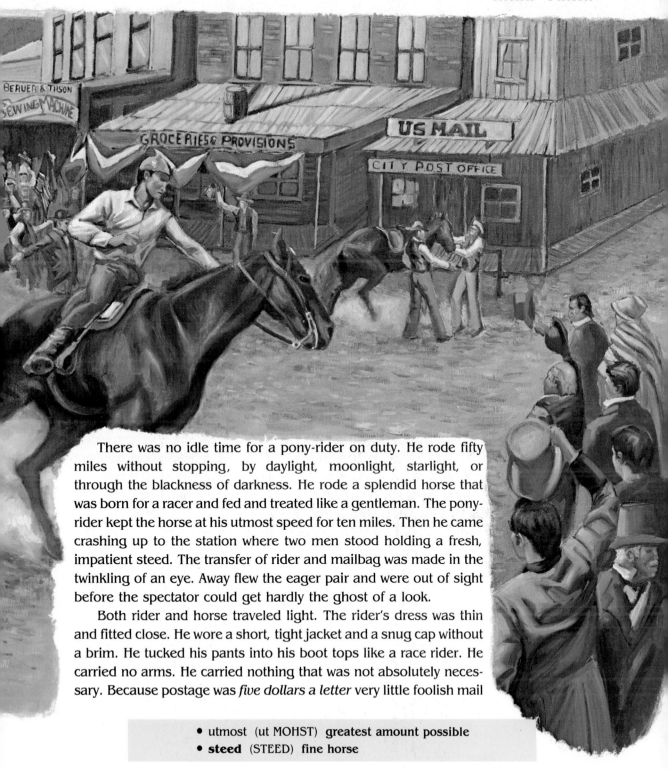

There was no idle time for a pony-rider on duty. He rode fifty miles without stopping, by daylight, moonlight, starlight, or through the blackness of darkness. He rode a splendid horse that was born for a racer and fed and treated like a gentleman. The pony-rider kept the horse at his utmost speed for ten miles. Then he came crashing up to the station where two men stood holding a fresh, impatient steed. The transfer of rider and mailbag was made in the twinkling of an eye. Away flew the eager pair and were out of sight before the spectator could get hardly the ghost of a look.

Both rider and horse traveled light. The rider's dress was thin and fitted close. He wore a short, tight jacket and a snug cap without a brim. He tucked his pants into his boot tops like a race rider. He carried no arms. He carried nothing that was not absolutely neces-sary. Because postage was *five dollars a letter* very little foolish mail

- utmost (ut MOHST) **greatest amount possible**
- **steed** (STEED) **fine horse**

53

was carried. His bag had business letters in it, mostly.

His horse was stripped of all unnecessary weight, too. He wore a little wafer of a racing saddle and no visible blanket. He wore light shoes or none at all. The little flat mail pockets strapped under the rider's thighs would each hold about the thickness of a child's first reader. They held many an important business and newspaper letter. These were written on paper nearly as airy and thin as a leaf. In that way, thickness and weight were economized.

The stagecoach traveled about a hundred to a hundred and twenty-five miles in a twenty-four hour day. The pony-rider covered about two hundred and fifty miles. There were about eighty pony-riders in the saddle all the time, night and day, stretching from Missouri to California. Forty flew eastward, and forty toward the west. Among them they made four hundred gallant horses earn a stirring living and see a deal of scenery every single day in the year.

We had had a great desire, from the beginning, to see a pony-rider. But somehow or other, all that passed us and all that met us managed to streak by in the night. So we heard only a whiz and a shout. The swift phantom of the desert was gone before we could get our heads out of the windows. But now we were expecting one along every moment. We would see him in broad daylight.

Before long, the driver exclaims, "Here he comes!"

Every neck is stretched further, and every eye strained wider. Away across the endless level of the prairie, a black speck appears against the sky. It is plain that it moves. Well, I should think so! In a second or two it becomes a horse and rider, rising and falling, rising and falling—sweeping toward us nearer and nearer—growing more and more clear, more and more sharp—nearer and still nearer. The sound of the hooves comes faintly to ear. Another instant a whoop and a hurrah from our stagecoach top, a wave of the rider's hand, but no reply. A man and horse burst past our excited faces and go winging away like a late fragment of a storm!

So sudden is it all, and so like a flash of unreal fancy, that except for the flake of white foam left quivering on a mail sack after the vision had flashed by and disappeared, we might have doubted whether we had seen any actual horse and man at all, maybe.

- strain (STRAYN) **to stretch beyond usual limits**
- fragment (FRAG munt) **small piece**

ALL THINGS CONSIDERED

1. The pony-rider was usually (a) small. (b) heavy. (c) armed.
2. Without stopping, a pony-rider usually rode (a) fifty miles. (b) one hundred miles. (c) two hundred fifty miles.
3. The transfer of horse was made very quickly every (a) mile. (b) ten miles. (c) fifty miles.
4. The reason that the horse and rider carried very little was that they (a) were afraid things would get lost. (b) didn't have many bags to hold things. (c) could travel faster with less weight.
5. The pony-rider carried the mail (a) in mail sacks. (b) in a knapsack. (c) under his thighs.
6. Only very important mail was sent by Pony Express because (a) very few people were allowed to send mail in that way. (b) sending mail that way was very expensive. (c) most people could not write.
7. The stagecoach traveled (a) about twice as far as a pony-rider each day. (b) about the same daily distance as a pony-rider. (c) less than half as far as a pony-rider did in a day.
8. The pony-riders traveled in the area between (a) New York and Florida. (b) Missouri and California. (c) Washington and Maine.
9. The reason that Twain did not see many pony-riders was that (a) they were going in a different direction. (b) many pony-riders went by at night. (c) only one pony-rider passed them during the whole trip.
10. The proof that the pony-rider had passed was (a) that they received their mail. (b) the rider dropped a letter. (c) a speck of foam on a mailbag.

THINKING IT THROUGH

1. The Pony Express lasted only a year, but many stories have been written about it. Why do you think this is so?
2. (a) When you send a letter to someone in your city or town, how long does it take to get there? (b) How long does it now take mail to travel across the country? (c) How does mail travel now?
3. (a) Would you have wanted to be a pony-rider? (b) Could you qualify? (c) Why or why not?

Building From Details

Visualizing From Details

Can you get a picture in your mind from what you read? Getting a picture in your mind is called **visualizing.** The details in a work of literature help you to visualize. You understand what you are reading better when you can picture it in your mind.

For example, read the two paragraphs on page 53 that begin "Both rider and horse traveled light."

1. Can you imagine what the horse and rider looked like? If you had to make up a costume for a movie based on these paragraphs, could you do it?
2. Look at the two drawings. Which one fits Twain's description? Which one does not? On a separate sheet of paper, write five details in the incorrect drawing that do not fit Twain's description. Use the two paragraphs to help you decide.

Composition

Follow your teacher's instructions before completing *one* of these writing assignments.

1. Write four sentences that describe what someone in the room is wearing. Do not mention the person. See if your classmates can figure out who you are describing.
2. People often wait to see an event that ends quickly. Think of an event that people wait to see and write a paragraph about it.

VOCABULARY AND SKILL REVIEW ——————————

Before completing the exercises that follow, you may wish to review the **bold-faced** words on pages 24–53.

I. On a separate sheet of paper, write the term in each line that means the same, or nearly the same thing, as the term in *italics*.

1. *bondage:* money, slavery, bandage, goodness
2. *bluff:* mountain, cliff, pond, valley
3. *heartfelt:* sincere, painful, sick, angry
4. *sentiment:* idea, feeling, greeting, desire
5. *steed:* metal, horse, boat, rider
6. *ascend:* rise, lower, keep, burn
7. *determine:* disagree, decide, desire, dislike
8. *shinny:* walk, climb, run, slide
9. *pursue:* escape, chase, wander, buy
10. *congregate:* complete, pray, meet, leave

II. Some of the following sentences are exaggerations. Some could really be true. On a separate sheet of paper, write the numbers 1 through 10. If the sentence shows exaggeration, write *E* next to the number. If the sentence could be true, write *T* next to the number.

1. The corn grew so high that it tickled the clouds.
2. He was six-feet tall and still growing.
3. We had the largest crop we had ever grown.
4. One sweep of his ax cleared the whole forest.
5. His voice hit the moon and echoed back on Earth.
6. The elephant was so fat that it weighed almost 400 pounds.
7. The meal was enough to feed 50 people.
8. The wind blew over trees and houses.
9. She was so skinny that you couldn't see her sideways.
10. The lake is so full of fish that they jump up and ask you to eat them.

WESTERN TOWN

by David Wadworth Cannon, Jr.

▶ Sometimes just a few lines give you a good picture. Can you imagine this town?

Dry Gap—a dingy general store.
A sign said, "Population Seven."
I found a universe for two:
One sun, one moon, and called it heaven.

WAYS OF KNOWING

1. What was the most noticeable place in Dry Gap?
2. How do you know that it was a small town?
3. Why does the speaker like the place? What does it have to offer?
4. Do you think that you would like a place like Dry Gap? Why or why not?

• **dingy** (DIN jee) very dirty looking, not clean

SHOES FOR HECTOR

from *El Bronx Remembered*

by Nicholasa Mohr

▶ Hector has a lot going for him at graduation. But he really feels that his parents have let him down when he opens the shoebox.

Hector's mother had gone to see Uncle Luis the day before graduation, and he had come by the same evening. Everyone sat in the living room watching Uncle Luis as he took a white box out of a brown paper bag. Opening the box, he removed a pair of shiny, light-caramel-colored shoes with tall heels and narrow, pointed toes. Holding them up proudly, he said, "Set me back 12 bucks, boy!"

Everybody looked at Hector and then back at Uncle Luis.

"Here you go, my boy. . . ." He gestured toward Hector. "Try them on."

"I'm not gonna try those things on!" Hector said.

"Why not?" asked Uncle Luis. "What's wrong with them? They are the latest style, man. Listen, boy, you will be ala moda with these."

"They . . . they're just not my type. Besides, they don't go with my suit—it's navy blue. Those shoes are orange!" Hector's younger brothers and sister looked at each other and began to giggle and laugh.

"Shut up, you dummies!" Hector shouted angrily.

"Hector, what is the matter with you?" his mother asked. "That's no way to behave."

"I'd rather wear my sneakers than those, Mami. You and Papi promised to buy me shoes. You didn't say nothing about wearing Uncle Luis's shoes."

"Wait a minute, now. Just a minute," Hector's father said. "We

- gesture (JES chur) **motion, hand signal**
- ala moda (AH lah MOHD ah) **in style**

59

know, but we just couldn't manage it now. Since your Uncle Luis has the same size foot like you, and he was nice enough to lend you his new shoes, what's the difference? We done what we could, son; you have to be satisfied."

Hector felt the blood rushing to his face and tried to control his embarrassment and anger. His parents had been preparing his graduation party now for more than a week. *They should have spent the money on my shoes instead of on a dumb party,* he thought. Hector had used up all the earnings from his part-time job. He had bought his suit, tie, shirt, socks, and handkerchief. His parents had promised to buy him the shoes. *Not one cent left,* he thought, *and it was just too late now.*

"It's not my fault that they lay me off for three days," his father said, "and that Petie got sick and that Georgie needed a winter jacket and Juanito some . . ."

As his father spoke, Hector wanted to say a few things. Like, *No, it's my fault that you have to spend the money for shoes on a party and a cake and everything to impress the neighbors and the familia. Stupid dinner!* But instead he remained quiet, looking down at the floor, and did not say a word.

"Hector . . . come on, my son. Hector, try them on, *bendito.* Uncle Luis was nice enough to bring them," he heard his mother plead. "Please, for me."

"Maybe I can get into Papi's shoes," Hector answered.

"My shoes don't fit you. And your brothers are all younger and smaller than you. There's nobody else. You are lucky Uncle Luis has the same size foot," his father responded.

"Okay, I'll just wear my sneakers," said Hector.

"Oh, no . . . no, never mind. You don't wear no sneakers, so that people can call us a bunch of *jíbaros!* You wear them shoes!" his mother said.

"Mami, they are orange!" Hector responded. "And look at them pointed fronts—they go on for a mile. I'm not wearing them!"

"Come on, please," his mother coaxed. "They look nice and brand new, too."

"Hector!" his father said loudly. "Now, your Uncle Luis was nice

• **lay off** put someone out of work for a while, often because there is not enough work to be done
• *jíbaro* (HEE bah roh) **peasant, a Puerto Rican word**

enough to bring them, and you are going to try them on." Everyone was silent and Hector sat sulking. His mother took the shoes from Uncle Luis and went over to Hector.

"Here, son, try them on, at least. See?" She held them up. "Look at them. They are not orange, just a light-brown color, that's all. Only a very light brown."

Without looking at anyone, Hector took the shoes and slowly put them on. No doubt about it, they felt like a perfect fit.

"How about that?" Uncle Luis smiled. "Now you look sharp. Right in style, boy!"

Hector stood up and walked a few paces. In spite of all the smiling faces in the living room, Hector still heard all the remarks he was sure his friends would make if he wore those shoes.

"Okay, you look wonderful. And it's only for one morning. You can take them right off after graduation," his mother said gently.

Hector removed the shoes and put them back in the box, resigned that there was just no way out. At that moment he even found himself wishing that he had not been selected as valedictorian and wasn't receiving any honors.

"Take your time, Hector. You don't have to give them back to me right away. Wear the shoes for the party. So you look good," he heard Uncle Luis calling out as he walked into his bedroom.

"That stupid party!" Hector whispered out loud.

With a pained expression on his face the next morning, Hector left his apartment wearing Uncle Luis's shoes. His mother and father walked proudly with him.

Hector arrived at the school auditorium and took his place on line. Smiling and waving at him, his parents sat in the audience.

"Hector López . . ." He walked up the long aisle onto the stage. He finished his speech and sat on a chair provided for him on the stage. They called his name again several times, and each time Hector received an honor or prize. Included were a wristwatch and a check for cash. Whenever Hector stood up and walked to the podium, he prayed that no one would notice his shoes.

- **sulk** (SULK) be silent and bad tempered
- valedictorian (val uh dik TAWR ee un) student who gives the farewell speech at graduation, usually the student who has the highest average

Finally, graduation exercises were over and Hector hurried off the stage, looking for his parents. People congratulated him on his many honors and on his speech. His school friends shook his hand and they exchanged addresses. Hector found himself engaged in long good-byes. Slowly, people began to leave the large auditorium, and Hector and his parents headed for home.

Hector sat on his bed and took off Uncle Luis's shoes. "Good-bye," he said out loud, making a face, and dropped them into the box. He sighed with relief. No one had even mentioned the shoes, he thought. Man . . . I bet they didn't even notice them. Boy! Was I ever lucky. . . . Nobody said a word. How about that? he said to himself. Reaching under the bed, he took out his sneakers and happily put them on. Never again, he continued, if I can help it. No, sir. I'm gonna make sure I got me shoes to wear! He remembered all the things he had won at graduation. Looking at his new wristwatch, he put it on. That's really something, he thought. He took out the check for cash he had received and read, *"Pay to the Order of Hector López. . . . The Sum of Twenty-Five Dollars and 00/100 Cents."* I can't wait to show everybody, he said to himself.

Hector left his room and looked into the kitchen. His mother and grandmother were busily preparing more food. He heard voices and music in the living room and quickly walked in that direction. When his younger brothers and sister saw him, they jumped up and down.

"Here's Hector!" Petie yelled.

"Happy Graduation Day, Hector!" everyone shouted.

The living room was full of people. His father was talking to Uncle Luis and some neighbors. Uncle Luis called out, "There he is. Hector! . . . There's my man now."

"Look." Hector's father pointed to a table that was loaded with platters of food and a large cake. The cake had the inscription "Happy Graduation to Hector." Behind the cake was a large card printed in bright colors:

HAPPY GRADUATION DAY, HECTOR
FROM ALL YOUR FAMILY
Mami, Papi, Abuelita, Petie, Georgie,
Juanito, and Millie

- exercise (EK sur size) ceremony
- **inscription** (in SKRIP shun) something written, often for a special occasion

Rows of multi-colored crepe-paper streamers were strung across the ceiling and walls. Lots of balloons had been blown up and attached to each streamer. A big bell made of bright-red crepe paper and cardboard was set up under the center ceiling light. The record player was going full blast with a loud marengue; some of the kids were busy dancing. Hector's face flushed when he saw Gloria. He had hoped she would come to the party, and there she was. Looking great, he thought.

Some neighbors came over and congratulated Hector. His friends began to gather around, asking him lots of questions and admiring his wristwatch.

"Show them the check, Hector," his father said proudly. "That's some smart boy; he just kept getting honors! Imagine, they even give him money. . . . "

Hector reached into his jacket pocket and took out the check for twenty-five dollars. He passed it around so that everyone could see it. Impressed, they asked him, "Hey, man. Hector, what you gonna do with all that money?"

'Yeah. Tell us, Hector, what you gonna do?"

Hector smiled and shrugged his shoulders. "Buy me a pair of shoes! Any color except orange!" he replied.

- multi-colored (MUL tee KUL urd) **having many colors**
- marengue (muh REN gay) **a kind of dance**

ALL THINGS CONSIDERED ───────────

1. Hector did not want to wear Uncle Luis's shoes because (a) the color and style did not go with his suit. (b) they did not belong to him. (c) they did not fit him.
2. Hector felt that his parents should have (a) borrowed the money to buy him shoes. (b) spent money on new shoes instead of a graduation party. (c) let him wear his brother's shoes.
3. Most of Hector's graduation clothes were paid for by (a) his parents. (b) his uncle. (c) Hector.
4. One reason that his father was short of money was that he (a) was layed off from his job. (b) had lent money to a friend. (c) had bought new furniture.
5. Hector wanted particularly to look good at graduation because (a) his friends used to make fun of his clothes. (b) he was the valedictorian. (c) his uncle would be there.
6. When he took off the shoes after the graduation exercises, he realized that (a) he liked them after all. (b) nobody seemed to notice them. (c) they really did match his suit.
7. One of Hector's prizes was a (a) gift certificate to a department store. (b) check for twenty-five dollars. (c) college scholarship.
8. Hector must have been one of the smartest students in the class because he (a) received a scholarship. (b) received several honors as valedictorian. (c) never got a poor grade.
9. At the party, Hector was especially glad when he saw (a) how proud his father was. (b) Gloria. (c) his new shoes.
10. At the party, Hector wore his (a) uncle's shoes. (b) sneakers. (c) new navy blue shoes.

THINKING IT THROUGH ───────────────

1. Did Hector's family care a lot about him? How do you know? Find some parts of the story that prove you are right.
2. Are Hector and his Uncle Luis very much like each other or very different from one another? How can you tell?
3. Hector was very unhappy about the shoes. In the end, did they really spoil his day?
4. Sometimes parents and children disagree about something important. What did Hector and his parents disagree about? Who do you think was right?

Building From Details

Getting the Facts

When you read a story, you should do what newspaper reporters do. Get the five *w*'s. The five *w*'s are question words that begin with a *w*. They are *who, what, when, where,* and *why.*

In thinking about "Shoes for Hector," ask the five *w*'s. On a separate sheet of paper, try to answer each of these *w*'s. Then write your own *why* question and answer.

1. *Who* are the important characters in the story?
2. *What* is the important problem in the story?
3. *When* does the story take place? When does it begin and when does it end?
4. *Where* does the story take place? Is there more than one setting?
5. *Why* can be many things. For example, it can be, Why is there a problem? Or, Why do the characters act the way they do?

Composition

Follow your teacher's instructions before completing *one* of these writing assignments.

1. Why is clothing so important to most people? Write three or four sentences that tell why you think people consider their clothing to be important.
2. What do you think Hector learned about his classmates from wearing his uncle's shoes to the graduation?

SPLIT CHERRY TREE

by Jesse Stuart

▶ Dave has to stay after school, and he knows his father is
going to be angry. But when his father says he will go to
school, Dave really begins to worry.

I don't mind staying after school," I says to Professor Herbert, "but
I'd rather you'd whip me with a switch and let me go home early. Pa
will whip me anyway for getting home two hours late."

"You are too big to whip," says Professor Herbert, "and I have to
punish you for climbing up in the cherry tree. You boys knew better
than that! The other five boys have paid their dollar each. You have
been the only one who has not helped pay for the tree. Can't you
borrow a dollar?"

"I can't," I says. "I'll have to take the punishment. I wish it would
be quicker punishment. I wouldn't mind."

Professor Herbert stood and looked at me. He was a big man. He
wore a gray suit of clothes. The suit matched his gray hair.

"You don't know my father," I says to Professor Herbert. "He
might be called a little old-fashioned. He makes us mind him until
we're twenty-one years old. I'll never be able to make him understand about the cherry tree. I'm the first of my people to go to high
school."

"You must take the punishment," says Professor Herbert. "You
must stay two hours after school today and two hours after school
tomorrow. I am allowing you twenty-five cents an hour. That is good
money for a high school student. You can sweep the schoolhouse
floor, wash the blackboards, and clean windows. I'll pay the dollar
for you."

I couldn't ask Professor Herbert to loan me a dollar. He never
offered to loan it to me. I had to stay and help the janitor and work
out my fine at a quarter an hour.

I thought as I swept the floor: "What will Pa do to me? What lie
can I tell him when I go home? Why did we ever climb that cherry
tree and break it down for anyway? Why did we run crazy over the
hills away from the crowd? Why did we do all of this? Six of us
climbed up in a little cherry tree after one little lizard! Why did the

66

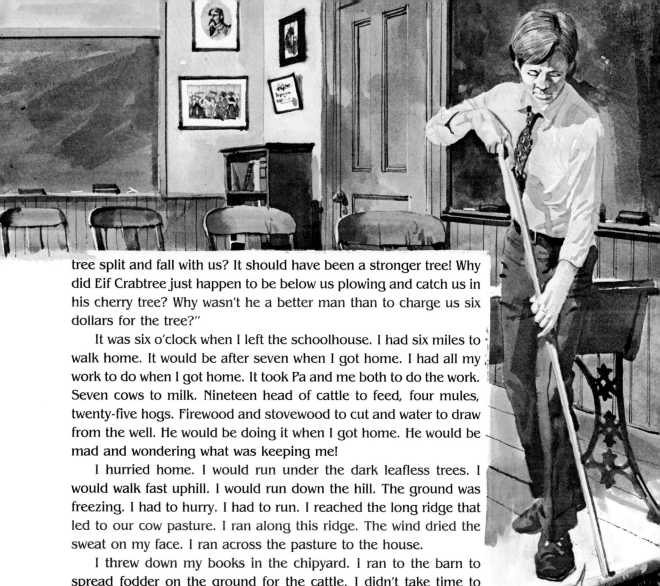

tree split and fall with us? It should have been a stronger tree! Why did Eif Crabtree just happen to be below us plowing and catch us in his cherry tree? Why wasn't he a better man than to charge us six dollars for the tree?"

It was six o'clock when I left the schoolhouse. I had six miles to walk home. It would be after seven when I got home. I had all my work to do when I got home. It took Pa and me both to do the work. Seven cows to milk. Nineteen head of cattle to feed, four mules, twenty-five hogs. Firewood and stovewood to cut and water to draw from the well. He would be doing it when I got home. He would be mad and wondering what was keeping me!

I hurried home. I would run under the dark leafless trees. I would walk fast uphill. I would run down the hill. The ground was freezing. I had to hurry. I had to run. I reached the long ridge that led to our cow pasture. I ran along this ridge. The wind dried the sweat on my face. I ran across the pasture to the house.

I threw down my books in the chipyard. I ran to the barn to spread fodder on the ground for the cattle. I didn't take time to change my clean school clothes for my old work clothes. I ran out to the barn. I saw Pa spreading fodder on the ground to the cattle. That was my job. I ran up to the fence. I says: "Leave that for me, Pa. I'll do it. I'm just a little late."

"I see you are," says Pa. He turned and looked at me. His eyes danced fire. "What in th' world has kept you so? Why ain't you been here to help me with this work? Make a gentleman out'n one boy in th' family and this is what you get! Send you to high school and you get too onery fer th' buzzards to smell!"

- **fodder** (FOD ur) food for cattle
- **onery** (OR nuh ree) ornery, mean and stubborn

67

I never said anything. I didn't want to tell why I was late from school. Pa stopped scattering the bundles of fodder. He looked at me. He says: "Why are you gettin' in here this time o' night? You tell me or I'll take a hickory switch to you right here on th' spot!"

I says: "I had to stay after school." I couldn't lie to Pa. He'd go to school and find out why I had to stay. If I lied to him it would be too bad for me.

"Why did you haf to stay after school?" says Pa.

I says: "Our biology class went on a field trip today. Six of us boys broke down a cherry tree. We had to give a dollar apiece to pay for the tree. I didn't have the dollar. Professor Herbert is making me work out my dollar. He gives me twenty-five cents an hour. I had to stay in this afternoon. I'll have to stay in tomorrow afternoon!"

"Are you telling me th' truth?" says Pa.

"I'm telling you the truth," I says. "Go and see for yourself."

"That's just what I'll do in th' mornin'," says Pa. "Jist whose cherry tree did you break down?"

"Eif Crabtree's cherry tree!"

"What was you doin' clear out in Eif Crabtree's place?" says Pa. "He lives four miles from th' County High School. Don't they teach you no books at that high school? Do they jist let you get out and gad over th' hillsides? If that's all they do I'll keep you at home, Dave. I've got work here fer you to do!"

"Pa," I says, "spring is just getting here. We take a subject in school where we have to have bugs, snakes, flowers, lizards, frogs, and plants. It is biology. It was a pretty day today. We went out to find a few of these. Six of us boys saw a lizard at the same time sunning on a cherry tree. We all went up the tree to get it. We broke the tree down. It split at the forks. Eif Crabtree was plowing down below us. He ran up the hill and got our names. The other boys gave their dollar apiece. I didn't have mine. Professor Herbert put mine in for me. I have to work it out at school."

"Poor man's son, huh," says Pa. "I'll attend to that myself in th' mornin'. I'll take keer o' 'im. He ain't from this country nohow. I'll go down there in th' mornin' and see 'im. Lettin' you leave your books and galavant all over th' hills. What kind of a school is it nohow!

- **biology** (by OL uh jee) the study of living things
- galavant (GAL i vant) gallivant, run about having fun

Didn't do that, my son, when I's in school. All fared alike, too."

"Pa, please don't go down there," I says. "Just let me have fifty cents and pay the rest of my fine. I don't want you to go down there! I don't want you to start anything with Professor Herbert!"

"Ashamed of your old Pap, are you, Dave," says Pa, "atter the way I've worked to raise you! Tryin' to send you to school so you can make a better livin' than I've made."

I thought once I'd run through the woods above the barn just as hard as I could go. I thought I'd leave high school and home forever! Pa could not catch me! I'd get away! I couldn't go back to school with him. He'd have a gun and maybe he'd shoot Professor Herbert. It was hard to tell what he would do. I could tell Pa that school had changed in the hills from the way it was when he was a boy, but he wouldn't understand. I could tell him we studied frogs, birds, snakes, lizards, flowers, insects. But Pa wouldn't understand. If I did run away from home it wouldn't matter to Pa. He would see Professor Herbert anyway. He would think that high school and Professor Herbert had run me away from home. There was no need to run away. I'd just have to stay, finish foddering the cattle and go to school with Pa the next morning.

The moon shone bright in the cold March sky. I finished my work by moonlight. Professor Herbert really didn't know how much work I had to do at home. If he had known he would not have kept me after school. He would have loaned me a dollar to have paid my part on the cherry tree. He had never lived in the hills. He didn't know the way the hill boys had to work so that they could go to school. Now he was teaching in a County High School where all the boys who attended were from hill farms.

69

After I'd finished doing my work I went to the house and ate my supper. Pa and Mom had eaten. My supper was getting cold. I heard Pa and Mom talking in the front room. Pa was telling Mom about me staying in after school.

"I had to do all th' milkin' tonight, chop th' wood myself. It's too hard on me atter I've turned ground all day. I'm goin' to take a day off tomorrow and see if I can't remedy things a little. I'll go down to the high school tomorrow. I won't be a very good scholar fer Professor Herbert nohow. He won't keep me in atter school. I'll take a different kind of lesson down there and make 'im acquainted with it."

"Now, Luster," says Mom, "you jist stay away from there. Don't cause a lot o' trouble. You can be jailed fer a trick like that. You'll get th' Law atter you. You'll jist go down there and show off and plague your own boy Dave to death in front o' all th' scholars!"

"Plague or no plague," says Pa, "he don't take into consideration what all I haf to do here, does he? I'll show 'im it ain't right to keep one boy in and let the rest go scot-free. My boy is good as th' rest, ain't he? A bullet will make a hole in a schoolteacher same as it will anybody else. He can't do me that way and get by with it. I'll plug 'im first. I aim to go down there bright and early in th' mornin' and get all this straight! I am to see about bug learnin' and this runnin' all over God's creation huntin' snakes, lizards, and frogs. Ransackin' th' country and goin' through cherry orchards and breakin' th' trees down atter lizards! Old Eif Crabtree ought to a-poured th' hot lead into 'em instead o' chargin' six dollars fer th' tree! He ought to a-got old Herbert the first one!"

I ate my supper. I slipped upstairs and lit the lamp. I tried to forget the whole thing. I studied plane geometry. Then I studied my biology lesson. I could hardly study for thinking about Pa. "He'll go to school with me in the morning. He'll take a gun for Professor Herbert! What will Professor Herbert think of me! I'll tell him when Pa leaves that I couldn't help it. But Pa might shoot him. I hate to go with Pa. Maybe he'll cool off about it tonight and not go in the morning."

- **plague** (PLAYG) pester, give trouble to
- **ransack** (RAN sak) **search through**
- plane geometry **branch of mathematics that studies flat shapes**

CHECKPOINT

> ▶ Stop here and answer the following questions.
>
> **1.** Why does Dave have to stay after school?
> **2.** What does Pa think about Dave's field trip with the class?
> **3.** How do you know that Pa expects more of Dave than he does of his other children?
> **4.** What does Pa hope to teach Professor Herbert by going to school?
> **5.** Why is Dave afraid of Pa going to school?

Pa got up at four o'clock. He built a fire in the stove. Then he built a fire in the fireplace. He got Mom up to get breakfast. Then he got me up to help feed and milk. By the time we had our work done at the barn, Mom had breakfast ready for us. We ate our breakfast. Daylight came and we could see the bare oak trees covered white with frost. The hills were white with frost.

"Now, Dave," says Pa, "let's get ready fer school. I aim to go with you this mornin' and look into bug larnin', frog larnin', lizard and snake larnin', and breakin' down cherry trees! I don't like no sicha foolish way o' larnin' myself!"

Pa hadn't forgot. I'd have to take him to school with me. He would take me to school with him. I was glad we were going early. If Pa pulled a gun on Professor Herbert there wouldn't be so many of my classmates there to see him.

I knew that Pa wouldn't be at home in the high school. He wore overalls, big boots, a blue shirt and a sheepskin coat, and a slouched black hat gone to seed at the top. He put his gun in its holster. We started trudging toward the high school across the hill.

It was early when we got to the County High School. Professor Herbert had just got there. I just thought as we walked up the steps into the schoolhouse: "Maybe Pa will find out Professor Herbert is a good man. He just doesn't know him. Just like I felt toward the Lambert boys across the hill. I didn't like them until I'd seen them and talked to them, then I liked them and we were friends. It's a lot in knowing the other fellow."

"You're th' Professor here, ain't you?" says Pa.

"Yes," says Professor Herbert, "and you are Dave's father?"

"Yes," says Pa, pulling out his gun and laying it on the seat in Professor Herbert's office. Professor Herbert's eyes got big behind his black-rimmed glasses when he saw Pa's gun. Color came into his pale cheeks.

"Jist a few things about this school I want to know," says Pa. "I'm tryin' to make a scholar out'n Dave. He's the only one out'n eleven youngins I've sent to high school. Here he comes in late and leaves me all th' work to do! He said you's all out bug huntin' yesterday and broke a cherry tree down. He had to stay two hours atter school yesterday and work out money to pay on that cherry tree! Is that right?"

"W-w-why," says Professor Herbert, "I guess it is."

He looked at Pa's gun.

"Well," says Pa, "this ain't no high school. It's a bug school, a lizard school, a snake school! It ain't no school nohow!"

"Why did you bring that gun?" says Professor Herbert to Pa.

"You see that little hole," says Pa as he picked up the long blue forty-four and put his finger on the end of the barrel. "A bullet can come out'n that hole that will kill a schoolteacher same as it will any other man. It will kill a rich man same as a poor man. It will kill a man. But after I come in and saw you, I know'd I wouldn't need it. This maul o' mine could do you up in a few minutes."

Pa stood there, big, hard, brown-skinned, and mighty beside Professor Herbert. I didn't know Pa was so much bigger and harder. I'd never seen Pa in a schoolhouse before. I'd seen Professor Herbert. He always looked big before to me. He didn't look big standing beside Pa.

"I was only doing my duty," says Professor Herbert, "Mr. Sexton, and following the course of study the state provided us with."

"Course o' study!" says Pa. "What study? Bug study? Takin' youngins to th' woods. Boys and girls all out there together a-galavantin' in the brush and kickin' up their heels and their poor old Mas and Pas at home a-slavin' to keep 'em in school and give 'em a education!"

Students are coming into the schoolhouse now. Professor Herbert says: "Close the door, Dave, so others won't hear."

I walked over and closed the door. I was shaking like a leaf in the wind. I thought Pa was going to hit Professor Herbert every minute. He was doing all the talking. His face was getting red. The red color was coming through the brown, weather-beaten skin on Pa's face.

"It jist don't look good to me," says Pa, "a-takin' all this swarm of youngins out to pillage th' whole deestrict. Breakin' down cherry trees. Keepin' boys in atter school."

"What else could I have done with Dave, Mr. Sexton?" says Professor Herbert. "The boys didn't have any business all climbing that cherry tree after one lizard. One boy could have gone up the tree and got it. The farmer charged us six dollars. It was a little steep, I think, but we had it to pay. Must I make five boys pay and let your boy off? He said he didn't have the dollar and couldn't get it. So I put it in for him. I'm letting him work it out. He's not working for me. He's working for the school!"

"I jist don't know what you could a-done with 'im," says Pa, "only a-larruped 'im with a withe! That's what he needed!"

"He's too big to whip," says Professor Herbert, pointing at me. "He's a man in size."

"He's not too big fer me to whip," says Pa. "They ain't too big until they're over twenty-one! It jist didn't look fair to me! Work one and let th' rest out because they got th' money. I don't see what bugs has got to do with a high school! It don't look good to me nohow!"

Pa picked up his gun and put it back in its holster. The red color left Professor Herbert's face. He talked more to Pa. Pa softened a little. It looked funny to see Pa in the high school building. It was the first time he'd ever been there.

"We're not only hunting snakes, toads, flowers, butterflies, lizards," says Professor Herbert, "but, Mr. Sexton, I was hunting dry grass to put in an incubator and raise some protozoa."

"I don't know what that is," says Pa. "Th' incubator is th' new-fangled way o' cheatin' th' hens and raisin' chickens. I ain't so sure about th' breed o' chickens you mentioned."

"You've heard of germs, Mr. Sexton, haven't you?" says Professor Herbert.

"Jist call me Luster if you don't mind," says Pa, very casual like.

- pillage (PIL ij) rob and destroy
- **steep** (STEEP) very expensive; costly
- larrup (LAR up) whip; beat
- withe (WYTH) thin, strong twig
- protozoa (proh tuh ZOH uh) one-celled animals that can be seen only under a microscope

"All right, Luster, you've heard of germs, haven't you?"

"Yes," says Pa, "but I don't believe in germs. I'm sixty-five years old and I ain't seen one yet!"

"You can't see them with your naked eye," says Professor Herbert. "Just keep that gun in the holster and stay with me in the high school today. I have a few things I want to show you. That scum on your teeth has germs in it."

"What," says Pa, "you mean to tell me I've got germs on my teeth!"

"Yes," says Professor Herbert. "The same kind as we might be able to find in a living black snake if we dissect it!"

"I don't mean to dispute your word," says Pa, "but danged if I believe it. I don't believe I have germs on my teeth!"

"Stay with me today and I'll show you. I want to take you through the school anyway. School has changed a lot in the hills since you went to school. I don't guess we had high schools in this country when you went to school."

"No," says Pa, "jist readin', writin', and cipherin'. We didn't have all this bug larnin', and findin' germs on your teeth and in the middle o' black snakes! Th' world's changin'."

"It is," says Professor Herbert, "and we hope all for the better. Boys like your own there are going to help change it. He's your boy. He knows all of what I've told you. You stay with me today."

"I'll shore stay with you," says Pa. "I want to see th' germs off'n my teeth. I jist want to see a germ. I've never seen one in my life. 'Seein' is believin',' Pap allus told me."

Pa walks out of the office with Professor Herbert. I just hoped Professor Herbert didn't have Pa arrested for pulling his gun. Pa's gun has always been a friend to him when he goes to settle disputes.

The bell rang. School took up. I saw the students when they marched in the schoolhouse look at Pa. They would grin and punch each other. Pa just stood and watched them pass in at the schoolhouse door. Two long lines marched in the house. The boys and girls were clean and well dressed. Pa stood over in the schoolyard under a leafless elm, in his sheepskin coat, his big boots laced in front with buckskin and his heavy socks stuck above his boot tops.

- **dissect** (dy SEKT) cut open and examine
- cipherin' (SY fur in) ciphering; arithmetic

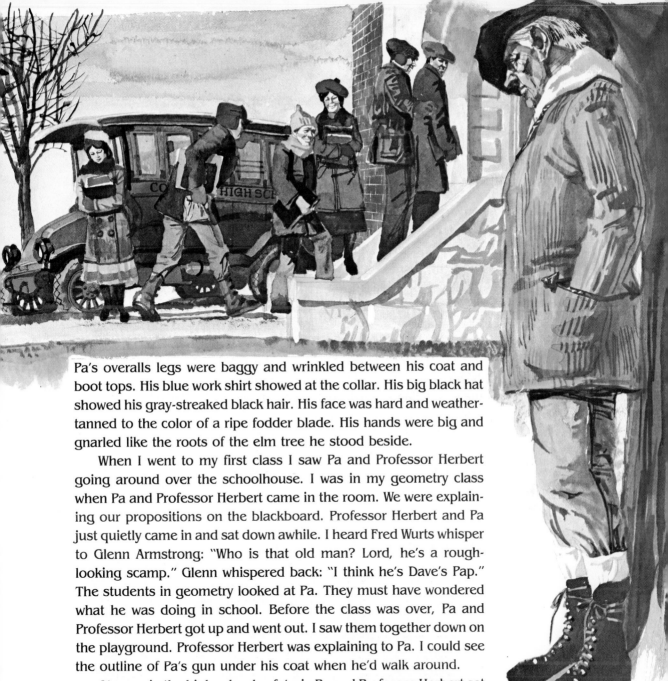

Pa's overalls legs were baggy and wrinkled between his coat and boot tops. His blue work shirt showed at the collar. His big black hat showed his gray-streaked black hair. His face was hard and weather-tanned to the color of a ripe fodder blade. His hands were big and gnarled like the roots of the elm tree he stood beside.

When I went to my first class I saw Pa and Professor Herbert going around over the schoolhouse. I was in my geometry class when Pa and Professor Herbert came in the room. We were explaining our propositions on the blackboard. Professor Herbert and Pa just quietly came in and sat down awhile. I heard Fred Wurts whisper to Glenn Armstrong: "Who is that old man? Lord, he's a rough-looking scamp." Glenn whispered back: "I think he's Dave's Pap." The students in geometry looked at Pa. They must have wondered what he was doing in school. Before the class was over, Pa and Professor Herbert got up and went out. I saw them together down on the playground. Professor Herbert was explaining to Pa. I could see the outline of Pa's gun under his coat when he'd walk around.

At noon in the high school cafeteria Pa and Professor Herbert sat together at the little table where Professor Herbert always ate by himself. They ate together. The students watched the way Pa ate. He ate with his knife instead of his fork. A lot of the students felt sorry

- gnarled (NAHRLD) twisted
- proposition (prop uh ZISH un) geometry problem to be solved

75

for me after they found out he was my father. They didn't have to feel sorry for me. I wasn't ashamed of Pa after I found out he wasn't going to shoot Professor Herbert. I was glad they had made friends. I wasn't ashamed of Pa. I wouldn't be as long as he behaved.

In the afternoon when we went to biology Pa was in the class. He was sitting on one of the high stools beside the microscope. We went ahead with our work just as if Pa wasn't in the class. I saw Pa take his knife and scrape one of his teeth. Professor Herbert put it under the lens and adjusted the microscope for Pa. He adjusted it and worked awhile. Then he says: "Now, Luster, look! Put your eye right down to the light. Squint the other eye!"

Pa put his head down and did as Professor Herbert said: "I see 'im," says Pa. "Who'd a ever thought that? Right on a body's teeth! Right in a body's mouth! You're right certain they ain't no fake to this, Professor Herbert?"

"No, Luster," says Professor Herbert. "It's there. That's the germ. Germs live in a world we cannot see with the naked eye. We must use the microscope. There are millions of them in our bodies. Some are harmful. Others are helpful."

Pa holds his face down and looks through the microscope. We stop and watch Pa. He sits upon the tall stool. His knees are against the table. His legs are long. His coat slips up behind when he bends over. The handle of his gun shows. Professor Herbert quickly pulls his coat down.

"Oh, yes," says Pa. He gets up and pulls his coat down. Pa's face gets a little red. He knows about his gun and he knows he doesn't have any use for it in high school.

"We have a big black snake over here we caught yesterday," says Professor Herbert. "We'll chloroform him and dissect him and show you he has germs in his body, too."

"Don't do it," says Pa. "I believe you. I jist don't want to see you kill the black snake. I never kill one. They are good mousers and a lot o' help to us on the farm. I like black snakes. I jist hate to see people kill 'em. I don't allow 'em killed on my place."

The students look at Pa. They seem to like him better after he said that. Pa with a gun in his pocket but a tender heart beneath his ribs for snakes, but not for man! Pa won't whip a mule at home. He won't whip his cattle.

Professor Herbert took Pa through the laboratory. He showed him the different kinds of work we were doing. He showed him our equipment. They stood and talked while we worked. Then they walked out together. They talked louder when they got in the hall.

When our biology class was over I walked out of the room. It was our last class for the day. I would have to take my broom and sweep two hours to finish paying for the split cherry tree. I just wondered if Pa would want me to stay. He was standing in the hallway watching the students march out. He looked lost among us. He looked like a leaf turned brown on the tree among the treetop filled with growing leaves.

I got my broom and started to sweep. Professor Herbert walked up and says: "I'm going to let you do that some other time. You can go home with your father. He is waiting out there."

I laid my broom down, got my books, and went down the steps.

Pa says: "Ain't you got two hours o' sweepin' yet to do?"

I says: "Professor Herbert said I could do it some other time. He said for me to go home with you."

"No," says Pa. "You are goin' to do as he says. He's a good man. School has changed from my day and time. I'm a dead leaf, Dave. I'm behind. I don't belong here. If he'll let me I'll get a broom and we'll both sweep one hour. That pays your debt. I'll help you pay it. I'll ast 'im and see if he won't let me hep you."

"I'm going to cancel the debt," says Professor Herbert. "I just wanted you to understand, Luster."

- chloroform (KLAWR uh fawrm) **use a chemical that produces sleep**

"I understand," says Pa, "and since I understand he must pay his debt fer th' tree and I'm goin' to hep him."

"Don't do that," says Professor Herbert. "It's all on me."

"We don't do things like that," says Pa; "we're just and honest people. We don't want somethin' fer nothin'. Professor Herbert, you're wrong now and I'm right. You'll haf to listen to me. I've learned a lot from you. My boy must go on. Th' world has left me. It changed while I've raised my family and plowed th' hills. I'm a just and honest man. I don't skip debts. I ain't larned 'em to do that. I ain't got much larnin' myself but I do know right from wrong atter I see through a thing."

Professor Herbert went home. Pa and I stayed and swept one hour. It looked funny to see Pa use a broom. He never used one at home. Mom used the broom. Pa used the plow. Pa did hard work. Pa says: "I can't sweep. Durned if I can. Look at th' streaks o' dirt I leave on th' floor! Seems like no work a-tall fer me. Brooms is too light 'r somethin'. I'll jist do th' best I can, Dave. I've been wrong about th' school."

I says: "Did you know Professor Herbert can get a warrant out for you for bringing your pistol to school and showing it in his office! They can railroad you for that!"

"That's all made right," says Pa. "I've made that right. Professor Herbert ain't goin' to take it to court. He likes me. I like 'im. We jist had to get together. He had the remedies. He showed me. You must go on to school. I am as strong a man as ever come out'n th' hills fer my years and th' hard work I've done. But I'm behind, Dave. I'm a little man. Your hands will be softer than mine. Your clothes will be better. You'll allus look cleaner than your old Pap. Jist remember, Dave, to pay your debts and be honest. Jist be kind to animals and don't bother th' snakes. That's all I got agin th' school. Puttin' black snakes to sleep and cuttin' 'em open."

It was late when we got home. Stars were in the sky. The moon was up. The ground was frozen. Pa took his time going home. I couldn't run like I did the night before. It was ten o'clock before we got the work finished, our suppers eaten. Pa sat before the fire and told Mom he was going to take her and show her a germ some time. Mom hadn't seen one either. Pa told her about the high school and the fine man Professor Herbert was. He told Mom about the strange school across the hill and how different it was from the school in their day and time.

ALL THINGS CONSIDERED _____

1. Dave has to stay after school because he (a) forgot to do his homework. (b) does not have his share of the money to pay for a tree he helped break. (c) fought with another student in class.

2. He asked the teacher to (a) lend him a dollar. (b) make his father understand. (c) whip him instead.

3. At first his father is angry because (a) Dave is late for his chores. (b) the teacher is unfair. (c) Dave did not break the tree.

4. His father thinks the school is wrong for (a) making children pay for the tree. (b) letting Professor Herbert teach. (c) teaching children about bugs and lizards.

5. Dave is worried because his father is (a) very angry with Professor Herbert. (b) not well educated. (c) not well dressed.

6. His father does not believe in (a) reading. (b) germs. (c) working hard.

7. Luster Sexton is (a) Dave's father. (b) a student in school. (c) the man whose cherry tree was broken.

8. Professor Herbert lets Luster Sexton use (a) the blackboard. (b) a microscope. (c) a hammer.

9. Luster Sexton does not want Professor Herbert to dissect the snake because (a) he thinks they are good mousers. (b) it will be too bloody and messy. (c) he thinks it's dangerous.

10. At the end of the story (a) Dave and his father have an argument. (b) Dave is angry at Professor Herbert. (c) Dave's father and Professor Herbert understand each other better.

THINKING IT THROUGH _____

1. (a) Do you think that Professor Herbert is being fair to Dave? (b) If the teacher understood more about Dave at the beginning, do you think he would have punished Dave differently?

2. How does Dave's way of looking at his father change from the beginning of the story to the end?

3. How does the author show that understanding between people works better than force? (Notice that the gun is never used in the story.)

4. (a) What does Dave's father think of the school and Dave's education at the beginning of the story? (b) What does he think about the school and education at the end of the story? (c) What is the reason for the change?

Literary Skills

Understanding Characters

Many good stories are about people changing and growing in understanding. In this story, each of the three main characters is a little different at the end of the story than at the beginning.

At the beginning, Dave is afraid to tell his father what happened. But he does not lie to his father. Dave is more able to talk to his father at the end of the story.

Dave's father is not sure that Dave should be going to the high school. At the end of the story, his opinion of the high school is different.

Professor Herbert does not understand how his students and their families live. At the end of the story, he understands them better.

Think about the story. What happens in the story to make each person change? How do the other characters help each character change?

Choose one of the three main characters in this story. On a separate sheet of paper, name one important way that character changes. Then list one thing each of the two other characters did to help create that change.

Composition

Follow your teacher's instructions before completing *one* of these writing assignments.

1. Write five sentences that tell some ways you have changed in the last two years.
2. The story is called "Split Cherry Tree." Write a paragraph that explains how the split tree makes it possible for the three main characters to meet.

VOCABULARY AND SKILL REVIEW ───────────

Before completing the exercises that follow, you may wish to review the **bold-faced** words on pages 58–76.

I. On a separate sheet of paper, mark each item *true* or *false*. If it is *false,* explain what is wrong with the sentence.

1. People often *sulk* when they are unhappy.
2. When there is more work to do, a boss has to *lay off* many workers.
3. *Biology* is the study of machines and tools.
4. A *plague* kills off many people.
5. You *dissect* a frog by sewing i back together.
6. An *inscription* on a building may tell when it was built.
7. People who do not have much money are glad when prices are *steep*.
8. Thieves may *ransack* a room to find money or jewels.
9. *Fodder* makes a delicious dessert.
10. People are proud of *dingy* laundry.

II. Use the five *w*'s. Think of a fairy tale you know—"The Three Bears," "Snow White," "Jack and the Beanstalk," or any other story you know.

On a separate sheet of paper list the five *w*'s. Next to each, write at least one thing from the story you chose.

1. who
2. what
3. when
4. where
5. why

Hint: The "when" is the same for most fairy tales. It is usually in the first sentence of the story.

UNIT REVIEW

I. Match the terms in column A with their definitions in column B.

A	B
1. characters	**a)** where and when a story takes place
2. plot	**b)** statement that could not possibly be true
3. setting	**c)** the people in a story
4. visualizing	**d)** who, what, where, when, and why
5. exaggeration	**e)** reading aloud with meaning
6. biography	**f)** story of one's own life
7. legend	**g)** story of someone else's life
8. autobiography	**h)** getting a picture in one's mind
9. oral interpretation	**i)** the action in a story
10. five w's	**j)** exaggerated story of someone who really lived

II. In this unit, you learned about four ways that readers learn about a character.

    1. the author's description
    2. what a character says
    3. how a character behaves
    4. what other characters say about that character

Different stories in this unit have examples of each way of learning about a character. Some stories have examples of more than one way. Look back over the stories and poems in this unit. Find one example of each way of learning about a character. On a separate sheet of paper write the numbers 1 through 4. Then write the page number in this unit where you found the example of each way of learning about a character.

III. What is an American to you? In this unit, you have met people who came to this country as immigrants, people who helped open up the West, and people whose families have been Americans for a long time. Choose one of the people you met in this unit. On a separate sheet of paper make a list of some details that you would put in a biography of that person. Use details you find in the story or poem.

UNIT REVIEW

IV. Have you ever heard someone say that a person is "a legend in his or her own time"? Pick some person living today. The person may be someone in sports or entertainment. It could be a world leader or a local leader. It could be a teenager or an adult.

Who will you choose?

First list some facts about the person. Try to take facts that are answers to some of the five w's. Then exaggerate the facts. Make up your own legend about that person. Give your legend some details that someone else can visualize.

Write your legend on a separate sheet of paper.

At the end of each Unit Review in this book, there is a selection for you to practice reading aloud. Reading aloud in front of a group helps you to become more comfortable speaking in front of people. It also helps improve your acting skill. It can also be a lot of fun. Here are some tips to help you do your best when reading aloud in front of people.

1. Read the piece silently to yourself before you read it aloud. Try to be sure that you understand the main idea of what you are reading.

2. Put the book on something in front of you, or hold the book away from you in one hand. That will leave one or both hands free for gestures.

3. Speak loud and clear, but do not shout. Try to speak loud enough for the farthest person in the room to hear you. If you happen to make a small mistake, forget it. Just go on with your acting.

4. Think about the person who is speaking. Pretend that you are that person. Soon, your gestures, the expressions on your face, and your tone of voice will be natural to the person who is speaking.

5. Don't be afraid to play either a male or female part. That is part of the fun of acting.

6. Rehearse, rehearse, rehearse. Put everything you can into the part. Use your voice, your body, your eyes.

The speech that follows was made by Chief Joseph of the Nez Perce Indian tribe. He made the speech when he surrendered to the United States government in 1877. Chief Joseph was one of the great Native American leaders. He had fought hard to help his people hold on to their land and their independence. In 1877, he realized that his people could fight no longer. Imagine how he felt when he had to make this speech.

Speaking Up

CHIEF JOSEPH'S SURRENDER SPEECH

I am tired of fighting. Our chiefs are killed. Looking Glass is dead. Toohulhulsote is dead. The old men are all dead. It is the young men who say no and yes. He who led the young men is dead. It is cold and we have no blankets. The little children are freezing to death. My people, some of them, have run away to the hills and have no blankets, no food. No one knows where they are. Perhaps they are freezing to death. I want to have time to look for my children and see how many of them I can find. Maybe I shall find them among the dead. Hear me, my chiefs, I am tired. My heart is sad and sick. From where the sun now stands I will fight no more forever.

Hear me, my chiefs! I am tired. My heart is sick and sad.

WRITING YOUR OWN DESCRIPTION

Who are these people? Do they seem interesting? What do you think they are like? Use your imagination and what you know about people to write a description of one of them.

1. **Prewriting:** Choose the person who seems most interesting, and name the person. That person will become the character in your paragraph. List several details that describe the character. Select about five details to include in your paragraph. The details can describe both looks and personality. For example, a character might have *dark* eyes. Or a character might have *sad* eyes.
2. **Writing:** Write a paragraph that creates a clear word picture of the person you have chosen. Use details you listed in the prewriting stage to describe the character.
3. **Revising:** Read your paragraph. Is the description interesting and complete? Have you included enough details to help readers picture the character? Does each sentence have a subject and a verb? Are the punctuation, capitalization, and spelling correct? Make corrections and rewrite your paragraph.

SEARCHING FOR YOURSELF

In a way, *searching for yourself* means almost the same thing as growing up. But searching for yourself suggests something more. It suggests an effort to discover who you are, a desire to become the best you can be.

Walt Whitman, a great American poet, expressed the theme of searching for yourself in this way.

> Afoot and light-hearted I take to the open road,
> Healthy, free, the world before me,
> The long brown path before me leading wherever
> I choose.
>
> *from "Song of the Open Road" by Walt Whitman*

Reading can be an exciting part of searching for yourself. Read. Ask questions. Look for honest answers. Use the stories in this unit as a starting point in searching for yourself.

THE CONFIDENCE GAME

by Pat Carr

▶ "Winning's not the most important thing; it's the only thing." Have you ever heard these words before? Do you agree or disagree with them? Tobi learns a lot about winning, and about herself, when Angela joins the swim team.

My confidence started draining out my toes the day Angela Brady showed up at the pool for workout. I even started to chew the inside of my cheek, a nervous habit I usually reserve for fighting the fear that clutches at me just before a race. In a way, I guess I knew it *was* a race between Angela and me for the backstroke position on our team relay for the National Championship.

I hadn't even seen her swim yet, but the whole team knew she had been swimming for a famous club in California. We were just a small city team, only two years old. But we had a coach whose middle name was motivation. He'd motivated me into swimming a killing three miles a day, and now I was actually in the running to compete at the Nationals. Or I was until Angela showed up.

"Okay, swim freaks, hit the water for an 800-meter freestyle warm-up!" barked Coach. Then he added in a more human voice, "Angela, why don't you try lane four today?"

Lane four was the fast lane, my lane. I'd had to earn my place in that lane by swimming 400 meters in less than five minutes. Now all Angela had to do was jump in. It wasn't fair.

I didn't think I could pretend friendliness, so I started the 800 before Angela hit the water. But I didn't even have time to settle into my pace when I felt the water churning behind me. I stroked harder, but I could still feel the churning water of someone closing in on me. I soon felt a light touch on my foot.

In swim workouts, it's one of the rules that when a teammate taps your foot, you move to the right to let that swimmer go ahead of you. I knew that, and I also knew that I was interfering with Angela's pace by not letting her pass me. My conscience told me to move over, but something stubborn kept my body in the middle of the lane.

At the end of the 800, I glanced up and saw Coach staring at me. Realizing that he had seen me refuse to let Angela

---

• **motivate** (MOH tuh VAYT) cause to act

88

pass, I took a deep breath and ducked underwater.

When the workout was over, everyone crowded around Angela, asking her if she knew any Olympic swimmers and stuff like that. Finding a quiet corner for myself, I slipped on my warm-up suit, draped a towel over my head and hurried toward my bike.

"Hey, Tobi! Where are you going?" someone shouted.

I didn't answer, just hopped on my bike and pedaled fast.

It was like that for the next two weeks. At every workout Angela was the star of the show. I was an invisible stagehand. Even worse, during time trials she beat me in all four strokes and took my place as lane leader.

I was miserable. And I was scared, too. I was scared that Angela was taking away my chance at the Nationals, a chance I had earned by a lot of hard work.

I started to show up late to workouts so that I wouldn't have to talk to anyone. I even walked on the bottom of the pool and faked my stroke, a swimmer's cheating trick I'd never used before. It was easy to catch up to Angela that way. And I always managed to be underwater when she gave our lane instructions.

I'll admit I wasn't very happy with my actions. But my jealous feelings were like a current I couldn't swim against.

The day before the Riverdale Meet, Coach called me over. At that moment I would rather have tried to talk to King Kong.

"Tobi, I want to talk to you about sportsmanship," he began.

"Sportswomanship, in this case, Coach," I quipped, hoping to distract him.

"Okay, sportswomanship," he said, taking me seriously. "Or whatever you want to call it when one athlete accepts

---

• **quip** (KWIP) make a witty remark

a better athlete in a spirit of friendly competition."

"Maybe the so-called better athlete is not as good as everyone thinks," I mumbled.

Coach left a big silence for my statement to fall into. I started to chew the inside of my cheek again.

"Let's stop talking about this athlete and that athlete," he said softly, "and talk instead about Tobi and Angela. She has made better time than you, Tobi. And that is an obvious fact, not something everyone thinks."

He paused. I stared at my toes, which were curling under my feet as if trying to hide.

"The worst of it, Tobi, is that your attitude is hurting your performance. Do you know that your times have become worse in the last two weeks? Maybe showing up late and walking on the bottom have something to do with that," he said. My face felt as if it had been splashed with hot pink paint.

"Do you have anything you want to say?" he asked. I shook my head. "That's all then, Tobi. I'll see you tomorrow at the Riverdale Meet."

The next morning I was too nervous to eat my special breakfast of steak and eggs. This meet would decide who was going to the Nationals.

The early skies were still gray when I arrived at the Riverdale pool for the warm-up session. The other swimmers were screeching greetings at each other like a flock of gulls. I jumped into the water to cut off the sound and mechanically began my stroke.

Half an hour later, I shuddered as the public address system squealed. The meet was about to start. After climbing out of the pool, I quickly searched the heat sheet for my name. Disappointed, I saw that I had just missed making it into the last, and fastest, qualifying heat. Angela's name, of course, was there. She'd taken my place just as she had at the trials.

Better not to think about Angela at all, I told myself, recalling Coach's words. Better to concentrate on my own race. Carefully, I went over Coach's instructions in my mind, shutting out the noisy crowd around me. In my mind I was swimming my race perfectly, over and over again, always perfectly.

"Would you like an orange?"

Without looking, I knew whose voice it was. "It's good for quick energy," continued Angela, holding the orange out to me.

"No thanks," I said. "I've got all I need." I saw that she was about to sit down next to me, so I added, "I don't like to talk before a race."

She nodded sympathetically. "I get uptight, too. The butterflies are free," she said with a nervous laugh.

For a moment I felt a little better toward her, knowing that she had the jitters, too. Then I remembered that she

---

• **obvious** (OB vee us) easily seen; clear

didn't have to worry.

"You'll be an easy winner," I said.

"You never know about that," she replied uncertainly.

My heat was called. Up on the blocks, I willed my muscles into obedience, alert for the starter's commands. At the gun, I cut into the top of the water smoothly.

I swam exactly as I had been imagining it before the race, acting out the pictures in my mind. I felt the water stream past me, smooth, steady and swift. When I finished, I was certain I had done my best in that heat.

Overwhelmed by exhaustion, I sat on the deck for several minutes, eyes closed, totally spent. I knew I was missing Angela's heat, but I was too tired to care.

The sound of the announcer's voice was like a crackling firecracker of hope bursting through my fatigue. Then I heard my name. I'd made it!

I also heard Angela's name, but it was several minutes before I realized that my name had been called last. That meant my time had been better. Figuring there must have been a mistake, I checked the official postings, but there were our times with mine four seconds faster.

Heading for the gym, where all the swimmers rest and wait for the heats to be called, I saw Angela sitting alone with her back against the wall. Her shoulders were rounded in a slump.

It could be me, I whispered to myself, remembering what it feels like to mess up a race. There's no worse anger than the kind you feel toward yourself when

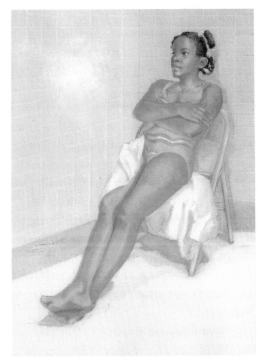

you've ruined something you care about. I knew how she felt, and I also knew there was no way I could make up for the way I had acted. But I just had to try.

"I don't talk before races, but I do talk after them. Sometimes it helps," I said, knowing Angela had every right to tell me to go drown myself.

"Talk if you want to," she murmured.

"Well, I will, but I was hoping you'd talk, too."

She hesitated, and I saw her trying to swallow. "I will as soon as I'm sure I'm not going to cry," she whispered.

So I babbled on for a few minutes about the meet, some of the other swimmers, the team standings, anything. I knew it didn't matter what I said as long as I kept talking.

All at once Angela interrupted my

opinion of the snack bar's hamburgers. "I do this all the time," she burst out. "I do great at workouts, then comes a meet, and something happens. I just can't do it."

"Maybe you don't know how to play the confidence game," I said. She looked at me suspiciously, but I went on. "How do you psych yourself up for a race?"

"I don't exactly." She was twisting the ends of the towel into tiny corkscrews. "I just try to block it out, not think about it."

"What about during a race?"

"I concentrate on not making mistakes."

"Very negative methods," I commented.

"What do you mean?"

"Well, take my positive approach. First, I think about all the good things I've done in previous races. Then I plan my upcoming race carefully, going over each detail in my mind, picturing myself the perfect swimmer. Then when I'm in the water, I tell myself to do it again, only this time for real."

"And you win," Angela added with a smile. Now I really felt bad, remembering how I had acted when Angela had done better than I in workouts.

"Listen, I have an idea," I said. Maybe I *could* make it up to her. "You swim faster than me, right?" Angela looked doubtful.

"Yes, you do, that's an obvious fact," I insisted. "Now, my idea is that you use me as a pacer in the backstroke final this afternoon."

At first Angela wasn't sure, but I soon had her convinced, and we were planning our strategy when Coach showed up.

"What's going on here?" He gave me an accusing look.

"We've got it all settled," Angela spoke up. "Tobi and I are going to be a team from now on."

"All right!" he said, giving us a smile usually reserved for winners.

As Angela and I sat together on the ready bench, I had conflicting thoughts about helping her. What was I doing anyway? Handing her my relay position on a silver platter, that's what.

I hadn't time to get worked up over it, though, because the whistle blew, and we stepped up to the blocks. At the sound of the gun I was into the water with barely a splash, skimming the surface like a water bug.

As I reached the wall, I pretended all my strength was in my legs as I flipped and pushed off. Pull hard, hard, hard, I told myself, muscles aching from the effort. Then on the last lap, I concentrated on a single word. Win! I shot through the water and strained for the finish.

- **negative** (NEG uh tiv) not helpful
- **positive** (POZ uh tiv) helpful
- pacer (PAY sur) one who sets the pace in a race
- **strategy** (STRAT uh jee) skillful planning
- **conflict** (KON flikt) lack of agreement; struggle

Immediately, I looked to Angela's lane. She was there, but it was too close to tell who had won. She gave me the thumbs-up sign, and I returned it.

I stared at the electronic scoreboard. Usually it didn't take long for the times to appear, but now it remained blank for so long I was beginning to worry that a fuse had blown.

Please, please let me be the winner, I whispered over and over. Finally, the winning times flashed on. I blinked away the chlorine haze, or maybe tears. Angela had won. I managed to give her a congratulatory hug.

"I couldn't have done it without you, Tobi," she bubbled.

"You did it, girls!" Coach couldn't keep himself from shouting, he was so excited. "You've just raced yourself to the Nationals!"

I had never felt so left out, so disappointed, in my whole life. "Well, at least Angela has," I said, struggling to smile.

Coach looked startled. "And you did, too, Tobi."

What was he talking about? "I saw that Angela won the place on our relay team."

"That's right, but you missed something. You both swam so fast that you made qualifying times for the *individual* backstroke event!"

I was stunned. I had concentrated so hard on the relay place I hadn't even thought about the individual events.

"So you'll both go to the Nationals!" Coach couldn't resist doing a couple of dance steps, and I was so ecstatic, I joined him. But a wet concrete swim deck is not an ideal dance floor.

"Look out!" yelled Angela, as we just missed falling into the water. "I don't want my partner to break a leg. We've got a long way to go before the Olympics."

"What?" I gasped.

"Just doing some positive mental rehearsing." She grinned.

"A little confidence sure goes a long way," I laughed.

Still, maybe that *is* something to think about!

• **ecstatic** (ek STAT ik) **full of joy**

ALL THINGS CONSIDERED

1. Before Angela joins the team, Tobi is the (a) best swimmer. (b) second best swimmer. (c) worst swimmer.

2. Tobi is afraid that (a) Coach doesn't like her. (b) Angela may be a better swimmer. (c) Angela will cheat.

3. When Angela becomes the swimming star, Tobi begins to (a) help her. (b) practice harder. (c) show up late for practice.

4. Tobi's attitude is (a) helping her swimming. (b) hurting her swimming. (c) hurting Angela's swimming.

5. The Riverdale Meet will decide who (a) is going to the Nationals. (b) is going to the Olympics. (c) will be the state champ.

6. Before the Riverdale meet, Angela (a) ignores Tobi. (b) makes a friendly gesture toward Tobi. (c) sits by herself.

7. In the first event, the best time is made by (a) another girl. (b) Angela. (c) Tobi.

8. Tobi tells Angela to (a) listen to Coach. (b) think positively. (c) avoid making mistakes.

9. Because of Tobi's advice, (a) both girls will go to the Nationals. (b) only Angela will go to the Nationals. (c) Angela asks Tobi to be her coach.

10. Tobi's willingness to help Angela tells you that (a) Tobi no longer wants to be the best swimmer. (b) Tobi has learned the true meaning of "sportswomanship". (c) Tobi knows that she cannot compete against Angela, so she may as well help her.

THINKING IT THROUGH

1. How does Coach define "sportsmanship" or "sportswomanship" for Tobi? (See page 89.) Do you think Tobi agrees with these definitions at first? Does Tobi eventually learn to be a good sport? If so, how does she show it?

2. Think of two or three more definitions of "sportsmanship." Explain why there can be more than one good definition of this word. Do you think one definition is better than the others? If so, why?

3. In the beginning, Tobi wants to win at all costs. At the end she has a different attitude. Which attitude do you think helps her swim better? Why?

Literary Skills

Fiction and Nonfiction

"The Confidence Game" is a work of **fiction**. It is a story about imaginary characters and events. Other stories you will read in this book tell of real characters and events. Such stories are called **nonfiction**.

Look through the selection you have read in Unit I. Find two examples of fiction and two examples of nonfiction. Write the titles of the stories you have chosen on a separate sheet of paper.

Understanding Plot

Plot is a series of events in a story. The plot begins when the main character is faced with a **conflict**, or problem. As the main character acts to resolve the conflict, the plot unfolds.

In "The Confidence Game," the main conflict is whether Tobi will keep her position on the swim team and go to the Nationals, or lose the position to Angela and not go to the Nationals.

On a separate sheet of paper, explain how Tobi resolves her conflict. Do you think Tobi has learned a valuable lesson by working to resolve the conflict? If so, what has she learned?

Composition

Follow your teacher's instructions before completing *one* of these writing assignments.

1. Tobi tells Angela, "Maybe you don't know how to play the confidence game." (See page 92.) In a short paragraph, explain what Tobi means by the "confidence game."
2. Imagine that Angela is the main character of the story. Write several sentences that tell (a) the conflict Angela faces and (b) how the conflict is resolved.

THICKER THAN WATER

by Paul Gallico

▶ The saying "Blood is thicker than water" refers to the close relationships among the members of a family. It is just a saying. For Joey White, however, it was something else—something real—and it made all the difference.

The other day I heard the story of how Tommy White came back from a South Pacific island. That's right, he came back from a grave where he sleeps under a wooden cross on which his helmet hangs, rusting in the tropic rains. He came back and knocked out Tony Kid Marino in the seventh round at the American Legion Stadium in our town.

Tommy White was a champion, but his kid brother Joey was a dog. You often run across things like that. They were both welterweights, and young Joey could box rings around Tommy. He could have boxed those same circles around any welterweight living if the geezer hadn't started to come out in him after the first solid smack.

Tommy, on the other hand, had the heart of a lion. That is why he became a world's champion. That is why he enlisted the day after Pearl Harbor. That is why he walked into the machine-gun fire that was coming from a Japanese pillbox and murdering his company. That is why he dropped a grenade into the slit, quietly and without fuss like a man posting a letter, before he died from being shot to pieces.

That sort of put the burden on Joey White, and it seemed to be more of a load than he could lug. Doc Auer, who had managed Tommy and been more like a father to him, helped out all he could. But Doc wasn't exactly rich. Tommy had won his championship in the days when nobody got rich.

There was Mom White, and Phil, the youngest. There was Anna, aged twelve, who had been living in a wheelchair ever since the

- welterweight (WEL tur wayt) **boxer who weighs between 136 and 147 pounds**
- geezer (GEEZ ur) **slang term for an odd old man**
- Pearl Harbor **harbor in Hawaii that was the location of Japanese attack on a U.S. naval base in 1941**

96

hit-and-run driver had tossed her like a broken doll into the gutter. And, of course, there was Ellie, Tom's widow and their year-old baby.

Joey was a good kid. He couldn't help the yellow streak that came out in him in the ring. It was just that he would begin to blink and wince at the first solid smack. Then pretty soon he would be down, and you knew he wasn't bothering to get up.

Joey wasn't happy about his weakness. He tried to overcome it by going back into the ring, but each time he dogged it. It nearly drove him crazy. He felt so ashamed. There was the time he got pneumonia after he quit cold to Young Irish, and he hoped it would kill him. It nearly did, too, because he wouldn't fight the bug in him. A blood transfusion saved his life. Tommy, who was home on leave at the time, went to the hospital and acted as donor, though Joey never knew about it. In the first place, hospitals don't tell. In the second, Tommy wasn't the kind who would mention such a trifle.

You hear a lot about fighters being no-goods and bums, but there are plenty of good kids in the game. The Whites were decent. When the news came about what had happened to Tommy in the Pacific, Joey went back to the ring. He might have got a job in a factory, but there were all the mouths to feed and the payments on the house. It wouldn't have been enough. And the ring was good for money now that there weren't too many classy boys around. Joey had picked up a ruptured eardrum in one of his early fights and was 4-F.*

Doc managed him, which was rough on Doc because he had loved Tommy like a son. Doc was a square shooter. He had a hook nose and tender hands that could soothe pain when he dressed damage in the corner. But he was a rough guy who couldn't stand ki-yi in his boys. What made it worse was that Doc knew Joey had it in him to be a bigger champion and a better fighter than Tommy ever was—if he didn't curl up inside when the going got rough.

You would think after Tommy being killed the way he was, it would have given Joey the guts to go in there and pitch leather. The kid had loved his brother with a sort of doglike affection. But it didn't

- **ruptured** (RUP churd) torn or broken apart
- ki-yi (KY yy) slang sports term for "quitter"

*During World War II anyone with a 4-F classification was disqualified from the armed forces for medical reasons.

work out that way. In his first fight he quit to Ruby Schloss after being out in front five rounds and having Ruby on the floor. It was a good enough brawl so that Doc could get Joey another match. But then he folded to Arch Clement, who wasn't much more than 138 pounds, from a left hook to the chin that shouldn't have bothered a flyweight. It wasn't so good.

Four-F, or no Four-F, the fans want a fight when they pay their money. You can't draw flies with a loser even in wartime. Besides, the ringworms were on to Joey. The promoters just said, "No, thanks," when Doc came around looking for a fight.

So the match with Tony Kid Marino was just sheer luck. "Soapy" Glassman, matchmaker for the American Legion Stadium, told Doc: "Lissen, if there was anybody around under 50 years old who could put his hands up, I wouldn't let a beagle like Joey into my club through the back door."

But there was nobody around, and Marino was a sensation. Discharged from the Army for some minor disability, he had swept through the South and the Middle West by virtue of a paralyzing left hook. He was headed for Madison Square Garden and the big dough. Glassman had to have an opponent in a hurry. Joey got the match, but everybody knew he was to be the victim in it. It was also plainly labeled "last chance."

Doc said to Joey: "I seen Marino train at Flaherty's Gym. He don't know nothin'. A smart boxer could stab him all night and he wouldn't catch up. But he hits you with that left hook, and you need a room in a hospital. You got to stay away from him. And if you get hit by a punch, you got to keep boxing."

Joey said, "I'll try, Doc. Honest, I will this time."

He always said that. He always meant it—until that first hard punch chunked home.

- hook boxing term for a kind of punch
- ringworms boxing fans; people who sit around the boxing ring
- matchmaker (MATCH may kur) one who arranges boxing matches
- **disability** (dis uh BIL uh tee) a handicap
- paralyze (PAR uh lyz) make an opponent powerless
- Madison Square Garden indoor sports arena in New York City

Doc said, "Yeah, I heard that before. If we could win this one, we go in the Garden instead of that bum. Ah, nuts! A guy can dream, can't he?"

Joey did try. He could box like a phantom. He was a tall, skinny boy with dark eyes and a serious face. His long arms and smooth shoulders fooled you because they packed an awful wallop any time he stayed on the ground long enough to get set. But the night he fought Marino he wasn't staying in one place long enough to throw dynamite. He was trying his level best to do what Doc told him—stay away, stab, box, and win.

There was a crowd of 8,000 packing the Legion Stadium when they rang the bell for round one. To a man, the crowd was there to see Marino, the new kayo sensation, stiffen somebody, and the fact that Joey White was in there made it just that much more certain. Nobody was even interested when Joey gave as pretty a boxing show as you could want to see in that first round. He jabbed Marino dizzy.

In fact, some wise guy started something by holding up one finger at the end of the round and shouting, "One!" That meant one round had gone by and Joey was still there. Pretty soon everybody in the stadium took it up at the end of each round. It went on that way: "Two!" "Three!" "Four!"

Marino was muscled like a bulldog. He moved forward with a kind of dark sneer on his face as he tried to herd Joey into a corner where he could club his brains out.

• kayo (KAY oh) slang for "knockout"

Doc wasn't daring to breathe when round six came up. Joey was still there and so far out ahead on points it wasn't even funny. He hadn't been hit yet. Four more rounds—then Madison Square Garden, the big dough, a shot at the championship, security for Tommy's family. In and out went Joey—feint and stab, jab and step away, jab and circle, pop-pop-pop, three left hands in a row.

So then it happened just before the end of the sixth. The ropes on the south side of the ring had got slack and didn't have the snap-back Joey expected when he came off them. This slowed him up just enough for Marino's hook to catch him. It hit Joey on the shoulder and knocked him halfway across the ring.

Now, nobody ever got knocked out with a punch to the arm. But it was all over. Everybody knew it. Everybody saw the look come into Joey's eyes, the curl to his mouth, and the cringe to his shoulders. It was the promise of things to come that did it. The swarthy Marino leaped after Joey to find an opening, but the bell rang ending the round.

The crowd stood up, held up six fingers, and yelled, "Six!" and the wag who had started it shouted, "Seventh and last coming up!" Everybody howled with laughter.

Joey went to his corner and sat down. Usually Doc was in the ring before the echoes of the bell had died away, cotton swabs sticking out of his mouth, sponge in hand, ready to loosen trunks and administer relief and attention. But this time Doc remained outside the ropes. He didn't so much as touch Joey. He just leaned down with his head through the space between the top and second strand, and talked out of the side of his mouth into Joey's ear.

He said, "Ya bum! You going to quit in the next round, ain't you?"

Joey moved on the stool and touched his shoulder. "My arm. It's numb."

Doc went right on talking quietly out of the side of his mouth as though he were giving advice: "Makin' out to quit and you ain't even been hurt yet. You got the fight won and you're gonna go out there and lay down, ain't you?"

Joey didn't say anything anymore but licked his lips and shuffled his feet in the resin. He tried to hide his eyes so nobody would see the fear that was in them.

Doc said, "I ought to bust the bottle over your head. You, with

• **feint** (FAYNT) **pretend a move in order to fool an opponent**

the blood of a champion in your veins, makin' to go out there and lay down like a dog."

Joey turned and looked at Doc, and his lips moved. Under the hubbub he said, "What are you talking about?"

"What I said. A guy you ain't even fit to think about. You got his blood in you. He give it to you when you was sick in the hospital and had to have a blood infusion.*

"I . . . I got Tommy's blood?"

The ten-second buzzer squawked.

Doc said, "Yeah. You got it, only it dried up when it come to your chicken heart. Okay, bum, go on out there and take the dive." Then he quietly climbed down the ring steps. The bell rang for the seventh round.

Everything happened then as expected. Joey came out with his hands held too low and he seemed to be trembling. Marino ran over and swept a clublike left to the side of his head, and Joey went down as everybody knew he would.

Only thereafter he did what no one expected or had ever seen him do before. He rolled over and got on one knee, shaking his head a little, and listened to the count until it got to eight. Then he got up.

His head was singing, but his heart was singing louder. Tommy's blood! His brother's blood, the blood of one of the gamest champions in the world, coursing through his veins. A part of Tommy's life was alive inside of him. . . .

The referee finished wiping the resin from his gloves and stepped aside. Marino shuffled over, his left cocked. Joey dropped his hands still lower and stuck out his chin. The stocky little Italian accepted the invitation and hit it with all his power, knocking Joey back into the ropes.

But he didn't go down. Marino followed up, pumping left and right to Joey's head, rocking him from side to side. The crowd was screaming and above the roar someone was shouting, "Cover up! Cover up, you fool!"

Cover up for what? This bum? He couldn't hit hard enough to knock out a man with a champion's blood in his veins. Joey seemed to feel his blood stream like fire all through his body. He could take it, take it, take it now. He could sop it up, punch after punch, and not

---

*Doc says "infusion" when he should have said "transfusion," as in "blood transfusion."

101

go down, never again go down as long as in his heart there beat and pulsed the warm life of his brother.

Marino fell back wheezing and gasping for air and strength to carry on the assault. Joey laughed and came off the ropes. Marino had punched himself out, had he? That was how Tommy used to get them.

Joey came down off his toes. His stance changed abruptly, hands at belt level, but nearer to his body. He edged close to Marino and chugged two short blows into his middle, whipping the punches with body leverage. The crowd roared to its feet. Men sitting in the back rows swore it was as though they were seeing Tommy White again.

Marino grunted, turned pale, and retreated. Strength coursed like hot wine through Joey's limbs. He pressed forward, anchored to the canvas floor like a sturdy tree, and raised his sights. The short, sharp, murderous punches whipped to Marino's jaw. Through the smoky air the gloves flew—punch, punch, punch!

When there was nothing more in front of him to punch, Joey leaned from a neutral corner and yelled at the body on the canvas as the referee's arm rose and fell, "Get up. . . .Get up and fight! I ain't finished yet."

- wheeze (HWEEZ) breathe hard
- stance (STANS) position of the feet

Then somehow he was in Doc's arms. Doc was kissing him and there were tears on Doc's face. He was crying, "Tommy . . . Tommy . . . Joey boy. . . It was just like Tommy was alive again. Joey, baby, there ain't nothing goin' to stop you now. . . ."

ALL THINGS CONSIDERED

1. The champion was (a) Tommy. (b) Joey. (c) Kid Marino.
2. The best boxer was (a) Tommy. (b) Joey. (c) Kid Marino.
3. Tommy was killed (a) in a boxing accident. (b) by his brother. (c) in the war.
4. Joey quit as soon as he (a) stepped into the ring. (b) was hit. (c) became tired.
5. Joey went back to the ring to (a) keep the championship in the family. (b) get revenge for his brother. (c) make money.
6. The winner of the Kid Marino fight would (a) be champion. (b) go on to Madison Square Garden. (c) get the chance to fight Tommy.
7. For almost six rounds Marino (a) never hit Joey. (b) was winning. (c) did not try to fight.
8. When Marino hit Joey on the arm, Joey (a) was ready to quit. (b) fought back. (c) never felt it.
9. Joey changed completely when he learned that he had (a) a good chance to become the next champion. (b) his brother's blood in his veins. (c) more talent than Marino.
10. As the story ends, you can conclude that Doc thinks Joey is (a) even braver than his brother. (b) a courageous fighter. (c) lucky to have gotten Tommy's blood.

THINKING IT THROUGH

1. Do you think that Joey will ever again be a quitter? Why or why not?
2. What made Joey change so suddenly? Was it something in his blood or something in his mind? Give reasons for your answer.
3. Do you think this story is realistic—that is, do you think it could have happened in real life? Why or why not?

Literary Skills

Plot and Conflict

The plot of a story begins when the main character is faced with a **conflict**, or problem. For example, in "Thicker Than Water," Joey, the main character, is faced with the problem of overcoming his cowardice in the boxing ring. That is his conflict.

There are three basic kinds of conflicts. There can be a conflict between persons. (Will Beth win the election over George for class president?) There can be a conflict between persons and things (objects or forces). (Will the lost hikers survive in the blizzard?) And there can be a conflict within a person. (Should Jenny keep the money she found or return it?)

What kind of conflict does Joey face in "Thicker Than Water"? How does he overcome this conflict?

Plot and Foreshadowing

An author will sometimes drop a hint about what is going to happen later on in the story. Such a hint is called **foreshadowing**. When the author of "Thicker Than Water" tells us that Joey once received a blood transfusion from his brother Tommy, we don't think much about it at the time. Only when we come to the end of the story do we remember the incident and its importance in the story.

Look back at the first paragraph of "Thicker Than Water." Which event that happens later is foreshadowed in this paragraph?

Composition

Follow your teacher's instructions before completing *one* of these writing assignments.

1. In "Thicker Than Water," Joey's main conflict is within himself. Suppose Joey's conflict is with another person or with an object or force. Write two sentences describing what these conflicts might be.

2. Suppose that Joey kept a diary. (a) Write three sentences that he might have written before his fight with Kid Marino. (b) Write three sentences that he might have written after the fight.

VOCABULARY AND SKILL REVIEW ─────────

Before completing the exercises that follow, you may wish to review the **bold-faced** words on pages 88–98.

I. On a separate sheet of paper, write the italicized term that best fills the blank in each sentence. Each term should be used only once.

conflict	*disability*	*ecstatic*	*motivate*	*negative*
obvious	*positive*	*quip*	*ruptured*	*strategy*

1. Our teacher can _____ us to do our homework.
2. Was her _____ within herself or with another girl?
3. On talk shows people often try to make a good _____ .
4. In boxing, _____ is just as important as it is in chess.
5. People who are happy with themselves have a _____ attitude.
6. Sam felt like a failure, and his _____ feelings about himself have hurt his performance in school.
7. The truth is often _____ to everyone, although sometimes it is not.
8. Marie's _____ makes it very difficult for her to swim.
9. Their friendship was _____ by the argument.
10. When our team won the championship, we were all _____ .

II. On a separate sheet of paper, write two or three sentences to answer each of the following questions.

1. Tobi had a conflict with Angela about a position on the swim team. She also had a conflict with herself about "sportswomanship." Which conflict was more important in this story? Why?
2. Joey had a conflict with Kid Marino in the boxing ring, but he also had a conflict with himself about courage. Which conflict was more important in this story? Why?
3. The theme of this unit is "searching for yourself." How were Tobi and Joey searching for themselves?
4. Which of the following sentences foreshadows the outcome of "Thicker Than Water"? Why?
   a. Tommy White was a champion, but his kid brother Joey was a dog.
   b. (Tommy White) came back from a grave and knocked out Kid Marino in the seventh round at the American Legion Stadium in our town.
   c. Tommy had the heart of a lion.

THE KIND OF MAN SHE COULD LOVE

by O. Henry

▶ This story was written many years ago, but its theme will never become old. It is about a young man who wants to get ahead in the world. Unfortunately, the way he tries to do this is his big mistake.

Mr. Owen Chandler is first seen in his rented room. He is pushing an iron back and forth, pressing into the pants the straight creases that will form two straight lines, front and back, from his polished shoes to the edge of his low-cut vest. Mr. Chandler, you see, lives in genteel poverty; that is, he tries not to *look* poor.

We next see Mr. Chandler as he descends the steps of his apartment. He is correctly clothed. He is calm, assured, handsome. He looks to be the typical New York up-and-coming young man-about-town, slightly bored, as he sets out to enjoy the pleasures of the evening.

Young Mr. Chandler was employed in the office of an architect. His pay was 18 dollars a week. He considered architecture to be the highest form of art, and he felt it an honor to be so employed.

Out of each week's earnings Chandler set aside one dollar. At the end of each ten weeks he took the ten dollars thus saved and had himself a gentleman's evening on the town. In his freshly pressed suit he felt like a millionaire, and he took himself where life was brightest and showiest and most expensive. There he dined among the wealthy. With ten dollars, a man may play the part of one who belongs to the upper crust of society—for an evening. For the next 69 evenings he would eat at lunch counters or cook for himself on the one-burner stove in his room. Chandler was willing to pay the price. Truly here was a son of the great city of razzle-dazzle. One

---

- **genteel** (jen TEEL) polite; well–mannered
- **razzle-dazzle** (RAZ ul-DAZ ul) glamour

evening in the limelight made up for seventy minus one in the lamp-light of his room.

Even on this wintry night young Mr. Chandler walked slowly in order to lengthen the pleasure of his evening. Suddenly, then, from around a corner came a girl. She stopped, to avoid bumping into him. Then she slipped on a patch of ice and fell to the sidewalk.

Chandler, always the gentleman, helped her to her feet. The girl hobbled to the wall of the building, leaned against it, and thanked him.

"I think my ankle is hurt," she said. "It twisted when I fell."

"Does it pain you much?" asked Chandler.

"Only when I rest my weight on it. I think I will be able to walk in a minute or two."

"Can I be of any further help?" suggested the young man. "I will call a cab or—"

"Thank you," said the girl softly but heartily. "I am sure you need not trouble yourself any further. It was so awkward of me."

Chandler looked at the girl and found her swiftly drawing his interest. She was pretty in a proper way. Her eyes were merry and kind. She was clothed in a plain black dress that suggested a sort of uniform such as shop girls wear. Her dark brown hair showed its

- **limelight** (LYM lyt) center of attention
- **heartily** (HAHRT uh lee) with spirit; with enthusiasm

107

curls beneath a cheap hat of black straw whose only ornament was a velvet ribbon and bow. She could have posed as a model for the self-respecting working girl of the best type.

A sudden idea came into the head of the young architect. He would ask this girl to dine with him. Here was something that had before been absent from his evenings out. Here was something that would double the pleasure of this long awaited night on the town.

"I think," he offered, "that your foot needs more rest than you are ready to admit. So please allow me to suggest something that will allow you to rest it and that will, at the same time, do me a favor. I was on my way to dine by myself when you fell, so to speak, at my feet. So why don't you come with me? We can have a warm dinner and pleasant talk. By that time your ankle will carry you home very nicely, I am sure."

The girl looked quickly up into Chandler's clear, pleasant face. Her eyes twinkled once very brightly, then she smiled. "But we don't know each other. It wouldn't be right, would it?" she said innocently.

"There is nothing wrong about it," said the young man. "I'll introduce myself—permit me—Mr. Owen Chandler. After our dinner, which I will try to make as pleasant as possible, I will bid you good evening or attend you safely to your door, whichever you prefer."

"But dear me!" said the girl, with a glance at Chandler's quite proper coat and scarf. "In this old dress and hat!"

"Never mind that," said Chandler cheerfully. "I'm sure you look more charming in them than anyone else we might see in the finest restaurant in town."

"My ankle does hurt yet," admitted the girl, trying a step or two. "I think I will accept your invitation, Mr. Chandler. You may call me—Miss Marian."

"Come then, Miss Marian," said the young architect, with perfect manners. "You will not have far to walk. There is a very respectable and good restaurant in the next block. You will have to lean on my arm—so—and walk slowly. It is lonely dining all by oneself. I'm just a little bit glad that you slipped on the ice."

When the two were seated at a candle-lit table, Chandler began to experience the real joy that his regular outings always brought to him. The restaurant was not so showy as one farther down Broadway, which he preferred, but it was nearly so. The tables were well filled with prosperous looking diners. There was an orchestra playing softly enough to make conversation a pleasure. The lighting,

and the menu too, were perfect. The young girl, even in her cheap hat and dress, held herself with an air that added distinction to the natural beauty of her face and figure. And it is certain that she looked at Chandler, with his calm manner and his warm dark eyes, with something not far from admiration.

Then it happened. The Madness of Manhattan, the Phony Fuss of the Fashionable, the Bug of Broadway bit our hero. There he was on the World's stage, so to speak. All eyes were on him. Yes, and he was dressed for the part. All his good angels had not the power to prevent him from acting out his role.

So he began to brag to Miss Marian about his clubs, his golf, his polo, his horses, his tours abroad. He even threw out hints of a yacht lying at Larchmont. He could see that she was impressed by this talk, and it egged him on. He spoke of great wealth. He mentioned familiarly a few names that he had read about on the society pages of the newspaper.

"This way of living you speak of," she said, "sounds so useless

• **distinction** (dis TING shun) special quality

109

and purposeless. Haven't you any work to do in the world that might interest you more?"

For a moment, then, Chandler saw the pure gold of this girl shine through the mist that his bragging had raised. But, alas, he went on: "Why my dear Miss Marian—work! Think of dressing every day for dinner, of making half a dozen calls in the afternoon. Think of having to play polo two evenings a week, of golf several whole afternoons, of having to take tea with the Rockefellers or Whitneys, if they so desire. We do-nothings are the hardest workers in the land."

The dinner was ended, the waiter generously tipped, and the two walked out to the corner where they had met. Miss Marian walked very well now. Her limp was hardly noticeable.

"Thank you for a nice time," she said. "I must run home now. I liked the dinner very much, Mr. Chandler."

He shook hands with her, smiling politely, saying something about a game of bridge at his club. He watched her walk rather rapidly eastward. Then he slowly walked homeward.

In his chilly bedroom, Chandler put away his evening clothes for a sixty-nine days' rest. He went about it thoughtfully. "That was a stunning girl," he said to himself. "She's all right, too, even if she is a working girl. Perhaps if I had told her the truth instead of all that razzle-dazzle, we might—but, confound it, I had to play up to my clothes."

Thus spoke the young architect who hoped, in his innocent way, to become one of the "best" in the great town of Manhattan.

As for the girl, she sped swiftly across town until she arrived at a handsome mansion. Here she entered and hurried up the stairs to a room where a young lady was looking anxiously out the window.

"Oh, you silly, reckless girl!" exclaimed the older girl. "When will you quit frightening us this way? It's two hours since you ran out in that rag of an old dress and Marie's hat. Mama has been so alarmed. She sent Louis in the auto to try to find you. You are a bad, thoughtless thing."

The older girl touched a button and, in a moment, a maid came in.

"Marie, tell Mama that Miss Marian has returned."

"Don't scold, Sister. I only ran down to Madame Theo's to discuss the dress she is making for me. My costume and Marie's hat were just what I needed. Everyone thought I was a shop girl, I am sure."

"Dinner is over, dear. You stayed so late."

"I know. I slipped on the sidewalk and turned my ankle. I could not walk, so I hobbled into a restaurant and sat there until I was better. That is why I took so long."

The two girls sat in the window seat, looking out at the lights and the steady stream of vehicles hurrying by. The younger one grew serious.

"We will have to marry someday," she said, dreamily. "We have so much money that we will not be allowed to disappoint the public. Do you want me to tell you the kind of man I could love, Sis?"

"Go on, you scatterbrain," smiled the other.

"I could love a man with dark and kind eyes, a man who is gentle and respectful to poor girls. I don't object to a handsome man so long as he is good and does not try to flirt. But I could love him only if he had an ambition, a goal in life, some work to do in this world. I would not care how poor he was if I could help him work his way up. But, dear Sister, the kind of man we always meet, the man who lives an idle life between society and his clubs, this kind of man I could not love even if his eyes were dark, even if he were kind to poor girls whom he met on the street."

ALL THINGS CONSIDERED _____

1. Mr. Chandler goes out for an expensive dinner once (a) a week. (b) every ten weeks. (c) a year.
2. At these times, Mr. Chandler always goes where (a) his friends eat. (b) the girls are prettiest. (c) the rich people eat.
3. By calling him a "son of the great city of razzle-dazzle," the author means that (a) Chandler is impressed by showy appearances. (b) Chandler is wealthy. (c) Chandler is a high-class thief.
4. Chandler and Miss Marian meet because they (a) bump into each other. (b) work in the same place. (c) are old friends.
5. To Chandler, Miss Marian looks (a) rich but nice. (b) strange but happy. (c) poor but attractive.
6. By saying "the bug of Broadway bit our hero," the author means that Chandler (a) wanted to become an actor. (b) was tempted to act like a wealthy man. (c) had too much to drink.
7. Chandler claimed to be (a) a great inventor. (b) the son of a powerful politician. (c) so rich that he never had to work.
8. Miss Marian responds by saying that (a) his way of life sounds useless. (b) she wishes she were wealthy. (c) she is also wealthy.
9. At the end, Chandler (a) is pleased with his behavior. (b) wonders if he should have told the truth. (c) decides money is more important than anything else.
10. We learn that Miss Marian could have loved Chandler if he had (a) told the truth. (b) been wealthy. (c) been more thoughtful.

THINKING IT THROUGH _____

1. Chandler saved his money so he could act like a wealthy New Yorker one evening out of seventy. What other things could he have done with his savings? Which of these would have been best for Chandler? Why?
2. Part of searching for yourself is acting out different roles—finding out which role seems best for you. How does this statement explain Chandler's behavior? How does it explain his failure as well as his success?
3. What might have happened if Chandler had told Miss Marian the truth about himself?

Literary Skills

Conclusion of a Plot

Every story has a beginning, a middle, and an end. The ending of a story is called the **conclusion**.

As explained earlier (p. 95), every plot has a conflict that the main character faces and must resolve. The actions that the main character takes to resolve the conflict lead to the climax or turning point of the story. Following the climax, comes the conclusion, in which the conflict is resolved.

Here are the three parts of "The Kind of Man She Could Love." On a separate sheet of paper, write a sentence that describes, in your own words, the conclusion of the story.

Beginning: Owen Chandler wants to appear richer than he actually is, so he saves his money for a night on the town. At the end of ten weeks, he gets dressed for his night on the town. He walks to the restaurant.

Middle: He meets Miss Marian. They have dinner. He lies to her about his wealth. He goes home, wondering if he made a mistake in bragging.

Conclusion: _____.

Composition

Follow your teacher's instructions before completing *one* of these writing assignments.

1. Below are four words from the story, "The Kind of Man She Could Love." Without copying any sentences from the story, use each of these words in a sentence about Owen Chandler. Write your sentences on a separate sheet of paper.

    genteel   razzle-dazzle   gentleman   bragging

2. Write a new conclusion to the story. Suppose that Miss Marian is a poor working girl. Describe how she secretly follows Owen Chandler to his room, where she watches him go in and shut the door. Tell what she thinks.

THE BUTTERFLY AND THE CATERPILLAR

A Fable Old Is Here Retold

by Joseph Lauren

▶ The following poem has a lesson to teach all of us. What
can we learn from a butterfly and a caterpillar? Read the
poem and find out.

A butterfly, one summer morn,
Sat on a spray of blossoming thorn
And, as he sipped and drank his share
Of honey from the flowered air,
Below, upon the garden wall,
A caterpillar chanced to crawl.
"Horrors!" the butterfly exclaimed,
"This must be stopped! I am ashamed
That such as I should have to be
In the same world with such as he.
Protect me from such ugly things!
Disgusting shape! Where are his wings!
Fuzzy and gray! Eater of clay!
Won't someone take the worm away!"

- **lure** (LOOR) attraction
- **endow** (en DOU) enrich
- **scorn** (SKORN) have a low opinion of
- miller (MIL ur) a kind of moth

The caterpillar crawled ahead,
But, as he munched a leaf, he said,
"Eight days ago, young butterfly,
You wormed about the same as I.
Just wait—a few weeks from today
Two wings will bear me far away
To brighter blooms and lovelier lures,
With colors that outrival yours.
So, flutter-flit, be not so proud;
Each caterpillar is endowed
With power to make it by and by
A bright and merry butterfly.
Remember, you who scorn me so,
Yes you who make so loud a show,
That you and other moths and millers
Are only dressed up caterpillars."

WAYS OF KNOWING

1. This poem is called a *fable*. A fable is a story with an important lesson, or moral. What is the moral of this poem?

2. The word *loud* in the last sentence has two basic meanings. One meaning has to do with sound and the other has to do with sight. (If you are not sure of these two meanings, look up *loud* in the dictionary.) Explain how both meanings apply in the poem.

3. Change the speakers in the poem to a six-year-old and a teenager. Which one would speak as the caterpillar? Which one would speak as the butterfly? Would the moral be the same? Why or why not? Then change the speakers to a teenager and an adult and answer the same questions.

4. How might the moral of the poem apply to different parts of your own life?

LAME DEER
REMEMBERS HIS
CHILDHOOD

by John Fire/Lame Deer and Richard Erdoes

▶ Growing up—anywhere in the world—can sometimes be difficult, and sometimes funny. Growing up as a Native American is a very special experience. In this story, Lame Deer tells how it was when he was a boy.

When I was sixteen I got the name Lame Deer. It was given to me after spending four days on a hilltop, alone, without food and water. I was waiting for a vision. When it came, I knew I was a man. And I got my name.

I was born a full-blood Indian in a twelve-by-twelve log cabin between Pine Ridge and Rosebud. *Maka tanban wicasa wan*—I am a man of the earth, as we say. Our people don't call themselves Sioux or Dakota. That's white man talk. We call ourselves Ikce Wicasa—the natural humans, the free, wild, common people. I am pleased to be called that.

As with most Indian children, much of my upbringing was done by my grandparents. Among our people the relationship to one's grandparents is as strong as to one's own father and mother. We lived in a little hut way out on the prairie, in the back country. For the first few years of my life I had no contact with the outside world. Of course we had a few white man's things—coffee, iron pots, a shotgun, an old wagon. But I never thought much of where these things came from or who had made them.

Most of my childhood days weren't very exciting, and that was all right with me. We had a good, simple life. One day passed like another. Only in one way was I different from other Indian kids. I was never hungry, because my dad had so many horses and cattle.

One of my uncles used to keep a moon-counting stick, our own kind of calendar and a good one. He had a special staff and every night he cut a notch in it until the moon "died"—that is, disappeared. On the other side of this staff he made a notch for every month. He started a new stick every year in the spring. That way we always knew when it was the right day for one of our ceremonies.

Every so often my grandparents would take me to a little celebration down the creek. Grandpa always rode his old red horse, which was well known in all the tribes. We always brought plenty of food for everybody. We had squaw bread, beef, the kind of dried meat we called *papa,* and *wasna,* or pemmican, which was meat pounded together with berries and kidney fat. We also brought a kettle of coffee, wild mint tea, or soup.

Grandfather was always the leader at the *owanka osnato*—the rehearsal ground. He prepared the place carefully. Only the real warriors were allowed to dance there—men like Red Fish or Thin Elk, who had fought in the Custer battle. With the years, the dancers grew older and older and fewer and fewer.

I was the *takoja*—the pampered grandson—and like all Indian children I was spoiled. I was never scolded, never heard a harsh word. "*Ajustan*—leave it alone"—that was the worst. No one ever spanked me—Indian children aren't treated that way. When I didn't want to go to sleep my grandma would try to scare me with the *ciciye*—a kind of bogeyman. "*Takoja, istima ye*—Go to sleep, sonny," she would say, or "the *ciciye* will come after you." Nobody knew what the *ciciye* was like, but he must have been something terrible. When the *ciciye* wouldn't work anymore, I was threatened with the *siyoko*—another kind of monster. Nobody knew what the *siyoko* was like, either, but he was ten times more terrible than the *ciciye*. Grandma did not have much luck. Neither the *ciciye* nor the *siyoko* scared me for long.

People said that I didn't take after my grandpa Good Fox, whom I loved, but after my other grandfather, Crazy Heart, whom I never knew. They said I picked up where he left off, because I was so daring and full of the devil. I was told that Crazy Heart had been like that. He was hot tempered. At the same time, he saved lots of people, gave wise counsel, urged the people to do right. He was a good speech-maker. Everybody who listened to him said that he was a very encouraging man. He always advised patience, except when it came to himself. Then his temper got in the way.

I was like that. I liked to play rough. We played shinny ball, a kind of hockey game. We made the ball and sticks ourselves. We played the hoop game, shot with a bow and arrow. We had foot races, horse races, and water races.

I liked to ride horseback behind my older sister, holding onto her. As I got a little bigger she would hold onto me. By the time I was nine years old I had my own horse to ride. It was a beautiful gray pony my father had given me together with a fine saddle and a very colorful Mexican saddle blanket. That gray was my favorite companion, and I was proud to ride him. But he was not mine for long. I lost him through my own fault.

Nonge Pahloka—the Piercing of Her Ears—is a big event in a little girl's life. By this ceremony her parents, and especially her grandmother, want to show how much they love and honor her.

- **pampered** (PAM purd) spoiled; allowed too many privileges
- **counsel** (KOUN sul) advice

They ask a man who is respected for his bravery or wisdom to pierce the ears of their daughter. The grandmother puts on a big feed. The little girl is placed on a blanket surrounded by the many gifts her family will give away in her name. The man who does the piercing is much admired and gets the most valuable gift. Afterward they get down to the really important part—the eating.

Well, one day I watched somebody pierce a girl's ears. I saw the fuss they made over it, the presents he got, and all that. I thought I should do this to my little sister. She was about four years old at the time and I was nine. I don't know anymore what made me want to do this. Maybe I wanted to feel big and important like the man whom I had watched perform the ceremony. Maybe I wanted to get a big present. Maybe I wanted to make my sister cry. I don't remember what was in my little boy's mind then.

Anyway, I found some wire and made a pair of "earrings" out of it. Then, when my sister and I were alone in our cabin, I asked her, "Would you like me to put these on you?" She smiled. "*Ohan*—yes." I didn't have the sharp bone one uses for the ear-piercing, and I

didn't know the prayer that goes with it. I just had an old awl but thought this would do fine. Oh, how my sister yelled. I had to hold her down, but I got that awl through her earlobes and managed to put the "earrings" in. I was proud of the neat job I had done.

When my mother came home and saw those wire loops in my sister's ears, she gasped. But she recovered soon enough to go and tell my father. That was one of the few occasions he talked to me. He said, "I should punish you and whip you, but I won't. That's not my way. You'll get your punishment later."

Well, some time passed and I forgot all about it. One morning my father announced that we were going to a powwow. He had hitched up the wagon and it was heaped high with boxes and bundles. At that powwow my father let it be known that he was doing a big *otuhan*—a give-away. He put my sister on a rug, a pretty Navajo blanket, and laid out things to give away—quilts, food, blankets, a fine shotgun, his own new pair of cowboy boots, a sheepskin coat, enough to fit out a whole family. Dad was telling the people, "I want to honor my daughter for her ear-piercing. This should have been done openly, but my son did it at home. I guess he's too small. He didn't know any better." This was a long speech for Dad. He motioned me to come closer. I was sitting on my pretty gray horse. I thought we were both cutting a very fine figure. Well, before I knew it, Dad had given my horse away, together with its beautiful saddle and blanket. I had to ride home in the wagon, and I cried all the way.

The old man said, "You have your punishment now, but you will feel better later on. All her life your sister will tell about how you pierced her ears. She'll brag about you. I bet you are the only small boy who ever did this big ceremony."

That was no comfort to me. My beautiful gray was gone. I was heartbroken for three days.

On the fourth morning I looked out the door and there stood a little white stallion with a new saddle and a silver-plated bit. "It's yours," my father told me. "Get on it." I was happy again.

• awl (AWL) **small tool for making holes**

ALL THINGS CONSIDERED ———————————————————

1. Lame Deer got his name when he was (a) born. (b) sixteen. (c) in school.
2. Lame Deer was raised by (a) his mother. (b) both parents. (c) his parents and his grandparents.
3. A moon-counting stick was a kind of (a) calendar. (b) story. (c) hunting tool.
4. According to the story, Indian children (a) had no horses. (b) were never spanked. (c) were not allowed to talk.
5. At the celebration down the creek, the dancers were (a) the children. (b) the women. (c) the real warriors.
6. To get him to go to sleep, his grandmother would say, (a) "Boo!" (b) "Your father will spank you!" (c) "The *ciciye* will come after you."
7. By the time he was nine years old, Lame Deer (a) had his ears pierced. (b) got his own horse. (c) went to school.
8. According to custom, a girl's ears were pierced by (a) a big brother. (b) a man of bravery and wisdom. (c) her mother.
9. Lame Deer was punished for (a) piercing his sister's ears. (b) stealing a horse. (c) playing too rough.
10. A few days after he was punished, Lame Deer (a) got a new horse. (b) was punished again. (c) brought his sister a horse.

THINKING IT THROUGH ———————————————————

1. In all societies, family life is important. How was Lame Deer's family life different from your own? What was good about his family life that you haven't experienced? What is good about your family life that Lame Deer probably never experienced?
2. Why is it good for a person to learn the ways of the larger society outside the home? Why is it good for a person to keep the ways of his or her own people? Do you think it is necessary to choose between these two ways of life, or is it possible to live happily with both?
3. Before punishing his son, Lame Deer's father says, "You have your punishment now, but you will feel better later on." Do you agree or disagree with that statement? Explain.

121

Building from Details

Paraphrasing

Once you understand clearly what you have read, you should be able to **paraphrase** it, or retell it in your own words. Reread the first paragraph of "Lame Deer Remembers His Childhood," on page 116. Then read the following paraphrase of it.

> Lame Deer got his name when he was sixteen. He spent four days alone on a hilltop with nothing to eat or drink. Then he had a vision and got his name.

A paraphrase should include the most important details of the story or passage. Although a paraphrase may not be exact, it should give the main idea of what you have read. It is, in short, a summary of the passage.

Look at the second paragraph of the story on page 116. Read it several times. On a separate sheet of paper, write a short paraphrase of it.

Composition

Follow your teacher's instructions before completing *one* of these writing assignments.

1. Lame Deer does not describe the cabin in which he was born. Using your imagination, write two or three sentences describing the cabin.
2. Two ceremonies are described in the story: Lame Deer's fast and vision on the hilltop, and a young girl's ear-piercing. Both of these ceremonies celebrate a young person's coming of age. What events in America today mark a child's coming of age? How do people celebrate these events? Write several sentences describing a modern coming-of-age celebration.

VOCABULARY AND SKILL REVIEW ————————

Before completing the exercises that follow, you may wish to review the **bold-faced** words on pages 106–118.

I. On a separate sheet of paper, mark each item *true* or *false.* If it is false, explain what is wrong with the sentence.

1. A person who enjoys the limelight is usually very shy.
2. Most kids would be proud of having parents of distinction.
3. He was bored by the razzle-dazzle of the city.
4. At a sports night banquet, most of the athletes eat heartily.
5. The musician was endowed with great talent.
6. Young people are foolish to listen to the counsel of their parents.
7. It is polite to scorn your friends.
8. The pampered child was a pleasure to know.
9. A lure is something unattractive, as the lure of snake-filled swamps.
10. The genteel woman was a charming guest.

II. Each sentence below gives a clue about one of the following:

character   setting   conclusion

On a separate sheet of paper, write the sentence and tell whether it gives a clue about character, setting, or conclusion.

1. Owen Chandler is first seen in his rented room.
2. The butterfly was very conceited.
3. A butterfly sat on a spray of blossoming thorn.
4. Truly here was a son of the great city of razzle-dazzle.
5. Lame Deer was punished for piercing his sister's ears, but in a few days he was given another pony.
6. The butterfly thought it was better than the caterpillar.
7. To get his name, Lame Deer spent four days and nights alone, without food and water, waiting for a vision.
8. Owen Chandler never knew what kind of a girl he had been talking with.
9. The action takes place during Lame Deer's childhood.
10. I was the *takoja*—the pampered grandson.

Robert Frost (1874-1963)

Robert Frost is probably the most popular American poet of the 20th century. He may also be the best. It is easy to see why he is so popular. He uses the rhythms and rhymes that people expect in a poem. He writes about everyday topics in everyday language. Frost seems to have an effortless skill of turning common speech into poetry and commonplace events into unique and important moments.

Frost's life—as well as his poetry—was filled with contradictions. He came from an old New England family but was born in California. The most American of all 20th-century poets, he had to go to England to be recognized. In many of his poems, the speaker is an uneducated farmer or laborer, while in others, the speaker is a delicate poet, a singer of words. Frost objected to awards, yet he won four Pulitzer prizes. He was a farmer, a working man, a college professor, and a poet. Most of his best poems grew out of minor events in a local setting, yet their themes are universal.

Although he expressed a deep love of life and a strong faith in people, Robert Frost was a doubter and a questioner. About himself, he wrote, "I had a lover's quarrel with the world." This statement summarizes both his life and his work.

THE RUNAWAY

by Robert Frost

▶ Two people stop to watch a colt, a young Morgan horse, that is frightened by the first snow of winter. They talk about it with each other. That's all there is to the poem. Or is it?

Once when the snow of the year was beginning to fall,
We stopped by a mountain pasture to say, "Whose colt?"
A little Morgan had one forefoot on the wall,
The other curled at his breast. He dipped his head
And snorted at us. And then he had to bolt.
We heard the miniature thunder where he fled,
And we saw him, or thought we saw him, dim and grey
Like a shadow against the curtain of falling flakes.
"I think the little fellow's afraid of the snow.
He isn't winter-broken. It isn't play
With the little fellow at all. He's running away.
I doubt if even his mother could tell him, 'Sakes,
It's only weather.' He'd think she didn't know!
Where is his mother? He can't be out alone."
And now he comes again with clatter of stone,
And mounts the wall again with whited eyes
And all his tail that isn't held up straight,
He shudders his coat as if to throw off flies,
"Whoever it is that leaves him out so late,
When other creatures have gone to stall and bin,
Ought to be told to come and take him in."

WAYS OF KNOWING

1. Who is the runaway in the poem? Why is he running away?

2. Will running away help the colt overcome his fear? Tell why or why not. Does running away from a problem ever help? Explain your answer.

3. What does the speaker think should be done to help the colt? Can this same help be given to a person who runs away? Explain your answer.

- colt (KOHLT) **a young horse**
- mount (MOUNT) **get up on**

RUNAWAYS

by Elizabeth Swados

▶ *Runaways* is a musical play that was performed in New York in 1978, and then made into a movie. Elizabeth Swados, who was not much older than the young people she wrote about, was the composer, the director, and the writer of the play. She hired nineteen actors between the ages of eleven and twenty-five. For over half a year, they worked together creating the songs, recitations, and scenes in the play. The only thing Liz didn't do was perform on the stage. She did, however, play the guitar—just off stage.

The following three poems come at the beginning of *Runaways.* They set the tone and introduce the themes. As you read, try to imagine how they might be performed on stage.

If you decide to make a play
about Runaways
don't expect that Runaways
    are only kids.
Look everywhere, in the eyes of everyone.
Start with yourself.
The world is full of people running.
You are a world full of questions.

When we made *Runaways*
we spent hours and days
running in place
as fast as we could
our thighs, our calves
our knees screaming.
We were sweating, our
hearts were pounding
we tried to find the sensation
of urgency
of *having* to leave.
We all wanted to erase different nightmares.
But we *all* had nightmares.

We discovered that fantasy saves us—
you can teach yourself to dream.
Out of a pile of paper towels
we made dolls, drums
even spaghetti and meatballs.
We made cousins out of empty shoes
boyfriends and girlfriends out of pillows.
Our parents became the elegant
photographs of antique furniture.
And we believed ourselves totally
as any loners would.

WAYS OF KNOWING

1. The first poem says that runaways are not just kids. Who else could be called runaways? How can you tell?

2. Why do the kids in the second poem run in place? What do they discover about people who run away?

3. The third poem says that "fantasy saves us." How is this so? What can fantasy do to help someone who wants to run away?

4. Does the poet approve or disapprove of running away? Do you think it is sometimes necessary to run away? Do you think it is sometimes better to stay and face your problems? Give examples to support your answer.

- fantasy (FAN tuh see) **imaginary happenings**
- elegant (EL uh gunt) **very pleasant; graceful; splendid**

127

Oral Interpretation

Choral Reading

Choral (KOR ul) reading is reading aloud in a group. The group may be as small as two or as large as 20 or more. Some poems sound more interesting when they are read chorally. This is probably the case with *Runaways*.

Before you do a choral reading, think about how you will organize the reading. First, decide which lines or words will be read by the entire group, which by a smaller group, and which by one person. Then, decide at what rate (fast or slow), at what volume (loud or soft), and with what pauses (where and for how long) the poem should be read.

Begin by reading the poem to yourself several times. Listen to the sounds. Imagine how a group might read it. Take notes on your ideas. Discuss your ideas with others in the group.

The following are suggestions for preparing a choral reading of the three poems from *Runaways*. They may help you get started.

Divide the first poem in the following manner:

Sentence 1: Read by the whole group.
Sentence 2: Read by two students.
Sentence 3: Read by one student.
Sentences 4 and 5: Read by the whole group.

For the second poem, you might run in place as you recite. Pause for a long time at each of the commas. Read some words louder and with more emphasis *(screaming, pounding, having, all)*. Read the last two sentences in whispers. Use creative gestures to make the third poem even more interesting.

LATHER AND NOTHING ELSE

by Hernando Téllez

▶ Imagine a barber in some distant country. One day, a powerful leader walks into his shop. What will this terrifying meeting tell him about himself?

He came in without a word. I was sharpening my best razor on the leather strop. When I recognized him I started to shake. But he did not notice. To cover my nervousness, I went on with the razor. I tried the edge with the tip of my thumb and took another look at it against the light.

Meanwhile, he was taking off his cartridge belt with the pistol holster suspended from it. He put it on a hook in the wardrobe and hung his cap above it. Then he turned full around toward me and, loosening his tie, remarked: "It's hot as the devil. I want a shave." With that he took his seat.

I estimated he had a four days' growth of beard. That would be the four days he had been gone on a raid on our men. His face looked burnt, tanned by the sun.

I started to work carefully on the shaving soap. I scraped some slices from the cake, dropped them into the mug, then added a little lukewarm water, and stirred with the brush. The lather* soon began to rise.

"We were gone long enough to get a good start on a beard," he said. I went on stirring up the lather.

"It was a good outing," he continued. "We caught the leaders. Some of them we brought back dead. Others are still alive. But they'll all be dead soon."

> • strop (STROP) a strip of leather used to sharpen a razor
> • **suspend** (sus PEND) hang down

* The word *lather* has two meanings: (1) the foam whipped up from soap to be put on the face for shaving, and (2) to be very excited, all fired up; to be nervously agitated, almost angry.

129

"How many did you take?" I asked.

"Fourteen. We had to go pretty far in to find them. But now they're paying for it. And not one will escape—not a single one."

He leaned back in the chair when he saw the brush in my hand, full of lather. I had not yet put the sheet on him. I was certainly flustered. Taking a sheet from the drawer, I tied it around this villain's neck.

He went on talking. He evidently took it for granted I was on the side of the existing government.

"The people must have gotten a scare with what happened the other day," he said.

"Yes," I replied, as I finished tying the knot on the back of his neck, which smelt of sweat.

"Good show, wasn't it?"

"Very good," I answered, turning my attention now to the brush. The man closed his eyes wearily and awaited the cool caress of the lather.

I had never seen him so close before. The day he ordered the people to file through the schoolyard to look upon the four rebels hanging there, my path had crossed his briefly. But the sight of those mutilated bodies kept me from paying attention to the face of the man who had been directing it all. And here he was now—I had him in my hands.

It was not a disagreeable face, certainly. And the beard, which aged him a bit, was not unbecoming. His name was Torres, Captain Torres.

I started to lay on the first coat of lather. He kept his eyes closed.

"I would love to catch a nap," he said, "but there's a lot to be done this evening."

I lifted the brush and asked, "A firing party?"

"Something of the sort," he replied.

"All of them?"

"No, just a few."

I went on lathering his face. My hands began to tremble again. The man could not be aware of this, which was lucky for me. But I

- flustered (FLUS turd) **confused**
- rebel (REB ul) **one who resists, or opposes, authority**
- mutilate (MYOO tuhl ayt) **to cut up in a cruel, or vicious, way**

130

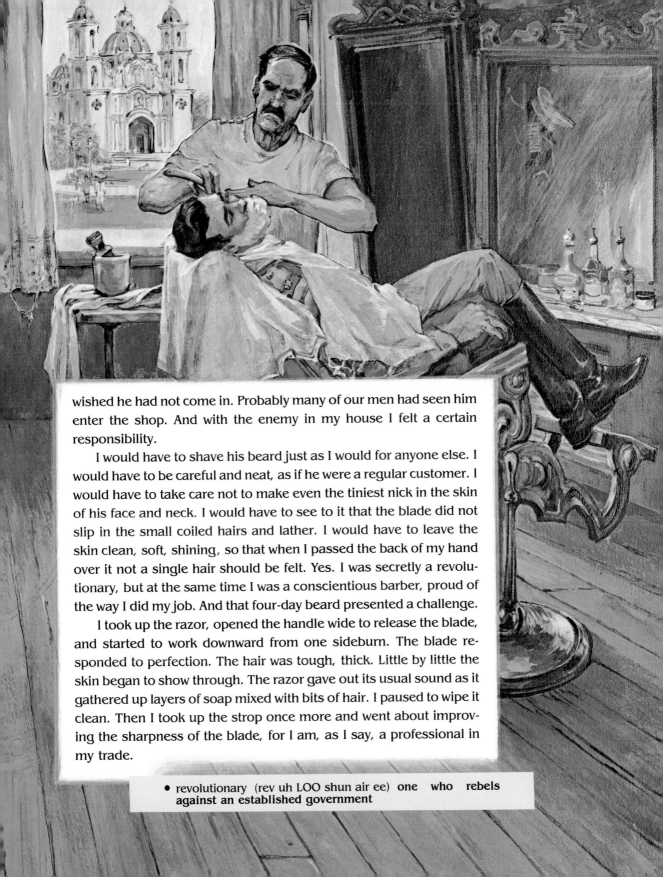

wished he had not come in. Probably many of our men had seen him enter the shop. And with the enemy in my house I felt a certain responsibility.

I would have to shave his beard just as I would for anyone else. I would have to be careful and neat, as if he were a regular customer. I would have to take care not to make even the tiniest nick in the skin of his face and neck. I would have to see to it that the blade did not slip in the small coiled hairs and lather. I would have to leave the skin clean, soft, shining, so that when I passed the back of my hand over it not a single hair should be felt. Yes. I was secretly a revolutionary, but at the same time I was a conscientious barber, proud of the way I did my job. And that four-day beard presented a challenge.

I took up the razor, opened the handle wide to release the blade, and started to work downward from one sideburn. The blade responded to perfection. The hair was tough, thick. Little by little the skin began to show through. The razor gave out its usual sound as it gathered up layers of soap mixed with bits of hair. I paused to wipe it clean. Then I took up the strop once more and went about improving the sharpness of the blade, for I am, as I say, a professional in my trade.

• revolutionary (rev uh LOO shun air ee) one who rebels against an established government

The man, who had kept his eyes closed, now opened them, put a hand out from under the sheet, felt the shaven part of his face, and said: "Come at six o'clock this evening to the school."

"Will it be like the other day?" I asked, stiff with horror.

"It may be even better," he replied.

"What are you planning to do?"

"I'm not sure yet. But we'll have a good time."

Once more he leaned back and shut his eyes. I came closer, the razor held high.

"Are you going to punish all of them?" I timidly ventured.

"Yes, all of them."

The lather was drying on his face. I must hurry. Through the mirror, I took a look at the street. It appeared about as usual: there was the grocery shop with two or three customers. Then I glanced at the clock—two-thirty.

The razor kept moving—up, down, up, down. Now from the other sideburn, up, down. It was a blue beard, a thick one. He should let it grow like some poets, or some priests. It would suit him well. Many people would not recognize him. And that would be a good thing for him, I thought, as I went gently over all the throat line. At this point you really have to handle your blade skillfully, because the hair, while scantier, tends to fall into small coils. And here at the throat the pores of the skin might open, allowing tiny drops of blood to emerge. A good barber like myself stakes his reputation on not permitting this to happen to any of his customers.

And this was indeed a special customer. How many of ours had he sent to their deaths? How many had he mutilated? It was best not to think about it. Torres did not know I was his enemy. Neither he nor the others knew it. It was a secret shared by very few, which made it possible for me to inform the revolutionaries about Torres's activities in the town, to tell them what he planned to do when he went on one of his raids to hunt down rebels. So it was going to be very difficult to explain how it was that I had him in my hands and then let him go in peace, alive, clean-shaven.

- **timid** (TIM ud) shy
- **venture** (VEN chur) express with caution
- **scanty** (SKAN tee) not enough; less of
- **reputation** (rep yuh TAY shun) the opinion of others
- **activities** (ak TIV uh teez) doings; movements

His face was now almost entirely clean-shaven. He looked younger, several years younger than when he had come in. I suppose that always happens to men who enter and leave barbershops. Under the strokes of my razor Torres was made young again. Yes, because I am a good barber, the best in this town, and I say this in all modesty.

A little more lather here under the chin, on the Adam's apple, right near the great vein. How hot it is! Torres must be sweating just as I am. But he is not afraid. He is perfectly relaxed, not even giving thought to what he will do to his prisoners this evening. I, on the other hand, I who am cleaning his skin with this razor but avoiding the drawing of blood, careful with every stroke—I cannot keep my thoughts in order.

Confound the moment he entered my shop! I am a revolutionary but not a murderer. And it would be so easy to kill him. He deserves it. Or does he? No, confound it! No one deserves to be sacrificed because someone else is dying to become an assassin. What is to be gained by it? Nothing. Others and still others keep coming. The first kills the second, and then these kill the next, and so on until everything becomes a sea of blood. I could cut his throat—so, swish, swish! With his eyes shut he would not even see the flash of the razor or the gleam in my eye. He would not even have time to moan.

But I'm shaking like a regular murderer. From his throat a stream of blood would flow on the sheet, over the chair, down on my hands, onto the floor. I would have to close the door. But the warm blood would keep flowing, along the floor, indelible. It would reach out to the street, like a scarlet stream.

I'm sure that with a good strong blow, a deep cut, he would feel no pain. He would not suffer at all. And what would I do then with the body? Where would I hide it? I would have to flee, leave all this behind, take shelter far away, very far away. But they would follow until they caught up with me. "The murderer of Captain Torres. He slit his throat while shaving him. What a cowardly thing to do!"

And others would say: "The avenger of our people! A name to remember! He was the town barber. No one knew he was fighting for our cause."

- **modesty** (MAHD us tee) **lack of conceit**
- indelible (in DEL uh bul) **cannot be erased; permanent**
- avenger (uh VENJ ur) **one who takes revenge**

133

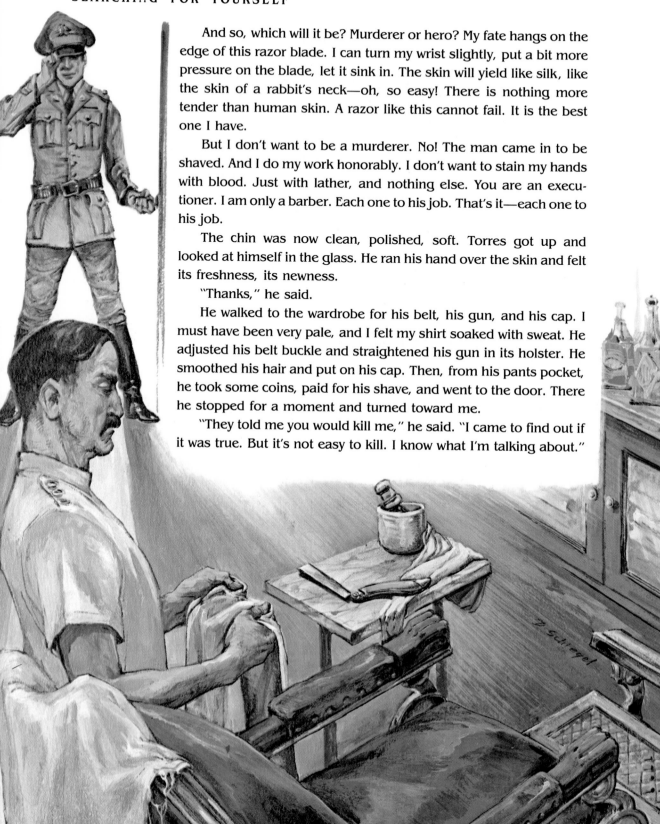

And so, which will it be? Murderer or hero? My fate hangs on the edge of this razor blade. I can turn my wrist slightly, put a bit more pressure on the blade, let it sink in. The skin will yield like silk, like the skin of a rabbit's neck—oh, so easy! There is nothing more tender than human skin. A razor like this cannot fail. It is the best one I have.

But I don't want to be a murderer. No! The man came in to be shaved. And I do my work honorably. I don't want to stain my hands with blood. Just with lather, and nothing else. You are an executioner. I am only a barber. Each one to his job. That's it—each one to his job.

The chin was now clean, polished, soft. Torres got up and looked at himself in the glass. He ran his hand over the skin and felt its freshness, its newness.

"Thanks," he said.

He walked to the wardrobe for his belt, his gun, and his cap. I must have been very pale, and I felt my shirt soaked with sweat. He adjusted his belt buckle and straightened his gun in its holster. He smoothed his hair and put on his cap. Then, from his pants pocket, he took some coins, paid for his shave, and went to the door. There he stopped for a moment and turned toward me.

"They told me you would kill me," he said. "I came to find out if it was true. But it's not easy to kill. I know what I'm talking about."

ALL THINGS CONSIDERED

1. Captain Torres has just (a) won the war. (b) lost many of his soldiers. (c) captured the leaders of the rebels.

2. A few days before, the captain (a) had taken over the government. (b) was rescued from the rebels. (c) displayed the bodies of dead rebels.

3. During the conversation, the barber is extremely (a) nervous. (b) relaxed. (c) happy.

4. The barber considers himself a rebel, but also a (a) skilled professional. (b) coward. (c) kind person.

5. That very night the captain plans to (a) invite the people to a party. (b) kill more rebels. (c) hold an election.

6. The barber tries hard to avoid (a) making even the tiniest nick in the skin. (b) sounding too friendly with the captain. (c) showing that he plans to kill the captain.

7. The barber regularly tells the rebels (a) how government leaders feel. (b) lies about the government soldiers. (c) what the captain plans to do.

8. The barber knows that he has the chance to become (a) a friend of the captain. (b) a hero. (c) a success in his profession.

9. The barber decides that he is not (a) a good barber. (b) a murderer. (c) a rebel.

10. You can tell that the barber is (a) a traitor to the rebels. (b) concerned with the lives of people in his country. (c) a coward.

THINKING IT THROUGH

1. On the surface, this story is about a barber shaving a customer. Not much seems to happen, but there is plenty of conflict. What kind of conflict takes place?

2. The conflict comes to an end when the barber makes a decision. What does he decide? Do you think his decision was right or wrong? Why?

3. The theme of this unit is "Searching for Yourself." What does this story tell the reader about that theme?

4. Do you remember the two meanings of the word *lather*? (See page 129.) With these meanings in mind, look again at the title of the story. What does the title mean to you now?

Literary Skills

The Main Parts of a Plot

On page 95, you learned that the plot of a story centers around a conflict, or problem, that is solved in a series of actions. On page 113, you saw how these actions reach a climax, or turning point, which leads to the conclusion of the story.

In this lesson you will see how **rising action** fits into this plan. Here are the four main parts of a plot:

Conflict—a question or problem that faces the main character

Rising action—the actions that lead up to the climax

Climax, or turning point—the action that brings about the conclusion

Conclusion—the ending of the story. This is what happens as a result of the decision made at the turning point. This is how the conflict is finally resolved.

Now look at the four parts of a plot in "Lather and Nothing Else." On a separate sheet of paper, complete items 1 through 4 by describing each part of the plot. The first one has been done for you.

1. *Conflict*: Will the barber take revenge on Captain Torres?

2. *Rising action*: _____.

3. *Turning point*: _____.

4. *Conclusion*: _____.

Relationships

Comparison and Contrast

A **comparison** is a way of showing how two or more things are alike. A **contrast**, on the other hand, points out the difference between two or more things. You will find examples of comparison and contrast in almost everything you read.

The author of "Lather and Nothing Else" uses both comparison and contrast to help readers understand the characters. Think about the barber and Captain Torres. Both live in the same country, under the same government. Both have very strong ideas. In another way, the characters are different. The barber is a revolutionary; Captain Torres is a powerful leader.

Here are five statements about "Lather and Nothing Else." On a separate sheet of paper, tell whether each statement is an example of comparison or contrast.

1. The main character is secretly a revolutionary, but he is also a skilled barber.
2. The barber is nervous. Captain Torres, on the other hand, is perfectly relaxed.
3. The barber does his work skillfully, like a true professional.
4. Captain Torres knows he is in great danger, but he shows no sign of fear.
5. When he left the barbershop, Captain Torres looked several years younger than when he came in.

Composition

Follow your teacher's instructions before completing *one* of these writing assignments.

1. The barber is never described in the story. Write two or three words that might describe his appearance. Next, write two or three words that describe his character. Then use these words in two or three sentences that describe the barber.
2. Suppose the barber made a different decision at the climax of the story. Write two short paragraphs to describe the following:
   a. the decision he makes
   b. the conclusion of the new story

AQUÍ SE HABLA ESPAÑOL

Leslie Jill Sokolow

▶ There can be problems when people of different backgrounds think about dating. And when different languages are involved, these problems can really be difficult to overcome. Is Andy making a mistake by dating Marina?

The pool had just opened for the summer, so there were plenty of new girls around. But it was Marina who caught my eye.

It took most of the morning before I got up the nerve to make a move. It just sort of happened. She was swimming lazily back and forth, so I dove in and made a long, slow ascent and bumped smack into her. When I surfaced, I started talking wildly so she wouldn't swim away.

"Gee! I'm sorry. I wasn't looking. Are you okay? Boy, for a little thing like you, you sure gave me a knock." I hated myself for talking so stupidly, but I couldn't collect my thoughts.

She smiled but said nothing. I tried again.

"How long have you been bumping guys at this pool? I bet all the guys go around black-and-blue 'cause of you!"

"I—I don't understand," she said, smiling faintly.

"Oh, of course. What a crazy fool I am. You know, *loco*. I don't know too much Spanish, you know. *No hablo español.* You *comprenda* me, huh?"

"Oh, yes," she replied. "I know the English, it's just the idioms that I have trouble in. Black-and-blue?"

The sun shone through her gleaming wet black hair. Tossing her head, she smiled up at me, her face shining like bright sunlight.

"My name's Andy. What's yours?"

She hesitated—that must have been the longest minute in my life—then she decided. "My name is Marina."

From then on, it was every Saturday night for the whole summer. But don't think we didn't have troubles. It was her parents. She was associating with me so much that she began to speak English, and it became a habit with her. I thought it was a good habit. Her mother didn't.

A month after I had met her, Marina invited me to her house for supper.

"Andy," she said, with that cute little accent of hers, "I did not ask my parents, you know, but please come to have supper tonight with me."

I must have looked startled, because right off she started saying how poor her home was and how they didn't have big meals like our family.

"Mari," I finally managed to answer when I'd gotten over my surprise, "that'd be great. I'd love to meet your family. I really would."

"Sure, Andy, at eight o'clock tonight, okay? We eat late."

"Sure, eight. That's fine, honey. I'll be there with bells on." I gave her a peck good-by.

The subway ride was long, hot, stuffy. I was slammed in between a pole and the door, facing a heavy woman. Sweat was pouring from everyone. The train lurched to a sudden stop—something was wrong; it would probably take a few minutes to get fixed. I couldn't stand it. There wasn't any fan, any draft, or any breeze. I had to stare at all those people jammed together, unsmiling, unhappy, staring ahead with eyes that refused to say anything. If the train hadn't started just then, I think I would have screamed.

At last I was there. I straightened my sky-blue-pink shirt, smoothed my hair, and knocked on the door. I started to shake.

A big mean-looking kid about my age stood at the door. He was the kind I was always too proud to admit I was afraid of at school.

"I'm Andrew Redina," I offered. "Marina invited me to supper tonight, you know."

"Oh, yeah." He broke into a big smile. "Come in. I'm Marina's brother, José. I got quite a sister, ain't I? Like my father was telling us," he said, ushering me to an easy chair. "Marina's got it over any girl on this here block."

He seemed pleasant, but I was relieved when Marina walked into the room. As always, she looked like something out of a story book, but then her mother was calling her. Marina turned and left, answering in rapid Spanish. Soon the living room was swarming with all the Chavez kids, ranging from seven to seventeen. An older guy who looked about twenty-two, with a little curly mustache, came over to me and smiled.

"I am Richie. Nice shirt you got there. You goin' with Carmen?"

"He's goin' with Marina, Richie."

"Wrong sister," he grinned. I felt good about his liking my shirt.

Soon we sat down to supper. Mrs. Chavez was a nice-looking woman, but her hair was unkempt. She was sweating from the stuffy room. Mr. Chavez was a rather short, stocky man who looked like an outcast sitting at the table. He spoke to no one and ate the little he did quickly.

José and Marina were speaking English. I think José did it for my sake; he was having great difficulty.

Then the trouble began. I think I must have symbolized America to the Chavezes. It started unnoticeably and ended with all the kids speaking English except little Johnny.

Then Johnny piped up, "'Ey, don't call me Juanito no more. Call me Johnny."

José laughed, "Sure we call you Johnny. Okay, everybody repeat Johnny. Carmen, say you Johnny. Marina, say you Johnny. Chico—" and so he went down the line.

- usher (USH ur) **lead someone into a place**
- unkempt (un KEMPT) **neglected; untidy**
- **symbolize** (SIM bul YZ) **be a sign or symbol of**

Suddenly Mrs. Chavez turned a sickly greenish-purple, matching her housedress, and started screaming in Spanish. She directed most of her accusations at José. He didn't act surprised. I guess he expected it.

"*Aquí se habla español,*" Mrs. Chavez screamed. Here you speak Spanish. It was horrible—she kept on repeating it until my ears rang and the chills ran up my spine. All the children kept their heads bent except José. Marina stole a glance at me, then she looked down, too.

Finally, in a low voice, the father uttered a command. Mrs. Chavez looked around the table and then marched into the kitchen. José, Marina, and I rose and went downstairs to the back alley. We stood there silently. José looked angry, Marina looked frightened, and I was bewildered.

"José—" Marina pleaded in a small, timid voice. He peered at us, his stern dark eyes narrowed.

"I'm sorry," he mumbled finally, his head bowed and his feet shifting. "I'm sorry." He turned to go.

"That's okay, that's okay," I said softly, but he was already gone.

- **accusation** (ak yoo ZAY shun) **a charge of wrongdoing**
- **bewilder** (bee WIL dur) puzzle; confuse

After that evening it was hard to see Mari. But in our few meetings I learned the only thing that mattered—she loved me, I loved her. I had to do something about it.

I went to see José. I knew where to find him. He looked as if he'd been through a lot, real punchy.

"Hi, José. How've you been?" I said. He didn't seem to know me.

"I'm Marina's boyfriend, remember? I was up the house and—"
He walked right past me. His face was blank.

"Hey, listen kid, what's the matter? Are you all right? I've gotta talk to you, José." I took a friendly but firm grip on his collar.

"Hey, 'ey—" He started shouting in Spanish that I should get off his coat collar, then stopped suddenly.

"Oh, you Marina's sweetheart, eh? What you want outta me?"

"Your sister and I want to go steady, Joe. We can't 'cause—"

"I know. I understand, Andy. But so what? What you wan' me to do, huh? It's hard makin' friends, you know, learnin' to speak American an' all. I bring friends, she won't like them. So say it short and quick."

"I wanna learn to speak Spanish. Mari is so upset—your old lady won't accept me. I mean, I understand Spanish okay, but I can't speak it."

"Why the world don't you go to some school? You loaded?" he bit off.

"Me?" I laughed. "I've got no more dough than you do."

He stared at me in disbelief.

"Listen," I went on, "at least your old lady cares who you go out with and all that. That's good. All parents should do that. Only in your mama's case, she's just—you know—a little mixed up."

"Okay! Okay, okay, okay. You know where to find me, it seems. Meet me after my work is out. Tomorrow," he mumbled abruptly.

We became pretty friendly. José took a lot of pleasure in expecting to knock his mother off her feet with my Spanish. I wasn't bad in grammar and things like that, but when José snapped a fast question at me I was at a loss for words.

I progressed, though, slowly but surely, and one day at the end of August, José and I, dressed in those sky-blue-pink Italian shirts, marched into the Chavez house. Marina nearly flipped when she saw us together. "José!" she exclaimed, surprise in her voice like a fourth of July sky rocket.

José's eyes softened for a split-second and then he was back to

his cool self. "Where's the ol' lady?" he asked, copying me.

"Don't do anything stupid, José, don't—she's in the kitchen."

"Good mornin', Mama. What's up? How's life down on the farm?"

Mrs. Chavez turned to him, wondering what he was up to now. He gave her a quick peck and whispered in Spanish too fast for me to catch. Then he began to talk very slowly.

"You remember Mr. Andrew Redina, don't you, Mama? Mr. Redina, this is my mother."

"I'm very glad to know you, Mrs. Chavez," I said in Spanish. "I didn't realize that Marina had such a nice mother and so pretty." I felt like a fool. José had made me say that. But Mrs. Chavez seemed pleased.

"Mr. Redina has taken pains to learn Spanish. He thinks it so beautiful," José added. "Even more than his own Italian." I choked. About all my Italian was "yes" and "no."

José went on and on. He had a good tongue—he was a natural-born flatterer.

Then came the big surprise. "Mr. Redina," said Mrs. Chavez—yes, in English. It wasn't perfect English by any means, but it was English all right. "Mr. Redina," she repeated, "please, we like you to come to dinner sometime."

I don't know who was more surprised, José, Marina, or me. We all smiled. Then José and Marina laughed and patted their mother on the back.

"Soon," said Mrs. Chavez.

So I came back for dinner the next night. Afterwards, Mari and I went downstairs to the alley. We both refused to give in—she spoke English, I spoke Spanish. We kissed under our mutual-speaking moon.

ALL THINGS CONSIDERED ————————————————

1. Andy met Marina (a) in school. (b) at a swimming pool. (c) at a dance.
2. Marina invited Andy to (a) dinner at her house. (b) a party. (c) a concert.
3. At dinner, everyone at the table began (a) singing. (b) arguing. (c) speaking English.
4. Mrs. Chavez wanted everyone to (a) be happy. (b) speak English. (c) speak Spanish.
5. After that dinner, Andy and Marina (a) still loved each other. (b) never saw each other again. (c) studied Spanish together.
6. Andy learned to speak Spanish (a) in school. (b) from Marina. (c) from José.
7. Mrs. Chavez was pleased that Andy (a) liked Marina. (b) spoke Spanish. (c) taught English to Marina.
8. Andy was surprised that Mrs. Chavez had learned (a) to speak English. (b) to cook. (c) to drive a car.
9. Mrs. Chavez (a) told Andy to speak English. (b) invited Andy to dinner. (c) taught Andy to speak Spanish.
10. You can conclude that (a) Mrs. Chavez will accept Andy. (b) Andy will learn to speak Spanish as well as Marina. (c) Spanish will no longer be spoken in the Chavez home.

THINKING IT THROUGH ————————————————

1. Why, in your opinion, does Mrs. Chavez want her children to speak Spanish? Why do you think her children want to speak English?
2. Mrs. Chavez becomes very angry when her children begin to speak English at home. What do you think is the real cause of her anger?
3. What problems and challenges do you think Andrew encountered in learning a new language?
4. Are there any advantages in knowing more than one language? If so, what are they?
5. Suppose Mrs. Chavez had refused to learn English. How might the story have ended?

Vocabulary and Sentence Meaning

Idioms

In "Aquí se Habla Español," Marina says that she knows English but has trouble with idioms. Andy talked about guys going around "black-and-blue," but Marina does not understand.

An **idiom** is a group of words with a special meaning. It is the whole word group that has the special meaning, not just the individual words. What a dictionary tells you about the individual words may have nothing to do with the meaning of the idiom. This is why Marina has trouble with idioms.

Here are two examples. The first sentence in each pair contains an idiom. The second sentence uses words according to their dictionary meanings.

A. { José blew his stack.
   { José became very angry.

B. { It was Marina who caught my eye.
   { It was Marina whom I noticed.

Did you notice that at the end of "Aquí se Habla Español" José had learned some idioms? Tell what each one means by rewriting the sentence on a separate sheet of paper.

1. What's up?
2. How's life down on the farm?

Composition

Follow your teacher's instructions before completing *one* of these writing assignments.

1. Pretend you are Andrew Redina, the main character in this story. Write a few sentences explaining the problems you face in dating a person whose native language is different from yours.
2. Imagine you are a teacher working with a student who can't speak English. Make a list of several idioms that the student might have trouble understanding and write an explanation of each.

E.E. Cummings (1894-1962)

E. E. Cummings wrote possibly the most unusual poetry of the 20th century. Cummings is well known for his unusual punctuation and phrasing. He didn't like capital letters at the beginning of sentences or even at the beginning of names. He wanted his own name to be printed e.e. cummings. Often, he experimented with word use, as in one of his poems that begins, "what if a much of a which of a wind." Even punctuation marks were written in his own way. In one of his poems, he wrote the word *thrushes* as t,h;r:u;s,h;e:s. That was his way of showing birds on a branch in the moonlight.

Cummings was born in Cambridge, Massachusetts. He attended Harvard University and was graduated with honors. In 1917 he volunteered to drive an ambulance in France during World War I. There, he was imprisoned because he refused to say he hated the Germans. He would only say "I like the French." All his life he believed that love was the only hope for a peaceful world. He also thought people are too easily bogged down by a need to own things. The curse of owning things and the need for love are themes in much of his poetry.

His book *The Enormous Room* (1922) relates his prison experience in France. It has been called the best book to come out of World War I. Cummings was a playwright and painter as well as a poet, but his plays and paintings are of minor importance compared with his poetry.

maggie and milly and molly and may

by e.e. cummings

maggie and milly and molly and may
went down to the beach(to play one day)

and maggie discovered a shell that sang
so sweetly she couldn't remember her troubles,and

milly befriended a stranded star
whose rays five languid fingers were;

and molly was chased by a horrible thing
which raced sideways while blowing bubbles:and

may came home with a smooth round stone
as small as a world and as large as alone.

For whatever we lose(like a you or a me)
it's always ourselves we find in the sea

WAYS OF KNOWING

1. Read the poem again, pausing at each punctuation mark. Use the following suggestions as a guide.
   Parentheses: Do not drop your voice, hesitate briefly.
   Comma: Drop your voice a little, pause briefly.
   Semicolon: Drop your voice, pause longer than for a comma.
   Colon: Drop your voice, pause still longer.
   Period: Drop your voice, with the longest pause.
   If you read the poem as suggested, you will pause longer and longer after each girl's experience. How does this reading change the way the poem sounds to you? What does it add to the meaning of the poem? Explain your answers.

2. Have you ever listened to a seashell, seen a starfish, watched a crab walk, or found a smooth, round stone on the beach? What is special about these experiences?

3. What might we lose if we lose a "you or a me"? What might we gain when "ourselves we find in the sea"? (As you answer these questions, keep in mind what the sea has always meant to people—it is ancient, changeless, and will undoubtedly go on in the same way forever.)

• languid (LANG wid) **lazy; weak; slow-moving**

BLIND SUNDAY

by Arthur Barron

▶ All the kids are at the pool. Jeff sees an attractive girl, but he is shy. She breaks the ice. They talk and smile. Then, suddenly, he realizes she is blind. What is it like to be blind, and just how should you treat a blind person? Jeff and the girl come up with an experiment that will help him find out.

CHARACTERS

Eileen, *a teenager*
Jeff, *a teenager*
Mrs. Hays, *a woman who works with blind people*
Dad, *Jeff's father*
Marge, *a friend of Eileen*

Eric, *a friend of Marge*
Waiter
Lifeguard
Cabdriver
Man
Ticket taker

Scene 1

Early June, late afternoon, at a public swimming pool. Eileen is swimming. Mrs. Hays is sitting at the side of the pool. Jeff tests the diving board, then executes a rather good jackknife. In a moment, he emerges from underwater.

Eileen: Hey, neat dive!
Jeff: Thanks.
Eileen: What do you call that?
Jeff: Jackknife.
Eileen: Oh—right. Can you do a half gainer?
Jeff: No. That's outta my class.

(There is a pause as Eileen waits for more conversation, but Jeff is shy. He nods at Eileen, swims over to the side of the pool, and gets out. As he dries himself, Eileen swims over to him and speaks from the edge of the pool.)

• execute (EKS uh kyoot) carry out; do

148

Eileen: I'm Eileen.

Jeff: Uh, I'm Jeff.

(Eileen *feels in front of her, then pushes herself out of the* *pool. She smiles. Jeff returns the smile but is confused* *and doesn't know what to say.*)

Eileen: Where do you go to school?

Jeff: Western.

Eileen: I go to Eastern.

(*At this moment,* Mrs. Hays *appears.*)

Mrs. Hays: Lee, hi! How's the water today?

Eileen: Great. Warmer than yesterday. Mrs. Hays, this is Jeff. He goes to Western. Jeff, this is Mrs. Hays. She's the librarian at Eastern—and my friend.

Jeff: Hi.

Mrs. Hays: Hello, Jeff. *(pause)* Well, this water looks terrific. I'm going to get some exercise. Nice to meet you, Jeff.

(Jeff *nods.*)

Eileen: Lee's my nickname. *(Jeff does not know what to say.)* Hey, you're the strong silent type, huh?

Jeff: Yeah, I guess so. *(trying to think of anything to say)* Hey, you want some peanuts?

Eileen: Why not?

Jeff: I've got some in my jacket. *(He stands, goes for the bag of peanuts and returns, setting the bag in front of Eileen.)* Help yourself.

Eileen: Thanks. *(She doesn't know where the bag is, of course, and has to feel for it. Jeff notices, watching intently. He is perplexed and shocked. Finally, he pushes the bag under her hand. She takes a handful.)* Unsalted, huh? *(Jeff can't speak.)* What's the matter? *(Jeff can't find the right words.)* So didn't you ever eat peanuts with a blind girl before? *(Jeff stares, his lips trying to say something.)* Hey, are you okay?

Jeff: Uh—yeah.

Eileen: Relax, will you?

Jeff: Sure.

Eileen: You're funny.

Jeff: I am?

Eileen: *(laughing)* You should see yourself.

Jeff: *(smiling finally)* Yeah, I guess so.

Eileen: Well now that you're okay again, hold the peanuts for me. I feel a half gainer coming on.

(She walks to the diving board, climbs the ladder, walks to the edge of the board. Jeff stares at her. The lifeguard watches. Mrs. Hays, just out of the water, watches with a smile.)

Mrs. Hays: Okay, Lee, it's all clear.

(Eileen gets set, takes a breath, executes a nice half gainer, and breaks from under the water with a smile.)

Eileen: Like it?

Jeff: That was fantastic!

Scene 2

Breakfast. Jeff is eating as his father enters.

Dad: Hi, Jeff.

Jeff: *(without enthusiasm)* Hiya, Dad.

Dad: How are you doing?

Jeff: Okay.

Dad: *(pouring himself a glass of orange juice)* You don't look any too terrific.

Jeff: I've been thinking. You know—wondering. How do you talk to somebody?

Dad: What?

Jeff: I mean, how do you make conversation? You know, when you just want to be friendly?

Dad: Oh—you mean like small talk?

Jeff: Yeah, that's it.

Dad: Maybe you try too hard.

Jeff: Yeah, I get tongue-tied. Nothing comes out.

Dad: I suppose you know that everything you say doesn't have to be earthshaking or super-ha-ha funny. Just relax. Be yourself.

Jeff: You know this school dance that's coming up, after the game?

Dad: Yes?

Jeff: I'd kinda like to go. You know—but if I did, what would I talk about?

Dad: Anything.

Jeff: Did you ever know a blind person?

Dad: *(pause)* I see you do.

Jeff: Yeah.

Dad: And this blind person's a girl?

Jeff: Yeah.

Dad: And you don't know how to talk to her?

Jeff: No.

Dad: But you kind of like her?

Jeff: *(pause)* Yeah. Guess so.

Scene 3

It is the end of the school day. Students are mixing outside school on the street. Eileen, *using her cane, enters with* Marge. Eric *joins them.*

Marge: Hi, Eric.

Eric: Hi, Marge. Hi, Lee.

Eileen: Hi.

(They stroll along the sidewalk.)

Eric: So how'd the French test go?

Marge: Awful!

Eric: Yeah?

Marge: If I made a D, I'm lucky.

Eric: Man, and your French is better than my English.

(They reach a corner. Marge and Eileen start to turn left, but Eric taps Marge on the shoulder and silently indicates she should stop.)

Eric: I got a history final tomorrow.

(While talking, he points to another boy and girl standing a few feet away to the right. In pantomime he indicates that Marge should leave Eileen and join him and the other couple. Marge shakes her head no, indicating she can't leave Eileen.)

Marge: Oh, well. I guess you'll have to hit the books tonight.

Eric: *(insisting she come, in pantomime)* Yeah, and there's this great movie on TV, too.

Marge: *(beginning to weaken)* Well, uh—well, I guess you'll have to miss it.

Eric: Yeah. *(He smiles as Marge shakes her head "yes.")* Yeah, it's too bad. *(He winks at Marge.)* Well, see you.

Marge: Okay, see you.

(Marge turns to Eileen, who has been listening to this encounter and sensing what's going on. Eric walks away and joins the other couple to wait for Marge to join them. Marge and Eileen walk a few steps along the sidewalk.)

Marge: Oh, gee—

Eileen: What's the matter?

Marge: I gotta go back, Lee. I forgot something.

Eileen: Okay. I'll wait here.

Marge: No! No—uh—I'll be awhile. I gotta find something.

Eileen: Hey, listen, Marge. If you want to go off with Eric, it's okay with me. Really.

• encounter (en KOUN tur) **a meeting**

Marge: *(feeling guilty)* What?

Eileen: I mean, don't you think I heard all that "signing"* going on? He did everything but send smoke signals.

Marge: What do you mean, Lee?

Eileen: I mean it's perfectly okay if you want to be alone. I know three's a crowd—only don't be hypocrites.

Marge: *(feeling bad)* Oh, gee, Lee. I—

Eileen: Hey, go on, willya. I'll get home all right. *(smiling)* I could do it in the dark.

Marge: *(turning to look at* Eric, *who waves impatiently)* Lee, I'm sorry. I didn't mean anything.

Eileen: Sure, I know. Look, I'll see you tomorrow. *(touching* Marge's *arm)* Have fun. Okay?

*(*Marge *walks off and joins the other couple.* Eileen *stands alone for a moment. Her face shows how she feels, but not for long.*

Across the street, Jeff *appears. He has been hurrying. He stops, looks, and notices* Eileen. Eileen *prepares to cross the street, sweeping her cane in front of her.* Jeff *quickly crosses the street and joins her.)*

Jeff: Uh—hi.

Eileen: Hi.

Jeff: Remember me?

Eileen: I think so. Say some more.

Jeff: Gee—uh—what should I say? Uh—the light changed. Can I help you cross?

Eileen: *(nicely)* No, thanks. I can manage.

(She crosses with Jeff *following along. She comes to the opposite curb.)*

Jeff: You're at the curb.

Eileen: Now I know who you are. You're Fido, the guide dog.

Jeff: *(hurt)* Oh.

Eileen: I'm sorry. You see, I like to manage myself. You're the guy I met at the pool, right?

Jeff: Yeah.

---

*Signing is the hand language of deaf people.

Eileen: You go to Western.

Jeff: Right.

Eileen: What are you doing over here?

Jeff: I had an errand do to.

Eileen: Well—it was nice seeing you.

(She starts to walk on. He pauses, then catches up with her.)

Jeff: My errand's done. I'm going this way. Maybe I can join you.

Eileen: Sure—it seems you already have.

Jeff: *(trying to relax)* I'm kinda hungry. Do you want a hamburger or something?

Eileen: *(pleased)* Why not? May I take your arm?

(Dissolve to*: A restaurant. Jeff and Eileen enter. Among the kids crowding the place are Marge and Eric. Marge notices Eileen and looks uncomfortable as Eileen walks by. Jeff and Eileen sit in a booth, Eileen feeling her way in.)

Jeff: *(making conversation)* Well, here we are.

Eileen: Yeah.

Jeff: Nice place.

Eileen: Uh-huh.

(Another silence is relieved by the waiter, who approaches, puts down glasses of water in front of them, and notices Eileen is blind.)

Waiter: *(to Jeff)* What'll you have?

Jeff: Uh, a burger—and a shake and—uh—fries.

Waiter: What's she gonna have?

Eileen: *(angry)* She will have a cheeseburger, a vanilla shake, and french fries.

(Waiter shrugs, gives Jeff a look, and leaves.)

Eileen: *That* makes me mad.

Jeff: I noticed.

---

*"Dissolve to" is a term used in television productions. It means that the original picture on the screen fades away to be slowly replaced by the new picture.

Eileen: Blind people aren't supposed to know what they want. *(pause)* Sometimes people ask me the dumbest things.

Jeff: Like what?

Eileen: Like—how do you find your mouth with your fork? A lady asked me that once. Or—do you sleep with your eyes open or closed? That's another.

Jeff: Dumb is hardly the word for it. *(He is still uncomfortable.)* You know—

Eileen: In case you're wondering—I can't remember ever being able to see.

(The waiter returns and puts their order on the table.)

Jeff: Thanks. *(He watches as Eileen carefully arranges her dishes.)* Can I help?

Eileen: No, thanks. I can manage.

Jeff: Sorry.

Eileen: You don't have to be sorry. Look, I just want to be treated like everybody else. You see that girl over there? The one with the long hair?

Jeff: Uh-huh.

Eileen: Well, that's my girlfriend Marge. Now would you ask her if she wanted help with her food?

Jeff: No. Hey, how'd you know she was there?

Eileen: I heard her when we passed by. Now here's how I manage my food. My plate's a clock.

Jeff: A clock.

Eileen: Uh-huh. And my cheeseburger's here at twelve o'clock. My french fries are at seven. And my pickles are at eleven. *(Pauses while* Jeff *studies.)* Now where's my shake?

Jeff: *(twisting his head around to see from her point of view)* Three o'clock.

Eileen: Thanks. *(She picks up the shake and pretends to pour it on her french fries.)* That's the way blind people eat french fries, right? *(Jeff laughs, then looks at her with appreciation and pleasure.)*

Scene 4

Jeff *and* Eileen *are walking to* Eileen's *house.*

Eileen: What color are your eyes?

Jeff: Blue.

Eileen: Color's the hardest thing.

Jeff: What do you mean?

Eileen: I mean the hardest thing to visualize. What's blue, for example?

Jeff: The sky—

Eileen: No. I mean, what *is* blue? I know what *things* are blue. But what does blue look like? *(Jeff doesn't answer.)* Stumped, huh?

Jeff: Guess so.

Eileen: Color's the thing I miss most—I guess.

(Dissolve to: Another street scene as they approach Eileen's *house.)*

Jeff: I don't know. I like working with my hands. An engineer maybe. What about you?

Eileen: A lawyer. Or maybe a model—the kind that just stands around looking glamorous, and they take pictures of you and you make hundreds of thousands. Hey, this is where I live. Want to come in?

Jeff: Uh, no thanks. I better get home.

Eileen: Okay. I had fun.

Jeff: Me too. Well—so long.

156

Eileen: Bye.
Jeff: Do you want to go to the park tomorrow?
Eileen: Oh, sure! Why not? That would be fun.
Jeff: Great! See you tomorrow.

Scene 5

The park. Jeff *and* Eileen *walk past someone sitting on a bench listening to a portable radio.*

Eileen: Do you like to dance?
Jeff: Well, I'm not very good at it.
Eileen: I love it. I love music. All kinds.
Jeff: Yeah?

(Dissolve to: The zoo. They are standing in front of a lion cage. The lion provides them with a roar.)

Eileen: Hey, there's a lion.
Jeff: It sure is.
Eileen: When I hear that, I expect a movie to start.

(They laugh. They wander past other cages. Jeff is holding a bag of peanuts. Eileen helps herself from time to time.)

(Dissolve to: Another zoo scene. Some people are feeding an elephant, whose trunk reaches through the bars. Eileen feeds the elephant some peanuts.)

Eileen: That's a vacuum cleaner, right?
Jeff: *(laughs)* Yeah—with big ears.

(They wander on, passing an area with gorillas.)

Jeff: Gee, they look sad.
Eileen: Who?
Jeff: Oh, I'm sorry!
Eileen: Don't be. Who looks sad?
Jeff: The gorillas. I hate seeing them penned up. Come on, let's go.

Scene 6

Another day, another park. Jeff and Eileen are riding a two-seater bicycle. Jeff is sitting in front and steering. They come down a hill, picking up speed. Jeff begins to brake.

Eileen: Don't brake! Come on, faster!
Jeff: Okay.
Eileen: Wow! I love it! Love it! Love it!

(Her hair is blowing. Her head is back as she enjoys the sensation of speed. Suddenly Jeff has to swerve to avoid hitting someone.)

Jeff: Oh, no! *(He slows, braking hard.)*
Eileen: What's wrong?
Jeff: I'm stopping.
Eileen: How come?

(Jeff gets off the seat, standing astride the bar.)

Eileen: Why'd you stop? That was some fantastic ride!
Jeff: It was dangerous.
Eileen: You were worried about me. Look, I told you, just treat me like everybody else. Can't you understand?
Jeff: Now wait a minute. I was worried about myself. *(After pause, he chuckles.)* And you, too.
Eileen: Chicken!
Jeff: I'm not kidding, Eileen. I just—
Eileen: Hey, call me Lee.

• **astride** (uh STRYD) with one leg on each side

Jeff: Okay, Lee. But you're changing the subject.

Eileen: Yeah, that's because nicknames are more interesting. What's yours?

Jeff: I don't have one.

Eileen: Well then I'll just have to think one up. *(pause)* So how about "chicken"?

(They laugh and ride off.)

Scene 7

Jeff's *house, in the driveway. His father is washing the car as Jeff enters.*

Jeff: *(cheerful)* Hi, Dad.

Dad: What's happening?

Jeff: Not much.

Dad: Hey, grab a rag, will you?

Jeff: Okay. *(He starts to work.)* You know that dance I was telling you about the other day?

Dad: Dance? Oh, yeah.

Jeff: *(Pause)* Well, it's a pretty important one. It's a dance sponsored by Western and Eastern. I've been thinking about taking somebody.

Dad: That nice girl you've been seeing?

Jeff: But I feel funny about it. I mean, everyone would be staring at us. They'd think I was desperate for a date or something.

Dad: You like being with her, don't you? You must have fun together. *(pause while they continue working)* And—uh—is she pretty?

Jeff: Yeah.

Dad: *(long pause)* Well, I guess you don't think too highly of yourself. Is that it?

Jeff: *(surprised)* What do you mean?

Dad: It seems to me you care more about what other people think than what you think.

Jeff: Oh, I don't know about that.

Dad: Well, let's face it. If you worry too much about what other people think, it means you lack self-confidence.

Jeff: *(starts working hard)* I'll have to think about that.

Scene 8

The school library. Mrs. Hays and Eileen are working quietly. After a moment, Eileen speaks.

Eileen: You know what I'd want more than anything if I could see just one thing?
Mrs. Hays: What?
Eileen: My face.
Mrs. Hays: You have a very nice face.
Eileen: I don't think so.
Mrs. Hays: Why not?
Eileen: I don't have dates. I mean, I have friends and all. People like me. But boys don't ask me out.
Mrs. Hays: What about Jeff?
Eileen: We have fun together. *(pause)* But I think he's more like a friend.
Mrs. Hays: Maybe it will develop into something else.
Eileen: But suppose I *am* ugly?
Mrs. Hays: But you're not. You're very attractive. What is all this, anyway? You know it's the person inside you that counts.
Eileen: I guess so.

Scene 9

The swimming pool. It is crowded. Eileen sits with Marge and Eric. Mrs. Hays is in the background, talking to a friend. The lifeguard is standing and yelling at some kids in the water to stop horsing around. Eric jumps in the water and yells to Marge.

Eric: Hey, Marge, hurry up.
Marge: Okay.
Eileen: *(to Marge)* You know that guy I've been seeing?
Marge: Jeff?
Eileen: Yeah. I was thinking of inviting him—to the dance. I mean—
Marge: That'd be neat, Lee.
Eileen: But you know—it was just a thought.
Marge: It sounds like a good idea to me.
Eric: *(from the water)* Hey, you guys, you coming in?
Eileen: Yeah, in a second.

(Marge jumps into the pool. Jeff walks over to Eileen.)

Jeff: Hi, Lee.
Eileen: Hi. Crowded today, huh?
Jeff: Yeah.

(There is a lot of activity, a lot of horseplay. A couple of boys are trying to throw girls into the pool. The girls are shrieking with mock fright, but really enjoying themselves. Soon Eric and Marge are out of the pool and joining the horseplay. Jeff watches as Eric throws Marge in. Marge shrieks with delight and swims away.)

Jeff: There goes Marge. She just got thrown in.
Eileen: Yeah. *(She sounds as if she is missing out on the fun. Jeff notices her tone of voice. He stares at her, looks at all the kids having a good time and makes up his mind.)*

Jeff: *(grabbing Eileen)* You're next. *(And he pushes her in.)*

(Eileen screams, and she isn't kidding. She's startled and frightened. She hits the water and goes under. After a moment, she comes to the top, but seems confused. She opens her mouth to yell, swallows a mouthful of water. She coughs, chokes, and becomes even more alarmed. The lifeguard dives into the pool. He tries to help Eileen, but this only infuriates her and she tries to push him away. Jeff has seen all this with horror. Kids rush to the side of the pool. Marge and Mrs. Hays join Jeff there.)

Jeff: Here, take my hand, Lee.
Eileen: I'm okay.

(Eileen climbs out herself. She slips on a wet tile, losing her balance, but she does not fall. She feels that all eyes are on her, and she is humiliated. Mrs. Hays offers her a towel, but Lee doesn't take it. She wants to be left alone.)

Jeff: Lee, I'm sorry. I'm awfully sorry.
Eileen: *(trying to hide her embarrassment)* It's okay. I'm fine.

• infuriate (in FYOOR ee ayt) **make angry**

161

Jeff: You said it seemed like fun. You know, I thought you wanted to be treated like everybody else. I didn't mean it like this.

Eileen: *(softly, pleadingly)* Please, I just want to get out of here. I've got to get out of here.

(She walks away quickly but with dignity. Jeff looks confused. Mrs. Hays walks over to him and puts her hand on his arm.)

Mrs. Hays: Jeff, let's have a talk, okay?

(Dissolve to: Jeff and Mrs. Hays off to one side, the pool and the noises in the background.)

Jeff: I feel terrible.

Mrs. Hays: I know you must feel bad about it.

Jeff: I mean, she's angry with me.

Mrs. Hays: I don't know about angry. She's embarrassed. She doesn't want her embarrassment to be the center of attention.

Jeff: I tried to understand what it means to be blind. I mean, *really* understand. It's like being in a different world—I mean, I can't imagine what it would be like.

Mrs. Hays: Shut your eyes, Jeff.

Jeff: Huh?

Mrs. Hays: Shut them. Keep them shut.

Scene 10

Sunday noon. Jeff is sitting in the back of a taxi. He is wearing dark patches over his eyes and dark sunglasses. The cab pulls up to Eileen's house. Jeff gets out, and walks to the front of the cab, feeling his way with a cane and his hands.

Jeff: How much?

Driver: Three-fifty.

Jeff: Thanks. Keep the change. *(gives the driver four bills)*

Driver: Thank you. Can I give you a hand, buddy?

Jeff: No, but you can put me in the direction of the front door.

Driver: Straight ahead up the driveway. Then up the steps to the right. Okay?

Jeff: Thanks.

(*The cab pulls away. Jeff turns in the direction of the house. He taps carefully with his cane, making agonizing progress. He comes to the steps, feels with his cane, and gently kicks the bottom step with his toe. It seems like Mt. Everest to him.*

He takes the steps one at a time, planting both feet solidly on the first, before going on to the second. He continues slowly. A truck passes on the street, grinding gears. Jeff tenses, freezing until it passes.

There is a slight concrete rise, not high enough to be called a step but high enough to create a raised level in front of the door. Jeff's cane passes over it without his noticing. He stumbles as his right foot hits it. He falls awkwardly, banging against the door. He fumbles for his cane, gets up, and searches for the bell. He feels everywhere but can't find it. He gives up and knocks on the door. No one comes. He knocks harder and harder until he is pounding.)

Jeff: It's me! Hello!

(*Someone comes to the door. Jeff hears the knob turning and steps back a bit as the door opens. It's Eileen.*)

Eileen: Jeff!

Jeff: It's me—Jeff.

Eileen: Why didn't you ring the doorbell?

Jeff: I couldn't find it.

Eileen: Why not?

Jeff: I'm blind.

(Dissolve to: Total blackness.)

Scene 11

(A park where Jeff and Eileen are walking. He is holding onto her elbow. She is guiding him.)

Jeff: So I decided I wanted to know how it felt to be blind. I mean, I've done so many dumb things.

Eileen: That's great.

Jeff: I mean, I felt real bad about making mistakes all the time. *(Eileen giggles.)* What are you laughing about?

Eileen: You're shouting.

Jeff: *(loudly)* I am? *(much quieter)* I am?

Eileen: That's one of the tricky things about being blind—learning just how loud to talk.

Jeff: I didn't know that.

Eileen: It's true.

(Dissolves to: Another area of the park. A hot dog stand is in the background. Eileen and Jeff are each eating a hot dog and holding a soda. Eileen eats with practiced ease. Jeff is having difficulty.)

Jeff: Do people cheat you with change and stuff?

Eileen: No. See, I always fold my bills differently so I know how much I'm giving. Like I fold fives in half and tens lengthwise and ones I don't fold at all. And of course I can feel change. Anyway, I think most people are pretty honest, don't you?

Jeff: Sure.

Eileen: I guess I'm a pretty positive person. I think life is great. *(Pause. Then she begins to giggle.)*

Jeff: What's so funny now?

Eileen: At this place for the blind where I trained they also train sighted people, like Mrs. Hays. And those people have to go around for a time like you—with goggles and stuff on. And once I went out with this man and we had lunch, right? And he asked me to order for both of us. So I ordered spaghetti for him. *(She laughs.)* What a time he had with that stuff. It was sliding all over the place.

Jeff: You're mean, you know that?

Eileen: *(laughing)* I know.

Jeff: *(smiling)* Like I probably have mustard all over me. *(He feels around on his shirt and touches something sloppy.)* Oh! oh! I feel something. *(They both laugh.)*

(Dissolve to: One of the tunnels in the park. It leads to the zoo. As they walk through the tunnel the camera and sound effects create the experience as Jeff undergoes it. The screen grows black. Sounds are loud, echoing. There are strange noises. The black screen wavers.

Dissolve to: A bear cage. Eileen and Jeff pass by.)

Jeff: What's that?

Eileen: A bear.

Jeff: How can you tell?

Eileen: He smells like a bear.

Jeff: What does a bear smell like?

Eileen: Like a bear.

Jeff: Do I have a smell?

Eileen: Sure!

Jeff: *(nervous)* What do I smell like?

Eileen: *(smiling)* Like a Jeff.

(Dissolve to: The bird house. Jeff and Eileen appear. Then we slowly move to Jeff's point of view—the screen goes black. We hear the weird, strange, frightening screams of birds—trills, caws, yelps, whistles, etc. Slowly, then, the screen grows light and we see Jeff and Eileen walking through the bird house. Jeff is growing nervous.)

Eileen: It's all right.

Jeff: Let's get out of here.

Eileen: Okay.

(They exit. Outside Jeff stops and Eileen turns to him.)

Jeff: Those noises were like a nightmare—if nightmares have noises. I'm not sure of anything. I mean, I feel disoriented—like I'm in space or something. I'm afraid if I take a step, I'll fall a million miles. Lee, I'm scared.

Eileen: It's okay, Jeff. Honest.

Jeff: Do you ever feel like this?

Eileen: No. You get over those things. You get your confidence.

Jeff: How long does it take?

Eileen: Well, see—I've been this way as long as I can remember. I've never known anything different. It's harder for people who lose their sight. They're much more scared. *(She takes his arm and they walk on.)* Hey, I just thought of something funny.

Jeff: What?

Eileen: The blind leading the blind.

Jeff: How do you know your way around so well?

Eileen: Oh, I've been here lots of times. When you're blind, you get maps in your head. I know exactly where I am right now. There's a phone booth right about here. *(She feels it with her cane.)* Excuse me. I promised to call Mom.

(She steps in and closes the door. There is a man sitting across the walk from Jeff. He has a dog with him, off the leash. It is a tiny dog, a toy poodle. The dog runs over to Jeff and begins barking. To Jeff, this tiny creature sounds like the Hound of the Baskervilles.)

Jeff: Go 'way. *(The dog barks louder.)* Hey, go away! *(The dog barks louder. Jeff begins to edge back and poke out with his cane. The dog snaps at the cane.)* Get out of here! *(Almost terrified, Jeff gets into the phone booth with Eileen.)*

Eileen: Hey, what's wrong?

Jeff: There's a ferocious dog after me.

Eileen: Huh?

Jeff: He tried to attack me.

(The man walks over to retrieve the dog.)

Man: Fluff! Come on, Fluff!

• ferocious (fur OH shus) **savage; vicious**

Eileen: Fluff?

Jeff: Yeah—

Eileen: That's a funny name for a monster.

(The man walks away with the dog on a leash. Jeff and Eileen wait inside for a moment.)

Eileen: Look, I think it's all right now. Come on.

(They leave the booth and start on their way. Dissolve to: Another area of the park. It is peaceful as they stroll by a pond. Across the way there appears an ice cream man riding a bicycle with attached freezer. As he pedals, the bells on the bar of the bicycle tinkle.)

Jeff: Wait—listen. *(They pause as Jeff listens.)*

Eileen: What?

Jeff: Sh-h! *(He holds his finger to his lips. We become very aware of the tinkling bells as they fade away.)* What a nice sound. I never realized how nice a sound that was before.

Eileen: Yeah.

Jeff: You really hear things like this.

(Eileen smiles and they stroll on. In the pond two ducks begin a dialogue in the chatty almost whispering way of contented ducks.)

Eileen: Hear the ducks.

Jeff: Yeah. *(pause)* It's as if I never heard ducks before.

Eileen: Hey, do me a favor, huh?

Jeff: Sure.

Eileen: I want to feel what you look like. *(She holds her hand up in front of his face.)* Okay? *(She runs her hand over his face, down his nose, across his forehead, and so on.)*

Jeff: *(trying to be casual)* Well?

Eileen: Well, your nose is kinda big.

Jeff: Thanks a lot.

Eileen: And your ears stick out.

Jeff: They do not.

Eileen: A little.

Jeff: Okay—a little. But not so's you'd notice. *(He smiles.)*

Eileen: That's a nice smile.

Jeff: I'm glad you like something.

Eileen: All in all, it's a nice face.

Jeff: You think so?

Eileen: Yeah, it's a really nice face.

Jeff: *(smiling)* You had me worried there for a minute.

(There is an embarrassed pause. Eileen lets her hand drop from Jeff's face.)

Eileen: Hey, come on, Nice Face.

(Dissolve to: Music and a colorful moving merry-go-round. Jeff and Eileen are standing beside it. The ticket taker is standing on the moving merry-go-round, holding onto a horse. As the horses pass by, we see a few teenagers riding on them and, of course, some kids with their parents. The machine slowly stops and the music runs down.)

Eileen: There's a step here, kinda high.

Jeff: Okay.

Eileen: You got it.

(They climb on. The ticket taker, a burly man, notices them and comes over.)

Ticket taker: Hey—you there.

Jeff: What?

Ticket taker: You've got to get off.

Jeff: What do you mean?

Ticket taker: I said you've got to get off. I can't take you people.

Jeff: What people? We just want a ride.

Ticket taker: It ain't allowed. I can't have blind people on the horses.

Eileen: Come on, Jeff. It's no big deal.

Jeff: No, wait a minute. We're all right. I've been on this ride a million times.

Ticket taker: Not with me here, buddy. I ain't covered.

Jeff: Huh?

• burly (BUR lee) **big and strong**

Ticket taker: I don't have insurance for your kind. Now look, I don't want to be mean. So come on. Let me help you off.

Jeff: Get your hands off me.

Ticket taker: *(takes Jeff's arm)* My customers want to ride.

Eileen: Come on, Jeff. It's all right. It's okay.

Ticket taker: Thanks, lady. Thanks.

Jeff: No, wait! It's not okay. Nothing's gonna happen. We just want a crummy ride, that's all.

(A kid sitting on a horse yells "Hey, mister, let's go" and is joined by a few other kids.)

Eileen: Come on, Jeff. Please.

(They go. Jeff stumbles, almost falling. The ticket taker walks to the lever on the merry-go-round. It begins to move. The music blares. The kids smile, laugh, wave. Jeff and Eileen stand helplessly on the side.

Dissolve to: A street in the park. Jeff and Eileen are standing on the curb, waiting to cross to the other side. Cars are whizzing by. The traffic light is green, but then there is a click. It turns to yellow, then red.)

Eileen: Hey, it's red.

(They begin to cross. Jeff moves slowly. He has trouble getting down the curb.)

Jeff: It's okay?

Eileen: Yeah, come on. They don't give you a lot of time.

(They move across. The engines seem to be running too loudly. One of them revs up as if readying for a race. A couple of drivers in back begin to honk.)

Jeff: *(angry and nervous)* Hold your horses!

(A driver beside Jeff suddenly revs his engine. Jeff jumps.)

Jeff: What's wrong with those guys?

Eileen: It's okay.

Jeff: *(The traffic light has just clicked.)* We're not even half way. *(He stumbles.)*

Eileen: It's all right. Come on.

Jeff: Don't they know we're blind?

Eileen: They'll wait.

Jeff: *(He has heard another click.)* It turned green!

(The cars in the lane behind them begin to move, taking off with a screech. The car nearest Jeff revs its engine.)

Jeff: *(turns to the car and waves his cane)* Shut up!

(Again the screen goes black, giving us Jeff's point of view. We hear the noise of the horns, tires, traffic become a roar. Then the picture gradually returns and we see Jeff frantically begin to take off his glasses, clawing at his face.)

Eileen: What are you doing?

Jeff: Taking this junk off!

Eileen: No! *(She takes his arm, firmly leading him on.)* Not yet! *(They are at the other side now. Jeff is breathing deeply.)* It's okay. Take it easy.

Jeff: I'm sorry. I panicked.

Eileen: Listen, it's all right. Just rest a minute.

Jeff: Such a coward. I'm sorry. *(Pause. Eileen takes his arm.)* How do you do it?

Eileen: You get used to it.

Jeff: Do you? Do you really?

Eileen: Hey, let's go.

(Dissolve to: Another part of the park. They are alone and pass a flowering lilac bush.)

Eileen: Hey, wait a minute. *(She stops at the bush.)*

Jeff: What?

Eileen: Come here. *(Jeff returns.)* Smell that. *(Jeff inhales.)* Feel. *(They both feel the same puff of flowers.)* Some kind of flowers.

Jeff: There's a big puff of them. And soft.

Eileen: What kind are they?

Jeff: I don't know.

Eileen: They're beautiful. I'd like to know.

Jeff: I'll ask somebody.

Eileen: There's no one around.

Jeff: Oh.

Eileen: Do me a favor.

Jeff: Okay.

Eileen: Take that stuff off your eyes.

Jeff: Now?

Eileen: Yes. Now.

(He hesitates, then begins to remove the glasses and the picture fades to Jeff's point of view. It is black and quiet. Then, as the last patch comes off, we see the lilac bush. The purple flowers are gorgeous.)

171

Jeff: *(showing surprise, pleasure)* Oh!

Eileen: Tell me. . . .

Jeff: Well, they're purple. Dark purple. Lots of little flowers on a stem. Four or five little petals on a flower. They're beautiful. . . .*(He turns around, slowly, with appreciation.)* Everything's beautiful. The sky . . . the trees . . . the grass. . . . *(laughs with pleasure)* It's like a fairy tale. I never realized— look, Eileen— *(He suddenly realizes with stunning clarity that she can never take off patches and see.)* I'm sorry.

Eileen: It's okay, Jeff. I can feel how nice it is from your voice.

Jeff: You can? *(He stares at her for a long moment.)* You know what's beautiful?

Eileen: What?

Jeff: You're beautiful.

Eileen: You mean that?

Jeff: I mean it. *(There is a long moment as she returns his stare by taking his arm. Then, embarrassed, they turn and start on their way.)* Hey, wait a minute. *(He goes back and picks a sprig from the lilac bush.)*

Eileen: What are you doing?

Jeff: I'm taking one of these. They'll forgive me just this once. *(He takes her hand and puts the sprig of flowers into it.)*

Eileen: Thank you. *(She smells it.)* Um-m-m. *(She puts it in her hair, takes his arm, and they walk on.)*

Jeff: *(casual, happy)* You know, I heard about this dance our two schools are having, after the game.

Eileen: *(casual and happy too)* Yeah, I've heard about it.

Jeff: Want to go with me?

Eileen: Why not?

Jeff: *(laughing)* Why not?

(The screen slowly fades to black.)

END

• clarity (KLAR uh tee) **clearness**

ALL THINGS CONSIDERED ──────────────

1. This play has (a) one main character. (b) two main characters. (c) three main characters.

2. Jeff is (a) athletic. (b) outgoing. (c) shy.

3. Because Eileen is blind, Marge and Eric (a) talk secretly with gestures. (b) help her home. (c) help her study.

4. The hardest thing for Eileen to imagine is (a) size. (b) shape. (c) color.

5. Eileen has (a) a sense of humor. (b) a big appetite. (c) very few friends.

6. Jeff pushes Eileen into the pool because (a) he wants to treat her the way he would treat everybody else. (b) she thinks the water is cold. (c) Eric told him to do it.

7. Jeff tries to understand what it means to be blind by (a) asking Mrs. Hays. (b) reading about blindness. (c) putting patches over his eyes.

8. On Sunday Jeff and Eileen (a) go to the dance. (b) read Braille together. (c) go to the park.

9. With the patches over his eyes, Jeff (a) learns to enjoy food more. (b) appreciates sounds more. (c) appreciates darkness more.

10. Jeff takes off his patches and glasses and tells Eileen (a) he enjoyed the experience. (b) everything is beautiful. (c) he will never again wear patches over his eyes.

11. At the end of the play, we feel sure that Jeff and Eileen will (a) get married. (b) go to the dance together. (c) soon stop seeing each other.

12. You can conclude that (a) Jeff has learned a valuable lesson from his experience. (b) blind people are often in great danger. (c) sight is more important than hearing.

THINKING IT THROUGH ──────────────

1. Which of these questions best summarizes the plot of "Blind Sunday"? Why?
   • How can Jeff and Eileen develop a good friendship?
   • Is it possible to love a blind person?
   • Are blind people as capable as sighted people?

2. Why does Eileen get so angry at the waiter in the restaurant? How do you think the waiter should have treated Eileen?

3. The ticket taker on the merry-go-round does not have insurance to cover accidents to blind people, so he will not let Jeff and Eileen ride. Do you think he is right or wrong? Why? What could be done to help solve this problem?

Vocabulary and Sentence Meaning

Synonyms

Synonyms are words that have almost the same meanings. But very few synonyms have exactly the same meanings. This small difference in meaning between similar words is important. It gives writers a chance to choose between words, a chance to choose the right word to express meaning.

For example, the first time Eileen speaks in "Blind Sunday," she says "Neat dive." Instead of *neat,* the writer could have chosen *fine* or *excellent.* But *neat* is the right word. It tells the reader that Eileen talks the way most high school students do and that, even though she is blind, she is very capable—in this case, she is able to use her hearing to know that Jeff made a good dive.

The following are examples of more choices between words in "Blind Sunday." On a separate sheet of paper, copy each example using the same choice of words that was made by the author of "Blind Sunday." You must choose between the three words in parentheses—the synonyms. Copy the sentence with your word choice, then write another sentence explaining why you made that particular word choice.

1. Page 150: Eileen has to feel for the bag of peanuts. Jeff watches intently. He is perplexed and (surprised, shocked, horrified).
2. Page 161: The kids are horsing around the pool. Boys are trying to throw girls into the water. The girls are (shrieking, crying, wailing) with mock fright.
3. Page 161: When Jeff throws Eileen into the water, she is really frightened. She comes up confused. She coughs, chokes, and becomes alarmed. The lifeguard dives in to help. This infuriates her, and she pushes him away. Jeff has seen all this with (amazement, anger, horror).
4. Page 164: Eileen says: "That's one of the (odd, tricky, touchy) things about being blind—learning just how loud to talk."
5. Page 166: When the little dog barks at him, Jeff jumps into the phone booth with Eileen and says: "There's a (bad, ferocious, violent) dog after me."

Composition

1. On a separate sheet of paper, copy the following part of the play, choosing between the expressions in brackets.

   (The bird house. We slowly move to Jeff's point of view—the screen goes black. We hear the weird, strange, $\begin{Bmatrix} \text{frightening screams} \\ \text{ugly cries} \end{Bmatrix}$ of birds—trills, caws, yelps, whistles, etc. Slowly, then, the screen grows light and we see Jeff and Eileen $\begin{Bmatrix} \text{strolling} \\ \text{walking} \end{Bmatrix}$ through the bird house. Jeff is growing $\begin{Bmatrix} \text{high strung.} \\ \text{nervous.} \end{Bmatrix}$

   Eileen: $\begin{Bmatrix} \text{It's all right.} \\ \text{Take it easy.} \end{Bmatrix}$

   Jeff: $\begin{Bmatrix} \text{Let's beat it.} \\ \text{Let's get out of here.} \end{Bmatrix}$

   Eileen: $\begin{Bmatrix} \text{You bet.} \\ \text{Okay.} \end{Bmatrix}$

2. Write a paragraph telling how Eileen has helped Jeff discover important things about himself. If you wish, start your paragraph with the following sentence:

   When he first met Eileen, Jeff felt ashamed to be seen with a blind girl.

   Then describe (1) the change in Jeff and (2) how Eileen helped him change.

VOCABULARY AND SKILL REVIEW

Before completing the exercises that follow, you may wish to review the **bold-faced** words on pages 129–141.

I. On a separate sheet of paper, write the *italicized* term that best fills the blank in each sentence. Each term should be used only once.

accusation   *activities*   *bewilder*   *modesty*   *reputation*
scanty   *suspend*   *symbolize* *timid*   *venture*

1. They made a poster for the school fair and planned to _____ it from a bridge over the river.

2. The small girl was _____ about asking the mayor a question.

3. She was so shy that she would not _____ to raise her hand.

4. Mr. Shields has such a _____ amount of hair that he can get a haircut in two minutes.

5. The captain had a _____ for scaring people, not for helping them.

6. Many of that man's _____ may not have been legal.

7. She thought herself in all _____ to be the best dancer in school.

8. In Mrs. Chavez's eyes, I came to _____ all American youth.

9. I defended myself against her _____ of wrongdoing.

10. They spoke Spanish fast in order to _____ me.

II. Below is a diagram of the parts of a plot with three parts labeled A, B, and C. On a separate sheet of paper, write the term (rising action, climax, conclusion) for each of these parts.

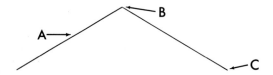

III. Each sentence below contains an idiom. On a separate sheet of paper, copy the sentence and explain what the idiom means.

1. "What's up?" José asked.

2. Andrew and Marina were going steady.

3. Andrew thought that Mrs. Chavez was mixed up.

4. José said, "What do you want outta me?"

5. Marina's old lady was really very nice.

UNIT REVIEW

I. Match the terms in column A with their definitions in column B.

<table>
<tr><td align="center">A</td><td align="center">B</td></tr>
<tr><td>1. conclusion</td><td>a) where and when a story happens</td></tr>
<tr><td>2. plot</td><td>b) a problem or question faced by a character</td></tr>
<tr><td>3. rising action</td><td>c) the actions or events in a story</td></tr>
<tr><td>4. conflict</td><td>d) actions leading to a climax</td></tr>
<tr><td>5. foreshadowing</td><td>e) the end of the story</td></tr>
<tr><td>6. synonyms</td><td>f) the turning point of a story</td></tr>
<tr><td>7. character</td><td>g) words with almost the same meaning</td></tr>
<tr><td>8. setting</td><td>h) hinting of something to come</td></tr>
<tr><td>9. climax</td><td>i) person or animal in a story</td></tr>
<tr><td>10. fiction</td><td>j) made-up story</td></tr>
</table>

II. A plot, as you know, is a series of actions that leads to the solution of a conflict. A good plot is one that holds the reader's interest throughout these actions. Below are the titles of stories in this unit. From the stories you have read, choose the one that you think has the best plot—that is, the one that best held your interest. On a separate sheet of paper, tell why it held your interest.

The Confidence Game   Blind Sunday

Thicker Than Water   Lather and Nothing Else

The Kind of Man She Could Love   Aquí se Habla Español

III. The theme of this unit is "searching for yourself." On a separate sheet of paper, answer the following questions.

1. Which story, in your opinion, best shows a character searching for herself or himself? Tell why.

2. In your opinion, which story best shows a character finding herself or himself? Tell why.

SPEAKING UP

The little poem below was written by the famous American poet Walt Whitman. Following it is a kind of continuation of the poem, asking you to respond by pronouncing your own name in different ways.

Try reading all of this aloud with a friend. Arrange a way for both of you to read the two stanzas by Whitman. One way would be to read the first stanza yourself and have your friend read the second. Either one of you can read the next four lines, with the other one responding by saying his or her name in different ways.

Finally, choose yet another way for both of you to read the final two lines.

WHAT AM I AFTER ALL?

by Walt Whitman

What am I after all but a child, pleased with the sound of my own name? repeating it over
        and over;
I stand apart to hear—it never tires me.

To you your name also;
Did you think there was nothing but two or three pronunciations in the sound of your name?

Go ahead, say your name . . . . (*respond*)
Good—say it again, a different way . . . . (*respond*)
That's right, say it again . . . . (*respond*)
Again . . . . (*respond*)
And then again . . . . (*respond*)

How many ways can you say your name?
They're all you!

WRITING YOUR OWN PLOT

What do you think is happening in this picture? What happened just before this picture was taken? What will happen next? Your answers to these questions will help you develop a plot paragraph.

1. **Prewriting:** Imagine that you are watching the people in this picture. List words and phrases that describe what you think they are doing. Then list some exciting action words. Finally, decide on the order of events.
2. **Writing:** Use your prewriting plan to write a paragraph that describes the action in the picture. Write your paragraph so that readers will experience the excitement of the event as though they were actually there.
3. **Revising:** Read your paragraph. Does it give a clear description of the action? Does the action move naturally from beginning to end? Have you used action words? Make corrections and rewrite your paragraph.

MONSTERS AND MYSTERIES

We dance round in a ring and suppose,
But the Secret sits in the middle and knows.
from "The Secret Sits" by Robert Frost

Imagine a world without secrets, a world without mystery. Imagine a world without stories and events that spark your imagination. Such a world would be dull.

There are mysteries all around us, in eerie places and unexplained events. In this unit, you'll have a chance to discover some of them. Be prepared for adventure and surprise as you enter the world of . . . monsters and mysteries.

STALEY FLEMING'S HALLUCINATION

by Ambrose Bierce

▶ The author of this story, Ambrose Bierce, was as much a mystery as some of his stories. For many years he wrote newspaper articles, stories, and books. Then, in 1913, he disappeared. Nobody knows what became of him.

As you read this strange and mysterious story, think about Staley Fleming's vision. Is it real or imaginary? Why doesn't it leave Staley Fleming alone?

Two men were talking. One was a doctor.

"I sent for you, Doctor," said the other. "But I don't think you can do me any good. Maybe you can recommend a specialist in psychiatry. I think I'm a bit loony."

"You look all right," the doctor said.

"You shall judge—I have hallucinations," said Staley Fleming. "I wake every night and see in my room—watching me—a big black Newfoundland dog with a white forefoot."

"You say you wake," replied the doctor. "Are you sure about that? Hallucinations are sometimes only dreams."

"Oh, I wake, all right. Sometimes I lie still a long time, looking at the dog as hard as he looks at me. I always leave the light going. When I can't stand it any longer I sit up in bed—and nothing is there!"

"Hmm, hmm. . . . What's the beast's expression?" asked the doctor.

"It seems evil to me. Of course I know that an animal's face always has the same expression—except in art. But this is not a real

- **recommend** (rek uh MEND) **suggest someone who would be good for a job**
- hallucination (huh loo sin AY shun) **seeing something that does not really exist**
- Newfoundland dog (NOO fun lund dawg) **a kind of large, strong dog with a thick black coat**

182

animal. Newfoundland dogs are pretty gentle looking, you know. What's the matter with this one?"

"Really, I can't give a diagnosis. I'm not going to treat the dog."

The doctor laughed at his own joke. But he watched his patient from the corner of his eye. Presently he said, "Fleming, your description of the beast fits the dog of the late Atwell Barton."

Fleming half rose from his chair. Then he sat again and tried not to look interested. "I remember Barton," he said. "I believe he was— it was reported that—wasn't there something suspicious in his death?"

Looking right into the eyes of his patient, the doctor said, "Three years ago, the body of your old enemy, Atwell Barton, was found in the woods near his home and yours. He had been stabbed to death. There have been no arrests. There was no clue. Some of us had theories. I have one. Have you?"

"I? Why, what could I know about it?" Fleming said. "You re-

- diagnosis (dy ig NOH sis) **a decision about the kind of illness a person has**
- presently (PREZ unt lee) **soon, before long**
- **theory** (THEE uh ree) **idea that is used to explain an event**

member that I left for Europe almost immediately afterward—quite a while afterward. In the few weeks since my return, you could not expect me to come up with a theory. In fact, I have not given the matter a thought. What about his dog?"

"It was the first to find the body. It died of starvation on his grave."

We do not know much about the law of coincidences. Staley Fleming did not either. Or perhaps he would not have sprung to his feet as the night wind brought in through the open window the long wailing howl of a distant dog. He strode several times across the room in the steady gaze of the doctor. Then, suddenly facing him, Fleming almost shouted, "What has all this to do with my trouble, Dr. Halderman? You forget why you were sent for."

Rising, the doctor laid his hand on his patient's arm and said gently, "Pardon me. I cannot diagnose your problem without giving it more time. Tomorrow, perhaps. Please go to bed. Leave your door unlocked. I will pass the night here with your books. Can you call me without getting up?"

"Yes, there is an electric bell."

"Good. If anything disturbs you, push the button without sitting up. Good night."

Comfortably settled in an armchair, the doctor stared into the glowing coals and thought deeply for a long time. But he frequently rose and opened a door leading to the staircase. He listened carefully. Then he went back to his seat. Presently, however, he fell asleep. When he woke, it was past midnight. He stirred the fire and lifted a book from the table at his side. He opened it at random and began to read.

"All flesh has spirit," the book said. "Flesh can take on the power of spirit. Also, the spirit can take on the power of the flesh. And there are those who say that beasts as well as humans can do this, and . . . "

The reading was interrupted by a shaking of the house, as if a heavy object had fallen. The doctor flung down the book, rushed

---

- **coincidence** (koh IN si duns) two or more things that happen at the same time, by accident
- **strode** (STROHD) walked; past tense of stride
- **at random** (at RAN dum) happening by chance, with no plan

184

from the room, and mounted the stairs to Fleming's bedroom. He tried the door, but it was locked—against his orders. He set his shoulder against it with such force that it gave way. On the floor near the disordered bed, in his nightclothes, lay Staley Fleming gasping away his life.

The doctor raised the dying man's head from the floor and observed a wound in the throat. "I should have thought of this," he said. The doctor believed it was suicide.

When the man was dead, an examination showed the unmistakable marks of an animal's fangs deeply sunken into the neck.

But no animal was to be found.

- unmistakable (un mi STAYK uh bul) clear; without being able to make a mistake about something

ALL THINGS CONSIDERED _____

1. Staley Fleming calls a doctor to his home because he (a) has a high fever. (b) thinks he sees a dog in his bedroom. (c) was bitten by a dog.

2. Fleming has hallucinations (a) when he awakens at night. (b) while he sleeps at night. (c) during the day.

3. The dog that Fleming sees has (a) a gentle expression. (b) a changing expression. (c) an evil expression.

4. Atwell Barton had been Staley Fleming's (a) enemy. (b) friend. (c) doctor.

5. Staley Fleming went to Europe (a) before the murder. (b) the day of the murder. (c) a little while after the murder.

6. After Atwell Barton's death, (a) his murderer was arrested. (b) clues were found. (c) no one was arrested.

7. The doctor tells Fleming to go to bed and (a) ring a bell if anything disturbs him. (b) read for a while. (c) lock all the doors in the house.

8. Atwell Barton's dog (a) is still alive. (b) died of starvation. (c) died of old age.

9. While the doctor is reading, (a) the house begins to shake. (b) he hears an electric bell. (c) a dog howls.

10. An examination of Fleming's body shows (a) stab wounds around the neck. (b) fang marks on the neck. (c) nothing unusual.

THINKING IT THROUGH _____

1. The doctor says he has a theory about the death of Atwell Barton. What do you think his theory is? What clues might have led him to this theory?

2. The book the doctor is reading states: "Flesh can take on the power of spirit. Also, the spirit can take on the power of the flesh." What do these statements mean? How are they related to Fleming's hallucination?

3. Were you surprised by the ending of the story, or did you guess how the story would end? Which clues help you guess what happens?

Literary Skills

Understanding Setting

As you know, every story has a **setting**. The setting tells you the *time* and *place* of the story. When the setting is not directly stated, you must look for clues in the story. By paying attention to these clues, you can figure out when and where a story takes place.

For example, when "Staley Fleming's Hallucination" begins, Staley Fleming is sitting in a chair. Later, he goes upstairs to his bedroom. The doctor reads in an armchair in front of the fire. Chairs and bedrooms are found indoors. So you know this story takes place in a home.

There are also clues to the time of day. Fleming goes to bed. The doctor says he will spend the night there. These clues tell you it is nighttime.

Here are four statements about the setting of "Staley Fleming's Hallucination." On a separate sheet of paper, write whether each statement is *true* or *false*. If it is false, rewrite the sentence so that it makes a true statement about the setting.

1. The story takes place before Fleming's trip to Europe.
2. The time of the story is after Edison invented electric gadgets.
3. The weather is extremely hot.
4. Staley Fleming's home is located in a big city.

Composition

Follow your teacher's instructions before completing *one* of these writing assignments.

1. The setting in this story helps create a feeling of mystery. Name three details about the setting that help make the story mysterious. Write a sentence about each telling how it adds to the feeling of mystery.
2. How would you explain what happens in this story? Write a paragraph explaining it in your own way. First state what you think causes Staley Fleming's death. After that, mention clues from the story that support your opinion.

187

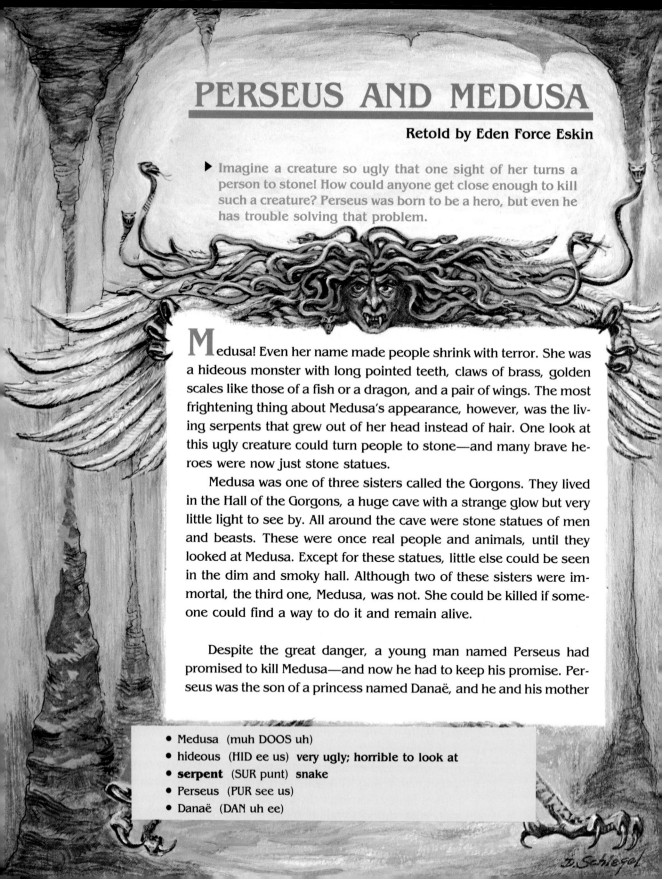

PERSEUS AND MEDUSA

Retold by Eden Force Eskin

▶ Imagine a creature so ugly that one sight of her turns a person to stone! How could anyone get close enough to kill such a creature? Perseus was born to be a hero, but even he has trouble solving that problem.

Medusa! Even her name made people shrink with terror. She was a hideous monster with long pointed teeth, claws of brass, golden scales like those of a fish or a dragon, and a pair of wings. The most frightening thing about Medusa's appearance, however, was the living serpents that grew out of her head instead of hair. One look at this ugly creature could turn people to stone—and many brave heroes were now just stone statues.

Medusa was one of three sisters called the Gorgons. They lived in the Hall of the Gorgons, a huge cave with a strange glow but very little light to see by. All around the cave were stone statues of men and beasts. These were once real people and animals, until they looked at Medusa. Except for these statues, little else could be seen in the dim and smoky hall. Although two of these sisters were immortal, the third one, Medusa, was not. She could be killed if someone could find a way to do it and remain alive.

Despite the great danger, a young man named Perseus had promised to kill Medusa—and now he had to keep his promise. Perseus was the son of a princess named Danaë, and he and his mother

- Medusa (muh DOOS uh)
- hideous (HID ee us) **very ugly; horrible to look at**
- **serpent** (SUR punt) **snake**
- Perseus (PUR see us)
- Danaë (DAN uh ee)

lived far from their own land, Argos. Danaë's father, the king of Argos, had sent them to sea in a great wooden chest because he was afraid for his life. A prophecy had warned the king that Danaë would have a son who would one day kill his grandfather. To keep the prophecy from coming true, the king forced Danaë and Perseus to leave Argos.

So the king sent a great wooden chest carrying Danaë and Perseus to sea. It landed on an island ruled by a man named Polydectus. Although Polydectus was not always kind to Danaë and Perseus, he did allow them to live on his island. On this island, the baby Perseus grew into a handsome young man, and it was to Polydectus that he made the promise to kill Medusa. If he did not keep his promise, he and his mother would be in serious trouble.

Polydectus was about to be married, and he demanded that Perseus bring him Medusa's head as a wedding present. Perseus was glad to promise almost anything, especially since Polydectus had stopped trying to marry Danaë, who disliked him. Nevertheless, this promise was more than he had planned on, and it was going to be very difficult to keep.

Perseus said good-bye to his mother and set out to find Medusa. He was not sure how to go about it, but help soon came to him in the form of the god Hermes and the goddess Athena. Hermes was the guide and the swift messenger of the gods. He gave Perseus a helmet of darkness that would make the wearer invisible, a curved sword of the strongest metal known, and a magic pouch. Then Hermes removed his own winged sandals and lent them to Perseus. Hermes told Perseus that he must first find the Gray Sisters; they were the only ones who knew how to find Medusa.

Athena, the goddess of wisdom, appeared to Perseus in a dream. She gave him her bright shield that shone like a mirror. She told him to look only at Medusa's image in the shield and never at the creature herself. If he did not look directly at her, he would be safe. Then she told him where to find the Gray Sisters.

- **prophecy** (PROF i see) **statement telling what will happen in the future**
- Polydectus (pol i DEK teez)
- Hermes (HUR meez) **guide and messenger of the Greek gods**
- Athena (uh THEE nuh) **Greek goddess of wisdom**

Perseus awoke and went in search of the Gray Sisters. He found them in a damp cave filled with cobwebs and insects. There was a smell of seawater and seaweed in their cave. The walls felt moist and chilly. The Gray Sisters were strange creatures with the bodies of swans and heads and hands that were almost human. Among them, the Gray Sisters had only one eye and one tooth, which they shared. They kept passing these treasures back and forth to each other.

As they were passing the eye, Perseus grabbed it and held it away from them. They screamed and tried to get it back, but he said he would return it only when they gave him directions for finding Medusa. They had no choice and soon told him that Medusa was in the Hall of the Gorgons. He returned the eye, but before the Gray Sisters had a chance to use it, he escaped quickly from the moldy cave.

When Perseus arrived at the Hall of the Gorgons, he found the hideous Medusa asleep in the strangely lit cave. Statues of long-lost heroes stood everywhere. They were caught in poses of action, and the expressions on their faces looked lifelike. Perseus put on the helmet and became invisible. He was very much tempted to look at the monster, but he thought of Athena's words and kept his eyes on her bright shield as he carefully approached the sleeping Medusa.

She and her sisters did not stir, but some of the serpents in her hair hissed in warning as Perseus came near. Then, still not looking at the creature except in the shield, he rushed forward and sliced off her head with one sweep of his super-strong sword.

While the serpents on the head still hissed and writhed, Perseus grabbed the head and put it quickly into the magic pouch. He knew that the head itself still had the power to turn people to stone, but the pouch would keep it safely out of sight.

Wearing Hermes' winged sandals, Perseus started to fly toward the island where he lived. As he flew over the country of Ethiopia, he saw a beautiful girl chained to a cliff near the sea. The sea waters were rough and often struck at her. A hideous sea monster swam below trying to devour her. The girl was Andromeda, the daughter of the king of Ethiopia. Like Perseus, she had been punished because of a prophecy although she had done no wrong. The prophecy had warned her father that chaining her to the rock was the only way to save his country from disaster.

Having seen Andromeda, Perseus fell in love with her beauty and decided to save her. He swooped down to fight the sea monster, whose body was covered with scales of iron. Perseus tried to find a place between the monster's scales to plunge his sword. Again and again they attacked each other. They fought hard and long until the cliff and waters were red with blood. Finally, Perseus gave the monster the final blow with his sword and freed Andromeda.

The princess fell in love with her brave and handsome rescuer, and her parents agreed to let them marry. Everyone was preparing to celebrate the wedding in the royal hall when another man came to claim her as his rightful bride. Andromeda had been promised in marriage to him earlier, but since he had never tried to rescue her from the sea monster, she did not think much of him. Nevertheless, now he was trying to stop her marriage to Perseus on her wedding day, and he had brought his soldiers with him. They began to attack Perseus and the wedding party. Perseus shouted to his friends to hide their eyes. Quickly he drew Medusa's head out of the magic pouch and showed it to his enemies. They all turned to stone where they stood.

- writhe (RYTH) twist and turn
- plunge (PLUNJ) jab

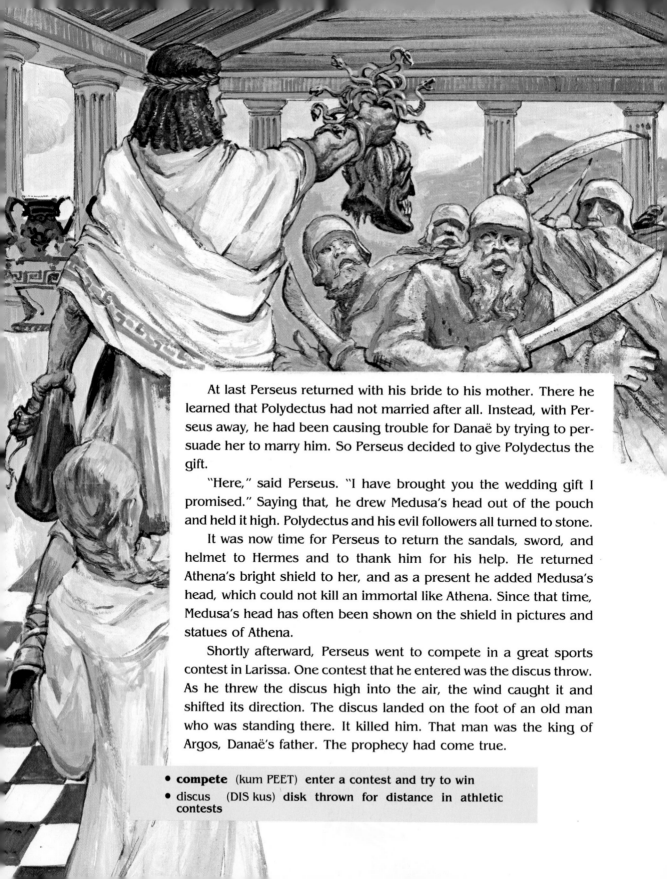

At last Perseus returned with his bride to his mother. There he learned that Polydectus had not married after all. Instead, with Perseus away, he had been causing trouble for Danaë by trying to persuade her to marry him. So Perseus decided to give Polydectus the gift.

"Here," said Perseus. "I have brought you the wedding gift I promised." Saying that, he drew Medusa's head out of the pouch and held it high. Polydectus and his evil followers all turned to stone.

It was now time for Perseus to return the sandals, sword, and helmet to Hermes and to thank him for his help. He returned Athena's bright shield to her, and as a present he added Medusa's head, which could not kill an immortal like Athena. Since that time, Medusa's head has often been shown on the shield in pictures and statues of Athena.

Shortly afterward, Perseus went to compete in a great sports contest in Larissa. One contest that he entered was the discus throw. As he threw the discus high into the air, the wind caught it and shifted its direction. The discus landed on the foot of an old man who was standing there. It killed him. That man was the king of Argos, Danaë's father. The prophecy had come true.

- **compete** (kum PEET) enter a contest and try to win
- **discus** (DIS kus) disk thrown for distance in athletic contests

ALL THINGS CONSIDERED

1. Medusa is (a) an immortal snake. (b) a sea monster. (c) a creature with snakes instead of hair.
2. Perseus promises to kill Medusa (a) as a present for Polydectus. (b) because she tried to kill him. (c) to keep Medusa from killing his grandfather.
3. Danaë is (a) the goddess of wisdom. (b) a princess of Ethiopia. (c) Perseus's mother.
4. Perseus gets help from (a) a god and goddess. (b) his mother and grandfather. (c) the Gorgons.
5. To find Medusa, Perseus first goes to (a) Danaë. (b) the Gray Sisters. (c) the Gorgons.
6. The Gray Sisters have (a) heads of swans. (b) one eye each. (c) bodies of swans.
7. When Perseus reaches the Hall of the Gorgons, Medusa is (a) sleeping. (b) writhing. (c) playing with snakes.
8. Andromeda is chained to a rock because (a) she won't marry the man favored by her parents. (b) a prophecy said it was the only way to save the country. (c) she is the bride of a terrible sea monster.
9. Perseus kills Polydectus with (a) a sword. (b) Medusa's head. (c) a discus.
10. On a picture of Athena's shield you might find (a) the head of Medusa. (b) a drawing of Perseus. (c) winged sandals like the ones that belonged to Hermes.

THINKING IT THROUGH

1. Think of the prophecy mentioned near the beginning of the story. (a) How does that prophecy force Danaë and Perseus to leave the land where they were born? (b) How does the prophecy come true at the end?
2. How are evil people punished and good people rewarded in this story? Give two examples.
3. This story is based on an old Greek legend. Why do you think Greeks told stories about heroes, gods, and goddesses? Why do you think people still enjoy this story today?

Relationships

Time Order

Time order—the order of events in a story—tells which events happen first, next, and last. Understanding time order is important to understanding and remembering a story. Clue words such as *first, next, then, later,* and *finally* help signal the order of events.

Here are some events from "Perseus and Medusa." On a separate sheet of paper, write the sentences in the correct time order. You may wish to look through the story to check your answers.

1. Perseus fell in love with Andromeda.
2. Perseus and Danaë landed on an island ruled by Polydectus.
3. Perseus threw the discus in games at Larissa.
4. Perseus grabbed the eye of the Gray Sisters.
5. A prophecy warned the King of Argos that his daughter's son would kill him.
6. Athena's shield helped Perseus kill Medusa.
7. Perseus promised that he would bring Medusa's head back to Polydectus.

Composition

Follow your teacher's instructions before completing *one* of these writing assignments.

1. Suppose you were telling a friend about "Perseus and Medusa." Write three sentences that tell what you think makes the story unusual.
2. Think about a story you know. Write a paragraph that tells the important events in that story in the correct time order. Use at least three clue words, such as *at first, then, next, after, later,* and *at last,* in telling the story.

THESEUS AND THE MINOTAUR

Retold by Eden Force Eskin

▶ The Minotaur is a monster that lives in a dark and gloomy Labyrinth. This monster likes to eat—people! From far away, however, comes a young hero named Theseus who believes he can kill the monster. Will he succeed?

The only son of Minos, the ruler of the island of Crete, had died when visiting the city of Athens. Minos's grief was more than he could bear, and he blamed Athens and its ruler for his son's death. Revenge was all that Minos could think of, so he invaded the city of Athens and threatened to burn it to the ground unless the Athenians followed his orders. And his orders were cruel! Every nine years, Athens would have to send seven young women and seven young men to Crete. There, they would be shut in the Labyrinth to meet their death.

The Labyrinth was a huge place—a kind of prison with winding paths that twisted and turned so that nobody could find the way out. It had been built by one of the great architects of the time. To those who were shut within its rough, rocky walls, it was dark, gloomy, and frightening. Sooner or later, anyone in the Labyrinth would run into the Minotaur. And meeting the Minotaur meant meeting death.

Minos had had the Labyrinth built to hold the Minotaur, a monster with the head of a bull and the body of a human. When the Minotaur found people inside the Labyrinth, it devoured them.

- Theseus (THEE see us)
- Minotaur (MIN uh tawr)
- Labyrinth (LAB uh rinth)
- Minos (MY nus)
- Crete (KREET) **an island in the Mediterranean Sea**
- Athens (ATH inz) **a city in Greece**
- Athenian (uh THEE nee un) **person from Athens, Greece**
- **architect** (AR ki tekt) **person who designs buildings**
- **devour** (di VOUR) **eat up quickly**

195

It was once again time for Athens to send seven young men and seven young women to Crete. And now the choice had to be made. One young man stepped forward to offer to go. It was Theseus, son of King Aegeus of Athens.

Theseus had been raised away from Athens and had grown up strong and courageous. He reached his father's home just before the time to send the young people off to their doom. The king did not want him to go. Father and son had known each other such a short time. But when Theseus explained that he intended to try to kill the Minotaur, King Aegeus had to agree.

Theseus promised his father that if he was successful, he would send a signal from the boat when it returned to Athens. The boat from Crete usually carried a black sail to show mourning for the victims of the Minotaur. Theseus promised that he would lower the black sail and raise a white sail as the ship approached Athens to show that he was still alive.

So Theseus and the others set sail for Crete. He still did not know how he would defeat the Minotaur and escape from the Labyrinth. But luck would surely be on his side.

When the Athenians reached Crete, they were paraded through the streets. Ariadne, who was Minos's daughter, saw Theseus—so strong, handsome, and brave looking. She fell in love with him and decided to help him. She found a way to meet Theseus secretly and told him that she would help him escape. In return he promised to take her back to Athens where they would marry.

Ariadne gave Theseus a spool of thread that she had gotten from the man who designed the Labyrinth. If Theseus would tie one end of the thread to the door at the entrance, he could unwind it as he made his way through the confusing paths. Then all he would have to do to find his way out was to follow the thread back to the entrance.

The thread would help Theseus escape from the Labyrinth, but he would have to fight the Minotaur on his own. Theseus strode boldly into the Labyrinth searching for the Minotaur. He made his

- Aegeus (uh JEE us)
- **mourning** (MAWRN ing) **showing and feeling sorrow after someone's death**
- Ariadne (are ee AD nee)

196

way carefully among the rocky, winding paths. Suddenly, he found himself looking straight at the sleeping monster.

Theseus realized he had no weapon, but he had to act quickly before the Minotaur awoke. He prayed for strength. Then he looked at his fists—they would have to be his weapons. Quickly, he pinned the Minotaur to the ground and began to attack him with his fists. The monster stirred and snorted, but it had been caught off guard. Theseus kept attacking with his fists as the Minotaur tried to stab him with its horns. The man kept attacking the beast with crushing blows. The Minotaur tried to get to its feet to fight back, but it was already weakened by the ironlike fists. It placed its four feet on the hard rock, staggered to a standing position, and lowered its head to attack. Theseus aimed one final blow at the weak spot in the Minotaur's neck, and the beast stumbled and collapsed. The life had gone out of this creature that had caused so much terror. Theseus had won.

Then he went searching for the other Athenians in the Labyrinth and found them all safe. He gathered them together and led them out of the dark gloom of the Labyrinth into the sunlight by following the spool of thread that Ariadne had given him.

Quickly, Theseus and the Athenians took Ariadne, fled to the ship that was waiting in the harbor, and started out for Athens. On the way, Ariadne became seasick, so Theseus set her on shore while he went back to the ship to make some repairs. But a storm carried the ship out to sea. Theseus remained on board and Ariadne still lingered on land. When the storm was over, he returned and found that Ariadne had died. He was heartbroken.

Perhaps it was his sadness that made Theseus forget to change the black sail for the white as they headed into Athens. King Aegeus

saw the black sail and plunged into the sea in his grief. The sea was named the Aegean Sea after the king. It is still called by that name.

After his father's death, Theseus ruled Athens as a wise and good king. Finally, he decided that the people should rule themselves. Athens became a city of liberty and democracy.

ALL THINGS CONSIDERED

1. King Minos wants revenge on Athens because (a) King Aegeus had killed his son. (b) his son had died there. (c) he had lost a war.

2. The Labyrinth is (a) the dark basement of a castle. (b) a place with winding paths. (c) part of the city of Athens.

3. The Minotaur is (a) a terrible human being. (b) half human and half animal. (c) a monster with snakes in its hair.

4. Theseus offers to go to Crete so that he can (a) meet Ariadne. (b) make peace with the king. (c) kill the Minotaur.

5. He kills the Minotaur (a) with a sword. (b) by strangling it with a magic thread. (c) with his bare hands.

6. He is able to find his way out of the Labyrinth with the help of (a) Ariadne. (b) Minos. (c) the 13 Athenians.

7. To find his way out of the Labyrinth, Theseus (a) uses a map. (b) follows a thread. (c) asks other Athenians for help.

8. Theseus loses Ariadne because (a) she doesn't follow the thread. (b) he lies to her. (c) a storm separates them.

9. King Aegeus plunges into the sea because he (a) thinks Theseus has died. (b) is unhappy about Ariadne's death. (c) loses the war with Crete.

10. Athens becomes (a) a huge empire. (b) a conquering city. (c) a city of liberty and democracy.

THINKING IT THROUGH

1. King Aegeus does not want Theseus to go to Crete. Why does he let him go? Do you think that he does the right thing?

2. Do you think that Ariadne is an important character in this story? Do you think that the story would have the same ending without her? Explain.

3. Do you think that the setting of this story could be changed to the world of today? Tell why or why not.

• Aegean (uh JEE un)

Relationships

Cause and Effect

In most stories one thing happens because of another. A **cause** is an event or idea that leads to a certain result, which is called an **effect.** In "Theseus and the Minotaur," for example, King Minos invades Athens because his only son died on a visit to that city. The *cause* is his son's death. The *effect* is that the king invades Athens.

Understanding causes and effects will help you to follow events in a story. The words "because," "so," "since," and "for that reason" are usually clue words to cause and effect.

On a separate sheet of paper, write a complete sentence by matching each of the following causes with its effect.

CAUSES	EFFECTS
1. King Minos wants revenge on Athens,	(a) . . . she offers to help him escape.
2. Because Ariadne falls in love with Theseus,	(b) . . . he uses his fists to kill the Minotaur.
3. Since Theseus has no weapon with him,	(c) . . . so he makes Athens send people to Crete to die.
4. King Aegeus sees a black sail on the ship,	(d) . . . so he thinks that Theseus is dead.

Composition

Follow your teacher's instructions before completing *one* of these writing assignments.

1. Here are three effects of events in the story. On a separate sheet of paper, complete each sentence by writing the cause.
(a) It was difficult to get out of the Labyrinth since _____ .
(b) Theseus wanted to go to Crete because _____ .
(c) Athens became a democracy because _____ .

2. Athens and Crete are real places. Theseus was probably a real person. Write a paragraph telling which parts of the story could be true and which parts have probably been invented.

VOCABULARY AND SKILL REVIEW

Before completing the exercises that follow, you may wish to review the **bold-faced** words on pages 182–196.

I.

1. A person who is in *mourning* (a) rises early. (b) is sad because someone has died. (c) always wants revenge.

2. If two events are a *coincidence* they (a) happen at the same time. (b) happen at different times. (c) never happen.

3. A person who *devours* food (a) eats it up quickly. (b) doesn't like it. (c) serves it in a restaurant.

4. If you *strode* into the room, you (a) tiptoed. (b) walked. (c) ran.

5. A person who *recommends* you for a job says you are a (a) good worker. (b) poor worker. (c) fast worker.

6. A *prophecy* tells (a) something that happened long ago. (b) a lie. (c) something that is going to happen in the future.

7. A *theory* is (a) a plan of action. (b) an idea that is used to explain something. (c) an excuse.

8. A person who is afraid of *serpents* is afraid of (a) fire. (b) monsters. (c) snakes.

9. An *architect* (a) invents puzzles. (b) designs buildings. (c) solves mysteries.

10. A person who *competes* (a) enters a contest. (b) finishes a job. (c) forces someone to do something.

II. When a writer changes the details in a setting, the feeling the story gives the reader can change, too. Change five of the setting details in the paragraph below. On a separate sheet of paper, write the paragraph with the changes. Check to see how the feeling of the paragraph has changed.

It gives me a strange feeling to sit alone in my furnished room with my head full of ghosts and the room full of voices of the past. All the Christmases of the past come back in a mad jumble. There is the childish Christmas with a house full of relatives, a tree in the window, a Christmas pudding, and the stocking in the dark morning. Then there is the teenage Christmas with mother and father, the War, the bitter cold, and letters from abroad. There is also my first grownup Christmas with a boyfriend, the snow and the enchantment, kisses, and the walk in the dark before midnight with the grounds so white and the stars diamond bright in a black sky. So many Christmases through the years. And now, the first Christmas alone.
—from "Christmas Meeting" by Rosemary Timperley

Thomas Stearns Eliot (1888-1965)

What would T.S. Eliot have thought if he had lived to see a Broadway musical based on his poetry? Nobody knows, but about 15 years after he died, *Old Possum's Book of Practical Cats* became the hit musical *Cats*.

Old Possum's Book of Practical Cats is one of the few humorous works by T.S. Eliot. Most of his poems are about serious subjects, such as the new ways people looked at things in the twentieth century.

Thomas Stearns Eliot was born and raised in St. Louis, Missouri. After graduating from Harvard University in 1910, Eliot studied in France and then in England. He eventually settled in England. In 1927, he became a British citizen. Now, although he was born in the United States, T.S. Eliot is considered a British writer.

THE NAMING OF CATS

by T. S. Eliot

▶ Many people think cats are very mysterious animals. T. S. Eliot thinks he knows one of the reasons for the mystery—their names. What do you think?

The Naming of Cats is a difficult matter,
    It isn't just one of your holiday games;
You may think at first I'm as mad as a hatter
When I tell you, a cat must have three different names.
First of all, there's the name that the family use daily,
    Such as Peter, Augustus, Alonzo or James,
Such as Victor or Jonathan, George or Bill Bailey—
    All of them sensible everyday names.
There are fancier names if you think they sound sweeter,
    Some for the gentlemen, some for the dames:

Such as Plato, Admetus, Electra, Demeter—
    But all of them sensible everyday names.
But I tell you, a cat needs a name that's particular,
    A name that's peculiar, and more dignified,
Else how can he keep up his tail perpendicular,
    Or spread out his whiskers, or cherish his pride?
Of names of this kind, I can give you a quorum,
    Such as Munkustrap, Quaxo, or Coricopat,
Such as Bombalurina, or else Jellylorum—
    Names that never belong to more than one cat.
But above and beyond there's still one name left over,
    And that is the name that you never will guess;
The name that no human research can discover—
    But the cat himself knows, and will never confess.
When you notice a cat in profound meditation,
    The reason, I tell you, is always the same:
His mind is engaged in a rapt contemplation
    Of the thought, of the thought, of the thought of his name:
        His ineffable effable
        Effanineffable
Deep and inscrutable singular Name.

WAYS OF KNOWING

1. Why do you think the poet believes a cat has three different kinds of names? What kinds of names are they? Can you think of another kind of name a cat might have?
2. Is the poem meant to be serious? Is it meant to be humorous? How can you tell?
3. Why does the poet think it is difficult to name cats? Do you agree? Why or why not?

- **perpendicular** (pur pen DIK yuh lur) **straight up**
- quorum (KWAWR um) **the required number**
- profound (pruh FOWND) **deep**
- contemplation (kon tem PLAY shun) **deep thought**
- ineffable (in EF uh bul) **impossible to put into words**
- inscrutable (in SKROO tuh bul) **very mysterious, impossible to figure out**
- peculiar (pi KYOOL yur) **strange; unusual**
- **cherish** (CHER ish) **treat with love and tenderness**
- rapt (RAPT) **in deep concentration about something**

Oral Interpretation

Choral Reading

Choral (KOR ul) **reading** is reading aloud in a group. It is like a chorus of voices speaking rather than singing. Some poems, such as "The Naming of Cats," sound especially good when they are read aloud. You can divide your class into sections to read different parts of the poem. Before reading the poem aloud as a group, plan the reading together so that it will sound right.

1. First read the poem silently and try to hear the sounds in your mind's ear. Pay particular attention to the way names are pronounced. Read the poem at least three times to yourself before the group begins to practice reading together.
2. Pay attention to the lines that have a thought carried over into the next line. These lines should be read without pausing or raising your voice at the end. Then look for pauses. They help give the poem its rhythm. Use the pauses well.
3. Decide where to make your voice mysterious, where to speak softly, and where to raise your voice. Remember that the poem is about a cat, not a person. Let the humor come through.
4. Stand up when you read aloud. One person may act as the director who gets everybody to start, pause, and end together.
5. Practice. Practice. Practice! Remember to S-L-O-W D-O-W-N. It will be easier to understand what you are saying and will also sound more mysterious.

Composition

Follow your teacher's instructions before completing *one* of these writing assignments.

1. Do you believe that cats are mysterious? If you do, write four sentences that give details explaining what makes cats mysterious. If you do not agree, give four details that explain why you believe cats are no more mysterious than other animals.
2. What would you think about before you named a cat? What would cause you to pick a particular name? Write a paragraph telling how you would go about choosing a name for a cat.

PUZZLE

by Robert Froman

▶ There are many puzzles in life. Before reading the poem, try to figure out the drawing. Then read the poem.

Map of a city with streets meeting at center?
Net to catch people jumping from a burning building?
Spider's web?
Burner on an electric stove?
Fingerprint?
No.
Frozen puddle after a hit by a rock.

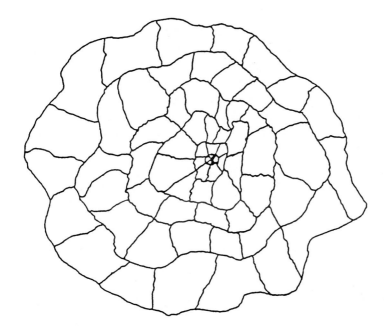

WAYS OF KNOWING

1. Think of other ideas for the drawing that the poet has not included. Name them.
2. Find out what some of your classmates thought the drawing was. Did everyone agree? What does this poem tell you about the way people see things?

Hector Hugh Munro (Saki) (1870-1916)

H. H. Munro lived what many people would consider a very romantic, exciting life. Although his parents were British, he was born in Burma, a country in Asia. During Munro's youth, Burma was ruled by Great Britain, and Munro's father was an inspector in the Burma police force.

When Munro was two years old, his mother died, and young Hector was sent to live in England with some strict aunts. Later, he attended boarding schools in England. When he was 17, his father retired and the two of them went traveling together through Europe.

Munro got a job with the Burma police force in 1893, but poor health forced him to resign. He returned to England and began to write. He chose the name "Saki" as a pen name. Many of his works first appeared under that name.

Most of his stories are written with either an odd sense of humor or a sense of horror. Sometimes both humor and horror are combined in one story.

When World War I began, Munro enlisted and went to France to fight. There he was known as a brave soldier. In 1916, he died while fighting.

THE OPEN WINDOW

by Saki (H. H. Munro)

▶ Mr. Framton Nuttel liked to go to the country to soothe his nerves. Unfortunately, this particular visit did not turn out to be very restful.

"My aunt will be down presently, Mr. Nuttel," said a very self-possessed young lady of 15. "In the meantime you must try and put up with me."

Framton Nuttel endeavored to say the correct something. But he doubted more than ever whether these visits to total strangers would do much to help cure his nerves, as they were supposed to do.

"I know how it will be," his sister had said when he was preparing to go to the country retreat. "You will bury yourself down there and not speak to a living soul. Your nerves will be worse than ever from moping. I'll just give you letters introducing you to all the people I know there. Some of them, as far as I can remember, were quite nice."

Framton wondered whether Mrs. Sappleton, the lady to whom he was presenting one of the letters, belonged in the "nice" division.

"Do you know many of the people here?" asked the niece.

"Hardly a soul," said Framton. "My sister was staying here, you know, some four years ago. She gave me letters to some of the people here."

He made the last statement in a tone of regret.

- self-possessed (SELF puh ZEST) very much in control of the way one behaves; calm and cool
- **endeavor** (en DEV ur) try; make an effort
- nerves (NURVZ) nervous condition
- **retreat** (ree TREET) a quiet place for rest
- **moping** (MOHP ing) being in a silent or sad mood

"Then you know practically nothing about my aunt?" the self-possessed young lady continued.

"Only her name and address," admitted the visitor. He was wondering whether Mrs. Sappleton was in the married or widowed state. Something about the room seemed to suggest that men lived there.

"Her great tragedy happened just three years ago," said the child. "That would be since your sister's time."

"Her tragedy?" asked Framton. Somehow in this restful country spot tragedies seemed out of place.

"You may wonder why we keep that window wide open on an October afternoon," said the niece, indicating a large French window that opened on to a lawn.

"It is quite warm for the time of the year," said Framton. "But has that window got anything to do with the tragedy?"

"Out through that window," replied the niece, "three years ago on this day, her husband and her two young brothers went off for their day's shooting. They never came back. In crossing the moor to their favorite snipe-shooting ground, they were all three trapped in a dangerous piece of bog. It had been that dreadful wet summer, you know, and places that were safe in other years gave way suddenly without warning. Their bodies were never recovered. That was the dreadful part of it." Here the child's voice lost its self-possessed note and faltered.

"Poor aunt always thinks that they'll come back some day," she continued. "They and the little brown spaniel dog that was lost with them will walk in at that window just as they used to do. That is why the window is kept open every evening till dusk. Poor dear aunt! She has often told me how they went out, her husband with his white raincoat over his arm, and Ronnie, her youngest brother, singing 'Bertie, why do you bound?' He always sang it to tease her because she said it got on her nerves. Do you know, sometimes on quiet evenings like this, I almost get a creepy feeling that they will all walk in through that window—"

- French window kind of tall window that can be used for an entrance or exit
- moor (MOOR) area of wild, open land used for hunting and shooting
- snipe (SNYP) a kind of bird found in marsh areas
- bog (BOG) wet ground; marsh
- **falter** (FAWL tur) speak in an unsure way; seem unsteady

She stopped with a little shudder. It was a relief to Framton when the aunt bustled into the room with apologies for being late.

"I hope Vera has been amusing you?" she said.

"She has been very interesting," said Framton.

"I hope you don't mind the open window," said Mrs. Sappleton briskly. "My husband and brothers will soon be home from shooting. They always come in this way. They've been out hunting snipe in the marshes today, so they'll make a fine mess over my poor carpets."

She went on cheerfully about the shooting and the scarcity of birds and the duck hunting in the winter to come. To Framton it was all purely horrible. He made a desperate effort to turn the talk to a less ghastly topic. He knew that his hostess was giving him only a part of her attention. Her eyes were constantly straying past him to the open window and the lawn beyond. It was certainly an unfortunate coincidence that he paid his visit on this tragic anniversary.

- bustle (BUS ul) **move quickly with a lot of energy**
- **ghastly** (GAST lee) horrible; frightful
- **constantly** (KON stunt lee) all the time; without changing

"The doctors agree in ordering me complete rest, no mental excitement, and nothing in the nature of violent physical exercise," announced Framton. He had the idea that total strangers were hungry for the least detail of his ailments and their cause and cure.

"On the matter of diet they are not so much in agreement," he continued.

"No?" said Mrs. Sappleton, in a voice which only replaced a yawn at the last moment. Then she suddenly brightened into alert attention—but not to what Framton was saying.

"Here they are at last!" she cried. "Just in time for tea, and don't they look as if they were muddy up to the eyes!"

Framton shivered slightly and turned toward the niece with a look that was meant to show sympathetic understanding. The child was staring out through the open window with dazed horror in her eyes. In a chill shock of fear, Framton swung round in his seat and looked in the same direction.

In the deepening twilight three figures were walking across the lawn toward the window. They all carried guns under their arms. One of them also carried a white raincoat over his shoulders. A tired brown spaniel dog kept close at their heels. They neared the house without any noise. Then a hoarse young voice chanted out of the dusk, "I said, Bertie, why do you bound?"

Framton grabbed wildly at his cane. The hall door, the gravel drive, and the front gate were hardly noticed in his headlong retreat. A cyclist coming along the road had to run into the hedge to avoid a collision.

"Here we are, my dear," said the man carrying the white raincoat as he came in through the French window. "We're fairly muddy, but most of it's dry. Who was that who raced out as we came along?"

"A most extraordinary man, a Mr. Nuttel," said Mrs. Sappleton. "He could only talk about his illnesses. He dashed off without a word of good-bye or apology when you arrived. One would think he had seen a ghost."

"I think it was the spaniel," said the niece calmly. "He told me he had a horror of dogs. He was once hunted into a cemetery somewhere in India by a pack of wild dogs. He had to spend the night in a newly dug grave with the creatures snarling and grinning and foaming just above him. Enough to make anyone lose their courage."

Fantastic stories at short notice were her specialty.

- **headlong** (HED lawng) very fast; without thinking
- **specialty** (SPESH ul tee) something a person does well

211

ALL THINGS CONSIDERED _____

1. Framton Nuttel goes to the country (a) to visit the Sappletons. (b) to visit his sister. (c) for his health.

2. He visits Mrs. Sappleton because (a) his sister has given him a letter of introduction. (b) her husband is an old friend. (c) he wants to get to know her niece.

3. The niece says Nuttel's sister must have visited the country (a) before the tragedy. (b) during the tragedy. (c) after the tragedy.

4. According to Vera, (a) Mr. Sappleton and his brothers-in-law disappeared in a marsh. (b) Bertie and Mr. Sappleton were shot while hunting ducks. (c) three men still lived in the house.

5. Vera says that the window is open (a) to let some fresh air in. (b) to give Framton a view of the countryside. (c) because Mrs. Sappleton thinks her husband and brothers will return in a short time.

6. Mrs. Sappleton upsets Framton Nuttel when she says that (a) her brothers disappeared with her husband. (b) she is expecting her brothers and husband. (c) she wants him to go hunting for ducks next winter.

7. Framton Nuttel talks mostly about (a) his illness. (b) the lost men. (c) diets.

8. Nuttel is terrified when the men come home because he (a) is not supposed to be visiting. (b) is afraid they will shoot him. (c) thinks they are ghosts.

9. The niece says he left because he is afraid of (a) dogs. (b) guns. (c) ghosts.

10. The niece is someone who (a) dislikes visitors. (b) makes up stories. (c) always tells the truth.

THINKING IT THROUGH _____

1. What kind of story did you think this was before you read page 211? How would the story have been different if it had ended before the last paragraphs? Which sentence helps the reader understand what has happened?

2. Unusual names for characters are sometimes a hint for the reader. How does the name Framton Nuttel fit the character?

3. Have you ever been fooled by someone who makes up wild stories? Perhaps you have even told some wild stories yourself. Give some examples of wild stories that might surprise certain people.

Building from Details

Inference

In every story, some of the facts or details are stated directly. For example, in "The Open Window" you know how old Vera is because you are told she is "a very self-possessed young lady of 15." You know that Vera is 15 because the writer has stated it directly.

In many instances, however, you have to use the details given and your own knowledge to figure something out. This is called making an **inference**.

In "The Open Window," the stated details and your own knowledge lead you to make inferences. Here are five sentences from the story. What inference does each one lead you to make?

1. Framton Nuttel's sister says to him, "You will bury yourself down there and not speak to a soul."
2. Vera says, "My aunt will be down presently, Mr. Nuttel. In the meantime you must try and put up with me."
3. "I hope you don't mind the open window," said Mrs. Sappleton briskly. "My husband and brothers will soon be home from shooting. They always come in this way."
4. "Here they are at last!" she cried. "Just in time for tea, and don't they look as if they were muddy up to the eyes!"
5. Fantastic stories at short notice were her specialty.

Composition

Follow your teacher's instructions before completing *one* of these writing assignments.

1. What, in your opinion, is the Sappleton's house like? Write five sentences that describe the setting. Make inferences from the details you read in the story.
2. Vera made certain inferences about Framton Nuttel before telling him the story. Write a paragraph explaining what inferences she made. Mention the facts on which she based these inferences.

Christina Georgina Rossetti (1830-1894)

You might see a painting of Christina Rossetti without realizing it. That is because her brother, Dante Gabriel Rossetti, and several other artists often used her as a model. Christina came from a very talented family. Her father was an Italian poet who escaped to England because of political differences with the Italian government. One brother, Dante, was a poet and painter and another brother, William Michael, wrote nonfiction.

Christina never went to school, but her mother taught her at home. She grew up speaking both Italian and English. A deeply religious person, many of her writings are about religious topics. She refused to marry the man she loved because they did not agree about religion.

Many people consider Christina Rossetti one of the greatest women poets of the English language.

Countée Cullen (1903-1946)

"Most of the things I write I do for the sheer love of the music in them." That is what Countee Cullen said about his poetry.

He was born in New York City, the son of a minister. When he was only 14, his first poem was published, and another poem won first prize in a literary contest a year later.

After graduating from high school, Cullen went on to college at New York University and then earned a master's degree at Harvard University. His university work earned him a Phi Beta Kappa key, an honor given only to the best students. He later worked as magazine editor and a teacher.

Countee Cullen continued to live in New York City for most of his life. At that time, the city was in the midst of a flowering of black art and literature. Cullen was an important part of that world.

▶ To many people all over the world, even the simplest things in life can be mysteries. For thousands of years, for example, the wind has been a mystery to poets and other people.

WHO HAS SEEN THE WIND?

by Christina G. Rossetti

Who has seen the wind?
   Neither I nor you:
But when the leaves hang trembling
   The wind is passing through.

Who has seen the wind?
   Neither you nor I:
But when the trees bow down their heads
   The wind is passing by.

THE UNKNOWN COLOR

by Countée Cullen

I've often heard my mother say,
When great winds blew across the day,
And, cuddled close and out of sight,
The young pigs squealed with sudden fright
Like something speared or javelined,
"Poor little pigs, they see the wind."

WAYS OF KNOWING

1. What question does the first poem ask? How does the first poem answer the question? How does the second poem answer the question?
2. According to the first poem, how do you know when the wind is passing? Is that the same as seeing the wind?
3. Christina Rossetti's poem has two stanzas. (a) What is the same about each stanza? (b) What is different about each stanza?
4. What do you think is meant by the title "The Unknown Color"? Does the poet think anyone knows the color? If so, who?

- javelined (JAV uh lind) **stabbed by a javelin, a long spear**
- squeal (SKWEEL) **make a sharp, shrill cry**

215

VOCABULARY AND SKILL REVIEW

Before completing the exercises that follow, you may wish to review the **bold-faced** words on pages 203–211.

I. On a separate sheet of paper, write the *italicized* word that best fills the blank in each sentence. Each word should be used only once.

perpendicular	*cherish*	*falter*	*headlong*	*moping*
constantly	*ghastly*	*retreat*	*endeavor*	*specialty*

1. She spent a week at a mountain _____ .
2. People who sit around _____ have very little fun.
3. The girl will always _____ the ring her grandmother gave her.
4. Hitting home runs is his _____ .
5. The shock caused her voice to _____ .
6. The walls of the old, creaking house were not _____ .
7. Did she _____ to become a better student?
8. After the battle, the injured people were a _____ sight.
9. They rushed _____ out of the burning building.
10. Some people complain _____ about their problems.

II. How good are you at making inferences? On a separate sheet of paper, copy the sentence (**a.**, **b.**, or **c.**) that is probably the best example of inference for the statement.

1. A cat has a collar around its neck.
   a. The cat has no owner.
   b. The owner's name is probably on the collar.
   c. The collar tells the cat's secret name.
2. People have trouble deciding what a picture really shows.
   a. People are not very smart.
   b. A picture can be seen in different ways.
   c. A picture is not a good way to show something.
3. A woman gives her brother letters to introduce him to people she knows.
   a. The brother has never met the people.
   b. The sister wants to meet the people.
   c. The brother already knows the people.
4. People cannot see the wind but know it is blowing hard.
   a. People cannot feel the wind.
   b. People can see things that the wind is blowing.
   c. People cannot be sure when the wind is blowing hard.

From TWO-MINUTE MYSTERIES

by Donald J. Sobol

▶ How good are your detective skills? Here's a chance for you to find out. As you read this short mystery, look for clues. Try to find some detail that does not make sense in the story. You may have to read the story several times. If you can't solve the mystery, don't worry. It takes practice to be a good detective!

THE CASE OF THE BLACKMAILER

"I don't mind telling you, Dr. Haledjian," said Thomas Hunt, "that inheriting the Hunt millions has had its nerve-racking moments. Do you remember Martin, the gardener?"

"A smiling and bowing little chap," said Haledjian, pouring his young friend a brandy.

"That's the fellow. I dismissed him upon inheriting the house in East Hampton. Well, three days ago he came to my office, bowing and smirking, and demanded 100,000 dollars.

"He claimed to have been tending the spruce trees outside my father's study when Dad drew up another will, naming his brother in New Zealand sole heir."

"You believed him?"

"I confess the news hit me like a thunderbolt. Dad and I had quarreled over Veronica sometime during the last week in November. Dad opposed the marriage, and it seemed plausible that he had cut me off.

"Martin asserted he possessed this second will, which he felt sure would be worth a good deal more to me than he was asking. As it was dated November 31—the day after the executed will—it would be legally recognized, he claimed.

- nerve-racking (NURV rak ing) **very difficult to deal with**
- **sole** (SOHL) **only**
- plausible (PLAW zuh bul) **seeming to be true; believable**
- assert (uh SURT) **say in a way that seems certain**

"I refused to be blackmailed. He tried to bargain, asking 50,000 and then 25,000."

"You paid nothing, I hope?" asked Haledjian.

"I paid—with my foot firm on the seat of his pants."

"Quite right," approved Haledjian. "Imagine trying to peddle a tale like that!"

What was Martin's blunder?

See below for solution.

ALL THINGS CONSIDERED

1. Dr. Haledjian is a (a) smiling and bowing little chap. (b) dishonest gardener. (c) friend of Thomas Hunt.
2. In the story, the gardener (a) claims to have the most recent will. (b) is supposed to inherit the money. (c) runs away to New Zealand.
3. The blackmailer says he wanted money for (a) hiding a will. (b) giving the real will to Thomas Hunt. (c) not telling anybody about Thomas Hunt's marriage.
4. Thomas Hunt (a) paid the gardener. (b) found the second will. (c) kicked the gardener.
5. The clue that Martin was lying is (a) that he seemed nervous. (b) the date he gives for the new will. (c) the mention of a brother in New Zealand.

THINKING IT THROUGH

1. Do you think this mystery is clever? Explain why or why not.
2. (a) Why do you think some authors write such short mystery stories? (b) Tell why you prefer either short mysteries or long ones.
3. Reread the story. How does the author include the clue without making it something you would notice easily?

SOLUTION:

No legal will could be dated November 31. November contains only 30 days.

Vocabulary and Sentence Meaning

Context Clues

Many words have more than one meaning. Some have more than one pronunciation, too. **Context clues,** or words surrounding a particular word, can help you to figure out the meaning of the word in a sentence. For example, how would you pronounce the word "read" in the sentence "I am going to read a book"? Did you say REED or RED? How did the rest of the sentence help you to know how to pronounce the word? Reread paragraphs 1 and 2 of "The Case of the Blackmailer." How did you pronounce the word "bowing"? Does the word as used in this story mean "bending politely" or "using a bow on a violin"? How do you know?

Here are some other words that can have more than one meaning. On a separate sheet of paper, write two sentences for each word. Use a different meaning for the word in each sentence.

1. spruce	**6.** bar
2. like	**7.** broke
3. deal	**8.** head
4. right	**9.** orange
5. firm	**10.** pass

Composition

Follow your teacher's instructions before completing *one* of these writing assignments.

1. Write five sentences. Each should contain two words that are spelled the same but have different meanings. Some words you might uses are *back, fire, pack,* and *rung*. Underline the two words. Here is an example:

Would you <u>mind</u> if I asked you to <u>mind</u> the baby?

2. Do you think being a detective is interesting work? Write a paragraph explaining why or why not.

THE TEN-ARMED MONSTER OF NEWFOUNDLAND

by Elma Schemenauer

▶ Do some monsters really exist? Can a legend be true? A young boy from Newfoundland has a chance to answer those questions.

"The mighty kraken floats quietly beneath the surface of the water like an underwater island," said the Norwegian storyteller. "Fishing people may row their boats to and fro in the shallow water above it. They will catch many fish. For the monster's strong smell draws the smaller sea creatures, who gather about it in great numbers.

"But the fishermen must always be watchful. If the water under their boats suddenly becomes shallower, they know that the powerful monster is raising itself out of the deep. They must then get away as fast as they can. For the terrible kraken has long arms that can reach as high as the mast of any ship. It can easily drag a fishing boat to the bottom, together with all those who are on board. . . ."

It's an old story—the legend of the kraken. Long before the Norwegian writer recorded it in 1752, sailors were telling tales of the long-armed monster.

"Ridiculous!" said most of the scientists who heard their reports. "We have no record of any such creature."

"But we saw it," protested the sailors. "Actually, it looked very much like the little squids that we sometimes catch in our nets. But it was much bigger. Could it be that the kraken is really a very large squid—bigger than anything you scientists have yet discovered?"

Over the years more and more people began to think this might be. But scientists continued to reject the theory. Until proof was of-

- kraken (KRAH kun) **sea monster in legends from Norway**
- Norwegian (nawr WEE jun) **from Norway, a country in Europe**
- squid (SKWID) **a kind of sea animal with ten arms**

fered, they preferred to regard the kraken as a legend.

Perhaps the kraken would have remained a legend forever, in the same class as mermaids, man-eating sea serpents, and other mysterious creatures of the deep. But in the 1870s a number of gigantic ten-armed bodies began to be washed up on the rocky shores of Newfoundland and Labrador.

Local fishing people who came upon the rubbery-looking giants often just hacked them up. They used the meat to bait their hooks or to feed their dogs. Maybe the fishermen simply didn't realize the importance of what they had found. Or maybe they thought people would laugh at them if they dared to suggest that there might be some connection between these monsters and the legendary kraken.

It was left to a twelve-year-old boy from Newfoundland to bring forward evidence proving that the giant squid did exist.

The boy's name was Thomas Piccot. On October 26, 1873, he and his father and another man named Daniel Squires went out fishing. The three set off very early, in the cold gray light before dawn. Thick fog still blanketed the little cove. Young Tom shivered in spite of his heavy coat. But he felt excited and happy. For this was the first time his father had ever taken him out for a full day's fishing.

He settled himself comfortably on a pile of nets in the big flat-bottomed, high-sided dory. Then he watched the fog slowly swallow up the little village as his father and Mr. Squires rowed the boat out into the bay. After a while, they stopped and let down the nets.

The morning passed quickly. By the time the noonday sun stood directly overhead, the three fishermen had netted a good catch of herring. They stopped to eat the lunch that they had brought along. Just as they were finishing, Tom's father happened to notice a flat, dark mass of something floating and bobbing in the choppy water not far from the dory. "Looks like a raft of seaweed," he said.

"Yes, or it could be part of a wrecked ship, I suppose," said Daniel Squires. "Let's go over and have a look."

- **regard** (ri GARD) **think about; consider**
- Newfoundland (NOO fun land) **province and island in east-ern Canada, on the Atlantic Ocean**
- Labrador (LAB ruh dor) **section of northeastern Canada, on the Atlantic Ocean, part of the province of Newfoundland**
- **legendary** (LEJ un deh ree) **found in legends**
- dory (DOR ee) **small boat with a flat bottom**

As they rowed the dory closer, they saw that the floating mass in the water was reddish brown. It was covered with a sort of shiny skin. And it was very, very big—nearly three times as large as the boat! "It almost looks like some kind of animal," said Mr. Squires.

"It's lying awfully still, if it is an animal," said Tom's father.

"Maybe it's dead," suggested Tom.

"We'll soon see," said his father. "Hand me that boat hook, will you, son?"

Grasping one end of the long pole, Mr. Piccot got up on his knees and leaned out over the water. Then, with a sudden quick movement, he jabbed the jellylike blob with the hook.

A great shudder rippled through the floating mass. Then a huge ugly beak raised itself straight up out of the water. Long arms like giant snakes began to thrash about wildly. The boat rocked and tipped dangerously. "Look out!" yelled Tom's father. He and Mr. Squires seized the oars. They turned the dory and started rowing furiously away.

But they weren't quick enough. A dark snakelike tentacle rose high in the air. It hovered there for a moment and then slithered down—right into the boat! Tom leaped back, gazing in wild-eyed horror at the thick rubbery arm with its rows and rows of sharp crown-shaped suckers. Suddenly the dory tipped to one side. The creature had wrapped another long arm around the outside of the boat and was beginning to draw it down into the water. At the same time it lifted its parrotlike beak once again and started to gnaw at the upper edge of the boat.

Tom's father and Daniel Squires raised their oars. They began pounding on the creature's long arms, desperately trying to force it to slacken its grip. As the waves sloshed over into the sinking dory, Tom's father seized a bucket and started bailing frantically.

- **blob** (BLOB) small lump or shapeless object
- **shudder** (SHUD ur) tremble, shake
- tentacle (TEN tuh kul) long, thin part of an animal, somewhat like an arm, used for feeling and touching
- **hover** (HUV ur) hang in the air
- slither (SLI ther) slide and move as a snake does
- sucker (SUK ur) part of an animal that can attach itself to objects by sucking and creating a vacuum between itself and the object
- **bail** (BAYL) dip water out of

222

Tom was about to snatch up the oar that his father had laid down. But suddenly his eyes fell on a hatchet lying in the bottom of the dory. It made him think of an old story he'd heard. Some Norwegian fishermen in a small boat had once been attacked by one of the dreaded krakens that haunt their cold waters. They had managed to save themselves by chopping off the creature's arms with an axe.

Tom crept as close as he dared to the long, sharp-suckered arm that clung to the inside of the dory. Clutching the hatchet in both hands, he raised it high. He paused for a second. Then he brought the sharp blade down with all his might on the tough, rubbery tentacle. Again he raised the hatchet and again he brought it down. Again and again and again! Like a madman he hacked at the arm until at last it was dangling by a mere thread of dark red flesh. The grip of its suckers loosened. And then the whole arm slowly slithered, lifeless, into the bottom of the boat.

But the creature's other arm was still trying to drag the boat down into the water. Tom's father and Mr. Squires were both bailing furiously, barely managing to keep the dory afloat.

223

Tom leaned out over the gunwale, and raising the hatchet once more, he began hacking at the arm that was wrapped around the outside of the boat. This one was harder to reach. But it wasn't quite as thick as the first. He finally managed to cut it off as well. His father turned and helped him heave it up over the gunwale into the boat. They flung it down beside the other one. Then they both wheeled around and prepared to meet the monster's next attack.

But the huge creature now seemed confused. It began to dart about in circles around and under the dory. It gave out great clouds of black ink that spread and colored the water for some distance around. At last it raised its great beak just once more, gasped, and then slowly sank from view beneath the dark waves.

Mr. Piccot's hands were shaking. Slowly and carefully he laid down the hatchet, which he had picked up waiting for fresh attack from the creature. He threw his arms around his son. "You did well, my boy," he said in a choked voice. . . .

All three were completely exhausted from their struggle. But they realized that they might still be in danger. As quickly as they could, they rowed the dory back towards the little village. "These will make good bait, Dan," said Tom's father as they were approaching the shore. He pointed at the two long suckered arms lying, coiled up, in the bottom of the boat.

"No, don't cut them up!" cried Tom in horror. "I'm going to keep them."

"Well, they're yours, I guess," said Mr. Squires with a smile. "You earned them, that's for sure. But you won't be able to keep them long anyway. They'll soon spoil, even in this cool weather."

The two men tied the boat to the dock. Then they set off into the village to tell their neighbors what had happened. They left Tom sitting in the dory with the souvenirs of the adventure.

The boy tossed the shorter arm up on the shore. As he sat in the boat examining the longer one, several hungry dogs came along. They snatched up the arm that was lying on the beach and trotted off with it. Tom leaped out of the boat and raced across the rocks after them. But he was too late. By the time he caught up with the dogs, they had torn the rubbery arm to shreds. Deeply disappointed, Tom slowly made his way back towards the dock where the dory was tied.

- gunwale (GUN ul) upper edge of the side of a boat
- **wheel** (HWEEL) turn quickly and suddenly

By this time his father and Daniel Squires had told a number of the villagers about their experience. But nobody believed them. The tale seemed too strange to be true.

It wasn't until the villagers came down to the dock and actually saw the gigantic snakelike arm that they began to take the men's story seriously. "If that's the size of its arm, just think how big the whole creature must have been," someone remarked.

"How many arms did you say it had, Dan?" asked someone else.

"Ten altogether," replied Mr. Squires. "Of course, thanks to young Tom here, it's missing a couple of them at the moment."

"I wonder what Reverend Harvey would make of it," said Tom's father suddenly. The Reverend Moses Harvey lived not far away, in the city of St. John's. He had spent years studying marine life. Local people often called upon him to identify sea creatures that were unknown to them.

When Reverend Harvey saw the huge tentacle, he became very excited. He had studied the stories of the legendary kraken and the giant squid. He felt sure that the two were actually one and the same. But he had never before had any really solid proof of the existence of either one.

The tentacle was carefully preserved in alcohol. The scientists who saw it had to admit that it definitely pointed to the existence of a giant squid. It corresponded exactly with the tentacles of the ordinary small squids that the fishermen often caught. But it was much, much larger! In the months that followed, several other Newfoundlanders came forward with parts or complete bodies of giant squids that they had either captured or found.

With this evidence, scientists all over the world finally changed their minds. They added the giant squid to their list of known sea creatures. At least part of the credit for the discovery belongs to a boy named Thomas Piccot. He showed great courage during his meeting with the dangerous creature. And he was curious enough and far-sighted enough to recognize the importance of keeping the proof of what he had experienced.

What about other mysterious creatures of the deep? Are they simply products of people's imagination? Or could some of them turn out to be just as real as the kraken? Perhaps the day will come when scientists will have solid proof of the existence of "Nessie," the monster who is said to lurk in the depths of Scotland's Loch Ness. And perhaps someday we'll know the true identity of other legendary monsters.

Some scientists claim that, even today, about half the existing forms of underwater life are still unknown to them. No wonder people still tell tales of mysterious creatures, just as our ancestors did in the past. In future years many of these legendary creatures of the deep may well prove to be just as real as the terrible kraken, or giant squid.

- **correspond** (kor ih SPOND) agree; match
- **far-sighted** (FAHR SY tid) smart enough to see what will be needed later
- **ancestors** (AN ses terz) people from whom one is descended

226

ALL THINGS CONSIDERED

1. The first stories about the monster are told by (a) sailors. (b) a Norwegian writer. (c) scientists.

2. The kraken looks very much like a (a) mermaid. (b) serpent. (c) squid.

3. When the ten-armed bodies first begin to wash up on shore, (a) people are afraid of them. (b) scientists come to study them. (c) fishing people use them for bait.

4. Proof that the giant squid exists is brought forward by (a) Daniel Squires. (b) Thomas Piccot. (c) Reverend Harvey.

5. At first, the people in the boat notice (a) a floating mass. (b) an ugly beak. (c) a snakelike tentacle.

6. The boat tips when (a) the creature swims under the boat. (b) two tentacles wrap themselves around the boat. (c) the fishermen row too fast.

7. Tom kills the creature with (a) an oar. (b) a boat hook. (c) a hatchet.

8. Reverend Harvey is called to (a) find the missing tentacle. (b) help identify the creature. (c) repair the boat.

9. Nobody believes the story until (a) the "monster" is caught. (b) they actually see the tentacle. (c) Daniel Squires tells what happened.

10. Today scientists believe that the kraken is (a) really a giant squid. (b) a mysterious sea monster. (c) simply the product of people's imaginations.

THINKING IT THROUGH

1. Today people talk about the existence of certain "monsters." Name some "monsters" if you can. Do you think that any of these monsters actually exist? How do you think these "monsters" can be explained?

2. Many of the creatures were seen before Thomas Piccot's time. Why is Piccot so important to the story?

3. Do you think that scientists should accept as true people's reports of "monsters" they have seen? Why or why not?

Building from Details

Visualizing Details

How well can you visualize what you read? **Visualizing** means forming a picture in your mind. The setting for a story is often described in several sentences. As you read, look for sentences that help you visualize the setting.

Here are five details about setting from "The Ten-Armed Monster of Newfoundland." Read them carefully and try to visualize what they describe. Then, on a separate sheet of paper, draw a picture of the setting as you visualize it.

1. On October 26, 1873, Tom Piccot and his father and another man named Daniel Squires are fishing.
2. The three set off very early, in the cold gray light before dawn.
3. Thick fog still hangs over the little cove.
4. Young Tom settles himself comfortably on a pile of nets in the big flat-bottomed, high-sided dory.
5. Tom's father and Mr. Squires rowed the boat out into the bay.

Composition

Follow your teacher's instructions before completing *one* of these writing assignments.

1. Try to visualize a place that you know well. You might choose your classroom or a room in your home. Write four sentences describing some of the details of that place.
2. This story is about a creature that for many years was thought to be a great mystery. Find out about another animal that was at one time considered to be a mystery. First gather information about it. Then write a paragraph describing it and telling where it is found. (Ideas: pandas, orangutans, okapis, capybaras, or any underwater creatures)

▶ Do you ever look at a creature you know and see a monster
in its place? Under what conditions might an animal suddenly seem to look like something else?

THE BAT

by Theodore Roethke

By day the bat is cousin to the mouse.
He likes the attic of an aging house.

His fingers make a house about his head.
His pulse beat is so slow we think him dead.

He loops in crazy figures half the night.
Among the trees that face the corner light.

But when he brushes up against a screen,
We are afraid of what our eyes have seen;

For something is amiss or out of place
When mice with wings can wear a human face.

WAYS OF KNOWING

1. What is the difference the speaker mentions between the bat during the day and the bat at night?
2. What is meant by "His fingers make a house about his head"?
   Describe the picture that the words make you see.
3. What does the poet mean by "For something is amiss or out of
   place"? Why is this frightening to people?
4. The wording of the poem begins simply—almost like a nursery
   rhyme—and then becomes more complicated. Why do you think
   the poet did this?

- pulse (PULS) beat of the heart
- crazy (KRAY zee) wild and excited
- amiss (uh MIS) wrong; not correct

VOCABULARY AND SKILL REVIEW

Before completing the exercises that follow, you may wish to review the **bold-faced** words on pages 217–226.

I. On a separate sheet of paper, write the word in each line that means the same, or nearly the same, as the word in *italics.*

1. *bail:* arrest, dip out, bubble up, package
2. *blob:* monster, light, lump, sack
3. *correspond:* agree, disagree, argue, answer
4. *far-sighted:* needing help, seeing ahead, working hard, helping others
5. *legendary:* not true, long-legged, light-headed, found in stories
6. *sole:* sunny, together, only, few
7. *shudder:* shake, break, shut, fall
8. *regard:* smile at, write to, think about, protect from
9. *wheel:* carry in a truck, turn quickly, improve, open slowly
10. *hover:* love deeply, hang in the air, live badly, steal openly

II. Read the sentences below and decide which meaning (**a, b,** or **c**) is correct for the words in italics. On a separate sheet of paper, write the number of the correct meaning next to the number of the sentence.

1. They *row* their boats in the shallow water.
   a. fight   **b.** line up in order   **c.** use oars to move
2. We have no *record* of such a monster.
   a. written history   **b.** musical performance   **c.** best performance
3. They noticed a *mass* of something floating in the water.
   a. weight   **b.** collection   **c.** religious service
4. The *bat* flew about at night.
   a. wink of an eye   **b.** baseball equipment   **c.** animal
5. Did his father leave him out of his *will*?
   a. statement of who gets belongings after the owner dies
   b. strong desire to do something
   c. feeling toward other people

PRONE

by Mack Reynolds

▶ The pleasant young man hardly looks like a monster, but Mitchie causes terrible things to happen. And the head of Earth's military forces certainly does not want to upset Mitchie's father, who has a very important government job. How is he going to deal with the mysterious troubles that Mitchie causes?

SupCom Bull Underwood said, "I continually get the impression that every other sentence is being left out of this conversation. Now, tell me, General, what do you mean *things happen around him*?"

"Well, for instance, the first day Mitchie got to the Academy a cannon burst at a demonstration."

"What's a cannon?"

"A pre-guided-missile weapon," the commander of the Terra Military Academy told him. "You know, shells and gunpowder. We usually demonstrate them in our history classes. This time four students were injured. The next day sixteen were hurt in ground-war maneuvers."

There was an element of respect in the SupCom's tone. "Your course must be rugged."

General Bentley wiped his forehead with a snowy handkerchief even as he shook it negatively. "It was the first time any such thing happened. I tell you, sir, since Mitchie Farthingworth has been at the academy things have been wild. Fires in the dormitories, small arms exploding, cadets being hospitalized right and left. We've just got to expel that boy!"

- SupCom?
- Terra (TEH ruh) Earth
- impression (im PRESH un) idea that is not very clear
- maneuvers (muh NOO vurz) exercises to practice military skills

"Don't be ridiculous," the SupCom growled. "He's the apple of his old man's eye. We've got to make a hero out of him if it means the loss of a battle fleet. But I still don't get this. You mean the Farthingworth kid is committing sabotage?"

"It's not that. We investigated. He doesn't do it on purpose, things just *happen* around him. Mitchie can't help it."

"Confound it, stop calling him Mitchie!" Bull Underwood snapped. "How do you know it's him if he doesn't do it? Maybe you're just having a run of bad luck."

"That's what I thought," Bentley said, "until I ran into Admiral Lawrence of the Space Marines Academy. He had the same story. The day Mitchie—excuse me, sir—Michael Farthingworth set foot in Nuevo San Diego, things started happening. When they finally got him transferred to our academy the trouble stopped."

It was at times like these that Bull Underwood regretted his shaven head. He could have used some hair to tear. "Then it *must* be sabotage if it stops when he leaves!"

"I don't think so, sir."

The SupCom took a deep breath, snapped to his secretarobot, "Brief me on Cadet Michael Farthingworth, including his early life." While he waited he growled under his breath, "A stalemated 100 year war on my hands with those Martian *makrons* and I have to get things like this tossed at me."

In less than a minute the secretarobot began: "Son of Senator Warren Farthingworth, Chairman War Appropriations Committee. Twenty-two years of age. Five feet six, one hundred and thirty, blue eyes, brown hair, fair. Born and spent early youth in former United States area. Early education by mother. At age of 18 entered Harvard but schooling was interrupted when roof of assembly hall collapsed killing most of faculty. Next year entered Yale, leaving two months

---

- apple of his eye **someone very dear to a person**
- sabotage (SAB uh tahzh) **act or acts of destroying an enemy's property on purpose**
- secretarobot?
- stalemated (STAYL mayt id) **caught in a situation where neither side can win**
- *makron?*
- appropriations (uh proh pree AY shunz) **deciding where to spend money and setting it aside for that purpose**

Cadet Michael Farthingworth
Son of
Senator Warren Farthingworth

after when 90 percent of the university's buildings were burnt down in the great fire of '85. Next attended University of California but failed to graduate owing to the earthquake which completely . . . "

"That's enough," the SupCom rapped. He turned and stared at General Bentley. "What is it? Even if the kid was a psychokinetic saboteur he couldn't accomplish all that."

The academy commander shook his head. "All I know is that, since his arrival at the Terra Military Academy, there's been an endless series of disasters. And the longer he's there the worse it gets. It's twice as bad now as when he first arrived." He got to his feet wearily. "I'm a broken man, sir, and I'm leaving this in your hands. You'll have my resignation this afternoon. Frankly, I'm afraid to return to the school. If I do, some day I'll probably crack my spine bending over to tie my shoelaces. It just isn't safe to be near that boy."

- **psychokinetic** (sy koh ki NET ik) **having to do with the ability to use mind control to make objects move**
- **saboteur** (SAB uh tur) **person who deliberately destroys an enemy's property**
- **resignation** (rez ig NAY shun) **statement that one is quitting a job**

233

For a long time after General Bentley had left, SupCom Bull Underwood sat at his desk, his heavy underlip in a pout. "And just when the next five years' appropriation is up before the committee," he snarled at nobody.

He turned to the secretarobot. "Put the best psychotechnicians available on Michael Farthingworth. They are to discover . . . well, they are to discover why things happen around him. Priority one."

Approximately a week later the secretarobot said, "May I interrupt you, sir? A priority-one report is coming in."

Bull Underwood grunted and turned away from the star chart he'd been studying with the two Space Marine generals. He dismissed them and sat down at his desk.

The visor lit up and he was shown the face of an elderly civilian. "Doctor Duclos," the civilian said. "Case of Cadet Michael Farthingworth."

"Good," the SupCom rumbled. "Doctor, what is wrong with young Farthingworth?"

"The boy is an accident prone."

Bull Underwood frowned at him. "A what?"

"An accident prone." The doctor continued with evident satisfaction. "There is indication that he is the most extreme case in medical history. Really a fascinating study. Never in my experience have I been—"

"Please, Doctor. What is an accident prone?"

"Ah, yes. Briefly, an unexplained phenomenon first noted by the insurance companies of the nineteenth and twentieth centuries. An accident prone has an unnaturally large number of accidents happen either to him, or less often, to persons in his vicinity. In Farthingworth's case, they happen to persons about him. He himself is never affected."

- psychotechnician (sy koh tek NISH un) **person who specializes in understanding and controlling the ways humans behave**
- priority (pry OR i tee) **first in importance**
- visor (VY zur) **part of a machine that shows words or images**
- evident (EV i dunt) **very clear; plain to see**
- extreme (ik STREEM) **greater than usual**
- phenomenon (fuh NOM uh non) **strange or remarkable happening**

234

The SupCom was unbelieving. "You mean to tell me there are some persons who just naturally have accidents happen to them without any reason?"

"That is correct," Duclos nodded. "Most prones are understandable. The death wish is at work and the prone *seeks* self-destruction. However, science has yet to discover the forces behind the less common type such as Farthingworth. It has been suggested that it is no more than the laws of chance at work. To balance out the accident prone, there should be persons at the other extreme who are blessed with abnormally good fortune. However . . . "

SupCom Bull Underwood's lower lip was out, almost fiercely. "Listen," he interrupted. "What can be done about it?"

"Nothing," the doctor said. "An accident prone seems to remain one as a rule. Not always, but as a rule. Fortunately, they are rare."

"Not rare enough," the SupCom growled. "These insurance companies, what did they do when they located an accident prone?"

"They kept track of him and refused to insure the prone, his business, home, employees, employers, or anyone or anything connected with him."

Bull Underwood stared unblinkingly at the doctor, as though wondering whether the other's whole explanation was an attempt to pull his leg. Finally he rapped, "Thank you, Doctor Duclos. That will be all." The civilian's face faded from the visor.

The SupCom said slowly to the secretarobot, "Have Cadet Farthingworth report to me." He added, "And while he's here have all persons keep their fingers crossed."

235

CHECKPOINT ─────────────────────

Stop here and answer the following questions.

1. Does this story take place in the past, present, or future? How do you know?
2. What is Mitchie's problem? What does *accident prone* mean?
3. What are some examples of things that go wrong around Mitchie?
4. (a) Who is Mitchie's father and what does he do? (b) Why does SupCom Bull Underwood want to avoid upsetting Mitchie's father?
5. How does the SupCom get information about Mitchie?
6. What do you think the SupCom will do about the problem?

The photoelectric-controlled door leading to the inner office of SupCom Bull Underwood glided quietly open and a lieutenant entered and came to a snappy attention. The door swung gently shut behind him.

"Well?" Bull Underwood growled.

"Sir, a Cadet Michael Farthingworth to report to you."

"Send him in. Ah, just a minute, Lieutenant Brown. How do you feel after talking to him?"

"Me, sir? I feel fine, sir." The lieutenant looked blankly at him.

"Hmmm. Well, send him in, confound it."

The lieutenant turned and the door opened automatically before him. "Cadet Farthingworth," he announced.

The newcomer entered and stood stiffly before the desk of Earth's military head. Bull Underwood appraised him with care. In spite of the stylish Academy uniform, Michael Farthingworth cut a sorry figure. His faded blue eyes blinked sadly behind heavy contact lenses.

"That'll be all, Lieutenant," the SupCom said to his aide.

"Yes, sir." The lieutenant about-faced snappily and marched to the door—which swung sharply forward and quickly back again before the lieutenant was halfway through.

- photoelectric (foh toh ih LEK trik) having electricity that is controlled by a light
- appraise (uh PRAYZ) look over and judge the nature of

SupCom Bull Underwood winced at the crush of bone and cartilage. He shuddered, then snapped to his secretarobot, "Have Lieutenant Brown hospitalized . . . and, ah . . . see he gets a Luna Medal for exposing himself to danger beyond the call of duty."

He swung to the newcomer and came directly to the point. "Cadet Farthingworth," he rapped, "do you know what an accident prone is?"

Mitchie's voice was low and sorrowful. "Yes, sir."

"You do?" Bull Underwood was surprised.

"Yes, sir. At first such things as the school's burning down didn't particularly impress me as being personally connected with me, but the older I get, the worse it gets, and after what happened to my first date, I started to investigate."

The SupCom said cautiously, "What happened to the date?"

Mitchie blushed. "I took her to a dance and she broke her leg."

The SupCom cleared his throat. "So finally you investigated?"

"Yes, sir," Mitchie Farthingworth said woefully. "And I found I was an accident prone and getting worse. Each year I'm twice as bad as the year before. I'm glad you've discovered it too, sir. I . . . didn't know what to do. Now it's in your hands."

The SupCom was somewhat relieved. Possibly this wasn't going to be as difficult as he had feared. He said, "Have you any ideas, Mitchie, ah, that is . . . "

"Call me Mitchie if you want, sir. Everybody else does."

"Have you any ideas? After all, you've done as much damage to Terra as a Martian task force would accomplish."

"Yes, sir. I think I ought to be shot."

"Huh?"

"Yes, sir. I'm expendable," Mitchie said miserably. "In fact, I suppose I'm probably the most expendable soldier that's ever been. All my life I've wanted to be a spaceman and do my share toward licking the Martians." His eyes gleamed behind his lenses. "Why, I've . . . "

- wince (WINS) **draw back as if in pain**
- cartilage (KAHR tuh lij) **tough body tissue; a soft kind of bone**
- woefully (WOH fuh lee) **sadly**
- expendable (ek SPEN duh bul) **capable of being lost, destroyed, or given up to gain something that is more important**

He stopped and looked at his commanding officer pathetically. "What's the use? I'm just a bust. An accident prone. The only thing to do is liquidate me." He tried to laugh, but his voice broke.

Behind him, Bull Underwood heard the glass in his office window shatter without seeming cause. He winced again, but didn't turn.

"Sorry, sir," Mitchie said. "See? The only thing is to shoot me."

"Look," Bull Underwood said urgently, "stand back a few yards farther, will you? There on the other side of the room." He cleared his throat. "Your suggestion has already been considered, as a matter of fact. However, due to your father's political importance, shooting you had to be ruled out."

From a clear sky the secretarobot began to say, "'Twas brillig, and the slithy toves did gyre and gimble in the wabe.'"*

SupCom Bull Underwood closed his eyes in pain and shrank back into his chair. "What?" he said cautiously.

"The borogoves were mimsy as all get-out," the secretarobot said and shut up.

Mitchie looked at it. "Slipped its cogs, sir," he said helpfully. "It's happened before around me."

"The best memory bank in the system," Underwood protested. "Oh, no."

"Yes, sir," Mitchie said apologetically. "And I wouldn't recommend trying to repair it, sir. Three technicians were electrocuted when I was . . . "

The secretarobot sang, "O frabjous day! Callooh! Callay!"

"Completely around the corner," Mitchie said.

"This," said Bull Underwood, "is too frabjous much! Senator or no Senator, appropriations or no appropriations, with my own bare hands—"

As he strode forward, he felt the rug giving way beneath him. He

- pathetically (puh THET ik lee) **in a manner that produces sympathy**
- liquidate (LIK wi dayt) **get rid of; kill**
- technician (tek NISH un) **person who is trained to do a special job, especially a job working with machines, electricity, etc.**
- strode (STROHD) **walked firmly**

*The words are from the nonsense poem "Jabberwocky" by Lewis Carroll.

grasped desperately for the edge of the desk, felt an ink bottle and water container go crashing over.

Mitchie darted forward to his assistance.

"Stand back!" Bull Underwood roared, holding an ankle with one hand, shaking the other hand in the form of a fist. "Get out of here, confound it!" Ink began to drip from the desk over his shaven head. It cooled him not at all. "It's not even safe to destroy you! It'd wipe out a regiment to try to assemble a firing squad! It—" Suddenly he paused, and when he spoke again his voice was like the coo of a condor.

"Cadet Farthingworth," he announced, "after considerable thought on my part I have chosen you to perform the most hazardous operation that Terra's forces have undertaken in the past 100 years. If successful, this effort will undoubtedly end the war."

"Who, me?" Mitchie said.

"Exactly," SupCom Underwood snapped. "This war has been going on for a century without either side's being able to gain that

- condor (KON dur) large bird of the vulture family
- considerable (kun SID ur uh bul) fairly large

slight edge, that minute advantage which would mean victory. Cadet Farthingworth, you have been chosen to make the supreme effort which will give Terra that superiority over the Martians." The Sup-Com looked sternly at Mitchie.

"Yes, sir," he clipped. "What are my orders?"

The SupCom beamed at him. "Spoken like a true hero of Terra's Space Forces. On the spaceport behind this building is a small spycraft. You are to report immediately to it and blast off for Mars. Once there you are to land, and hide the ship, and make your way to their capital city."

"Yes, sir! And what do I do then?"

"Nothing," Bull Underwood said with satisfaction. "You do absolutely nothing but live there. I estimate that your presence in the enemy capital will end the war in less than two years."

Michael Farthingworth snapped him a brilliant salute. "Yes, sir."

Spontaneous combustion broke out in the wastebasket.

Through the shattered window, SupCom Bull Underwood could hear the blast-off of the spyship. Half a dozen miles away the flare of a fuel dump going up in flames lighted up the sky.

Seated there in the wreckage of his office he rubbed his ankle tenderly. "The only trouble is when the war is over we'll have to bring him home."

But then he brightened. "Perhaps we could leave him there as our occupation forces. It would keep them from ever recovering to the point where they could try again."

He tried to get to his feet, saying to the secretarobot, "Have them send me in a couple of medical corpsmen."

"'Beware the Jabberwock,'" the secretarobot sneered.

- minute (my NOOT) **very small; tiny**
- advantage (ad VAN tij) **anything that makes one side more likely to succeed than another**
- superiority (suh peer ee OR i tee) **condition of being better**
- spontaneous combustion (spon TAY nee us kum BUS chun) **when a fire starts by itself**
- occupation (ok yoo PAY shun) **controlling an enemy territory**
- corpsmen (KOR mun) **military person who helps the wounded**

ALL THINGS CONSIDERED

1. Mitchie is a problem because (a) he likes to destroy things. (b) terrible things happen when he is near. (c) his father expects too much of him.

2. Whenever Mitchie leaves a place (a) troubles begin for that place. (b) his father fires someone. (c) troubles end for that place.

3. A Martian *makron* is probably (a) a soldier from Mars. (b) a machine used to fight on Mars. (c) an Earth soldier who fights on Mars.

4. Lieutenant Brown gets a medal when he (a) is injured by a door. (b) explains what to do about Mitchie. (c) wins a battle on Mars.

5. Mitchie Farthingworth first realized he causes problems when (a) his school burns down. (b) his date breaks her leg. (c) Doctor Duclos explains what is wrong.

6. Mitchie tells the SupCom that (a) his father made him become a Space Cadet. (b) he doesn't want to fight the Martians. (c) he always wanted to be a spaceman.

7. Mitchie suggests that the only way to prevent more accidents is to (a) keep everybody far away. (b) shoot him. (c) destroy the robots.

8. When Mitchie enters the office, the secretarobot suddenly begins to (a) argue with the SupCom. (b) explain what to do. (c) talk nonsense.

9. The SupCom gets a bright idea after (a) Mitchie shoots him. (b) the wastebasket catches fire. (c) he decides it's not safe to destroy Mitchie.

10. The problem in the story is settled by (a) sending Mitchie to Mars. (b) calling Mitchie's father. (c) executing Mitchie.

THINKING IT THROUGH

1. (a) Do you think that some people are really accident prone? In what ways? (b) Could anybody really be as accident prone as Mitchie?

2. (a) What kind of person do you think Mitchie is? (b) Would you want him for a friend if he didn't have this problem?

3. (a) Were you surprised by the ending of the story? (b) Which problems did the ending solve?

4. Some of the words in this story were made up. Guess what each of the following made-up words means. Use context clues to help you decide.

SupCom, secretarobot, makron

UNIT REVIEW

I. Match the terms in column A with their definitions in column B.

	A		**B**
1.	cause	a)	figuring out things from what you already know
2.	choral reading	b)	thing that makes something else happen
3.	detail	c)	more than one meaning
4.	effect	d)	thing that happens because of something else
5.	familiar	e)	small part of a whole picture
6.	inference	f)	known to you
7.	multiple meanings	g)	reading aloud as a group
8.	setting	h)	not something you know
9.	unfamiliar	i)	where and when a story takes place
10.	visualizing	j)	getting a picture in your mind

II. Try to remember the settings of some of the stories in this unit. Choose two stories. Write a few sentences to describe their settings. Try to include the time, place, and some details about each story.

III. What are the characteristics of a monster? Does a monster have to look strange? Must a monster always act in unusual ways? Think of the monsters you read about in this unit. In your own words, describe the characteristics of a monster.

IV. Which of the stories in this unit was the most mysterious? Explain why you think so?

SPEAKING UP

Charles Osgood is a reporter on radio and television. In addition to reporting news stories, he often reads humorous pieces. "The Great Sock Mystery" is one piece he read on the radio.

Read this aloud as if you were reading it on the radio. You will have to speak more slowly than you usually do. It is also important to pronounce each word clearly because listeners can hear your voice, but they can't get clues from the expression on your face. Try not to let your voice drop too low. Low voices are hard to hear on the radio.

THE GREAT SOCK MYSTERY

by Charles Osgood

Have you ever wondered what happened to the socks that disappear in your washer? Or maybe it's your dryer that they disappear in. At any rate, they do disappear. This is not an occasional or unusual incident. Socks disappear all the time, and this has been going on now for years. Furthermore, an independent survey I've done on the subject indicates that sock disappearance is an almost universal experience. Everybody's socks disappear.

You would think, since sock disappearance is such a widespread and unexplained problem, that many Congressional committees would have studied the problem by now, investigated the mystery, held hearings, suggested legislation.

But they have not. So we must begin our own investigation.

In a bureau drawer at home, I have maybe 20 socks. Not 20 pairs of socks, mind you, just 20 socks. All without mates. Each at one time belonged to a pair, but somewhere along the line, through a process not understood, the other socks disappeared. Now and again, a missing sock turns up under a bed or behind a bureau. But most socks, once they disappear, are never seen again.

- universal (yoo nuh VUR sul) **something that happens to almost everyone**

243

SPEAKING UP

Do washing machines eat socks? Washing machine manufacturers insist that they do not. Do dryers eat socks? Drying machine manufacturers (who turn out, incidentally, to be the same people) insist that they do not.

Where, then, are the socks? Is there some conspiracy to take socks out of circulation for the benefit of the sock companies? Has anybody looked into whether the sock industry is making huge profits because of the sock replacement caused by the sock disappearance?

One great problem is that there are no dependable figures upon which one can base intelligent decisions on the subject. However, there are approximately 220 million Americans now, almost all of whom wear socks, two at a time. That's 440 million socks, just for openers. And most of us have several pairs of socks. Indeed, if each of us is missing as many socks as I personally am, the missing-sock figure is up into the billions. This is not small potatoes.

Among the questions I would like answered are these: Why is it that, of the 20 socks in a given bureau drawer, not one of them matches any of the others? Why is that, even if you do find two of approximately the same color, one will come up to your ankle and the other darned sock will reach up to your knee? And speaking of darned socks, people used to darn socks. Nobody ever does any more. Why not? I would like to know.

Is there a nationwide sock-stealing ring, with agents who sneak into people's houses and steal socks out of washers, dryers, and hampers? And, if so, why do they never steal a whole pair, but only one sock at a time? And what is the market for the single socks they steal? What do they do with them anyway? Is there an underground supply of single socks, socked away somewhere? And finally, why this conspiracy of silence? Why has nobody blown the whistle on the great sock-disappearance scandal until now?

If you can unravel the mystery, let me know.

- conspiracy (kun SPEER uh see) **secret, evil plan**
- darn (DAHRN) **repair a hole by sewing or weaving**
- underground (UN dur ground) **secret and sneaky**
- unravel (un RAV ul) **solve, clear up; pull out threads**

WRITING YOUR OWN SETTING

A setting creates a mood, or a feeling, for a story that is about to unfold. What mood does this picture create? Does it create a feeling of cheerfulness? Mystery? Gloom?

1. **Prewriting:** Look closely at the picture. Then close your eyes and try to visualize it. List five or more details that describe the setting. For instance, what season of year and time of day is it? What are the surroundings of the house like?
2. **Writing:** Use your prewriting plan to write a paragraph about the setting. Include enough details so that a reader can visualize the setting. Use phrases such as *to the left of, in front of*, and *at the center of* to tell where objects are located.
3. **Revising:** Read your paragraph. Have you described all the important details in the picture? Will a reader be able to visualize the setting? Check your spelling, punctuation, and capitalization. Make corrections and rewrite your paragraph.

TRYING HARDER

I do not ask for any crown
But that which all may win;
Nor try to conquer any world
Except the world within.

—Louisa May Alcott

Read Louisa May Alcott's words again. Think about their meaning. What is the "world within"? What does the speaker mean by "conquer"? What is the "crown" that "all may win"?

These are the questions for you to think about as you read the selections in this unit. Each selection tells about people who try hard in different ways to conquer inner and outer worlds. In their efforts, these people experience both failure and success. But they also discover that anything worthwhile must be won by trying harder.

MY HERO

by Zoltan Malocsay

▶ A flat tire was just the beginning of Jackson's troubles. Before he knew it, both he and his dog were trying their hardest to save their own lives. Even then, could they both get away alive?

Jackson heard his dog yelping off in the pines and he sighed. First a flat tire and now what? He hoped she wasn't learning about skunks or porcupines.

Tossing the tire iron and jack into the trunk of his subcompact, he slammed down the trunk lid and called her. "Here, Detta. Come on, girl. Ready to go now." He shaded his eyes, tried to peer deeper into the Montana woods.

Her yelping got closer; then she dashed into view, her eyes white-rimmed with fright. "Come here—" Jackson started, then he flinched. She was running from a bear, a huge, angry, determined bear. A grizzly!

"H-hey, don't come . . ." Jackson muttered, backing up. He jumped into the car. Reaching for the ignition switch, he remembered that the keys were still in the trunk lid. *No time now.* Detta howled a DON'T LEAVE ME! and the grizzly gained fast behind her, all claws and teeth and great roaring rage. Jackson rolled up windows and slapped down door locks, holding his own door open until Detta could bound in. Then he slammed it shut.

The grizzly reached out with one paw, punched at the glass. Jackson saw the window spiderweb, break inward with a dull crunch that sent little cubes of safety glass spraying. Gasping, he ducked to avoid the clawing paw that swept inside. Then the grizzly caught the panel and yanked, tearing away the locked door.

- **tire iron** short piece of steel with a flat end used for taking a tire off the rim of a wheel
- **flinch** (FLINCH) draw back from something painful or dangerous
- **spiderweb** (SPY dur web) to break in a pattern that looks like a spider's web
- **safety glass** window glass made so that if it breaks, the pieces will not scatter about

248

Jackson hit the door on the other side and rolled out, with his retriever howling and climbing all over him. He scrambled a few feet on his hands and knees, then got to his feet and ran for the tree-covered slope that fell away beside the road.

Too big to make it through the car, the grizzly had to back out and come around—a tiny head start for Jackson. Yet he couldn't help remembering what he'd read somewhere: For a short distance, a grizzly can outrun a horse!

Detta raced ahead, easily outrunning Jackson. *Am I the slowest one here?* he asked himself. *I'm—I'm the slowest one here!*

With the claws cutting ground close behind him, he angled down the hillside, catching trees first with one hand and then the other, using his speed to swing him in wide zigzags. It worked. The grizzly's bulk wouldn't let him run his fastest downhill or along the hillside: He had to slow down to keep his balance.

- retriever (re TREE vur) **a breed of dog used for hunting; also one who gets something and brings it back**
- **scramble** (SKRAM bul) **climb quickly up or down, especially on the hands and knees**
- angle (ANG gul) **to move at an angle or in a slanting way**
- bulk (BULK) **large body**

Jackson could see a grassy meadow below. *Musn't go down there and run out of slope,* so he turned to run straight along the mountainside. *Got to wear him down,* he told himself. *Bears are sprinters, not distance runners.*

Yet neither was Jackson. Just another tourist from the lowlands, not used to this thin air. Soon the altitude had him puffing; the soft ground wore out his ankles.

Detta ran just ahead, every once in a while stopping to bark at the grizzly. *What'd you do to get him so mad?* Jackson wondered.

Suddenly, they came to a place where an old rock slide cut across their path, a spill of black flaky stuff that reached all the way down the mountain. Still running, Jackson tried to scramble across it, but that rock was slate, dull little brittle bits that slipped and slid over each other. With a whoosh, he rocketed away down the slope. Rolling, sliding, he tried for a hold, but then he heard another swooshing noise above and looked up to see the grizzly sliding down after him, madder than ever.

When he reached the bottom, he didn't have the strength to try running uphill, so he struck out across the flat meadow, elbows and legs churning.

The grizzly kept after him, eating up the distance between them. Jackson didn't have to look back. He could hear the paws falling closer and closer behind him.

Suddenly he caught one foot in the grass, tripped, and went down. Halfway to the ground he knew he was a goner, so when he hit, he froze. He tried to tell himself that some animals depend on playing dead, but it was pretty hard to pretend with his chest heaving.

Then he heard the dry grass crunching near him, felt the grizzly's hot breath move over him, and he died a little. Jackson held his breath and kept his eyes shut hard, waiting . . .

Detta barked, came suddenly. *That wonderful dog!* The bear roared and dashed out in pursuit again. *Saved! Oh, that marvelous dog!*

- sprinter (SPRINT ur) **person or animal that runs very quickly for a short distance**
- spill (SPILL) **place into which water or dirt sometimes spills**
- **goner** (GAW nur) **someone who appears to be impossible to save**

With the bear drawn away, Jackson leaped to his feet, but as soon as he was up and running, Detta joined him again. "Go away!" he yelled at her. "Go away!"

So she did, running out ahead of him again, and that put the grizzly back on his heels. *Pick a tree!*

Running to the first big tree at the edge of the woods, Jackson leaped for the lowest branch. Both fists closed on it and he pulled himself up, grabbed the tree trunk high with his legs, and started up, using his knees, chin, elbows, anything.

He didn't get far before the grizzly galloped up to the tree and stood up, reaching. That bear would've had him right there, but Detta charged up behind and took a nip at his tail.

Whirling, the bear went after Detta again and Jackson got his chance to climb high out of reach. *Oh, that dog! If she hadn't nipped that grizzly*—He watched her, yelping, scared, running with her tail between her legs, but he knew that she was a hero just the same. He promised her special goodies for the rest of her life.

Then a rifle cracked, once, twice. The bear stopped, looked toward the sound, and started running away. A jeep drove up, a jeep with a ranch brand painted on the side. The rancher got out to pet Detta.

Jackson hurried down to thank him.

"Don't mention it," said the old man. "Maybe you won't believe this, but most folks around here don't have much trouble with bears. Even grizzlies. You've just got to make enough noise. If they know you're coming, they're glad to get out of your way. You'll never even see one, if they can help it. But if I were you, young fella, I'd get myself another dog."

"What?" Jackson flared. "Another—why she's the best dog! She saved my life. Twice."

"Hold on." The old man grinned. "I just meant you need two dogs in this country—that's all. Two or none."

"What?"

"Sure. You know how dogs are. They'll go sniff out a bear and bark at him and antagonize him. Grizzlies won't put up with that. They hate that."

"But you said two dogs."

"Yeah. Two dogs protect each other. You know, they get on each side. The bear can't go for one without the other jumping in. But that's with two dogs. One dog can't do that. One dog can't do anything but make a grizzly real mad and then RUN! Understand?"

Jackson nodded slowly. Then he saw his golden retriever slinking away sheepishly, and his eyes sharpened. *My hero!* he simmered.

The rancher's voice was amused. "That's why folks around here won't go near the woods with just one dog, son. You never know when she might turn out to be a retriever!"

- **antagonize** (an TAG uh nyz) make an enemy of someone by annoying him or her
- slink (SLINGK) move in a way that shows shame or fear
- **sheepishly** (SHEEP ish lee) in an embarrassed way

ALL THINGS CONSIDERED —————————————————

1. In this story, italics are used to show (a) what Jackson is thinking. (b) words Jackson shouts. (c) what the dog is thinking.

2. When Jackson hears his dog yelping in the woods, he thinks (a) she is having trouble with a bear. (b) she has found a skunk or porcupine. (c) she's telling him it is time to leave.

3. The first thing that Jackson does when he sees the bear is (a) start the motor of his car. (b) run to save his dog. (c) jump into his car.

4. Jackson knows he is in trouble when the grizzly (a) unlocks the car door. (b) breaks the car window. (c) jumps on the car.

5. When the bear, dog, and man start running, Jackson realizes that (a) he is the slowest of the three. (b) bears run fast for long distances. (c) he can outrun the bear.

6. When he trips and the bear comes close, Jackson decides the best thing to do is (a) roll down the hill. (b) get up and run. (c) play dead.

7. Jackson is saved for the first time when (a) the bear is fooled. (b) Detta bites the bear. (c) Detta's bark draws the bear away.

8. Jackson is saved again when (a) the bear falls into a ditch. (b) Detta nips the bear's tail. (c) Detta jumps on the bear's back.

9. Jackson and his dog are finally saved when (a) Jackson reaches his rifle. (b) a rancher kills the bear. (c) a rifle shot scares the bear off.

10. The rancher tells Jackson that in this kind of country (a) a person needs two dogs. (b) Detta is the wrong kind of dog. (c) dogs need to be trained to hunt.

THINKING IT THROUGH —————————————————

1. How does Detta get herself and Jackson into trouble in the first place? How does she help save Jackson's life? What finally saves both their lives?

2. Why is the story called "My Hero"? Do you think it is a good title for the story? Tell why or why not.

3. Why was Jackson's car an unsafe place to hide from a bear? What did Jackson forget that made the car even less safe?

4. An author often uses strong, vivid verbs, or action words, to help make the story more exciting. An example would be, "He *yanked* the door." Find examples of verbs that make the story more exciting.

Literary Skills

Author's Purpose

Why does a person write a story, a poem, a play, or an essay? Every author has a **purpose**, or reason, for writing. The usual purposes for writing are:

1. to explain or teach something to the reader
2. to entertain the reader
3. to try to make the reader agree with the author's ideas

How do you figure out the author's purpose? One way is to turn to this list. Which purpose best describes what you are reading? An author usually has only one purpose for each work.

The author's purpose in writing "My Hero" was probably to entertain the reader with a good, exciting story. By reading this story, you may learn something about going into the woods with dogs, but that was not the author's real purpose. Above all else, the story tells about an exciting adventure.

Look back through the selections you have already read in this book. Find one work that fits each of the purposes discussed earlier. (Do not use "My Hero.") On a separate sheet of paper, write the following information for each of the three selections you choose:

title   main character(s)
author   purpose

Composition

Follow your teacher's instructions before completing *one* of these writing assignments.

1. What do you think is the best kind of pet? Write a sentence that begins, "The best kind of pet is _____." Then write three sentences to try to convince other people that you are right. Remember, your purpose is to try to make others agree with you.

2. People may not know what to do when they are in a different part of the country. Imagine, for example, a city person in the woods, or a small-town person in a large city. Write a paragraph telling (1) where the person came from, (2) what the new place looks like, and (3) what kinds of strange or new conditions the person will have to get used to.

OOKA AND THE STOLEN SMELL

by I. G. Edmonds

▶ Can someone steal a smell? That's what a shopkeeper accuses a student of doing. Now Ooka, the great and wise judge, must decide the case.

Now it so happened in the days of old Yedo, as Tokyo was once called, that the storytellers told marvelous tales of the wit and wisdom of His Honorable Honor, Ooka Tadasuke.

This famous judge never refused to hear a complaint, even if it seemed strange or unreasonable. People sometimes came to his court with the most unusual cases, but Ooka always agreed to listen. And the strangest case of all was the famous Case of the Stolen Smell.

It all began when a poor student rented a room over a *tempura* shop—a shop where fried food could be bought. The student was a most likable young man, but the shopkeeper was a miser who suspected everyone of trying to get the better of him. One day he heard the student talking with one of his friends.

"It is sad to be so poor that one can only afford to eat plain rice," the friend complained.

"Oh," said the student, "I have found a very satisfactory answer to the problem. I eat my rice each day while the shopkeeper downstairs fries his fish. The smell comes up, and my humble rice seems to have much more flavor. It is really the smell, you know, that makes things taste so good."

The shopkeeper was furious. To think that someone was enjoying the smell of his fish for nothing! "Thief!" he shouted. "I demand that you pay me for the smells you have stolen."

"A smell is a smell," the young man replied. "Anyone can smell what he wants to. I will pay you nothing!"

- **wit** (WIT) understanding and intelligence
- **likable** (LY kuh bul) pleasant and easy to like
- tempura (TEM poor uh) vegetables or fish fried in a batter

255

Scarlet with rage, the shopkeeper rushed to Ooka's court and charged the student with theft. Of course, everyone laughed at him, for how could anyone steal a smell? Ooka would surely send the man about his business. But to everyone's astonishment, the judge agreed to hear the case.

"Every person is entitled to time in court," he explained. "If this man feels strongly enough about his smells to make a complaint, it is only right that I, as city magistrate, should hear the case." He frowned at the amused spectators.

Gravely, Ooka sat on the dais and heard the evidence. Then he delivered his verdict.

"The student is obviously guilty," he said severely. "Taking another person's property is theft, and I cannot see that a smell is different from any other property."

The shopkeeper was delighted, but the student was horrified. He was very poor, and he owed the shopkeeper for three months' smelling. He would surely be thrown into prison.

"How much money have you?" Ooka asked him.

"Only five *mon*, Honorable Honor," the boy replied. "I need that to pay my rent, or I will be thrown out into the street."

"Let me see the money," said the judge.

- **magistrate** (MAJ i strayt) **judge**
- gravely (GRAYV lee) **in a slow and serious way**
- dais (DAY is) **raised platform or place of honor**
- obviously (OB vee us lee) **in a way that is easy to see; clearly**

256

The young man held out his hand. Ooka nodded and told him to drop the coins from one hand to the other.

The judge listened to the pleasant clink of the money and said to the shopkeeper, "You have now been paid. If you have any other complaints in the future, please bring them to the court. It is our wish that all injustices be punished and all virtue rewarded."

"But, most Honorable Honor," the shopkeeper protested, "I did not get the money! The thief dropped it from one hand to the other. See! I have nothing." He held up his empty hands to show the judge.

Ooka stared at him gravely. "It is the court's judgment that the punishment should fit the crime. I have decided that the price of the *smell* of food shall be the *sound* of money. Justice has prevailed as usual in my court."

- clink (KLINGK) a sharp, ringing sound, as of metal hitting metal
- **virtue** (VUR choo) goodness
- **prevail** (pri VAYL) win out

ALL THINGS CONSIDERED _____

1. This story takes place in (a) the United States about 100 years ago. (b) Tokyo, Japan, today. (c) Yedo, the former name for Tokyo, long ago.

2. The student lived (a) in a food store. (b) above a food store. (c) with a shopkeeper.

3. Although he can only afford rice, the student enjoys his meals because (a) the shopkeeper gives him leftover food. (b) he smells fish cooking as he eats the rice. (c) he steals fried fish from the shop.

4. The shopkeeper demands money for the stolen (a) fish. (b) rice. (c) smells.

5. The student says (a) he enjoys the smell of rice. (b) the extra fish is thrown out anyway. (c) anyone can smell things for free.

6. When Ooka agrees to hear the case, (a) people are astonished. (b) no one is surprised. (c) everyone knows that the shopkeeper will win.

7. Ooka decides that the student (a) must go to prison. (b) has to pay his rent. (c) is guilty of theft.

8. A *mon* is a (a) kind of fish. (b) Japanese coin. (c) prison.

9. The student pays for the stolen smell (a) by giving the shopkeeper all his money. (b) by paying a fine to the judge. (c) with the sound of his money.

10. Ooka tells the shopkeeper that (a) people should not steal smells. (b) the punishment should fit the crime. (c) nobody should waste time on such foolish cases.

THINKING IT THROUGH _____

1. Do you think most judges would take a case like this one? Why do you think Ooka took the case?

2. What does Ooka mean by saying, "Justice has prevailed in my court"? Do you agree? Do you think his decision was a wise one? Why or why not?

3. How is Ooka different from a modern American judge? How is he like one?

Literary Skills

Topic and Theme

The **topic** is what a piece of writing is about. It can usually be expressed in a word or just a few words. Some topics you might find in your reading are Friendship, Getting Used to a New Place, Winning, and Fighting for Freedom.

The **theme** is different from the topic. The theme expresses the writer's ideas about the topic. Usually, the theme is stated in a full sentence. Here are some possible themes about the above topics: Friends should be honest with each other; Other people can help you feel comfortable in a new country; Winning is best when you win fairly; People who fight for their own freedom often win freedom for others.

Look at the topics and themes listed below. Decide which is the topic for "Ooka and the Stolen Smell." Then decide which is the theme.

1. Smells and Sounds
2. Judges are not always right.
3. Justice
4. Old Japan
5. A fair punishment should fit the crime.

Composition

Follow your teacher's instructions before completing *one* of these writing assignments.

1. Choose one of these topics. Then write three sentences that could be themes for a story with that topic.
Topics: Baseball   Television   Music   The Future

Here is an example showing a topic and theme.

Topic: Weather
Theme: Some activities can be done in any weather, but others depend on certain kinds of weather.

2. What food smells do you like the best? Write a paragraph that tells about your favorite food smells.

259

THE PENNY FIDDLE

by Robert Graves

▶ Some people seem to have a special something that allows them to perform better than you or I. What do you think this special something is or might be?

Yesterday I bought a penny fiddle
    And put it to my chin to play,
But I found that the strings were painted,
So I threw my fiddle away.

A gypsy girl found my penny fiddle
    As it lay abandoned there;
When she asked me if she might keep it,
    I told her I did not care.

Then she drew such music from the fiddle
    With help of a farthing bow,
That I offered five shillings for the secret,
    But alas, she would not let it go.

WAYS OF KNOWING

1. Why couldn't the poet play the fiddle? How was the gypsy girl able to play it?

2. What does the speaker want to buy from the girl? Do you think it is something the girl could sell? Explain your answer.

3. Why do you think some people seem to do better than others with the same equipment?

- farthing (FAHR thing) a coin, no longer in use, worth one fourth of a British penny
- shilling (SHIL ing) a coin worth 12 times a British penny

William Butler Yeats (1865-1939)

The great love of William Butler Yeats was Ireland, and Ireland loved him in return. Yeats was Ireland's greatest poet and one of its greatest playwrights. He was also the only Irish writer to receive a Nobel Prize for Literature.

Born in Dublin, Ireland, Yeats spent many years in London, England. In fact, his early schooling was in England. During his youth, Yeats thought he might become a painter, but he soon discovered that his true talent was writing poetry.

In 1898, Yeats and several other playwrights founded the Irish Literary Theatre, later known as the Abbey Theatre. It was created as a showplace for Irish plays and Irish actors. The Abbey Theatre was a great success and is still active today.

Yeats admitted to believing in the supernatural. Many people thought he was joking when he said he believed in fairies, but he probably did believe in some kind of supernatural beings. Yeats expressed his views of life and the supernatural through Irish history, tales, and legends.

Yeats was always humble about his work, but his contributions to Irish literature were great. In 1923, William Butler Yeats won the Nobel Prize for Literature.

Many poets begin well when they are young, but their poetry does not improve as they age. William Butler Yeats is one poet whose work seemed to grow better as he grew older. For this reason, Yeats is often considered one of the greatest poets of his time.

DOWN BY THE SALLEY GARDENS

by William Butler Yeats

▶ Some people try too hard, as the young man in the poem found out.

Down by the salley gardens my love and I did meet;
She passed the salley gardens with little snow-white feet.
She bid me take love easy, as the leaves grow on the tree;
But I, being young and foolish, with her would not agree.

In a field by the river my love and I did stand,
And on my leaning shoulder she laid her snow-white hand.
She bid me take life easy, as the grass grows on the weirs;
But I was young and foolish, and now am full of tears.

WAYS OF KNOWING

1. The young woman asks the poet to take two things easy. What are these things? How did he respond to her request?
2. The poet compares taking things easy to the way "the leaves grow on the tree" and "the grass grows on the weirs." What do these words help you visualize? What do you think the poet means?
3. When is the poet telling this story? What do you think has happened? What leads you to think so?

• weir (WEER) small dam in a stream

VOCABULARY AND SKILL REVIEW

Before completing the exercises that follow, you may wish to review the **bold-faced** words on pages 248-257.

I. On a separate sheet of paper, write the *italicized* term that best fills the blank in each sentence. Each term should be used only once.

wit	*virtue*	*magistrate*	*flinch*	*goner*
sheepishly	*prevail*	*antagonize*	*scramble*	*likable*

1. The comedian had won fame for his charm and _____.
2. If you behave rudely, you will _____ the people around you.
3. Do you believe that justice will _____ in the trial?
4. After the accident, the doctors thought he was a _____, but he was fine in a few months.
5. The new student was a _____ fellow, with a warm smile and a friendly handshake.
6. Since the girl was shy, she lowered her head and answered the question _____.
7. Before he delivered a verdict, the _____ considered all the evidence.
8. Most people automatically _____ when an object is thrown at them.
9. The hikers were tired, but they had enough energy to _____ up the mountainside.
10. He was respected as a leader because he was a person of the highest _____.

II. Choose four of your favorite stories in this book. On a separate sheet of paper, make a list of the stories, their topics, and their themes. Write one topic and one or more themes for each story. Tell whether the topic and theme of each are stated or unstated. You can set up your list in this way.

Story	Topic	Stated or Unstated	Theme(s)	Stated or Unstated
1.				
2.				
3.				
4.				

Emily Dickinson (1830-1886)

If no one had looked through Emily Dickinson's dresser drawers after her death, America would have lost one of its greatest poets. Dickinson wrote more than a thousand poems in her lifetime but published only a handful. Her sister Lavinia discovered all the poems in Emily's dresser. The first two books of poetry were not published until 1900.

The daughter of a lawyer, Emily Dickinson grew up in the town of Amherst, Massachusetts. She was better educated than most girls at the time. As a young woman, she enjoyed the life of the village and the companionship of her school friends. But during her thirties, Emily began to go out less and less. She continued to see people, however, because her father was an important man in the town, and many interesting people came to the house.

Some people believe there may have been a secret love in her life. They think that she fell in love with a man she met while on a trip with her parents. There are other people who say that she wanted to marry another man but her father refused to allow the marriage. No one is really sure, since Emily Dickinson led a very private life, and we know her mainly through her poetry.

POEMS BY EMILY DICKINSON

▶ Emily Dickinson tried hard to tell us what she was feeling and thinking. Sometimes, however, these thoughts-made-into-poems can be difficult to understand. The following poems may make you work a little harder, but they are worth it.

SUCCESS

Success is counted sweetest
By those who ne'er succeed.
To comprehend a nectar
Requires sorest need.

Not one of all the purple host
Who took the flag today
Can tell the definition
So clear of victory

As he defeated, dying,
On whose forbidden ear
The distant strains of triumph
Burst agonized and clear.

WAYS OF KNOWING

1. According to the poet, who appreciates success the most? What examples does she give to support her view? Do you agree with her? Why or why not?
2. Who does the poet think can give the best definition of victory—the winner or the loser? Find the lines in the poem that tell this. Explain why you agree or disagree with the poet's explanation.

- ne'er (NAYR) **never**
- comprehend (kom pri HEND) **understand**
- nectar (NEK tur) **delicious, heavenly drink**
- host (HOHST) **great number of people; army**
- strains (STRAYNZ) **sounds or songs**
- **agonized** (AG uh nyzd) **suffering greatly, in great pain**

265

"HOPE" IS THE THING WITH FEATHERS

by Emily Dickinson

"Hope" is the thing with feathers
That perches in the soul,
And sings the tune without the words,
And never stops at all.

And sweetest in the gale is heard.
And sore must be the storm
That could abash the little bird
That kept so many warm.

I've heard it in the chillest land,
And on the strangest sea.
Yet, never, in extremity,
It asked a crumb of me.

WAYS OF KNOWING

1. By saying "'Hope' is the thing with feathers," the poet compares hope to something else. To what is she comparing hope? What other words or phrases in the poem help create the image?

2. When and why is hope important to the poet? Do you think it helps her try harder? Do you think hope is important to most people? How does hope "sing" to you?

3. Does hope ask anything from most people? Explain.

• abash (uh BASH) **make uneasy**

Building from Details

Paraphrasing

Paraphrasing is stating the meaning of a passage in your own words. When you really understand what you are reading, you should be able to put the writer's ideas into your own words.

For example, if you were going to paraphrase the poem "Hope Is the Thing with Feathers," you might say, "Hope is like a little bird that manages to survive bad times. It calls most strongly to us when we think everything is at its worst."

Choose two poems that you have already read in this book. On a separate sheet of paper, write a paraphrase of each poem. Before you begin, look through each poem for key words and phrases. These words and phrases are clues to the poet's meaning. Try to state the poet's meaning in your own words.

Composition

Follow your teacher's instructions before completing *one* of these writing assignments.

1. Write down the lyrics, or words, of a favorite song. (You do not have to write the entire song, just a part of it.) Then paraphrase the song's lyrics.
2. Think of some ideas such as beauty, love, happiness, misery, or anger. Write a short poem or paragraph in which you compare each idea to some real thing in the world of nature.

THE KICK

by Elizabeth Van Steenwyk

▶ Even when a person knows she cannot win a race, she can still try her hardest and do her best. But doing one's best can be especially difficult when all the others in the race are boys.

The announcer's voice boomed over the loudspeaker, "Last call for frosh-soph milers." The moment she stepped on the track with the guys, she heard the snickering start again. Why couldn't the spectators get used to her presence, too? Why couldn't people understand that girls loved to run as much as boys?

The starter called out their names and assigned lanes; she was seeded in the fifth.

"Boys," he began, then looking at her, "I mean, boys and girl, this is the mile run, four laps around the track. Stay in your lanes until you come to the red markers down there." He pointed to the far turn. "Then you can cut for the pole. There will be two commands to start, the whistle and the gun. Have a good race, boys, I mean, boys and girl."

She assumed the beginning stance and tried to wash her mind of everything but the race before her. Today was no ordinary meet, but League prelims, and she was the first girl ever to be entered from any school. Sure she felt nervous, but she had a good feeling about the meet. Maybe today was her day.

The starter blew the whistle; she tensed. He fired the gun. They were off. For a couple of glorious moments, she ran ahead of the pack because of her advantage in the fifth lane, but it didn't last. The

- frosh (FROSH) freshman, person in first year of a school
- soph (SOF) sophomore, person in the second year of a school
- seeded (SEED id) placed or arranged in the order of ability
- stance (STANS) way of standing
- prelims (PREE limz) sports event you must pass to enter the main event
- advantage (ad VAN tij) something that gives a person a better chance

kid from Springdale passed her, but she'd expected this. He was a real hotshot; he'd probably be a class runner by this time next year. She stayed with the other three boys until the first stretch. Then gradually, two more pulled away and she was left with the Crown City boy.

"You're doing fine, Mary Beth," she heard someone shout from the infield and recognized the voice of her friend, Bones, the varsity two-miler. He was a senior and captain of the team. She'd been so proud and grateful when he took a special interest in her, a lowly freshman.

"Keep those arms down," he called again.

She tried to think about form. She knew its importance as a part of the training strategy she'd practiced for so many months. Milers had to have a good combination of stamina and speed and all the training had been directed to that. Would it pay off for her?

Fortunately, speed came naturally. Dad had been a sprinter on his college team and her three brothers lettered in track before her. Bill, now a senior and a class runner in the mile, discovered her speed last summer when he clocked her running the junior high track and suggested she go out as a freshman. Then, when she did,

- varsity (VAHR si tee) **belonging to a school's team**
- stamina (STAM uh nuh) **strength and ability to last**
- sprinter (SPRINT ur) **one who runs quickly for a short distance**

269

he had acted like a total stranger. If it hadn't been for Bones, she might have quit. He was the only one on the team who acknowledged her membership in the human race.

She and the Crown City kid rounded the far turn on the first lap and crossed their lanes. She felt a prickly sensation on her legs and knew it to be a spray of fine gravel he'd kicked up as he pulled away from her. Now, as they passed the grandstand, she heard voices but no words, and she hoped it would stay that way. If she heard Mom shouting, she'd just die.

The next lap seemed easier and she felt light, almost airborne, hardly feeling the ground when her feet touched it. That was a bad sign, and fearing that sort of self-hypnosis most of all, she shook it off. Then she heard Bones calling again, "Keep him in sight, Mary Beth. Hang in there." Good, she needed that. She pulled closer to the Crown City kid, but they had nearly two more laps to go and she had to hold something back for the kick.

What was a kick anyway? Jim Ryun talked about it, so did Francie Larrieu and the rest of the running world, but no one ever could define it exactly. Oh, she knew a kick was that last hard sprint at the finish line, but it was more than that. Was it courage, strength, competitiveness, or just plain guts? The coach said he didn't know for sure, she'd have to find it out for herself.

They passed the grandstand for the third time and then she heard it, Mom's voice shouting, "Come on, Honey Bunch."

Crumb, she thought. Why does she have to call me that? For a minute she thought she'd broken her rhythm she got so upset, but then she retrieved it and held the Crown City kid in tight. The lead boy from Springdale was a half lap ahead of them, he was really kicking and the other two boys were fighting for second and third.

She made up her mind. I'm not going to be last, she thought. I won't be last. She picked up her speed, but the Crown City kid sensed it ahead and kept the distance between them.

- **acknowledge** (ak NOL ij) **admit that something is true**
- prickly (PRIK lee) **full of sharp points; tingling**
- self-hypnosis (SELF hip NOH sis) **putting oneself in a condition resembling a trance**
- **competitiveness** (kum PET i tiv nis) **trying hard to win against others**
- retrieve (ri TREEV) **get something back again**

She wondered what his nickname was, or if he had one. Nicknames were a status symbol, or at least they were on her team. It was a sign that you'd really arrived when the boys bestowed a special name on you. Well, she was still Mary Beth and probably always would be, except to Mom. *"Honey bunch,"* Ugh!

But she should be concentrating on the event. She closed the gap on the Crown City kid at the final turn. This was the moment she'd trained for, hoped for, and yes, prayed for. Did she have the will to win? Could she at least beat a boy? A sudden thought grabbed her. Did the Crown City kid have a good kick? She couldn't remember from their dual meet.

She heard Bones yelling again, "Kick it on home, Mary Beth."

Now she knew it was now or never. Would she have it, that kick, when she wanted it? Her mouth was parched and dry as a day-old sandwich. She was afraid that her kick wouldn't be there when she needed it most.

She ran even with the Crown City kid now. Neck and neck. Was it his breathing or hers that she heard?

Then she reached way back in her brain and told every cell in her body, every screaming tendon, every breath, every pounding beat of her heart to kick and soon, slowly, then quickly, it washed over her with a flood of strength and desire and sweat. She was kicking it on home and the spectators saw it and knew magic was in the air. They rose as one and roared and shouted their approval. The girl, she felt them thinking, the girl was going to beat that boy, actually beat a boy for the first time in the history of the league.

Then she heard Bill's voice shouting at her from the infield. "You've got him, Honey Bunch."

Crumb, she thought. Why that name, now at a time like this? Then she knew and just the knowing enveloped her like a soft garment. They'd given her a special nickname, like everyone else, just like Bones and Brick and Spider and Zap. She'd been accepted.

- status symbol (STAY tus SIM bul) **something used to show how important a person is**
- concentrate (KON sun trayt) **give all one's attention to**
- **parched** (PAHRCHD) **dried out**
- tendon (TEN dun) **part of the body that connects a muscle to a bone**
- envelop (en VEL up) **wrap; surround**

271

She pulled away for good then, and crossed the finish line two steps ahead of the Crown City kid, kept her lane for another 20 feet, stopped, and leaned over to gasp and catch her breath. Sweat dripped from her, her hair felt like a soggy mop hanging down her back but she didn't care. Victory was sweet.

The team surrounded her. She gloried in their praise, and listened intently as the announcer spoke her name.

"Mary Beth Barkley of Walnut Hill, fourth place in the time of 5:21.04."

She walked out to the center of the track and waved to the grandstand just like Olga Korbut.

Finally, the magic softened to a warm glow within her, the cheering stopped, and she couldn't wait to drink some tea, that super honey tea the mothers provided for every meet. Set up on an old bench at the grandstand's far corner, cups and jugs were ready and waiting. She walked over, grateful to be alone, and poured herself a cup.

Then she saw him. At first she glimpsed only a pair of legs sticking out from under the grandstand. But when she bent over and looked underneath, she recognized the kid from Crown City in his green and orange uniform. His shoulders heaved with dry sobs and he pounded the dirt with his fists in frustration and rage.

She knew, of course. She knew what he felt, because she'd been last so many times herself. But it was more than that with him. He'd been beaten by a girl and somehow, he'd have to live with it for a long time.

She put her tea down so suddenly, it sloshed out of the cup. Crumb, she thought. Why didn't someone tell her there's more to a victory than winning? She kicked off her spikes and walked barefoot back to the dressing room.

- intently (in TENT lee) **with sharp attention**

- frustration (fruh STRAY shun) **disappointment people feel when they cannot get what they had hoped for**

273

ALL THINGS CONSIDERED ———————————————————

1. Mary Beth is the first girl (a) to lose all her races. (b) from any school to enter the race. (c) to have won more than two races.

2. At first, she is running ahead of the others because (a) the others are slow starters. (b) she was allowed to start out first. (c) the lane she is in gives her an advantage.

3. The person who helps her by calling out encouragement and advice is (a) Bones, a friend who is also a runner. (b) her brother Bill. (c) her mother.

4. The person who discovered that she could run fast is (a) her friend Bones. (b) her father, who had been a sprinter. (c) her brother Bill, who is a runner.

5. For most of the race, she is trying to beat (a) the boy from Crown City. (b) the hotshot from Springdale. (c) Bones.

6. In the middle of the race, she makes up her mind that she will (a) beat the others by hypnotizing herself. (b) come in second or third. (c) not be last.

7. She is upset when (a) her mother calls her "Honey Bunch." (b) Bones calls her "Mary Beth." (c) the Crown City kid calls her by a nickname.

8. The spectators are on her side when they realize that (a) she is going to win. (b) a girl is going to beat a boy. (c) she will come in last.

9. A "kick" is (a) a last hard run at the end of a race. (b) a trophy a runner gets for winning a race. (c) passing a runner and spraying him or her with gravel.

10. At the end, Mary Beth realizes that (a) she should not have beaten a boy. (b) she feels bad because she didn't win. (c) the Crown City kid feels bad that a girl has beaten him.

THINKING IT THROUGH ———————————————————

1. How did Mary Beth "win" the race? What did she accomplish that was important to her? Do you think that she was a winner?

2. At the beginning of the race, the starter says "Boys . . . I mean boys and girl . . . " Why does he say this? Would his words bother you if you were Mary Beth? Tell why or why not.

3. Why is a nickname important? Does Mary Beth have a runner's nickname at the beginning of the story? Does she have one at the end? How does she feel about nicknames? How do you feel about nicknames? Explain.

Building from Details

Topic Sentence and Supporting Details

Every paragraph has a topic, or main idea. Many paragraphs also have a **topic sentence**. The topic sentence gives the most important idea of the paragraph. The other sentences in the paragraph give **supporting details**. Supporting details together add up to the idea in the topic sentence.

Look at the paragraph on page 271 that begins "She wondered what his nickname was . . . " The topic sentence in that paragraph is the second sentence, "Nicknames were a status symbol, or at least they were on her team." Two supporting details in that paragraph are: (1) nicknames are a sign that you had arrived, and (2) Mary Beth does not yet have a nickname.

On a separate sheet of paper, write the topic sentence for each of the following paragraphs. Under the topic sentence, write two supporting details.

Page 269, paragraph beginning, "Fortunately, speed came naturally."

Page 270, paragraph beginning, "What was a kick anyway?"

Page 273, paragraph beginning, "She knew, of course."

Composition

Follow your teacher's instructions before completing *one* of these writing assignments.

1. Write a topic sentence about your favorite sport or hobby. Then write a list of three or more details that could be supporting details for your topic sentence.

2. Do you think girls should be allowed to compete in the same leagues as boys, or should they compete in separate girls' leagues? Write a topic sentence that gives your opinion. Develop this into a paragraph by writing at least four sentences with supporting details to convince people of your opinion.

from DEAR LOVEY HART, I AM DESPERATE

by Ellen Conford

▶ Have you ever read an advice column in the newspaper? Could Carrie Wasserman, a high school student, write an advice column? Should she? How hard would she have to try to come up with answers that were both interesting to read and gave good advice? Would you give the same advice Carrie gave?

For almost a year I was the best-kept secret at Lincoln High. That is, my identity was—or actually, the identity of *Lovey Hart.*

The whole thing started one bright fall afternoon in the office (such as it was) of the school paper, the *Lincoln Log.*

"Carrie, wait a minute. I have to ask you something important." Chip Custer, the editor of the *Log*, walked toward me, his face solemn.

"Listen," he began, pulling over a chair, "I had an idea, and I think you'd be just the person to pull it off."

"Uh-oh," I said.

He grinned. He turned the chair around backward and sat, his arms leaning against the back. "I've been fooling around with the idea of an advice to the

lovelorn column, and I think you'd do a great job with it."

"Advice? To the lovelorn? *Me?*"

"It's just that I think you'd have the right touch for this sort of thing. Those sample columns you wrote when you tried out for the paper showed real potential. What I'd want is light, lively stuff, you know, bringing out the 'funny side of human foibles.' Of course, you could throw in a couple of serious ones, too, if you think you can handle them."

If I thought I could handle them! Who spent hours on the phone, listening to the problems Terry and Claudia brought me to solve?

"Well, of course I can handle it!" I said indignantly.

"Great!" Chip cried, clapping me on

- lovelorn (LUV lawrn) **suffering for lack of love**
- **potential** (puh TEN shul) **ability that is not yet used**
- foibles (FOI buls) **weaknesses**
- indignantly (in DIG nunt lee) **in a way that shows anger at something considered unfair**

276

my shoulder. "I knew you could. Now listen, the first thing is, this has to be kept absolutely secret."

"What does?" I asked, confused. "The column?"

"No, no, the fact that you're Lovey Hart."

"I'm *who?*"

"Lovey Hart. That's the name we're going to use for the column. 'Dear Lovey Hart.' Isn't that a great name?"

"Chip," I said gently, "that's not exactly one of your top ten names."

"Are you kidding? It's a terrific name."

"Chip, it's corny."

"Well, naturally. It's *supposed* to be corny. Carrie, where's your sense of humor? The thing is mostly in fun anyway."

"What are we going to do for letters?" I asked suddenly. "I mean, the first issue? No one will know about the column—"

"Ah, that's what you think." He whipped a wadded piece of looseleaf paper out of his shirt pocket. He unfolded it and spread it out before me on the desk.

"Posters," he announced. "All over school."

"LET LOVEY HELP!" it read.

"Read 'Lovey Hart' in the *Lincoln Log!* Write to Lovey Hart c/o the *Log* office. Lovey Hart answers your questions, solves your problems, with snappy suggestions for happy solutions!! No names, please—Lovey Hart wants just the facts! Lovey listens—so listen to Lovey!"

"But look," he went on gravely, "this whole thing has got to be kept quiet. You can't tell anyone. And that's for your own protection."

- wadded (WAD id) **crumpled up into a ball**
- gravely (GRAYV lee) **seriously**

"Not even my family?" I asked dubiously.

"Especially not your family!" he groaned. "Caroline, have you forgotten who your father is?"

Ridiculous as that sounds, I had. And I immediately realized that Chip was right—of all the people who mustn't know that I was Lovey Hart, my father was right up there at the head of the list—the head guidance counselor at Lincoln High.

"And besides," Chip was saying, "you lose all the—the—mystery, if people know Lovey Hart is just Caroline Wasserman."

"*I don't like it.*" My father's forehead settled into anxious furrows. "Whoever this Hart is, she certainly isn't qualified to give 'snappy solutions' or 'instant relief' or whatever those posters say."

"Oh, Dad, you're taking the whole thing much too seriously!"

The posters had been up for two weeks, and they had stirred up more interest than usual in the paper. And they'd already inspired some letters, which Chip was holding for me.

"And you're not taking it seriously *enough*," my father replied. "The thought of some mixed-up kid giving out advice to other mixed-up kids is absolutely—"

"That's not fair!" I said indignantly. "How do you know she—or *he*," I added quickly, "is a mixed-up kid? Maybe she or he is very sensible."

"I'm really tempted," he went on, as if he hadn't even heard me, "to put a stop to the whole thing before it starts."

"Dad! You can't do that. Remember our rule!"

Our rule was that since we were both at the same school, the best way to maintain cordial relations was to never interfere or intrude in the other's sphere of activity.

"This doesn't involve you," he said innocently.

"Dad," I said carefully, "I work on the paper, and you want to censor it. That *involves* me. They'd all resent me if you did that. Anyway, it's mostly for laughs."

"Sometimes things that start out as laughs end up being very unfunny," he said.

"Oh, *Dad*," I sighed.

- anxious (ANGK shus) **worried**
- furrow (FUR oh) **wrinkle**
- **inspired** (in SPY urd) **having the idea or spirit to do something**
- **cordial** (KOR jul) **friendly and warm**
- sphere (SFEER) **area or place**
- dubiously (DOO bee us lee) **doubtfully**
- **censor** (SEN sur) **refuse to allow something to be printed because you disagree with what is said**
- **resent** (ri ZENT) **show anger because of hurt feelings**

"Here's one," Chip said, handing me a letter.

We were in the *Log* office. Chip had had the idea of coming before school instead of staying on after meetings.

"Let's see." I took the letter from him.

Dear Lovey Hart:

I really like this boy, and most of the time we have no problems, except during lacrosse season. During lacrosse season, he doesn't even know I'm alive. All during the year he's considerate, attentive, and everything you could want. But for four months out of the year I don't see him, he hardly ever calls, and he spends all his time and energy practicing. What can I do to make him pay attention to me during lacrosse season?

Yours truly,
Anonymous

"Hmm," I said. "A nice problem. Nothing life or death about that one."

I pondered a moment. Then, inspired, I scrawled across the bottom of the letter:

Dear Anonymous:

Everyone has her lacrosse to bear. Take up tennis and get yourself as involved in that as he is in his sport. That way, even though he isn't paying attention to you, you won't have time to notice.

I went on to the next letter.

Dear Lovey:

How can I get a boy who sits in front of me in one of my classes to notice me? The only time he ever turns around is when he has to pass papers back. What can I do to get him interested in me?

Sincerely,
B.G.

- **lacrosse (luh KRAWS) team sport played on a field with a ball, long-handled rackets, and goals at each end of the field**

"Aren't there any letters from boys in there?" I asked Chip. "This whole column is going to be how girls can get boys to pay attention to them. That'll get pretty boring after a while."

"We'll go through the whole bunch of them, and then you can pick out the ones you like best," he said absently.

I sighed, and set my mind to thinking how a girl could get the right boy to notice her.

"Tickle the back of his neck," I wrote, and had trouble hiding a silly giggle. Chip looked up at me; I just smiled mysteriously. "Eventually," I continued scribbling, "he'll turn around to see what's going on. After that, you're on your own."

This isn't bad, I thought, reaching for the next letter. As a matter of fact, it's kind of fun.

"That's a more serious one," Chip warned. "I thought we might throw it in for—you know—tragic relief."

Dear Lovey Hart:

A year ago I was in with a crowd that was involved in the drug scene. It wasn't that I wanted the drugs so much—it was just that these were the only friends I had. So I went along. But I realized I was doing bad things to myself, so after a couple of months I stopped. But now I have no friends, and I'm lonely and all I can think of is that if I get back into drugs I'll have these friends again. At least I'll have someone to talk to,

instead of being by myself all the time. I know this is a school paper, so I'm sure you'll tell me to stay straight, but <u>then</u> <u>what</u>? [The words were underlined twice.] I'm getting so tired of being lonely.

Friendless

I slapped the letter down on the desk.

"Tragic relief is right!" I groaned. "I can't answer that!"

"Why not? You have a good head and—I guess—a reasonably good heart. You haven't even tried."

"But, Chip, you said this was supposed to be for laughs."

"I said, 'mostly for laughs.' A serious note now and then makes a good column."

I sighed and picked the letter up again. I didn't even know if the writer was a boy or a girl; all I knew was that it was depressing to read.

Dear Friendless: [I wrote slowly.]

To have a friend you must first be one. It's not easy to make friends, but it's not easy to get off drugs, either, and you managed to do <u>that</u>. [I wrote faster now.] Start by making friends out of acquaintances. Ask one person you like but don't know very well over to your house after school. Or to go to the movies with you. You must take the first step. Since you've been out of touch with people for a while, they don't realize you want to be back in again.

• **acquaintance** (uh KWAYN tuns) person you know, but not very well

Maybe the first person you ask will reciprocate; maybe not. But whatever happens, don't stop there. Ask another person to do something with you. If you keep on doing this, soon you will have plenty to do, and plenty of people to do it with. I know it's hard, but you owe it to yourself to <u>try</u>.

Good luck!

I put down my pencil with a satisfied sigh.

"Not bad," I said. "Hey, Chip, I think this is pretty good."

"Whatever it is," he said vaguely, shuffling through the pile of letters, "don't worry about it too much. Mr. Gross checks all the copy anyway before it's printed up."

Mr. Gross was the *Log's* faculty adviser. I felt a wave of relief remembering that he'd go over my answers; at least that way, I was sort of off the hook. I mean, if I gave bad advice, he could tell me and I could change it. And once he okayed the column, I could be sure I hadn't told anyone anything they shouldn't be told.

- reciprocate (ri SIP ruh kayt) **give or do something in return for something given or done**
- faculty adviser (FAK ul tee ad VY zer) **teacher who helps and guides a group of students in a club**

ALL THINGS CONSIDERED

1. The idea for the advice to the lovelorn column comes from (a) Chip Custer. (b) Caroline Wasserman. (c) Mr. Gross.

2. Most of the answers are supposed to be (a) serious. (b) funny. (c) dull.

3. Lovey Hart gets the first letters by (a) writing them herself. (b) putting up posters. (c) advertising in the school paper.

4. Chip tells her not to (a) use the name Lovey Hart. (b) tell anybody except her family who Lovey Hart is. (c) tell anybody at all who Lovey Hart is.

5. Caroline's father is the (a) faculty adviser to the school paper. (b) principal of the school. (c) head guidance counselor at the school.

6. He tells Caroline that (a) he does not like the idea of an advice column. (b) it is a good idea for students to help each other solve problems. (c) she should write the column.

7. The first letter is from a girl who (a) likes a boy who plays lacrosse. (b) used to be on drugs. (c) likes the boy who sits in front of her.

8. Carrie is not sure whether she should answer (a) silly letters. (b) letters with serious problems. (c) letters about problems she has not solved for herself.

9. Before anything is printed in the school paper, it has to be checked by (a) Mr. Gross. (b) Mr. Wasserman. (c) the principal.

10. Caroline is probably a girl who (a) has many boyfriends. (b) talks over friends' problems with them. (c) does not care about people.

THINKING IT THROUGH

1. Do you think that teenagers can give good advice to other teenagers? When should a teenager go to an adult for advice?

2. Many of Lovey Hart's letters are written in a humorous tone. Do you think her advice is meant to be serious? Do you think her advice is good?

3. Do you read any advice columns in your school or local paper? How do you decide when the writer is giving good advice? What qualifications should a writer have in order to give advice?

Relationships

Fact and Opinion

A **fact** is something you can check and prove to be true or false. An **opinion** is a person's belief about something or someone. It cannot be proven true or false. Most of Lovey Hart's advice is an expression of her opinion.

Which of the sentences below are facts and which are opinions? On a separate sheet of paper, copy the numbers of the sentences below. Write **F** for fact or **O** for opinion next to the number for each sentence.

1. Chip Custer was the editor of the *Log.*
2. Carrie would be the best person to write the advice to the love-lorn column.
3. Carrie has a lot of potential as a writer.
4. Lovey Hart is really Caroline Wasserman.
5. Carrie's father does not like the idea of Lovey Hart.
6. Carrie's father is wrong to object to Lovey Hart.
7. Carrie should tell her father that she is Lovey Hart.
8. Tennis is a better sport than lacrosse.
9. To have a friend you must first be one.
10. Mr. Gross checks the articles for the school paper.

Composition

Follow your teacher's instructions before completing *one* of these writing assignments.

1. Make a list of five problems with which teenagers may want help. Write each as a complete sentence. Then tell which problems only an adult should help solve, and which problems other teenagers could help solve.
2. How would you answer a letter if you were Lovey Hart? Look at the letters in this selection. Pretend that you are Lovey Hart and write an answer to one of them.

VOCABULARY AND SKILL REVIEW

Before completing the exercises that follow, you may wish to review the **bold-faced** words on pages 265–280.

I. **1.** A person who is *agonized* is (a) ready to do something. (b) in great pain. (c) alive and well.

2. If land is *parched*, it is (a) full of plants. (b) too muddy. (c) very dry.

3. Someone who *censors* writing (a) fixes the incorrect grammar. (b) refuses to allow certain ideas to be printed. (c) buys books for a school.

4. If the young man *resents* criticism, he (a) is glad to get useful ideas. (b) offers his own ideas on how to make improvements. (c) does not like what other people say.

5. If *competitiveness* is important to a team, the members (a) like to try to win. (b) travel a lot. (c) are more interested in fun than in winning.

6. An *acquaintance* is (a) a very good friend. (b) someone you know, but not very well. (c) a person you don't want to know.

7. She was *inspired*, so she (a) did not want to work. (b) had to rest for a while. (c) really wanted to do important work.

8. If we have *cordial* relations with another country, our two countries (a) are friendly. (b) have the same leaders. (c) share the same customs.

9. When you *acknowledge* a mistake, you (a) try to hide it. (b) correct it before anyone knows about it. (c) admit that you made it.

10. A ballplayer who has *potential* (a) is already a star. (b) has problems. (c) has the ability to do well.

II. On a separate sheet of paper, paraphrase the sentences below.

1. I pledge allegiance to the flag of the United States of America.

2. O say does that Star-Spangled Banner yet wave?

3. We hold these truths to be self-evident.

4. The buck stops here.

5. I regret that I have but one life to give for my country.

THE WOLF OF THUNDER MOUNTAIN

by Dion Henderson

▶ His grandpa had been after the wolf for years. Now he was going up the mountain to see his grandpa—and the wolf.

All the way to the station my mother kept giving me the same instructions she'd been giving me for a week. This was the first time I was allowed to take the train up north by myself to see Grandpa. Finally I reminded her how old I was. Then she said a funny thing. Growing up or growing old, my mother said, it doesn't make much difference how many birthdays you have. And all the way up north on the train I tried to figure out whether she was talking about me or Grandpa.

At the Settlement, the train stopped just long enough to let me off. The conductor helped me with the duffel bag. It was so heavy I could hardly lift it. I looked around for Grandpa, but he wasn't there yet. It wasn't hard to tell. Grandpa was about nine feet tall.

The lumberjacks sitting on the bench in front of the general store watched me. When I got close, one of them said did I figure I could stay overnight without any more gear than that. I put the duffel bag down and said politely that I figured I had enough gear to spend a year on Thunder Mountain. "Thunder Mountain," one of the other ones said. He was kind of polite, too, all of a sudden. He said, "You the boy that goes up there to see the wolf?"

I said, "That's the boy I am, all right."

Later on it turned out we meant different things when we talked about the wolf of Thunder Mountain. I meant the old gray wolf who got the moonlight in his eyes. The people in the Settlement meant Grandpa.

Just then there was a commotion up at the end of the street, and the people on the sidewalk started to go indoors. The street was empty, and then I heard Grandpa. He was singing a Chippewa war song.

Pretty quick he came in sight, driving the red horse on the dog cart. He never bothered with a car, because the first thing you had to cross on the way up the mountain was the Little Warrior. He said

- duffel bag (DUF ul BAG) large canvas bag, shaped like a closed tube, used for carrying clothing
- Chippewa (CHIP uh wah) a Native American group that lives in the northern United States and southern Canada

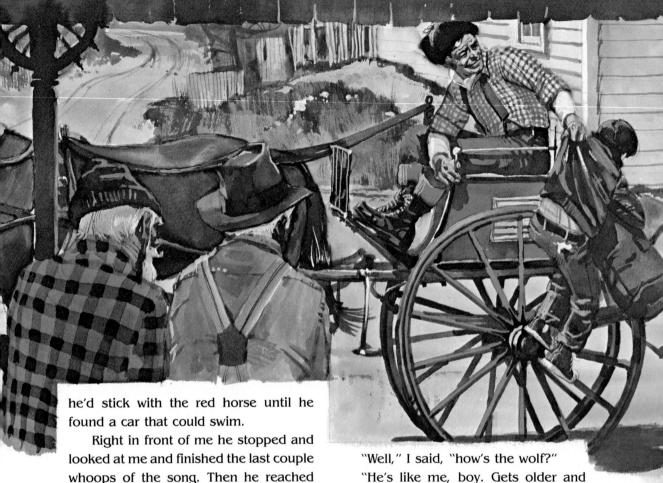

he'd stick with the red horse until he found a car that could swim.

Right in front of me he stopped and looked at me and finished the last couple whoops of the song. Then he reached down smiling and picked up me and the duffel bag together and put us on the seat.

I said, "I'm glad to see you aren't real puny yet."

"How's that?" Grandpa said.

"My mother said you ought to come back down to the city with me this fall, because you're getting too old and puny to stay on the mountain all winter."

"Might have known it," Grandpa said. "Your mother's been saying that for 30 years."

"Well," I said, "how's the wolf?"

"He's like me, boy. Gets older and maybe even a mite smarter, but no punier."

"Has he got a family this year?"

"No," Grandpa said, a little sadly. "Not anymore."

"Did you catch them?"

"I didn't fix to catch them, boy. But wolves are something like people. You fix to catch the smartest one of all, you have to catch all the young ones and the foolish ones and the ignorant ones first. That's what it is."

"Did you catch the puppies, too?"

- **puny** (PYOO nee) small and weak
- **mite** (MYT) little bit

286

"No." He sounded disappointed that I'd asked. "I ain't caught a pup since that first one, and that was an accident. I caught the she-wolf before there were any pups."

"I suppose you had to."

"Yes," Grandpa said. "I had to. He brought her down last year, and he showed me to her. Got so I knew they were following me and watching me. The old wolf was saying to his mate, 'See the way he does and learn all about him.'"

"So you had to catch her, all right."

"Yes." Grandpa felt better because I understood. "The old wolf knew it and I knew it."

"Does he know you're going to catch him, too?"

"I couldn't rightly say," Grandpa said. "I reckon he figures there's some question about that."

"But you will."

"Yes," Grandpa said. "I got to."

While we were talking, the red horse was picking his way up the logging road that led through the Norway pine and spruce trees.

"They wanted to build a road up Thunder Mountain." Grandpa said.

He meant the forestry people from the Settlement.

"What'd you tell them?"

Grandpa looked over at me, and the dark blue eyes twinkled and he smiled. "I told 'em that if any of them needed any toothpicks, they could come up and whittle them, one at a time."

Now we were across the stream, and the red horse was working hard, up the trail on Thunder Mountain.

Grandpa said, "You can't change a place like this a little bit. Either you don't change it at all, or you change it altogether."

"Maybe," I said, "maybe they'll build the road while you're down in the city spending the winter."

"That'll be the day," Grandpa said. "When I go down to the city to spend the winter, they're welcome to build the road."

It appeared I said the wrong thing again. So I asked him to tell me about how he and the wolf first met.

Of course, that was five or six years ago, when it started. The old wolf was a young wolf then, just another wolf. That was the spring there was no snow in the North country. The deer ranged widely from the yards where ordinarily they gathered in a herd. And the wolf came down early, following the deer.

Although Grandpa didn't trap much anymore, he saw the wolf's sign beside the body of a fawn and put out a trap, just to keep in practice. Because in the days when he trapped seriously, he was the kind of trapper that some violin players are musicians. The next day when he came back to the place where the trap was, he saw the wolf sitting there quietly.

Wolves are very intelligent. When a wolf like that is caught in a trap and he knows that he can't escape, he won't struggle. Instead, he will sit quietly full of hate and wait to see the man who has brought him to the end of his splendid journey. Grandpa said he understood this very well. The wolf, he said, looked at him while he prepared his revolver.

Then Grandpa looked at the wolf for the first time as an individual, and the wolf looked back at him fiercely.

But suddenly, the wolf came smoothly to his feet and with the magical wolf grace bounded beautifully and rapidly into nowhere, and he was gone. He wasn't caught in the trap after all. But he had been, Grandpa said. The wolf had stepped in the trap and two toes of his forefoot were still there.

The wolf had waited at the trap for him, to see the man so that he could recognize him again. And that was fair enough, Grandpa said, because the footprint with the toes missing let him recognize the wolf. But they did not meet again, face to face, for a long time, although they came close.

In the spring, the wolf brought a bride down while there still was snow. On the cold nights of late spring Grandpa would lie in his cabin and hear the signal yelps of the two wolves hunting.

Maybe he would not have trapped anymore for this wolf if it had not been for the people of the Settlement. There was a terrible situation, they said. A wolf pack had descended on the community. The people of the Settlement said, "Will you catch them?"

Grandpa put out his traps for the wolves. The pup was caught accidentally in a weasel set and drowned. Grandpa felt so bad about that, that he stopped trapping for that year. The next year he caught the she-wolf before she had pups. But he did not meet the old wolf face to face again until the night I remembered.

Grandpa did not have to tell me about that again. Maybe I was pretty young then, but I remembered all right. I was in my bunk in the cabin. Suddenly I was not asleep anymore. I was wide awake, straining my ears to hear something, and there was nothing. That was the trouble, there was no sound at all. There was silence all around.

I got out of my bunk and went to the door of the cabin. I went out on the porch and put my bare feet against fur. When I bent over to look, I saw it was Grandpa's cat. Dead. I looked around the clearing,

- bound (BOWND) leap; jump
- set (SET) trap placed to catch wild animals
- **strain** (STRAYN) cause to work as hard as possible

and there at the edge the heifer was lying, and I walked over there. The heifer was dead, too. And in their yard, the geese too—dead, dead, dead. I turned, suddenly frightened then, more frightened than I'd ever been, to run back to the cabin. But out of nowhere the wolf was there, in the yard, sitting between me and the cabin. I stood still. The wolf sat there, and the moon was in his eyes.

I don't know what would have happened then because by the wolf's reckoning I belonged to Grandpa, too. But it did not come to that. Suddenly my grandfather spoke from the cabin. The wolf turned smoothly and swiftly. Then the carbine crashed from the porch, and crashed again. The wolf fell heavily, and Grandpa came off the porch running. I tell you he was nine feet tall in the moonlight. But the wolf was gone.

Grandpa said, "I touched him that time, boy."

Now, riding up into the clearing behind the red horse, I recalled how frightened I had been. I felt that I must be very strong and brave to make up for it.

Grandpa went and sat on the porch. I unhitched the red horse and put him in the barn and rubbed him down. Then I said, "How about a trout for supper?"

"That's fine," Grandpa said.

"You want to catch him?"

"I believe I'll let you do it," Grandpa said.

I found a cricket and went down to the pool. I put the cricket on the hook and tied a little stick on the line a foot above it. Then I let it into the pool gently. Suddenly the rod bent and the line hummed, and I had a trout hooked.

When I went back up to the cabin, Grandpa still was sitting on the porch. He looked kind of tired. He said he'd let me fix supper, too. So I cleaned the trout, rolled it in cornmeal, and fried it in bacon grease. I fixed some beans in the skillet. For dessert I opened a can of peaches.

- heifer (HEF ur) **young cow**
- reckoning (REK uh ning) **way of thinking**
- carbine (KAHR byn) **short, lightweight rifle**

Right after we ate, Grandpa said he believed he'd go to bed, if I could clean things up.

"That'll be fine," I said. "I believe I'll sit up awhile."

The red horse had to be fed and turned out, but there weren't any other chores outside. When I was through, I built up the fire and sat down on the bearskin and looked around at the things in the cabin.

Next thing I knew it was morning and the fire was out. Grandpa was still sleeping. That was kind of funny. When I stopped to think, I didn't remember ever seeing Grandpa asleep before. But by the time I had the fire built up and breakfast ready, he was sitting on the edge of the bunk. He still looked tired.

"Reckon I won't eat any breakfast just now," he said. I must have had some sort of expression on my face, because he said, "Well, maybe just a mite."

He didn't eat much. When I finished he said, "I believe you'll have to go out and look at a couple of traps this morning."

"Yes, sir," I said. "Where are they?"

"Well, I'll draw you a kind of map," Grandpa said.

"Wolf traps?" I asked eagerly.

"Yes. Wolf traps." Grandpa smiled at me. "I calculate the old wolf was going to cross that way last night, and he won't cross there again for a year."

"He won't?"

"No," Grandpa said. "I understand him. To understand a wolf, you need only to think like a wolf. I have had more experience than the wolf has. That is my advantage."

"All right," I said. "If you will draw me the map."

"Be careful," Grandpa said. "You haven't had hardly any experience thinking like a wolf. One trap is in the trail, and you may find a hare in it. But there is another set, above the first, where a wolf might go in order to inspect the trap in the trail. You must be careful not to step in that yourself."

"Yes, sir," I said. "I'll bring them back."

"No," Grandpa said. "Spring them and leave them."

That was when I realized that Grandpa was sick. "Leave them?"

"Yes," Grandpa said. "If I have not caught him now, I will not try again. The wolf and I are both growing old. And maybe"—he smiled at me—"maybe as your mother says, puny."

I said, "Before I go to the traps, I could ride up and find Doc Champion."

"First the traps," Grandpa said.

He was very firm. I took the map and saddled the red horse. Then I came back into the house for the carbine. Grandpa was lying down again. I paused, worried, and he did not open his eyes, but he said, "First the traps."

So I went to the traps. It was a good

- **advantage** (ad VAN tij) something that helps one person win against another
- spring (SPRING) release a trap so that it cannot work

thing I was leading the horse when we got close to the traps, because suddenly he snorted and reared and almost pulled the reins out of my hand. I tied him to a tree and went on to the crossing place.

And there was the wolf, waiting, the old gray wolf with the white streak across the top of his head that must have been from Grandpa's bullet. He looked at me the same way he had looked that night when the moon was in his eyes. But he looked surprised to see me. His foreleg was caught deeply in the trap. There was no use struggling and he hadn't struggled.

I looked at the wolf and my hands were sweating so I almost dropped the carbine. When I brought it up I could not hold the barrel steady until I braced it against a tree. The old wolf sat there with his leg in the trap, looking at me with that strange expression, surprised at seeing me instead of someone else. He did not believe it when I brought the barrel steady on him. He did not believe any of it, not the trap nor the gun nor me nor the shot either. He did not believe any of it at all, and then he was dead.

I saw him lying there and smelled the powder smoke, and I did not believe it either. I went over and touched him with my foot and turned his head. Then I saw his eyes and I believed it. The eyes did not hate anymore.

Afterward I went back for the red horse. I took the rope from the saddle and tied it to the wolf and tied the other end to the saddle. I could not get the red horse any closer than that to the wolf, even if the wolf was dead. The red horse did not believe it either. That was how we got back to the cabin.

Grandpa still was lying down. Without opening his eyes, he said, "Was there a rabbit in the lower set?"

"Yes," I said. "And the wolf was in the other."

"Yes," Grandpa said. "To be sure."

"Really," I said. "The wolf."

"A wolf," Grandpa said, opening his eyes. "Some wolf."

"No," I said. "The old wolf. With the two toes missing and the bullet mark on his head."

• **brace** (BRAYS) make steady; hold firm

"No," Grandpa said. He sat up suddenly on his bunk. "No. Not after all this time."

"Yes," I said. "It was just the way you said. He was caught in the trap when he went to look at the place where you put the other trap."

"Where is he now?" Grandpa said, looking hard at me.

"He's out in the yard. I had to drag him behind the red horse. I thought you would want to see him."

"Drag him," Grandpa said, the beginning of a strange expression on his face. "He is not dead?"

"He is dead all right," I said. "He did not believe and the horse did not believe it and you do not believe it, but he is dead all right."

"No," Grandpa said. "He can't be dead."

The expression was getting clear on his face now.

"He is dead as anything. If you will come outside you can see him."

"No," Grandpa said.

I started to say something, then I saw quite suddenly the expression on Grandpa's face. He was not looking at me now. He was looking beyond me.

"I'm sorry," I said to my grandfather, without knowing why. "Did I do something wrong?"

"No," Grandpa said. "No."

"Maybe I could have let him go."

Grandpa said, "He did not ask you to."

"No," I said. "He looked at me with his teeth showing, he looked surprised."

"Yes," Grandpa said. "All right. He was old then, but not too old."

I didn't understand him.

"You must not worry," Grandpa said. "But neither a man nor a wolf should get too old."

"I didn't mean to do wrong."

"You did very well," Grandpa said. "You mustn't worry. But perhaps you will bury him now."

"All right," I said. "But shouldn't I go for Doc first?"

"No," Grandpa said. "Maybe after you bury the wolf, you will hitch up the red horse, and we will go down to the Settlement. I believe maybe your mother knows best."

"You mean about how you're getting —" I couldn't say it.

"Maybe she does," Grandpa said. "Maybe I ought to go back to the city with you, after all."

For a little while I didn't say anything. Then I said, "She didn't really think you'd come. She didn't think you'd leave the mountain."

Grandpa lay back on the bunk. He was smiling. "Things change, boy."

He looked at the ceiling, still smiling. "You come back here, boy, when you're grown up. There'll be a road. And the pine'll be gone. And you know what? There won't hardly be a mountain anymore."

He lay there. I went out and buried the wolf and hitched up the red horse. Afterward I went back and helped Grandpa out of the cabin and into the dogcart. He wasn't really nine feet tall. All the way to the Settlement I kept one arm around him and did my best not to cry.

ALL THINGS CONSIDERED ─────────────────────

1. At the beginning of the story the boy believes that his grandpa is (a) nine feet tall. (b) a wolf. (c) growing weak.

2. When Grandpa comes into town, the people seem to be (a) glad to see him. (b) amused at him. (c) afraid of him.

3. When they meet, the boy asks his grandpa (a) how the wolf is. (b) when he will leave the mountain. (c) when they will eat.

4. In this story, Grandpa is compared to the wolf because they both (a) are old and cunning. (b) are puny and helpless. (c) live on a mountain.

5. The wolf lost its toes (a) from a gunshot wound. (b) in a trap. (c) when they froze.

6. The wolf killed the cat, cow, and geese because (a) it was hungry. (b) they belonged to Grandpa. (c) they helped kill his mate.

7. The boy knows his grandpa is sick when Grandpa (a) goes to bed early. (b) wants the boy to look at the traps. (c) tells him to spring the traps and leave them.

8. The wolf is killed by (a) the boy. (b) Grandpa. (c) the trap.

9. When the boy returns, his grandpa does not believe (a) there was anything but a rabbit in the trap. (b) the dead wolf is the same wolf he had been hunting. (c) the boy did the right thing.

10. At the end, Grandpa agrees to (a) let the forestry people build a road. (b) return to town with the boy. (c) go to a doctor.

THINKING IT THROUGH ─────────────────────

1. How does the boy feel about his grandpa at the beginning of the story? How has his idea of his grandpa changed at the end? What causes the change?

2. What details in the story show that the boy is growing up?

3. What do you think the wolf means to Grandpa? Why does the wolf's death make Grandpa change his mind about going to the Settlement?

4. Who is the "Wolf of Thunder Mountain"? Can there be more than one answer to that question? Explain.

Literary Skills

Topic, Theme, and Character Growth

Often you can see a character change from the beginning of a story to the end. In this story, as in many others, the character's growth is related to the topic and the theme.

Can you find the stated topic? Reread the first paragraph. You can see that the topic is stated in the mother's words: "Growing up or growing old." The theme, however, is not stated directly. In your own words, state the theme of the story.

Find three details from the story that show the boy growing up. Next find three details that show the grandfather growing old. Compare your responses to those of your classmates.

When you are finished, see if you can figure out what the mother meant when she said, "Growing up or growing old, it doesn't make much difference how many birthdays you have."

Composition

Follow your teacher's instructions before completing *one* of these writing assignments.

1. The boy in this story can handle himself like an adult in several ways. He can fix a meal; he can take care of the horse without being asked; he can go out in the woods by himself; and he can take care of his grandfather's traps. Think of three ways in which you can handle yourself like an adult. Write a sentence describing each one.

2. In this story, Grandpa doesn't want to see the mountain change. Do you think that natural places should be left alone, or should they be changed to meet people's needs? Write a topic sentence that tells what you think. Then write several sentences of supporting details to explain your opinion.

THINGS

by Eloise Greenfield

▶ Some things last, some things do not. It's not just a matter
of how hard you try, but of what you choose.

Went to the corner
Walked in the store
Bought me some candy
Ain't got it no more
Ain't got it no more

Went to the beach
Played on the shore
Built me a sandhouse
Ain't got it no more
Ain't got it no more

Went to the kitchen
Lay down on the floor
Made me a poem
Still got it
Still got it

WAYS OF KNOWING

1. What three things did the speaker get or make? Which did not
   last, and which did? Explain.
2. How is a poem different from candy or a sandhouse? What
   makes a poem important to a person?
3. What other things can people keep, in the way that the speaker
   keeps the poem?

MY FIRST AUDITION

by Ingrid Bergman and Alan Burgess

▶ Sometimes it's hard to keep trying when you think you've failed. But that's when it's most important to try harder. Here's the story of a famous actress who learned that lesson when she was still a teenager.

There was a sense of urgency about the young girl in the wool skirt, tan sweater she had knitted herself, and common-sense walking shoes as she hurried toward the bright, open waterfront in Stockholm. Almost eighteen, Ingrid had been "the thinnest child ever."

She lacked confidence. She was terribly shy. She was frightened of people and of the world in general. And at that moment, she was extremely nervous. This was, without a doubt, the most important morning of her life. If she lost this opportunity, the world would end. She could forget her dreams of huge audiences applauding as she made her tenth bow at the conclusion of a successful opening night.

She had made her promise to Uncle Otto. If this attempt failed, she might become a salesperson or somebody's secretary. But her dreams of theatrical fame would have to stop.

Uncle Otto was convinced that actresses led wicked lives. She wouldn't even attempt to argue with him. She knew that he was trying to fill in for her father by seeing that she had a good education and was brought up properly. Her strong interest in playacting, her urge to go on the stage, distressed him a great deal. As a religious man, he felt it was his duty to save her from what he thought was a life of shame. As her guardian, he owed that to her father's memory. But he knew that she was stubborn and determined. He knew that to dismiss this dream of hers, not to give her even the opportunity, would leave her heartbroken. That would not be fair. Therefore, he had given her one chance.

"All right," he said. "You shall have the money you need for the extra lessons. You can try for the Royal Dramatic

- urgency (UR jun see) **great importance**
- waterfront **section of a town or city facing a body of water**
- Stockholm (STOK hohm) **capital city of Sweden**
- theatrical (thee AT ri kul) **having to do with theater or acting**

School. Take the examinations. Do whatever auditions you have to do. But if you fail, that's the end of it. Understand that! No more of this actress nonsense! And I want your promise because I know you will keep that promise. Do you accept this?"

Accept it? She had leaped at it. Without training, her chances of success would be small. She needed money for acting lessons—her own money, it was true, left in trust to Uncle Otto by her father. As for failing, that was unthinkable.

Certainly she knew that there were seventy-five applicants this year. Only a very few would be selected. But if the judges had to choose only *one*, then she *had* to be that one. Otherwise life would be unbearable.

She paused in front of the pale gray theater building. Beyond stretched the waterfront, backed by the curve of seven-story apartment buildings, shops and offices, and the copper domes turned green by the salty winds from the seas. She breathed in deeply. She belonged to this city of lakes and ferryboats and glittering water. She had been born no more than a hundred yards from this theater, in the apartment above her father's photography shop.

She looked at the theater's broad stone steps. Then she went around to the stage door and crossed to the office. The porter was peering at the list of applicants to be auditioned that morning.

She went outside again, crossed the road to the small park near the waterfront, and rehearsed her opening lines in her mind. Then she made one or two leaps to prepare for her magnificent entrance. After that she wandered around a bit, looked at the seagulls, and returned to the theater still fifteen minutes before her time.

- **audition** (aw DISH un) **a test for a part; tryout**
- **unthinkable** (un THINGK uh bul) **too terrible to think of or imagine**
- **applicant** (AP luh kent) **person who asks for something; one who applies**
- porter (POR tur) **doorkeeper**

Some weeks previously, she had delivered to the Royal Dramatic Theater her big tan envelope. It contained the three pieces she had chosen for her audition. The jury would select the two she was to perform. She knew that she could be failed at either the first or second test. If she failed, the porter would give her back the big tan envelope. That would be the end of her. But if she passed, she would get a smaller white envelope. That would tell her the date of the next audition and which of her audition pieces the jury wanted to hear.

Ingrid had discussed her choice with her drama teacher. "The first audition must be the most important," Ingrid said. "Practically everybody else will be doing serious dramatic pieces and wailing and weeping all over the stage. I think the jury will be so bored having to watch a parade of young girls breaking their hearts. Can't we make the jury laugh?"

Her teacher had agreed with her. "Good idea. And I know a play that would be just right. A peasant girl, pretty and happy, is teasing this bold country boy who's trying to flirt with her. She's even bolder than he is. She leaps across a small stream toward him. And she stands there, hands on hips, laughing at him.

How's that for an entrance? You make a flying jump out of the wings onto the stage. And then you stand there, legs apart, hands on hips, as if to say, 'Here I am. Look at me! Are you paying attention?'"

So this was the play Ingrid worked on.

You do the audition on the stage all by yourself. Any other dialogue is thrown at you from the wings. In my case, it was by the boy who was playing the country lad. He also acted as prompter in case I forgot my lines.

I wait in the wings. Suddenly I'm called. A run and a leap into the air, and there I am in the middle of the stage with that big joyful laugh that's supposed to stop them dead in their tracks. I pause and get out my first line. Then I take a quick glance down over the footlights at the jury. And I can't believe it! They are paying not the slightest attention to me. In fact, the jury members in the front row are chatting to the others in the second row. I froze in absolute horror. I simply can't remember the next line. The boy throws the cue at me. I get the line out. But now the jury members are talking in loud voices. I go blank with despair. At least they could hear me out and let me

- **wings** (WINGZ) **areas to the right or left side of a stage**
- dialogue (DY uh lawg) **words people say in a play**
- prompter (PROMP tur) **person who reminds actors and actresses of their lines but does not appear on stage**
- cue (KYOO) **signal that reminds an actor or actress of what to do next**

stage after about thirty seconds. I have to say, "They didn't listen to me. They didn't even think I was worth listening to." Now I can't think of becoming an actress ever again. So life isn't worth living. I walk straight across to the waterfront. And I know there's only one thing to do. Throw myself into the water.

Ingrid stood near the little booth where ferry tickets were sold. There was no one about. A few seagulls screamed in the distance; two or three floated on the water. The water was dark and shining. She took a step closer and peered at it. It was dark and shining . . . and *dirty*. She would be covered with dirt when they pulled her out. She'd have to swallow that stuff. Ugh! That was no good.

For now, the idea was forgotten. But still in despair, she turned and began the uphill walk through the shops and streets up to the apartment block where she lived. Her long slender legs had no life in them now.

In the apartment, her two cousins were waiting for her. They were the last people she wanted to see. Oh, for the comfort of her room where she could throw herself on the bed and weep and weep and weep and weep. . . . If only

finish. I can't concentrate, can't remember anything. I hiss to the boy, "What's my next line?" But before he can say it, I hear the voice of the chairperson of the jury, "Stop it, stop it. That's enough. Thank you, thank you miss . . . Next please, next please."

I walk off the stage. I don't see anybody or hear anything. I walk out through the lobby. I walk out into the street. And I'm thinking that now I have to go home and face Uncle Otto. Now I have to tell him that I'm thrown off the

- concentrate (KON sun trayt) **get one's mind to pay careful attention**
- **despair** (di SPAIR) **loss of hope**

Mama or Papa were alive and could comfort her. And now Britt and Margit just wouldn't leave her alone. "What's taken you so long?" "Yes, where have you been?" Stupid questions! How could she tell these two horrible, grinning girls how she felt?

"Lars Seligman was on the phone." Lars? What could he want? They were close friends. He was also trying to pass his auditions. "He said he'd been down to the office to collect his white envelope. And he asked what sort of envelope you got. And they said you got a white envelope too."

A white envelope? She got a white envelope! Could they be telling the truth? There was no time for discussion. She turned and ran. She raced down the stairs; she ran into the street. It was downhill all the way, but she would swear that her feet never touched the ground until she reached the theater. She arrived at the office as if blown in by a storm.

"What sort of envelope have I got? Please tell me what sort of envelope I've got!"

The porter smiled, "A white one, Miss Bergman. We wondered where you'd been. Here it is. Good luck!"

She tore it open. "Your next audition will be. . . ." She couldn't read the date. But she read the name of the piece they wanted her to audition. She floated out in the sweet summer air. Oh, how wonderful life was! Oh, how lucky she was to have Britt, and Uncle Otto, and Aunt Hulda. Wasn't Stockholm the most beautiful city in the world? And that dark shining water stretching away to some dis-

tant enchanted horizon was the most glorious thing she had ever seen.

I was so happy to be accepted that I didn't bother to ask why they had paid no attention to me after I leaped onto the stage. It was not until many years later in Italy that I got the answer. I was in Rome, and there was Alf Sjoberg who was one of the jury at the audition. And it all came back to me.

I said, "Tell me, please tell me, why at that first audition did you all treat me so badly? I could have killed myself, you treated me so nastily and disliked me so much."

Alf stared at me as if I'd gone mad. "Disliked you so much! Dear girl, you're crazy! The minute you leaped out of the wings onto the stage and stood there laughing at us, we turned around and said to each other, 'Well, we don't have to listen to her, she's in! Look at that confidence. Look at that stage presence. Look at that boldness.' You jumped out onto the stage like a tigress. You weren't afraid of us. We said to ourselves, 'No need to waste another second, we've got dozens more to look at. Next please.' So what are you talking about? You might never make as good an entrance in your life again."

- **enchanted** (en CHAN tid) under a spell; charmed
- stage presence a controlled, self-confident way of acting on stage

ALL THINGS CONSIDERED _____

1. In this story, Ingrid Bergman is (a) trying out for a part in a play. (b) hoping to get into acting school. (c) asking her Uncle Otto to change his mind about acting.

2. Her Uncle Otto believed that (a) actresses are bad people. (b) Ingrid would not be a good actress. (c) Ingrid was too skinny to be an actress.

3. The money to be used for the acting lessons was (a) money that Ingrid earned. (b) money left to Ingrid by her father. (c) Uncle Otto's money.

4. Before her audition, Ingrid went to (a) the waterfront. (b) a photography shop. (c) her drama teacher's home.

5. If applicants got back the big tan envelope, it meant they (a) passed. (b) failed. (c) must audition again.

6. For her first audition, Ingrid decided to play (a) a clown. (b) an unhappy child. (c) a young peasant girl.

7. She made an entrance by (a) leaping onto the stage. (b) coming out weeping. (c) falling.

8. She got upset when she realized that the jury members were (a) watching her prompter. (b) laughing at her. (c) not paying attention to her.

9. Right after the audition, she thought the best thing to do was (a) learn to be a secretary. (b) jump into the water. (c) start studying her next part.

10. Lars called and left a message that (a) he was sorry that she did not pass. (b) she had forgotten to meet him. (c) she had passed the first audition.

THINKING IT THROUGH _____

1. Ingrid Bergman says she was once very shy and lacked confidence. What did Alf Sjoberg say about her? What made the difference? Do you think pretending to be confident can help a person become more confident? Why or why not?

2. Do you think that Ingrid could have gotten what she wanted if she had not taken acting lessons? How important is it to train yourself to become good at what you want to do? Do you think that there are people with natural talent who do not need practice or training?

3. Ingrid Bergman nearly made a terrible mistake because she was disappointed and did not understand what was really happening. What else could she have done after the audition? How can people deal with disappointment?

Oral Interpretation

Reading Narrative and Dialogue

Oral interpretation is reading a selection aloud so that it can be understood and enjoyed by listeners. Many people like to read stories aloud. To read well, a person must first decide whether he or she is reading **narrative** or **dialogue**. Narrative is the part that tells the story. Dialogue gives the words spoken by the characters in the story.

Work with a group of classmates to read a section of "My First Audition" aloud. Each reader should choose one or more paragraphs. Include at least one paragraph of dialogue, such as Uncle Otto's words on page 296, or the drama teacher's words on page 298, or Alf Sjoberg's words on page 301.

Read the paragraphs through once. When you read narrative, think about the important ideas. When you read dialogue, think about what the character is feeling. Make sure each reader understands everything he or she is reading. Help each other with ideas for reading clearly.

Then practice. Practice several times until everyone is satisfied with his or her reading. You are now ready to read the section of the story aloud to the rest of the class.

Composition

Follow your teacher's instructions before completing *one* of these writing assignments.

1. Think of something you would like to be or become, such as an actress, a ballplayer, or a scientist. Write five things you should do to prepare yourself for what you want to be.
2. What would have happened if . . . ? That's a question many people often ask. Choose any story you have read in this book. Name the story. Then change one thing in that story and write a paragraph that tells how the story would have turned out differently.

VOCABULARY AND SKILL REVIEW

Before completing the exercises that follow, you may wish to review the **bold-faced** words on pages 286-301.

I. On a separate sheet of paper, mark each item *true* or *false.* If you write *false,* explain what is wrong with the sentence.
   1. A *puny* person can probably beat just about anyone in a wrestling match.
   2. It's easy to deal with a *mite* of difficulty.
   3. The sprinter was willing to *strain* himself in order to win the race.
   4. Being tall is an *advantage* for a basketball player.
   5. If your hand trembles, *brace* it against the arm of the chair.
   6. The actress waited in the *wings* to hear her cue.
   7. The actress planned to *audition* for the part.
   8. There were several *applicants* for the job, but only one was qualified.
   9. The sad news made them *despair.*
   10. The forest was *enchanted* from the witch's spell.

II. Choose two characters that you enjoyed reading about in this book. On a separate sheet of paper, tell how each character grew and changed. Then explain how the theme of the story helped you to understand that growth and change.

III. Choose a character from another story in this book or another book. Find dialogue in that story. Practice reading that dialogue. If you can, memorize part of it. When you know it well, practice reading the dialogue in front of a mirror and watch the expressions on your face until you feel you are speaking and acting naturally.

THE FINISH OF PATSY BARNES

by Paul Laurence Dunbar

▶ Things looked pretty bad for young Patsy and his mother. They had little money, and Patsy's mother was sick. Patsy was trying hard to help, but the only thing he knew about was horses. What were Patsy and his mother going to do?

His name was Patsy Barnes, and he lived in Little Africa. In fact, he lived on Douglass Street. By all the laws governing people and their names, he should have been Irish. But he was not. He was black, and very much so. That was the reason he lived on Douglass Street. Patsy's mother had found her way to Little Africa when she had come North from Kentucky.

Patsy was beyond reform. The truant officer and the terrible penalty of the compulsory education law had come into Little Africa. Time and time again, poor Eliza Barnes had been brought up on account of that son of hers. She was a hard-working, honest woman. Day by day, she bent over her tub, scrubbing away to keep Patsy in shoes and jackets that would wear out so much faster than they could be bought. But she never murmured, for she loved the boy with a deep affection, though his behavior was a sore thorn in her side.

She wanted him to go to school. She wanted him to learn. She had the idea that he might become something better, something higher than she had been. But for him, school had no charms. His school was the cool stalls in the big livery stable nearby. The arena of his activity was its sawdust floor. The height of his ambition was

- truant (TROO unt) **person who plays hooky from school**
- compulsory (kum PUL suh ree) **required (by the government, for example)**

to be a horseman. Either here or in the racing stables at the Fairgrounds he spent his truant hours. It was a school that taught much, and Patsy was as good a pupil as he was a constant visitor. He learned strange things about horses though he had only turned into his fourteenth year.

A man goes where he is appreciated. Then could this slim black boy be blamed for doing the same thing? He was a great favorite with the horsemen. He picked up many a dime or nickel for dancing or singing, or even a quarter for warming up a horse for its owner. He was not to be blamed for this. First of all, he was born in Kentucky. He had spent his baby days about the paddocks near Lexington where his father had lost his life on account of his love for horses. The little fellow had shed no tears when he looked at his father's bleeding body, bruised and broken by the wild young two-year-old horse he was trying to tame. Patsy did not sob or whimper, though his heart ached. Along with all his feeling of grief was a mad, burning desire to ride that horse.

His tears were shed, however, when they moved to Dalesford with the idea that times would be easier up North. Then, when he learned that he must leave his old friends, the horses and their masters whom he had known, he wept. The rather simple Fairgrounds at Dalesford proved a poor exchange for what he had known. For the first few weeks Patsy had dreams of running away—back to Kentucky and the horses and stables. Then after a while he settled himself to make the best of what he had. With a mighty effort, he took up the burden of life away from his beloved home.

Eliza Barnes, older and more experienced though she was, took up her burden less cheerfully than her son. She worked hard and made a scanty living, it is true. But she did not make the best of what she had. Her complainings were loud in the land. Her wailings for her old home struck the ears of any who would listen to her.

They had been living in Dalesford for a year nearly, when hard work and exposure brought the woman down to bed with pneumonia. They were very poor, too poor even to call in a regular doctor.

- paddock (PAD uk) **fenced-in area for horses**
- burden (BUR din) **heavy weight; great load**
- scanty (SKAN tee) **very small; hardly enough for what is needed**
- exposure (ek SPOH zhur) **being outside in bad weather**

There was nothing to do but to call in the city physician. Now this medical man had too many calls into Little Africa, and he did not like to go there. So he was very rough when anyone called him. It was even said that he was careless of his patients.

Patsy's heart bled as he heard the doctor talking to his mother.

"Now, there can't be any foolishness about this," he said. "You've got to stay in bed and not get yourself damp."

"How long you think I got to lay hyeah, doctah?" she asked.

"I'm a doctor, not a fortune-teller," was the reply. "You'll lie there as long as the disease holds you."

"But I can't lay hyeah long, doctah, case I ain't got nuffin' to go on."

"Well, take your choice—the bed or the boneyard."

Eliza began to cry.

"You needn't sniffle," said the doctor. "I don't see what you wanted to come up North for anyhow. Why didn't you stay down South where you belong?"

There was an angry being in the room, and that was Patsy. His eyes were full of tears that scorched him and would not fall. He dared not let his mother hear him swear. Oh! to have a stone, to be across the street from that man!

When the physician walked out, Patsy went to the bed, took his mother's hand, and bent over to kiss her. The little mark of affection comforted Eliza greatly. The mother-feeling overwhelmed her in one burst of tears. Then she dried her eyes and smiled at him.

"Honey," she said, "mammy ain' gwine lay hyeah long. She be all right putty soon."

"Nevah you min'," said Patsy with a choke in his voice. "I can do somep'n', an' we'll have anothah doctah."

"La, listen at de chile. What kin you do?"

"I'm goin' down to McCarthy's stable and see if I kin git some horses to exercise."

A sad look came into Eliza's eyes as she said, "You'd bettah not go, Patsy. Dem hosses'll kill you yit, des like dey did yo' pappy."

But the boy, used to doing pretty much as he pleased, was stubborn. Even while she was talking, he put on his ragged jacket and left the room.

• boneyard (BOHN yahrd) **slang term for a cemetery**

CHECKPOINT ────────────────────────────

Stop here and think about what you have read so far. Choose the answer that best completes each of the following sentences.

1. Patsy Barnes was born (a) on Douglass Street. (b) in Kentucky. (c) in Dalesford.

2. His mother loves him but worries because he (a) refuses to work. (b) doesn't like Kentucky. (c) is not interested in school.

3. His father died (a) in an accident with a horse. (b) of pneumonia. (c) because the family couldn't find a doctor.

4. Their difficult life becomes more difficult when (a) Patsy's mother gets sick. (b) Patsy runs away from home. (c) Patsy loses his job.

5. The city doctor (a) does the best he can. (b) won't come to Patsy's house. (c) does not seem to care.

Patsy was not wise enough to be diplomatic. He got right to the point with McCarthy, the stable man.

The big red-faced fellow slapped him until he spun round and round. Then he said, "Ye little devil, ye! I've a mind to knock the whole head off o' ye. Ye want harses to exercise, do ye? Well, git on that 'un an' see what ye kin do with him."

The boy's honest desire to be helpful had tickled the big, generous Irishman's peculiar sense of humor. From now on, instead of giving Patsy a horse to ride now and then as he had formerly done, he put into his charge all the animals that needed exercise.

It was with a king's pride that Patsy marched home with his first considerable earnings.

They were small yet, and would go for food rather than a doctor, but Eliza was very proud of him. It was this pride that gave her strength and the desire of life to carry her through the coming days of the crisis of her disease.

- diplomatic (dip loh MAT ik) **careful and wise in dealing with people**
- considerable (kun SID uh ruh bul) **fairly large**
- crisis (KRY sis) **dangerous time when a disease or problem can get better or worse**

Patsy saw his mother growing worse. He saw her gasping for breath. He heard the rattling as she drew in the little air that kept going through her clogged lungs. He felt the heat of her burning hands. He saw the pitiful appeal in her poor eyes. Soon he became convinced that the city doctor was not helping her. She must have another. But the money?

That afternoon, after his work with McCarthy, he was at the Fairgrounds. The spring races were on. He thought he might get a job warming up the horse of some independent jockey. He hung around the stables, listening to the talk of men he knew and some he had never seen before. One of those he had not seen before was a tall, thin man, speaking to a group of men.

"No, suh," he was saying to them. "I'm goin' to withdraw my hoss, because thaih ain't nobody to ride him as he ought to be rode. I haven't brought a jockey along with me, so I've got to depend on pick-ups. Now, people are set again my hoss, Black Boy, because he's been losin' regular. But that hoss has lost for the want of ridin', that's all."

The crowd looked in at the slim-legged, bony horse, and walked away laughing.

"The fools!" muttered the stranger. "If I could ride myself I'd show 'em!"

Patsy was gazing into the stall at the horse.

"What are you doing thaih?" called the owner to him.

"Look hyeah, mistah," said Patsy, "ain't that a bluegrass hoss?"

"Of co'se it is, an' one o' the fastest that evah grazed."

"I'll ride that hoss, mistah."

"What do you know 'bout ridin'?"

"I used to be roun' Mistah Boone's paddock in Lexington, an'—"

"Aroun' Boone's paddock—what! Look here, if you can ride that hoss to a winnin' I'll give you more money than you ever seen before."

"I'll ride him."

Patsy's heart was beating very wildly beneath his jacket. That horse. He knew that glossy coat. He knew that bony body and those flashing nostrils. That black horse there owed something to the orphan he had made.

• bluegrass (BLOO gras) a type of horse raised in Kentucky

The horse was to ride in the race before the last. Somehow out of odds and ends, his owner scraped together a suit and racing colors for Patsy. The colors were maroon and green, a curious combination. But then it was a curious horse, a curious rider, and a more curious combination that brought the two together. Long before the time for the race, Patsy went into the stall to become better acquainted with his horse. The animal turned its wild eyes upon him and neighed. He patted the long, slender head and grinned as the horse stepped aside as gently as a lady.

"He sholy is full o' spirit," he said to the owner, whose name he had found to be Brackett.

"He'll show 'em a thing or two," laughed Brackett.

"His dam was a fast one," said Patsy, without thinking.

Brackett whirled on him in a flash. "What do you know about his dam?" he asked.

The boy would have taken it back, but it was too late. Stammering, he told the story of his father's death and the horse's connection with him.

"Well," said Brackett, "if you don't turn out to be a hoodoo, you're a winner for sure. I'll be blessed if this don't sound like a story! But I've heard that story before. The man I got Black Boy from told it to me."

- curious (KYOO ree us) very strange; odd
- dam (DAM) mother, said of animals
- stammering (STAM ur ing) talking unevenly
- hoodoo (HOO doo) something that brings bad luck

When the bell sounded and Patsy went to warm up, he felt as if he were riding on air. Some of the jockeys laughed at his outfit. But there was something in him—or under him, maybe—that made him rise above their laughter. He saw a sea of faces about him, then saw no more. Only a shining white track appeared ahead of him. A restless steed was running with him around the curve. Then the bell called him back to the stand.

They did not get away at first, and back they trooped. A second start was also a failure. But at the third, they were off in a line as straight as a chalk mark. There were Essex and Firefly, Queen Bess and Mosquito, galloping away side by side, and Black Boy a neck ahead. Patsy knew the family reputation his horse had for endurance as well as fire. He began riding the race from the first. Black Boy came of blood that would not be passed. To this his rider trusted. At the eighth, the line was hardly broken. But as the quarter was reached, Black Boy had moved a length ahead, and Mosquito was at his flank. Then, like a flash, Essex shot out ahead under whip and spur, his jockey standing straight in the stirrups.

- steed (STEED) fine horse
- endurance (en DOO runs) the ability to keep on going
- flank (FLANGK) side near the back leg; hip
- spur (SPUR) metal piece attached to a rider's shoe to make the horse go faster

The crowd in the stands screamed. But Patsy smiled as he lay low over his horse's neck. He saw that Essex had made her best move. His only fear was for Mosquito, who hugged and hugged his flank. They were nearing the three-quarter post. He was tightening his grip on the black. Essex fell back; his move was over. The spurs dug him in vain.

Black Boy's breath touches the leader's ear. They are neck and neck—nose to nose. The black stallion passes him.

Another cheer from the stands. Again Patsy smiles as they turn into the stretch. Mosquito has gained a head. The black boy flashes one glance at the horse and rider who are so surely gaining upon him. His lips close in a firm line. They are halfway down the stretch, and Mosquito's head is at the stallion's neck.

For a single moment Patsy thinks of the sick woman at home and what that race will mean to her. Then his knees close against the horse's sides with a firmer dig. The spurs shoot deeper into the steaming flanks. Black Boy shall win. He must win! The horse that has taken away his father shall give him back his mother. The stallion leaps away like a flash and goes under the finish wire—a length ahead.

Then the band thundered. Patsy was off his horse. Very warm and very happy, he followed his mount to the stable. There, a little later, Brackett found him. He rushed to him and flung his arms around him.

"You little devil," he cried. "You rode like you were kin to that hoss! We've won! We've won!" And he began sticking money at the boy. At first Patsy's eyes bulged. Then he seized the money and got into his clothes.

"Goin' out to spend it?" asked Brackett.

"I'm goin' for a doctah fu' my mother," said Patsy, "She's sick."

"Don't let me lose sight of you."

"Oh, I'll see you again. So long," said the boy.

An hour later, he walked into his mother's room with a very big doctor, the greatest the druggist could direct him to. The doctor left his medicines and his orders. But, when Patsy told his story, it was Eliza's pride that started her on the road to recovery. Patsy did not tell her his horse's name.

ALL THINGS CONSIDERED ――――――――――――――

1. Patsy goes to the stable to ask if he can (a) exercise some horses. (b) be a jockey. (c) find a bluegrass horse.

2. At first, the money he earns goes to pay for (a) doctor bills. (b) food. (c) clothing.

3. After working for McCarthy, Patsy sees a (a) horse he knows. (b) man he knows. (c) tall, thin stranger.

4. A horse owner is looking for someone (a) to ride his horse in a race. (b) who knows how to exercise horses. (c) from bluegrass country.

5. Patsy knows that the horse (a) is a winner. (b) killed his father. (c) has a strange way of running.

6. Patsy slips when he lets the owner know he never (a) rode a horse. (b) rode a horse in a race. (c) liked horses.

7. When the horses start out, they run (a) across in a line. (b) with Black Boy at the rear. (c) with Black Boy in front.

8. Patsy remembers that the horse (a) starts slow and then gains speed. (b) lasts well through a race. (c) runs fast only at the start.

9. During the race he thinks of (a) Mr. Brackett. (b) his father. (c) his mother.

10. With the money he wins, Patsy gets (a) new clothing for his mother and himself. (b) a better doctor for his mother. (c) the medicines he could not afford before.

THINKING IT THROUGH ――――――――――――――

1. What special skills does Patsy have that help him earn money? Where did he learn those skills?

2. This story was written many years ago. What details in the story would be different now? What would be the same? Do you think Patsy could do the same thing if he lived today?

3. The author writes some of the dialogue the way people's words sound to him. There are three different ways of speaking in the story. Compare the ways Patsy, McCarthy, and Mr. Brackett speak. What are the differences?

4. What does the author mean by "The horse that has taken away his father shall give him back his mother"? Does the story work out that way? Does the ending satisfy you?

5. Do you think "Patsy" is an unusual name for a boy? How do you think he got such a name? Do you think a name can affect the way a person feels about himself or herself? If so, how?

UNIT REVIEW

I. Match the terms in column A with their definitions in column B.

A		B	
1.	author's purpose	**a)**	something that can be proved
2.	fact	**b)**	say something in your own words
3.	opinion	**c)**	the idea a story is about
4.	oral interpretation	**d)**	told by the author
5.	paraphrase	**e)**	a writer's ideas about a topic
6.	supporting detail	**f)**	sentence that tells the main thought of a paragraph
7.	stated	**g)**	reason for writing
8.	theme	**h)**	way something is read aloud
9.	topic sentence	**i)**	idea that cannot be proved
10.	topic	**j)**	something that adds to the topic sentence

II. Do people who try harder always win? Find one story in this unit in which the character is a winner and one story in which the character is not a winner. On a separate sheet of paper, write the name of each story. Then tell each story's topic and theme. Did the character grow in the story? If so, tell how. Also, tell what you think the author's purpose was in writing the story. Was it to entertain you, give you information, convince you of something? What does the purpose have to do with the theme?

III. Did you have to try harder to understand any selections in this unit? Which pieces made you try harder? What did you have to do to understand? Did you succeed? If so, how did you feel about yourself?

SPEAKING UP

Some writers help us see ways of trying harder to become better people. Here are speeches by two great writers of the English language. Each one creates an image that gets the idea across.

Choose one or both to read aloud. First read it to yourself. Make sure you understand the image and the theme of each. Practice reading it so that the most important ideas become clear.

NO MAN IS AN ISLAND

by John Donne

No man is an island entire of itself. Every man is a piece of the continent, a part of the main. . . . Any man's death diminishes me because I am involved in mankind. And therefore, never send to know for whom the bell tolls. It tolls for thee.

- main (MAYN) **mainland; land that is not separated by water**
- diminish (di MIN ish) **make smaller or less important**

315

FROM OTHELLO

by William Shakespeare

Good name in man and woman, dear my lord,

Is the immediate jewel of their souls.

Who steals my purse steals trash. 'Tis something, nothing.

'Twas mine, 'tis his, and has been slave to thousands.

But he that filches from me my good name

Robs me of that which not enriches him

And makes me poor indeed.

- 'tis (TIZ) **it is**
- 'twas (TWUZ) **it was**
- filch (FILCH) **steal**

WRITING YOUR OWN SKETCH

A *sketch* is a short word picture. Use the photograph to help you write a sketch. Combine what you have learned about character, setting, and plot.

1. **Prewriting:** First, select about two characters as the subjects of your sketch. Name your characters. Write a few sentences comparing or contrasting them. Next, list a few words or phrases that describe the setting. Finally, decide what is happening in the photograph and the order of the events.
2. **Writing:** Use your prewriting plan to write an opening paragraph that describes the characters. In the next paragraph, describe the setting. In the last paragraph, describe the plot.
3. **Revising:** Read your sketch. Have you included the most important details in the setting? Did you describe the characters' looks as well as their personalities? Have you described an action from beginning to end? Are your spelling, punctuation, and grammar correct? Make corrections and rewrite your paragraphs.

GREAT IDEAS

What is a great idea? If you asked a hundred people this question, you would probably get a hundred different answers.

Their answers would tell you two things. One, there are hundreds of great ideas in the world. Two, what's a great idea for one person may not be great for another.

In this unit, you'll read about a great idea from the world of science and a great idea from the Texas plains. You'll read about a familiar article of clothing that was once considered a great idea. In fact, you'll discover that reading itself can be a great idea.

As you'll see, you can come across a great idea almost anywhere. Keep your eyes and ears open—you won't want to miss out when a great idea comes your way.

319

THE SUBSTANCE AND THE SHADOW

An Aesop Fable

▶ The first great idea you'll read about comes from one of the oldest kinds of stories we have—a fable. This fable is an updated version of one of the oldest fables still told—a fable by Aesop (EE sop), a Greek slave who lived around 600 B.C. Can this old fable teach an important lesson to modern people?

Once upon a time a traveler was stuck in Azcan, a town that was no more than a watering place in the desert. Anxious to be on his way (the truth is, he was running from the police), the traveler went to the post office for help. There he met a stubby little man and introduced himself as Jack.

"Tell me, friend," he said, "is there someone in town who will rent me a horse for a day?"

"Jackie, my friend," said the stubby little man, "I, Felix, will be delighted to rent you my horse."

"Excellent," said Jack. "And how much will you charge?"

"Well," said Felix, "I think about—no, that is too much. Let's say—no, that is too much, too. Ten dollars is enough. Ten puny dollars."

"Felix, my friend," said Jack, "ten dollars is highway robbery."

"All right," said Felix. "Five dollars then. He is a very strong horse."

But having agreed on a price, they had to figure out a way for Jack to return the horse at the end of the day. If Jack traveled alone, as he wanted, how would the horse get back to Azcan? If they rode together on the horse, as Felix wanted, it would no longer be worth five dollars to Jack.

"He is a very strong horse," said Felix. "He will carry you, Jackie, and me, Felix, as easy as two little babes."

- **substance** (SUB stuns) the important part; the real part
- stubby (STUB ee) short and thick

320

"Ha!" laughed Jack, for he had seen the bony nag outside. "He looks pretty skinny to me."

"How can you say that?" said Felix, deeply hurt. "He is the biggest and strongest horse in all of Azcan."

"Felix, my friend," said Jack, "don't kid me. Your horse is the *only* horse in all of Azcan."

So they reached a compromise. Jack, since he was getting only half a horse, would pay only half of five dollars.

And they started on their way.

It was a very hot day (in Azcan, all days are hot), so at noon they stopped to rest. The sun burned down upon them in all its fury. It seemed there was no protection from it, but Felix knew what to do. He lay down in the shadow of the horse.

Jack, observing that this was a splendid idea, tried to share the shadow with Felix. But the shadow was not large enough to shade two men, a fact that stopped Jack for merely a moment. Looking mournfully at Felix, he said as gently as he possibly could, "I am sorry, Felix, but that shadow is mine."

"No, friend Jackie," answered Felix. "I was here first."

- nag (NAG) a horse of poor quality
- compromise (KOM pruh myz) settle a difference of opinion by agreeing that each person will give up part of what he or she demands

"First does not matter," said Jack. "I rented the horse, so I have the right to his shadow."

"Oh, no, Jackie!" answered Felix. "You rented the horse, not his shadow."

"Nonsense," said Jack. "When one rents a horse, the shadow is always—is necessarily—part of the deal."

"Jackie, you fool!" said Felix, raising his voice. "I own the horse, so I own his shadow, too."

"But I rented it!" Jack responded, raising his own voice.

"You rented just the horse," Felix shouted, sitting up now. "If you wanted the shadow, you should have rented it."

"Felix, you cheater!" cried Jack, shaking his fist. "Give me my shadow or I'll have you arrested when we get to town." (Jack would not, of course, go near a policeman.)

The two men argued, shouting and shaking their fists, until Jack stamped his foot and sent a cloud of sand into the face of Felix. At this, Felix leaped to his feet and attacked Jack with his fists. Jack fought back. Soon the two were at it hand and foot. Swinging with their arms and kicking with their legs, they threw themselves against the horse.

The angry blows sent the horse running off across the desert. This stopped the fight, of course, and the two men sat there, exhausted and sore and hot, watching both the horse and his shadow disappear into the distance.

They had learned, though too late to do them any good, that if you fight over the shadow you may lose the substance.

ALL THINGS CONSIDERED

1. The setting of this fable is (a) a mountain top. (b) a hot desert-like area. (c) a jungle.
2. Jack wants to (a) hitchhike to a city. (b) rent a horse. (c) buy a car.
3. Jack thinks that Felix is trying to (a) charge too much. (b) sell a horse. (c) rob him.
4. Because of the compromise, Felix goes with Jack but (a) walks alongside the horse. (b) asks Jack to walk alongside the horse. (c) charges half as much.
5. When they rest, Felix lies down (a) by a stream. (b) under a tree. (c) in the shadow of the horse.
6. Jack argues that he (a) rented the shadow. (b) bought the horse. (c) needs to rest.
7. Felix argues that he owns the horse, so he (a) can ride it. (b) owns the shadow, too. (c) can take it away from Jack.
8. The argument leads to (a) Jack's running off. (b) Felix's victory. (c) a fight between Jack and Felix.
9. They fight over the shadow and (a) lose their friendship. (b) lose the substance. (c) lose their patience.
10. You can conclude that both Felix and Jack (a) owned the shadow. (b) learned an important lesson. (c) searched for a new horse.

THINKING IT THROUGH

1. State the moral of this fable in your own words. Is it an important lesson to learn? Why is a fable a good way to teach a lesson?
2. Suppose Jack and Felix had each behaved a little less selfishly. Do you think the fable would have ended differently? Explain.
3. Suppose the moral of this fable were "First come, first served." Change the ending of the fable so that it now illustrates this very different moral.

Literary Skills: Review

If you wish to review any term in *italics* in this exercise, refer to the Glossary of Terms.

I. On a separate sheet of paper, answer each question by writing a complete sentence. Give details to support your answers.

1. What is the *setting* of "The Substance and the Shadow"?
2. What is the *theme* of "The Substance and the Shadow"?
3. Is "The Substance and the Shadow" *fiction* or *nonfiction*?

II. On a separate sheet of paper, choose the best ending for each statement. Write the complete sentence.

1. The horse could be considered a *character* in "The Substance and the Shadow" because (a) it talks to its owner. (b) its action leads to the conclusion of the story. (c) it fools the two men.
2. The *conflict* in "The Substance and the Shadow" is between (a) people. (b) people and nature. (c) people and machines.
3. The *conclusion* of "The Substance and the Shadow" comes immediately after the men (a) agree on a price for renting the horse. (b) stop to rest. (c) fight over the shadow.

Composition

Follow your teacher's instructions before completing *one* of these writing assignments.

1. Write a sentence that shows an important characteristic of Jack, and a separate sentence that shows an important characteristic of Felix. Your sentence might begin like this: "Jack is the kind of person who . . . "
2. A fable is usually a story with a moral. Tell another story showing that by fighting over the shadow, you may lose the substance. You might tell about two members of a musical group who argue about who will play the lead guitar. What might happen? (Your characters must do something to show that by fighting over the shadow, they might lose the substance.)

THE MAN WHO WAS A HORSE

by Julius Lester

▶ How do cowboys learn about the animals they work with? One way is the way of the experts—to learn to do what others before you have done. Another way is the way of Bob Lemmons, a black cowboy.

Bob Lemmons was a real person. This story tells how he did what no other cowboy had ever done before.

It wasn't noon yet, but the sun had already made the Texas plains hotter than an oven. Bob Lemmons pulled his wide-brimmed hat tighter to his head and rode slowly away from the ranch.

"Good luck, Bob!" someone yelled.

Bob didn't respond. His mind was already on the weeks ahead. He walked his horse slowly, being in no particular hurry. That was one thing he had learned early. One didn't capture a herd of mustang horses in a hurry. For all he knew, a mustang stallion might have been watching him at that very moment. And if he were galloping, the stallion might get suspicious and take the herd miles away.

As far as Bob could see, the land was flat, stretching unbroken like the cloudless sky over his head until the two seemed to meet. Nothing appeared to be moving except him on his horse. But he knew that a herd of mustangs could be galloping near the horizon line at that moment and he would be unable to see it until it came much closer.

He rode north that day, seeing no sign of mustangs until close to evening, when he came across some tracks. He stopped and dismounted. For a long while he stared at the tracks until he was able to identify several of the horses. As far as he could determine, it seemed to be a small herd of a stallion, seven or eight mares, and a couple of colts. The tracks were no more than three days old, and he half expected to come in sight of the herd the next day or two. A herd didn't travel in a straight line, but ranged back and forth within what the stallion considered his territory. Of course, that could be the size of a county. But Bob knew he was in it, though he had not seen a horse.

He untied his blanket from behind the saddle and laid it out on the ground. Then he removed the saddle from the

- mustang (MUS tang) **wild horse**
- dismount (dis MOUNT) **get off a horse, bicycle, etc.**

horse and hobbled the animal to a stake. He didn't want a mustang stallion coming by during the night and stealing his horse. Stallions were good at that. Many times he had known them to see a herd of tame horses and, for who knew what reason, become attracted to one mare and cut her out of the herd.

He took his supper out of the saddlebags and ate slowly as the chilly night air seemed to rise from the very plains that a few short hours before had been too hot for a man to walk on. He threw the blanket around his shoulders, wishing he could make a fire. But if he had, the smell of wood-smoke in his clothes would have been detected by any herd he got close to.

After eating he laid his head back against his saddle and covered himself with his thick Mexican blanket. The chilliness of the night made the stars look to him like shining slivers of ice. Someone

had once told him that the stars were balls of fire, like the sun. Bob didn't feel them that way. But he wasn't educated, so he wouldn't dispute with anybody about it. Just because you gave something a name didn't mean that that was what it actually was, though. The thing didn't know it had that name, so it just kept on being what it thought it was. And as far as he was concerned, people would be better off if they tried to know a thing like it knew itself. That was the only way he could ever explain to somebody how he was able to bring in a herd of wild horses by himself. The way other people did it was to go out in groups of two and three and run a herd until it almost dropped from exhaustion. He guessed

- hobble (HAHB ul) a horse is hobbled when two legs are tied loosely together so it cannot move freely
- **dispute** (dis PYOOT) argue

326

that was all right. It worked. But he wouldn't want anybody running him to and fro for days on end, until he hardly knew up from down or left from right.

Even while he was still a slave, he'd felt that way about mustangs. Other horses, too. But he had never known anything except horses. Born and raised on a ranch, he had legally been a slave until 1865, when the slaves in Texas were freed. He had been 18 at the time and hadn't understood when Mr. Hunter had come and told him that he was free. That was another one of those words, Bob thought. Even as a child, when his father told him he was a slave, he'd wondered what he meant. What did a slave look like? What did a slave feel like? He didn't think he had ever known. He and his parents had been the only black people on the ranch and he guessed it wasn't until after he was "freed" that he saw another black person. He knew sometimes, from the names he heard the cowboys use, that his color somehow made him different. He heard them talking about "fighting a war over slavery," but it meant nothing to him. So when Mr. Hunter had told him he was free, that he could go wherever he wanted to, he nodded and got on his horse and went on out to the range to see after the cattle like he always had. He smiled to himself, wondering how Mr. Hunter had ever gotten the notion that he couldn't have gone where he wanted.

A few months after that he brought in his first herd of mustangs. He had been seeing the wild horses since he could remember. The first time had been at dusk one day. He had been playing near the corral when he happened to look toward the mesa and there, standing on top of it, was a lone stallion. The wind blew against it, and its mane and tail flowed in the breeze like tiny ribbons. The horse stood there for a long while. Then, without warning, it suddenly wheeled and galloped away. Even now Bob remembered how seeing that horse had been like looking into a mirror. He'd never told anyone that, sensing how people might think him a little touched in the head. Many people thought it odd enough that he could bring in a herd of mustangs by himself. But, after that, whenever he saw one mustang or a herd, he felt like he was looking at himself.

One day several of the cowboys went out to capture a herd. The ranch was short of horses and no one ever thought of buying horses when there were so many wild ones. He had wanted to tell them that he would bring in the horses, but they would have laughed at him. Who'd ever heard of one man bringing in a herd? So he watched them ride out, saying nothing. A few days later they were back, tired and disgusted. They hadn't even been able to get close to a herd.

That evening Bob timidly suggested to Mr. Hunter that he be allowed to try.

• mesa (MAY suh) ?

327

Everyone laughed. Bob reminded them that no one on the ranch could handle a horse like he could, that the horses came to him more than anyone else. The cowboys acknowledged that that was true, but it was impossible for one man to capture a herd. Bob said nothing else. Early the next morning he rode out alone, having asked the cook to leave food in a saddlebag for him on a tree in the north pasture every day. Three weeks later the cowboys were sitting around the corral one evening and looked up to see a herd of mustangs galloping toward them, led by Bob. Despite their amazement, they moved quickly to open the gate, and Bob led the horses in.

That had been some 20 years ago, and long after Bob left the Hunter Ranch he found that everywhere he went he was known. He never had trouble getting a job. But capturing mustangs was only a small part of what he did. Basically he was just a cowboy who worked from sunrise to sunset, building fences, herding cattle, branding calves, pitching hay, and doing everything else that needed to be done.

Most cowboys had married and settled down by the time they reached his age, but Bob had long ago relinquished any such dream. Once he'd been in love with a Mexican girl named Pilar, but her father didn't want her to marry a "colored" man. It was another lesson he had to learn about people—or about some people. Some people thought that Bob's skin color somehow made a difference. It made a big enough difference to Pilar's father for him to stop Pilar from marrying Bob. After that, he decided not to be in love again. It was a decision he never regretted. Almost every morning when he got up and looked at the sky lying full and open and blue, stretching toward forever, he knew he was married to something. He wanted to say the sky, but it was more than that. He wanted to say everything, but he felt that it was more than that, too. How could there be more than everything? He didn't know, but there was.

The sun awakened him even before the first arc of its roundness showed over the horizon. He saddled his horse and rode off, following the tracks he had discovered the previous evening. He followed them west until he was certain they were leading him to the Pecos River. He smiled. Unless it was a herd traveling through, they would come to that river to drink every day. Mustangs never went too far from water, though they could go for days without a drop if necessary. The Pecos was still some distance ahead, but he felt his horse's body quiver slightly, and she began to strain forward against his tight hold on the reins. She smelled water.

"Sorry, honey. But that water's not for you," he told the horse. He wheeled

---

- corral (kuh RAL) **pen for horses and cattle**
- relinquish (ruh LING kwish) **?**
- **arc** (ARK) **any part of a circle**

around and galloped back in the direction of the ranch until he came to the outermost edge of what was called the west pasture. It was still some miles from the ranch house itself, and today Bob couldn't see any cattle grazing up there.

But on a tree at the outer edge of the ranch was a saddlebag filled with food. Each day one of the cowboys would bring a saddlebag of food up there and leave it for him. He transferred the food to his own saddlebags. He was hungry but would wait until evening to eat. The food had to have time to lose its human odor, an odor that mustangs could pick out of the slightest breeze. He himself would not venture too close to the horses for another few days, not until he was certain that his own odor had become that of his horse.

He rode southward from the pasture to the banks of the Nueces River. There he dismounted, took the saddle off his horse, and let her drink her fill and wade in the stream for a while. It would be a few days before she could drink from the Pecos. The mustangs would have noticed the strange odor of horse and man together, and any good stallion would have led his mares and colts away. The success of catching mustangs, as far as Bob was concerned, was never to hurry. If

necessary he would spend two weeks getting a herd accustomed to his distant presence once he was in sight of them.

He washed the dust from his face and filled his canteen. He lay down under a tree, but its shade didn't offer much relief from the heat of high noon. The day felt like it was on fire and Bob decided to stay where he was until the sun began its downward journey. He thought Texas was probably the hottest place in the world. He didn't know, not having traveled much. He had been to Oklahoma, Kansas, New Mexico, Arizona, and Wyoming on cattle drives. Of all the places,

- pasture (PAS chur) **a grassy field or hillside**
- grazing (GRAYZ ing) **feeding on growing grass**
- Nueces River (noo AY says) **a river in southern Texas flowing into the Gulf of Mexico**
- canteen (kan TEEN) **a small container for carrying water and other liquids**

he liked Wyoming the most, because of the high mountains. He'd never seen anything so high. There were mountains in Texas, but nothing like that. Those mountains just went up and up and up until it seemed they would never stop. But they always did, with snow on the top. After a few days, though, he wasn't sure that he did like the mountains. Even now he wasn't sure. The mountains made him feel that he was penned in a corral, and he was used to spaces no smaller than the sky. Yet he remembered Wyoming with fondness and hoped that some year another cattle drive would take him there.

The heat was still intense when Bob decided to go north again and pick up his trail. He would camp close to the spot where his mare had first smelled the Pecos. That was close enough for now.

In the days following, Bob moved closer to the river until one evening he saw the herd come streaming out of the hills, across the plain, and to the river. He was some distance away, but he could see the stallion lift his head and sniff the breeze. Bob waited. Although he couldn't know for sure, he could feel the stallion looking at him, and for a tense moment Bob didn't know if the horse would turn and lead the herd away. But the stallion lowered his head and began to drink and the other horses came down to the river.

Bob sighed. He had been accepted.

The following day he crossed the river and picked up the herd's trail. It was not long after sunrise before he saw them grazing. He went no closer, wanting only to keep them in sight and, most important, make them feel his presence. He was glad to see that after a moment's hesitation, the stallion went back to grazing.

Bob felt sorry for the male horse. It always had to be on guard against dangers. If it relaxed for one minute, that just might be the minute a nearby panther would choose to strike, or another stallion would challenge him for the lead of the herd, or some cowboys would throw out their ropes. He wondered why a stallion wanted the responsibility. Even while the horses were grazing, Bob noticed that the stallion was separate, over to one side, keeping a constant lookout. He would tear a few mouthfuls of grass from the earth, then raise his head high, looking and smelling for danger.

At various times throughout the day Bob moved a few hundred yards closer. He could see it clearly now. The stallion was brown, the color of the earth. The mares and colts were black and brown. No sorrels or duns in this herd. They were a little smaller than his horse. But all mustangs were. Their size, though, had nothing to do with their strength or

---

- penned (PEND) **shut in; confined**
- intense (in TENS) **?**
- **hesitation** (hez uh TAY shun) **failure to act promptly**
- sorrel (SOHR ul) **reddish brown**
- dun (DUN) **dull brown**

endurance. There was no doubt that they were the best horses. He, however, had never taken one from the many herds he had brought in. It wasn't that he wouldn't have liked one. He would have, but for him to have actually ridden one would have been like taking a piece of the sky and making a blanket. To ride with them when they were wild was all right. But he didn't think any man was really worthy of riding one, even though he brought them in for that purpose.

By the sixth day he had gotten close enough to the herd that his presence didn't attract notice. The following day he moved closer until he and his mare were in the herd itself. He galloped with the herd that day, across the plain, down to the river, up into the hills. He observed the stallion closely, noting that it was a good one. The best stallions led the herd from the rear. A mare always led from the front. But it was only at the rear that a stallion could guard the herd and keep a mare from running away. The stallion ran up and down alongside the herd, biting a slow mare on the rump or ramming another who threatened to run away or to bump a third. The stallion was king, Bob thought, but he worked. It didn't look like much fun.

He continued to run with the herd a few days more. Then came the critical moment when, slowly, he would begin to give directions of his own, to challenge the stallion in little ways until he had completely taken command of the herd and driven the stallion off. At first he would simply lead the herd in the direction away from the one the stallion wanted to go. Then, just before the stallion became enraged, he would put it back on course. He did this many times, getting the stallion confused as to

- **endurance** (en DOOR uns) ability to keep going
- **critical** (KRIT uh kul) at an important moment

whether or not there was a challenger in his midst. But enough days of it and the stallion gradually wore down, knowing that something was happening but unable to understand what. When Bob was sure the herd was in his command, he merely drove the stallion away.

Now came the fun. For two weeks Bob led the herd. Unlike the stallion, he chose to lead from the front, liking the sound and feel of the wild horses so close behind. He led them to the river and watched happily as they splashed and rolled in the water. Like the stallion, however, he kept his eyes and ears alert for any sign of danger. Sometimes he would pretend he heard something when he hadn't and would lead the herd quickly away simply as a test of their willingness to follow him.

At night he stopped, unsaddled his horse, and laid out his blanket. The herd grazed around him. During all this time he never spoke a word to the horses, not knowing what effect the sound of a voice might have on them. Sometimes he wondered what his own voice sounded like. And sometimes he even wondered if he would return to the ranch and find himself able only to snort and neigh, as these were the only sounds he heard. There were other sounds though, sounds that he couldn't reproduce, like the flaring nostrils of the horses when they were galloping, the dark, bulging eyes, the

flesh quivering and shaking. He knew that he couldn't hear any of these things—not with his ears at least. But somewhere in his body he heard every ripple of muscles and bending of bones.

The longer he was with the herd, the less he thought. His mind slowly emptied itself of anything relating to his other life and refilled with sky, plain, grass, water, and shrubs. At these times he was more aware of the full-bodied animal beneath him. His own body seemed to take on a new life and he was aware of the wind against his chest, of the taut muscles in his strong legs and the strength of the muscles in his arms, which felt to him like the forelegs of his horses. The only thing he didn't feel he had was a tail to float in the wind behind him.

Finally, when he knew that the herd would follow him anywhere, it was time to take it in. It was a day he tried to keep away as long as possible. But even he began to tire of going back to the west pasture for food and sometimes having to chase a horse that had tried to run away from the herd. He had also begun to weary of sleeping under a blanket on the ground every night. So one day, almost a month after he had left, he rode back toward the ranch until he saw one of the cowhands and told him to get the corral ready. Tomorrow he was bringing them in.

The following morning he led the

- **reproduce** (ree proh DOOS) **copy**
- flare (FLAIR) **spread out**
- taut (TAWT) **?**

herd on what he imagined was the ride of their lives. Mustangs were made to run. All of his most vivid memories were of mustangs, and he remembered the day he had seen a herd of what must have been at least a thousand of them galloping across the plains. The earth was a dark ripple of movement, like the swollen Nueces River at floodtime. And though his herd was much smaller, they ran no less beautifully that day.

Then, toward evening, Bob led them east, galloping, galloping, across the plains. And as he led them toward the corral, he knew that no one could ever know these horses by riding on them. One had to ride with them, feeling their hooves pound and shake the earth, their bodies glistening so close by that you could see the thin straight hairs of their

shining coats. He led them past the west pasture, down the slope, and just before the corral gate, he swerved to one side, letting the horses thunder inside. The cowboys leaped and shouted, but Bob didn't stay to hear their congratulations. He slowed his mare to a trot and then to a walk to cool her off. It was after dark when he returned to the ranch.

He took his horse to the stable, brushed her down, and put her in a stall for a well-earned meal of hay. Then he walked over to the corral, where the mustangs mingled restlessly. He sat on the rail for a long while, looking at them. They were only horses now. Just as he was only a man.

After a while he climbed down from the fence and went into the bunkhouse to go to sleep.

• **mingle** (MING gul) mix together

ALL THINGS CONSIDERED

1. Bob Lemmons was basically a (a) cowboy. (b) horse thief. (c) horse trainer.

2. Bob's special skill was (a) capturing wild horses. (b) taming wild horses. (c) training other cowboys.

3. Bob learned that it was best to approach the horses (a) from the rear. (b) from the side. (c) very slowly.

4. Bob thought he could know a thing by (a) studying it in books. (b) talking to it. (c) knowing it the way it knew itself.

5. Others caught wild horses by (a) setting traps. (b) running them until they became tired. (c) lassoing them.

6. Bob could round up a herd of wild horses in (a) an afternoon. (b) about a week. (c) about three weeks.

7. Bob approached the wild horses only after (a) they became tired. (b) his own odor mixed with his horse's. (c) they reached the river.

8. Bob's method was to (a) take the place of the leader slowly. (b) shoot the leader. (c) chase the leader away suddenly.

9. When Bob became the leader of the herd, he (a) led them back to the corral. (b) acted as their leader for two weeks. (c) talked to them gently all day.

10. You can conclude that Bob Lemmons (a) understood horses better than most cowboys did. (b) always owned horses. (c) was smarter than any other cowboy of the time.

THINKING IT THROUGH

1. How do you think Bob Lemmons learned his special skill? What kind of person did he have to be to learn this skill? Do you think other cowboys could have learned this skill? Why or why not?

2. On page 327 you learned that Bob never told anyone how he could put himself in the place of the horse. He sensed that people might think him a little touched in the head. Why would people have thought he was a little crazy? What do you think about Bob's ability to put himself in the place of the horse? Can humans ever put themselves in the place of animals?

3. Bob Lemmons was a slave before he became a cowboy. Do you think this was unusual? Why? What was the background of other cowboys you have learned about?

Vocabulary and Sentence Meaning: Review

Here are four words from "The Man Who Was a Horse." Next to each word is the number of the page and paragraph where it appears. Look back at the story for context clues that will help you figure out the meaning of each word. When you know the meanings, match each word in column **A** with its correct meaning in column **B**.

A	**B**
1. mesa (page 327, paragraph 3)	**a.** very strong
2. relinquish (page 328, paragraph 3)	**b.** tight
3. intense (page 330, paragraph 2)	**c.** give something up
4. taut (page 332, paragraph 4)	**d.** a flat-topped hill

Building from Details: Review

Write one sentence that answers each of the five **W** questions about "The Man Who Was a Horse."

1. Who was Bob Lemmons?
2. What did he do?
3. Where did he do this?
4. When did he do this?
5. Why did he do this?

Composition

Follow your teacher's instructions before completing *one* of these writing assignments.

1. Look at the first two sentences of the story again. Notice what they tell about the setting and main character. Rewrite these sentences using your own words. If you want, you can use three or even four sentences in your rewriting.

2. Write a paragraph that tells what you think of Bob Lemmons. Try to use at least four of the following words in your paragraph:

interesting   different   odd   nature   expert

FUELED

by Marcie Hans

▶ Sometimes, it is easy to overlook small, everyday events.
But small, everyday events often deserve as much attention
as big, dramatic ones.

Fueled
by a million
man-made
wings of fire—
the rocket tore a tunnel
through the sky—
and everybody cheered.
Fueled
only by a thought from God—
the seedling
urged its way
through the thicknesses of black—
and as it pierced
the heavy ceiling of the soil—
and launched itself
up into outer space—
no
one
even
clapped.

WAYS OF KNOWING

1. How is the flight of a rocket like the growth of a seedling? How
   are these two events different?

2. Why do you suppose people would cheer a rocket launching but
   not notice the growth of a seedling? Do you think an event such
   as the growth of a seedling deserves to be cheered? Explain.
   What other little events that happen each day deserve to be
   cheered?

- fueled (FYOOLD) supplied with power
- seedling (SEED ling) a young plant grown from a seed
- pierce (PEERS) go through

336

THE BLACK BOX
A SCIENCE PARABLE

by Albert B. Carr

▶ For some problems, there is no sure answer. What can we do to try to solve problems like these? This science parable tells you what scientists do.

A parable (PAR uh bul)—like a fable—is a short story that teaches a lesson. In a fable the lesson is directly stated. In a parable, however, the reader must look for meaning hidden in the story.

Once upon a time some boys and girls were walking on the beach, just looking for what there was to find. But their findings had not been very good. Except for a few shells, their pockets were empty. They had just about decided to give up their looking and go swimming when they saw it lying there on the sand. It was black, all black—a black box.

The boys and girls approached the box carefully, for they had never seen a box quite like it before. They wondered what it could be, what it was doing there, where it might have come from, and what it might contain. They looked at it, all six sides of it. It wasn't shiny; it wasn't dull. It wasn't heavy; it wasn't light. It wasn't rough; it wasn't smooth. It wasn't big; it wasn't small. It really wasn't anything special—just a black box.

The girls and boys picked up the box and tried to open it, but they couldn't. No matter how hard they tried, they could not open the black box. They used their hands. They used their feet. They shook it. They banged it with rocks. They soaked it in the ocean water. They threw it down hard on the sand. They even used their teeth and tried to bite it open. But no matter what they did, they could not open the black box.

Then one of them said: "Maybe it's not a box at all, and that's why it can't be opened! Maybe it's just a black block!" But they knew it

wasn't a block. They knew it was a box because they heard something moving inside when they shook it. And the harder they shook, the more they were able to hear. And the more they heard, the more they wondered about what was inside the box.

They wondered out loud: "Maybe it's something valuable, like gold or jewelry."

"Maybe it's something dangerous, like poison or a bomb."

"Maybe it's something from outer space that no one has ever seen before."

"Maybe it's like a seed pod filled with seeds."

"Maybe it's filled with things to eat, like bars of candy." "Maybe . . . ," "Maybe . . . ," "Maybe . . . ." And the more "maybes" there were, the more the boys and girls wondered what was inside the black box.

They decided to take the black box home where there were tools they could use to open it. On the way, they stopped at the fire station. Perhaps a fireman could open the box, but he couldn't. No matter how hard he tried with his axe and other pieces of equipment, he could not open the black box. So they continued on their way, leaving behind a confused fireman with a bent and broken axe.

As the girls and boys passed along Main Street, they stopped several times to see if anyone could open the black box. But no one could. The policeman, the grocer, the pharmacist, and the others— none of them could open the box.

The dentist had a very good idea. He thought that he could use his X-ray machine and take a picture of the inside of the box. But he couldn't. The X-rays passed easily through the box in every direction—but produced no picture of what was inside the black box!

Even a stop at the library, with all its books, gave no clue to what might be inside the box.

When the boys and girls arrived home, they tried hammers, chisels, saws, and even power tools. But no matter what they used, they could not open the black box. That night they all talked with their parents, for parents were usually very good at solving problems. But this time their parents could not help. And the mystery of what was inside the black box became even more perplexing.

Since the next day was Sunday, one of them took the black box to church. Perhaps the minister could help with their problem. He

---

• **perplexing** (pur PLEKS ing) puzzling; bewildering

had been helpful at times in the past. But the minister said: "I'm sorry, this is not a problem for a minister. It seems to me that what you have here is a scientific problem. Why not take your black box to the university? Show it to the scientists and see if they can help you."

So the next day, after school, the girls and boys took their black box to the university to see the scientists.

They went to a laboratory where some young scientists were working on an experiment. The scientists were intrigued by the black-box problem. They tried every approach they could think of to discover what was inside the black box. But they were unsuccessful. The young scientists could not pry into or open the box even with their most powerful scientific equipment. They finally said: "We cannot open the box. We cannot tell you what is inside. But perhaps the professor, our teacher, can answer your question." And so the boys and girls took their black box and went to see the professor.

The professor was very old. He had a beard, and it was obvious that he was very wise indeed. In his office he was surrounded by many books—some he had even written himself. The professor had studied for a very long time. In fact he said that he was still studying. He had been almost everywhere that there was to go. He had done almost everything that there was to do. The boys and girls felt very confident in his presence. They felt sure that the professor would answer their question about what was inside the black box.

The professor took the box in his hands and listened carefully as the girls and boys told their story about the black box. Finally the professor said: "It seems to me that your black box is similar to other scientific problems. There appear to be no sure answers to the question you have raised. But this does not mean that there are no answers. It means that you will need to invent an answer—or perhaps several answers to your question." The professor paused and looked at the boys and girls. They looked at one another, wondering if they understood what the professor had said.

Then the professor continued: "You must observe as much as possible—from the outside of the box. And then, on the basis of these observations, construct a model of what you think is inside. As you make more observations and gather more information, your model of what is inside may change. And this is good. It means your

• intrigued (in TREEGD) to be very curious about something

model is getting more and more like what really is inside the black box.

"This is the way it has always been in science and the way it will always be. We invent the best explanations we can on the basis of our best observations."

The girls and boys did not completely understand everything the professor said. They realized, however, that the absolute authority—someone with the right answer to their question—just did not exist in science.

And they managed to agree on the following model. Inside the black box, there was a slightly smaller box with a slightly smaller box inside of it with a slightly smaller box inside of it with a slightly smaller box inside of it with a slightly smaller box inside of it with a slightly smaller box inside of it with a slightly smaller box inside of it with a slightly smaller box inside of it with a slightly smaller box inside of it with a slightly smaller box inside of it

• **absolute** (AB suh loot) complete; final; perfect

ALL THINGS CONSIDERED ─────────────

1. The boys and girls find a mysterious (a) shiny box. (b) locked box. (c) black box.

2. The box is mysterious because it (a) is empty. (b) is large. (c) cannot be opened.

3. The problem is: (a) What is inside the box? (b) Who owns the box? (c) Why is the box black?

4. No one they show the box to (a) can guess what is inside. (b) can open it. (c) is interested in the box.

5. An X-ray picture (a) shows how to open the lock. (b) shows what is inside the box. (c) does not show what is in the box.

6. The young scientists (a) cannot solve the problem. (b) laugh at the boys and girls. (c) perform an experiment on the box.

7. The professor says they should make a model by (a) taking an X-ray of the box. (b) observing the box. (c) observing other boxes.

8. The professor says their model (a) will probably change. (b) must be correct. (c) must look like a small box.

9. Their model tells the girls and boys (a) that there is no answer to the problem. (b) the correct answer to the problem. (c) that there are boxes inside boxes.

10. You can conclude that constructing a model is (a) the only way to solve a problem. (b) one of the best ways to solve a problem. (c) the only way scientists solve problems.

THINKING IT THROUGH ─────────────

1. How does constructing a model help the boys and girls find an answer to their problem? Can you think of any problem that you could solve by constructing a model?

2. When a scientist makes a model, does it give the one true answer to a problem? Why or why not?

3. Compare the problem of the black box with the problem that scientists have in discovering the cause of a disease. How are these problems similar? How are they different?

Building from Details: Review ————

The selection does not directly state the answers to the following questions. It does, however, give you details that allow you to make an inference. On a separate sheet of paper, answer each question "yes" or "no." Then write a sentence telling what detail allowed you to make your inference.

1. Is the black box heavy?
2. Does the black box have a lid?
3. Had anyone ever seen another box like this one?
4. Was the dentist surprised that his X-ray machine could not take a picture of the inside of the box?
5. Was the professor disappointed because he could not open the box?

Composition ————

Follow your teacher's instructions before completing *one* of these writing assignments.

1. Suppose that you have found a mysterious sealed container on a beach. Before opening it, you try to find out what might be inside. Write five questions you would ask to help you find out what's inside the box.
2. Write an essay of two paragraphs. In the first paragraph, describe a problem for which you have no answer. In the second paragraph, describe a "model" that might help you solve this problem.

VOCABULARY AND SKILL REVIEW ────────────────

Before completing this exercise, you may wish to review the **bold-faced** words on pages 320–340.

I. On a separate sheet of paper, write the *italicized* word that best fills the blank in each sentence. Each word should be used only once.

absolute	*dispute*	*hesitation*	*arc*	*reproduce*
critical	*endurance*	*mingle*	*perplexing*	*substance*

1. The two men had a ――――― over who had a right to use the horse.
2. Is a scientist an ――――― authority on questions of science?
3. During the party, the guests seemed to ――――― quite happily.
4. Some clever people can ――――― the calls of birds.
5. The conflict of the main character is usually the ――――― of a story.
6. Bob volunteered without ――――― to bring in the herd of wild mustangs.
7. After the shower, the brilliant ――――― of a rainbow appeared in the sky.
8. The answers to some problems are difficult and ―――――.
9. Does a mule have more strength and ――――― than a horse?
10. The ――――― moment came when Bob first acted as leader of the herd.

II. Read the short selection on the next page; then answer the questions. This little story is by Alexander Solzhenitsyn, a famous Russian writer who now lives in Vermont.

from A CAMPFIRE AND ANTS

by Alexander Solzhenitsyn

I threw a small rotten log onto the fire and didn't notice that its insides were thickly settled with ants.

The log began to crackle. Ants tumbled out and ran off in despair. They ran along the top and writhed, burning in the flames. I grabbed the log and rolled it aside. Now many of the ants escaped—they ran down to the sand, to the pine needles.

But what was strange: they didn't run away from the fire.

Barely having overcome their terror, they turned, swung around, and—some sort of power drew them back, to the abandoned home!—and there were many of these who again ran onto the burning log, rushed along it, and perished there.

1. The plot of this story is based on the question, (a) Will the man put out the fire? (b) What will the ants do about the fire? (c) Who will win the fight?

2. You can tell from the context that *writhed* means (a) moved quickly. (b) twisted in pain. (c) turned back.

3. The theme in this story may be stated in the following way: (a) The desire for your home is very strong. (b) Fire is always dangerous. (c) Ants have no sense of danger.

4. The main character is (a) the writer. (b) a camper. (c) the ants.

AMELIA'S BLOOMERS

by Linda Schechet Tucker

▶ This story actually happened. It is history. It tells about a simple idea, a useful idea, and—even more important—a liberating idea. That makes it a great idea. So why didn't someone do something about it before Elizabeth Smith Miller?

It was spring in the year 1850, and Elizabeth Smith Miller was working in her garden. She was not thinking about the weeds she was pulling out or the flowers she was transplanting. She was thinking about how awful she felt.

"I don't know why I continue to wear these horrid clothes when they make me so uncomfortable," she said to herself. Elizabeth was wearing long underwear trimmed with lace, a stiff petticoat that stood out like a bell, a flannel petticoat with a scalloped hem, another flannel petticoat, a plain white petticoat, a fancy white petticoat, and finally a huge skirt that went down to the ground.

Around her middle, under her dress, she wore stays, whalebone strips that were pulled in tight to make her waist look small. Over that she wore a camisole which protected her dress from the stays. Unfortunately, nothing protected Elizabeth's body from the stays, and her ribs hurt her where the stays were pressing against them. Elizabeth panted. It was hard for her to breathe in her tightly laced stays, and it was always difficult for her to stand up straight with the pieces of whalebone jabbing into her back.

This was Elizabeth's gardening outfit. In 1850, it was the outfit women wore all the time. They cooked in it, cleaned in it, and even took care of their babies in it. When they were at home, they didn't always pull their stays quite as tight as they did in public. Sometimes they also took off one or two petticoats, but they always wore their long dresses. Elizabeth had just been married, and she was quickly learning how impossible it was to keep house in such cumbersome clothing.

Elizabeth was angry. "I simply cannot go on wearing clothes that I know are ridiculous. I don't care what the fashion

- bloomers (BLOOM urz) loose-fitting pants that are gathered below the knee
- stays (STAYZ) corset; a close-fitting undergarment worn around the waist and hips
- camisole (KAM uh sohl) a woman's undergarment that looks like the top part of a slip
- **cumbersome** (KUM bur sum) clumsy; difficult to manage

345

is." She got up from her garden and went into the house. She went right to her sewing room and took out some fabric she had bought to make a new dress. She took out her pins, needle, thread, and scissors. Elizabeth was soon busily working. She was not making just another dress.

Earlier, Elizabeth had visited a rest home where women were recuperating from the effects of tightly laced stays. They had welts on their bodies and cracked ribs. Some of them even had hurt the inside parts of their bodies because of lacing the outside too tightly. Their waists had looked tiny, but their bodies were not healthy.

While they were recovering, the women wore special outfits given to them at the rest home. They wore loose-fitting pants that were tied closed at the

ankle. Over the pants they wore dresses that did not go down to the floor but stopped about four inches below the knee. They were the first outfits Elizabeth had ever seen where you could actually tell that a woman had legs.

The dresses were not pulled in at the waist, and, of course, the women wore no stays. These outfits were called Turkish outfits because people in Turkey wore this style of pants. Elizabeth had decided to make herself a Turkish outfit.

The next morning Elizabeth came downstairs wearing her new clothes. Her pants were full and were gathered in with an elastic band at the ankle. Her dress was loose at the waist and reached a little below her knee. She wore no petticoats. Elizabeth felt comfortable. Her husband looked astonished. "Whatever are you wearing, Elizabeth?" he asked her.

"I'm sick and tired of wearing stays and petticoats. I don't see why I have to be uncomfortable all the time. This is my new outfit, and I don't care what you or anybody else thinks of it!"

"Just a minute, Elizabeth," he said. "In fact, I think your outfit is very sensible and looks much more comfortable than what you usually wear. I only asked you what it was."

Elizabeth was embarrassed that she had jumped down Charles's throat. Of course, she should have realized that he would approve of her new clothes. It was just that she was so worried about what people would say.

Elizabeth knew that her father would be very pleased when he saw her. He had often said that women would never win their rights until they started wearing clothes they could move in. When she was a child, Elizabeth had been the only girl in Peterboro, New York, who wore comfortable play clothes as the boys did. Her father had refused to dress her in long proper skirts.

Unfortunately, Elizabeth's neighbors did not find her outfit as sensible as her husband and father did. They could not believe that Elizabeth would walk out of her house in such clothes. Mrs. Williams in her stays and petticoats and long dress said to Mrs. Johnson in her stays and petticoats and long dress, "Have you seen Mrs. Miller?"

"I have indeed," said Mrs. Johnson to Mrs. Williams as their skirts dragged through the mud. "Imagine a woman wearing pants. Who does she think she is—a man?"

But Elizabeth continued to wear her Turkish outfit. She had worn the fashionable clothes long enough. Now she was determined to be comfortable. She made herself more Turkish outfits and began to wear them every day. She wore them at home and, despite disapproving glares of her neighbors, wore them into town as well.

It wasn't long after Elizabeth began wearing her new clothes that she decided to pay a visit to Elizabeth Cady Stanton. Besides being cousins, the two Elizabeths had been friends for many years. Elizabeth was sure that Lizzie would approve of her Turkish outfit. They had both long agreed that women could never expect to be able to do all the things that men could do as long as they could hardly move in their stays and petticoats.

Elizabeth arrived at Lizzie's house in Seneca Falls wearing full Turkish pants, a short dress, and a Spanish cloak all made of black broadcloth. She also wore dark furs and a beaver hat with feathers. Lizzie was astonished.

"How wonderful!" she said. "You must feel so comfortable and free. I've never seen such an outfit."

"You should make yourself one, Lizzie," Elizabeth said. "I've never felt so good. Look at how I can move." Elizabeth twirled around to show her cousin her freedom, as well as to show her how the outfit looked from the back.

• **glare** (GLAIR) angry look

"Oh, I don't know if I could wear such clothes in Seneca Falls," answered Lizzie.

The two women walked toward the house together, one with a tight waist and long dress, the other walking more briskly with her loose waist and Turkish pants. As soon as they entered the house, Lizzie heard her baby crying upstairs. She gathered up her skirts and climbed the stairs. She came down a few minutes later holding little Theodore in one arm and her skirt and petticoats in the other. It was late in the day, and it was difficult to see on the stairway.

"Lizzie, you should carry a candle. You could fall and hurt yourself and your baby walking downstairs in the dark like that."

Lizzie laughed. "Now how am I going to do that?" One hand was busy with skirts and petticoats, and the other was busy with a baby. "I only have two hands."

Elizabeth took Theodore out of his mother's arms and picked up a candle with her free hand. She walked up the stairs quickly and easily. When she reached the landing, she turned and looked at Lizzie at the foot of the stairs. "It's really quite simple," she said.

Lizzie was convinced. The next day she sat down and made herself a Turkish outfit of black satin. The two women could now be seen walking through Seneca Falls together in their loose pants and short skirts. They had never enjoyed walking so much. The disapproving looks of Lizzie's neighbors did not bother them. With no long skirts to get in their

way and no stays to hamper their breathing, the cousins could walk for miles.

One day they stopped at the post office. Amelia Bloomer, the postmaster's wife, was busily working in a room next to the post office. She was the publisher of a monthly newspaper called The Lily. Amelia claimed that The Lily was the first paper in the United States that was owned, edited, and published by a woman. When Lizzie and Elizabeth arrived at the post office, Amelia was wrapping and addressing her newspapers for mailing. She had already written many of the articles for the new issue, edited the articles that other people had written, and arranged for the paper to be printed.

Just by coincidence, in this issue of The Lily, Amelia had written an article on how much women needed more comfortable clothing than the stays and petticoats that she was wearing. Imagine her surprise when Lizzie and Elizabeth walked into the post office wearing their Turkish pants and short skirts! "Excuse me for not bothering with pleasantries, but please tell me all about your outfits. It just happens that I have been writing in my newspaper about the need for a change in women's dress. I must describe your clothing in The Lily."

Elizabeth gladly told Amelia all about how she had come to wear the Turkish outfit. Amelia realized the time had come to put into practice what she had been writing about. At home that night, she made herself a Turkish outfit.

Now Mrs. Miller, Mrs. Stanton, and Mrs. Bloomer could all be seen walking through Seneca Falls breathing deeply

and moving briskly. The town talked of nothing else. Young boys taunted them as they walked.

Heigh! ho!
Thro' sleet and snow.
Mrs. Bloomer's all the go.
Twenty tailors take the stitches,
Mrs. Stanton wears the breeches.
Heigh! ho!
The carrion crow.

Mrs. Stanton's own son, who was away at boarding school, wrote to his mother to ask her please not to visit him in her new clothes. She wrote back to him.

"Now suppose you and I were taking a long walk in the fields and I had on three long petticoats. Then suppose a bull should take after us. You with your arms and legs free could run like a shot,

---

• taunt (TAWNT) *mock; laugh at*

but I, alas, should fall a victim to my graceful flowing drapery. My petticoats would be caught by the stumps and the briars, and what could I do at the fences? Then you in your agony, when you saw the bull gaining on me, would say, 'Oh, I wish Mother could use her legs as I can.'

"Now why do you wish me to wear what is uncomfortable, inconvenient, and many times dangerous? I'll tell you why. You want me to be like other people. You do not like to have me laughed at. You must learn not to care for what foolish people say."

It was hard for a young boy to learn, but the three women truly did not care what foolish people said. They did what they wanted to do no matter who laughed at them.

Elizabeth went home to Peterboro and continued to wear her Turkish outfit in spite of her neighbors' stares and comments. Her husband, Charles, and her father always supported her decision to wear the new clothes. Elizabeth even wore her outfit to Washington, D.C., where her father was a congressman.

Lizzie also continued to wear her Turkish outfit. She carried her baby safely and comfortably up and down the stairs in her house. She wore her new clothes all over New York State, where she traveled to talk to people about rights for women.

And in the next issue of *The Lily,*

Amelia wrote about the Turkish outfit and announced to her readers that she was now wearing it herself. Hundreds of women wrote to her asking for sewing patterns so that they could make their own Turkish outfits. But thousands of people were still shocked at the very idea of women wearing pants and short skirts.

Articles began to appear in other newspapers about the Turkish outfit. Most of them said that it was terrible for women to wear pants. Amelia wrote back to one newspaper saying, "If gentlemen really think they would be comfortable in long, heavy skirts, well, let them wear them." More and more women began to wear Turkish outfits.

Since the other newspapers had first learned about the Turkish outfit from Mrs. Bloomer's articles, they called it "Mrs. Bloomer's outfit." Then they began to call it "the Bloomer outfit," and finally just "bloomers." The women who wore bloomers were called "bloomerites," and the whole idea of wearing the new clothes was called "bloomerism." Amelia insisted over and over again that it was Mrs. Miller who had first worn the outfit in public and that she should be given credit for her idea and her courage.

"They should be called 'millers,' not 'bloomers,'" said Amelia. But nobody listened. The name "bloomers" stuck. There was nothing that anybody could do about it.

• **inconvenient** (in kun VEEN yunt) troublesome; not easy to do

ALL THINGS CONSIDERED

1. At the beginning of the story, Elizabeth thought her clothes were (a) ugly. (b) uncomfortable. (c) expensive.

2. Whalebone strips called "stays" were used to (a) give support to the back. (b) make the dress attractive. (c) make the waist look small.

3. The Turkish pants Elizabeth invented gave her more (a) freedom. (b) support. (c) beauty.

4. Most people thought that a woman wearing pants was (a) sensible. (b) illegal. (c) terrible.

5. Two people who immediately approved of Elizabeth's pants were (a) her cousin Lizzie and Amelia Bloomer. (b) her son and Amelia Bloomer. (c) her cousin Lizzie and Lizzie's son.

6. In her newspaper, Amelia Bloomer (a) made fun of the new pants. (b) described the new pants. (c) sold the new pants.

7. Lizzie's advice to her son was that he should (a) get new clothes. (b) wear comfortable clothes. (c) not care what foolish people say.

8. Because of the article in her newspaper, Amelia Bloomer (a) was elected to Congress. (b) received hundreds of requests for the pattern to make the pants. (c) was forced to stop publishing.

9. Because the article appeared in Amelia Bloomer's paper, the pants were called (a) bloomers. (b) amelias. (c) paper pants.

10. The idea of wearing the new clothes was called (a) bloomerism. (b) ameliana. (c) milleritis.

THINKING IT THROUGH

1. In this selection, the author has two basic purposes. She wants to tell the truth about what happened, but she also wants to make the story as interesting as possible. This means that she has invented some parts of her story. Which parts are most likely to be historically accurate? Which parts are most likely to have been invented?

2. What could women do while wearing the new clothes that they could not do wearing the old clothes? Make a list. How do these activities allow women to enjoy greater freedom?

3. Elizabeth thought that wearing uncomfortable clothes was ridiculous and stupid. Do you agree? Why do you think women were willing to wear clothes that were so uncomfortable? If you had been alive at the time, do you think you would have agreed with Elizabeth? Why or why not?

Literary Skills: Review

Each of the terms below describes one of the following sentences. On a separate sheet of paper, match the letter of the term with the number of the sentence it describes.

    a. cause and effect
    b. compare and contrast
    c. idiom
    d. opinion
    e. fact

1. "The dress was impossible to wear," Elizabeth told her husband.

2. She was sick and tired of wearing stays and petticoats.

3. She was uncomfortable because of her clothes.

4. The women walked to the house together, one with a tight waist and long dress, the other with her loose waist and Turkish pants.

5. Amelia Bloomer was the publisher of *The Lily*.

Composition

Follow your teacher's directions before completing *one* of these writing assignments.

1. Copy the sentences below, filling in the missing parts.
Perhaps women wore terribly uncomfortable and dangerous clothes because. . . . It was . . . to wear such clothes because. . . .

2. Suppose that you are Elizabeth Cady Stanton's son. You have just received a letter in which your mother explains the benefits of wearing her new clothes (page 349). Write an answer to this letter, trying to respond as you think he might have. Begin your letter like this:

September 30, 19—

Dear Mother,

THE PARABLE OF THE EAGLE

by James Aggrey

▶ Could a bird with the heart of an eagle be content to live in a chicken coop? Or, with a great idea, could it soar to the sky?

One day not so very long ago a man caught an eagle in a trap. He brought it home to his chicken farm and put it in a cage with his chickens. Although he knew it was an eagle, the king of birds, he fed it chicken food. After a while the eagle was walking around in the cage and eating off the ground just like the chickens.

When the eagle was fully grown, a naturalist visited the farm. He saw the eagle and said, "Why do you treat that eagle like a chicken?"

"You may think it's an eagle," said the chicken farmer, "but I have trained it to be a chicken. Its wings measure ten feet across, but it is no longer an eagle. It is just a big chicken."

"Oh, no!" said the naturalist. "If it has the heart of an eagle, it is an eagle. Give it a chance and it will soar above the clouds."

"You are wrong," said the chicken farmer. "It is a chicken. It will only hop along the ground."

Each man swore he was right, so they agreed to give the eagle a test.

The naturalist held up the eagle and spoke to it. "You are an eagle, the greatest of birds," he said. "Spread your wings and fly."

The eagle's head turned to the right and left. Then, looking down at the chickens, it hopped to the ground and began eating the chicken food.

"There," said the chicken farmer. "Just as I told you, it's a chicken."

"Give the eagle another chance," said the naturalist. "If it has the heart of an eagle, it must be an eagle."

• naturalist (NACH ur uh list) **a person who studies plants and animals**

The next day the two men took the eagle to the roof of the house. There the naturalist spoke to it and said, "Eagle, listen. You are an eagle. Spread your wings and fly."

But the eagle didn't fly. Seeing the chickens on the ground, it hopped down from the roof and began eating the chicken food.

"Now do you see that I am right?" said the chicken farmer.

"No," said the naturalist. "Give it one more chance. It has the heart of an eagle, so it must be an eagle."

The next morning at sunrise, the naturalist and chicken farmer took the eagle to a hilltop. Over the distant mountains the sun was rising, spreading its golden glory across the land.

The naturalist once again picked up the eagle and spoke. "You are an eagle," he said. "Go and live with the wind on the mountains. Spread your wings and fly."

The eagle looked to the right and left. Its body began to tremble. It did not jump down, but it did not fly either.

"Eagle," said the naturalist, "behold the sun!"

And the eagle saw the sun. It lifted its head and spread its wings. Then up, up into the sky it soared. Higher and higher, on and on it went, screaming like an eagle.

The eagle never returned. It may have been trained to be a chicken, but it was an eagle.

• behold (bi HOHLD) **see; look at**

ALL THINGS CONSIDERED ———————————

1. The chicken farmer treats the eagle like (a) a caged bird. (b) an ordinary chicken. (c) a special pet.

2. The naturalist says that the eagle (a) looks like an ordinary chicken. (b) will always be a proud eagle. (c) can learn to act like a chicken.

3. The two men test the eagle to see if it (a) will obey. (b) is happy. (c) is truly an eagle.

4. The naturalist holds up the eagle and tells it to (a) spread its wings and fly. (b) hop to the ground. (c) scream in the wind.

5. The first time the naturalist speaks to it, the eagle (a) flies away forever. (b) tries to fly but fails. (c) hops to the ground like a chicken.

6. The eagle flies up into the sky when it sees (a) the sun. (b) the mountain. (c) the naturalist.

7. After the eagle flies into the sky, it (a) builds a nest near the chicken farm. (b) returns to the chicken farmer. (c) never returns to the farm.

8. You can conclude that the eagle flew away because (a) the naturalist believed in it. (b) it had the heart of an eagle. (c) it never liked the chicken farm.

THINKING IT THROUGH ———————————

1. Do you think this parable has an important lesson for people to learn? If so, what is the lesson?

2. Pretend you are the author and do not want to use the word *parable* in the title of this story. Write three good titles. Each title should express the main idea of the selection. Then draw a line under the one that you like best.

3. If the naturalist had not come to the chicken farm, do you think the eagle would have eventually learned to fly? Why or why not?

4. What idea made it possible for the eagle to finally soar into the sky? State this idea in your own words.

Building from Details: Review

Paraphrasing—telling a story in your own words—is an important skill. It is one of the best ways to show you understand what you have read.

Try paraphrasing "The Parable of the Eagle." First, reread the selection. Close your eyes and try to form clear images of the characters and events in your mind. Then, review the order of events in the selection. Finally, relate the story in your own words.

Relationships: Review

On a separate sheet of paper, write the following sentences in the correct time order.

1. A naturalist visited the chicken farm and tried to get the eagle to fly.
2. The eagle hopped to the ground and continued to act like a chicken.
3. A man caught an eagle in a trap.
4. Once it saw the sun, the eagle soared into the sky.
5. After a while, the eagle began to act like a chicken.

Composition

1. Describe the eagle at two different times. First, describe how it looks and acts at the beginning of the story. Describe the look in its eyes and the weak flapping of its wings as it walks along the ground like a chicken. In another paragraph, describe how the eagle looks at the end of the story. Describe the changes in the eyes and in the way the wings flap as it soars into the sky.
2. A parable can be very short. In a few paragraphs, write your own parable—a story that teaches a lesson.

THE PATHWAY FROM SLAVERY TO FREEDOM

by Frederick Douglass

▶ Frederick Douglass (1817–1895) is one of the great figures in black history. His autobiography is perhaps the best expression we have of the effects of slavery on the mind and body of a human being.

This selection is taken from Douglass's autobiography, *Narrative of the Life of Frederick Douglass, an American Slave*. It tells how he learned to read, which was—for a slave—a secret and dangerous adventure.

Mrs. Auld, my new mistress, had never before had a slave under her control. And before her marriage, she had to earn her own living. For these reasons, I believe, she had been in a good degree saved from the dehumanizing effects of slavery. In the simplicity of her soul, she began to treat me as she supposed one human being ought to treat another. In entering upon the duties of a slaveholder, she did not seem to understand that I was a mere slave, a non-human being, a creature to be treated like any other piece of property, no better than a cow or pig. She was a pious, warm, and tender-hearted woman. There was no sorrow or suffering for which she had not a tear. She had bread for the hungry, clothes for the naked, and comfort for every mourner that came within her reach.

I was utterly astonished at the goodness of Mrs. Auld. I scarcely knew how to behave towards her. She was entirely unlike any other white woman I had ever seen. I could not approach her as I had learned to approach other white ladies. The crouching dog-like behavior, usually so acceptable in a slave, did not gain her favor. Indeed, she seemed to be disturbed by it. She did not think it bold or improper for a slave to look her in the face. The meanest slave was put fully at ease in her presence, and none left without feeling better for having seen her. Her face was made of heavenly smiles, and her voice of gentle music.

- **dehumanize** (dee HYOO muh nyz) to treat in a cruel manner
- pious (PY uhs) religious

But, alas! this kind heart had but a short time to remain such. Slavery soon proved its ability to steal from her these heavenly qualities. Under its influence, the tender heart became stone, and the lamb-like character gave way to one of tiger-like fierceness. The fatal poison of irresponsible power began its infernal work. That cheerful eye, under the influence of slavery, soon became red with rage. That voice, made all of sweet harmony, changed to one of harsh and horrid discord. And that angelic face gave place to that of a demon.

Thus slavery proved to be as injurious to her as to me. Very soon after I went to live with Mr. and Mrs. Auld, she very kindly began to teach me the ABC's. After I had learned this, she assisted me in learning to spell words of three or four letters. Just at this point of my progress, Mr. Auld found out what was going on. He at once forbade Mrs. Auld to instruct me further. He told her to let well enough alone. And he explained to her that it was unlawful to teach a slave to read. "If you give a slave an inch, he will take an ell*. A slave should know nothing but to obey his master—to do as he is told to do. Learning would *spoil* the best slave in the world. Now," said he, "if you teach this new slave of yours how to read, there would be no keeping him. It would forever unfit him to be a slave. He would at once become unmanageable, and of no value to his master. As for himself, reading would do no good, but a great deal of harm. It would make him discontented and unhappy."

These words sank deep into my heart. They stirred up sentiments that lay slumbering and called into existence an entirely new train of thought. It was a new and special revelation, explaining dark and mysterious things with which my youthful understanding had hopelessly struggled. I now understood what had been to me a most perplexing difficulty—I mean, the white man's power to enslave the black man. From that moment, I understood that the pathway from slavery to freedom was books. It was just what I wanted, and I got it at a time when I the least expected it. Whilst I was saddened by the

- **irresponsible** (ir ree SPON suh bul) **not responsible**
- infernal (in FURN ul) **devilish**
- **discord** (dis KORD) **lack of harmony**
- **injurious** (in JOOR ee us) **harmful**
- revelation (rev uh LAY shun) **something made known; something made clear**

*An old measure of length equal to 45 inches.

thought of losing the aid of my kind mistress, I was gladdened by the precious instruction which, by the merest accident, I had gained from my master. Though conscious of the difficulty of learning without a teacher, I set out with high hope, at whatever cost, to learn how to read. The very decided manner with which he spoke about the evil consequences of giving me instruction served to convince me of the absolute truth of his words. What he most dreaded, that I most desired. What he most loved, that I most hated. That which to him was a great evil, to be avoided at all costs, was to me a great good, to be sought at all costs. In learning to read, I owe almost as much to the bitter opposition of my master as to the kindly aid of my mistress. I acknowledge the benefit of both.

My mistress soon began to follow her husband's advice. In time she became even more violent in her opposition than her husband himself. She was not satisfied with simply doing as well as he had suggested. She seemed anxious to do better. Nothing seemed to make her more angry than to see me with a newspaper. She seemed to think that here lay the danger. I have had her rush at me with a face made all up of fury, and snatch from me a newspaper, in a manner that fully revealed her concern. She was an intelligent woman; and a little experience soon demonstrated to her that education and slavery were incompatible.

From that time on I was most closely watched. If I was in a separate room any length of time, I was sure to be suspected of having a book. And I was at once told to give an account of myself. All this, however, was too late. The first step had been taken. Mistress, in teaching me the alphabet, had given me the *inch,* and nothing could then prevent me from taking the *ell.*

The plan which I adopted, and the one by which I was most successful, was that of making friends of all the little white boys whom I met in the street. As many of these as I could, I turned into teachers. With their kindly aid, obtained at different times and in different places, I finally succeeded in learning to read. When I was sent on errands, I always took my book with me. Then, by doing one part of my errand quickly, I found time to get a lesson before my

- **opposition** (op uh ZISH un) action against
- **acknowledge** (ak NOL ij) admit; willingly state
- **incompatible** (in kum PAT uh bul) not in agreement; unable to get along with

return. I used also to carry bread with me, enough of which was always in the house and to which I was always welcome. As for food, I was much better off than many of the poor white children in our neighborhood. This bread I used to give to the hungry little boys. They, in return, would give me that more valuable bread of knowledge. I am strongly tempted to give the names of two or three of those little boys, as an expression of the gratitude and affection I bear them. But it might not be wise. It would not injure me, but it might embarrass them, for it is almost an unpardonable offense to teach slaves to read in this Christian country.

I used to talk this matter of slavery over with them. I would sometimes say to them, I wished I could be as free as they would be when they got to be men. "You will be free as soon as you are 21, *but I am a slave for life!* Have not I as good a right to be free as you have?" These words used to trouble them. They would express genuine sympathy and comfort me with the hope that something would happen that would make me free.

I was eager to hear any one speak of slavery. I was a ready listener. Every little while, I could hear something about the abolitionists. It was some time before I found what the word meant. It was
always used in such connections as to make it an interesting word to
me. If a slave ran away and succeeded in getting clear, or if a slave
killed his master, set fire to a barn, or did any thing very wrong in the
mind of a slaveholder, it was spoken of as the fruit of *abolition*.
Hearing the word in this connection very often, I set about learning
what it meant. The dictionary afforded me little or no help. I found it
was "the act of abolishing," but then I did not know what was to be
abolished. Here I was. I did not dare to ask any one about its meaning, for I was satisfied that it was something they wanted me to
know very little about. Finally, I got one of our city papers containing
an account of the number of petitions from the north praying for the
abolition of slavery. From this time I understood the words *abolition*
and *abolitionist*. I always drew near when that word was spoken,
expecting to hear something of importance to myself and fellow-
slaves.

I went one day down to the wharf where two Irishmen were un-
loading stone. I went, unasked, and helped them. When we had
finished, one of them came to me and asked me if I were a slave. I
told him I was. He asked, "Are ye a slave for life?" I told him that I
was. The good Irishman seemed to be deeply affected by the statement. He said to the other that it was a pity so fine a little fellow
should be a slave for life. He said it was a shame to hold me. They
both advised me to run away to the north. They said I should find
friends there, and that I should be free. I pretended not to be interested in what they said, acting as if I did not understand them. You
see, I feared they might be treacherous. White men have been
known to encourage slaves to escape, and then, to get the reward,
catch them and return them to their masters. I was afraid that these
seemingly good men might use me so; but I nevertheless remembered their advice. From that time I resolved to run away. I looked
forward to a time at which it would be safe for me to escape. I was
too young to think of doing so immediately. Besides, I wished to
learn how to write, as I might need to write my own pass. I comforted myself with the hope that I should one day find a good
chance. Meanwhile, I would learn to write.

• **resolve** (ree ZOLV) determine; decide

ALL THINGS CONSIDERED _____

1. Owning slaves caused Mrs. Auld to become (a) a helpless person. (b) a kind person. (c) an evil person.

2. Douglass learned his ABC's (a) by himself. (b) from Mrs. Auld. (c) from another slave.

3. Mr. Auld said that if Douglass learned to read, he would (a) never be a good slave. (b) learn to do more work. (c) become a house servant.

4. The pathway from slavery to freedom was (a) reading. (b) Mrs. Auld. (c) escape.

5. Mr. Auld taught Douglass (a) the evil of slavery. (b) the importance of reading. (c) how to get to the North.

6. Douglass's next teachers were the (a) other slaves. (b) newspapers. (c) young white boys.

7. It was difficult for Douglass to learn how to read because he (a) was a poor student. (b) disliked reading. (c) was closely watched.

8. One day at the wharf, two Irishmen (a) offered to help Douglass escape. (b) advised Douglass to run away to the North. (c) offered to teach Douglass how to write.

9. Douglass learned the word *abolition* by (a) reading a dictionary. (b) asking Mrs. Auld. (c) using context clues.

10. Douglass wanted to learn how to write (a) in case he would have to write his own pass. (b) because he wanted to write a book. (c) because all free people knew how to write.

THINKING IT THROUGH _____

1. How were Mr. and Mrs. Auld both important in Douglass's learning to read? Do you think Mr. Auld or Mrs. Auld had more of an effect on making Douglass want to read? Why?

2. How could knowledge free a person from slavery? Is this as true today as it was in Douglass's day?

3. When Adolf Hitler became the dictator of Germany in the 1930s, he burned books. Why would he have done that? Do you think it was for the same reason that slaveowners wanted to keep their slaves ignorant? Why or why not?

Literary Skills: Review

Match the term in column **A** with the definition in column **B**.

A	**B**
1. biography	**a.** the ending of a story
2. autobiography	**b.** the sequence of actions in a story
3. fiction	**c.** the story of a person's life told by that person
4. nonfiction	**d.** the story of a person's life told by another person
5. parable	**e.** any kind of made-up story
6. fable	**f.** a story that teaches a lesson
7. conclusion	**g.** a story with a moral that is directly stated
8. plot	**h.** any writing that is not a made-up story
9. conflict	**i.** a detail in a story that gives a sign of what is to come
10. foreshadowing	**j.** the problem faced by a character

Composition

Follow your teacher's instructions before completing *one* of these writing assignments.

1. Why was reading important to Frederick Douglass? Write a short paragraph answering this question. Your first sentence might begin like this:
"Reading was important to Frederick Douglass because . . ."
The rest of your paragraph might then give examples of what reading did for Frederick Douglass.
2. Write a paragraph explaining how reading is important in your life. Your first sentence should be similar to either a or b:
a. "Reading is important to me because . . ."
b. "Reading is just as important today as it was in the time of Frederick Douglass."
The rest of your paragraph should give reasons supporting what you have claimed in the first sentence.

VOCABULARY AND SKILL REVIEW ————————

Before completing the exercises that follow, you may wish to review the **bold-faced** words on pages 345–361.

I. Notice the use of the *italicized* word in each sentence. On a separate sheet of paper, mark each use of a word as correct or incorrect. If it is incorrectly used, rewrite the sentence so the word is used correctly.

    1. The *cumbersome* clothes made the woman feel extremely uncomfortable.

    2. As Amelia Bloomer walked through the town in her new clothes, people *glared* at her.

    3. Modern music often experiments with *discord*.

    4. Reading will often *dehumanize* people.

    5. Since the two girls became close friends, they have been *incompatible*.

    6. Players on the same team are called the *opposition*.

    7. I *resolve* to do well in school.

    8. Since her house is located by the train station, visiting her is often *inconvenient*.

    9. The fall was *injurious* to her health.

    10. The wise old judge is seldom *irresponsible*.

II. On a separate sheet of paper, complete each sentence so it shows a cause and effect.

    1. It snowed all night . . .

    2. Because I like to read . . .

    3. After learning about Frederick Douglass . . .

    4. Because I read the book . . .

    5. When I won the race . . .

Pearl Buck
(1892-1973)

The daughter of American missionaries, Pearl Sydenstricker grew up in China, where she developed a love for the people and their traditional ways of life. She returned to the United States during her college years. Once back in China she taught at Nanking University and married John Buck. She intended to live her life in China, but those were years of great political and social change, and it became impossible for her to stay on while the China she loved was torn apart by violence. So in 1932 she returned to the United States.

The Far East was the focus of her writing. Most of her stories are about the people and places of the Orient. During her lifetime, she wrote and had published 85 volumes of novels, stories, and essays.

Her first full-length book, *East Wind, West Wind* (1930), attempted to explain Chinese culture to the West. *The Good Earth* (1931), her most famous book, is about a peasant family and their struggle for survival. In 1932 the book earned her the Pulitzer Prize for "rich and genuine portrayals of Chinese life. . . ." In 1938 she was awarded the Nobel Prize for Literature, which is given each year to one writer for an overall contribution to literature.

Concern for the people of the Orient made up a nonwriting career as well. Pearl Buck adopted and raised nine children of Asian parentage. During the 1940s, she founded The East and West Association, Welcome House, and The Pearl Buck Foundation. All these organizations were founded to insure the care of Asian children and to promote better East-West relations.

365

THE BIG WAVE

by Pearl Buck

▶ Pearl Buck turned one of her fine stories into this television play. As you read, visualize the action on your TV screen. Pay attention when the directions say "dissolve to." These words mean the image on the screen fades from one picture into the next.

The setting for the story is Japan of long ago. It is a story about families and their closeness to nature.

CHARACTERS

Narrator
Kino Uchiyama *(KEE noh oo chee YAH mah), a farmer's son*
Mother
Father, *the farmer*
Setsu *(SET soo), Kino's younger sister*
Jiya *(JEE yah), a fisherman's son*
Jiya's Father, *the fisherman*
Old Gentleman, *a wealthy landowner*
Two Servants
Gardener
First Man
Second Man
Woman
Child

Act One

Open on: A scene in Japan, sea and mountainside, and in the distance Fuji. *

Dissolve to: A small farmhouse, built on top of terraces.

This, as the Narrator speaks, dissolves to: The inside of the house, a room with the simplest of Japanese furniture.

---

*Fuji (FOO jee) a volcano that has been extinct for over 300 years. It is the highest mountain in Japan.

Narrator: Kino lives on a farm. The farm lies on the side of a mountain in Japan. The fields are terraced by walls of stone, each one of them like a broad step up the mountain. Centuries ago, Kino's ancestors built the stone walls that hold up the fields. Above the fields stands this farmhouse, which is Kino's home.

(Dissolve to: Kino *comes into the room. He is a sturdy boy of about 13, dressed in shorts and a Japanese jacket.)*

Kino: Mother!

(Mother hurries in. She is a small, serious-looking woman dressed in a kimono. She is carrying a jar of water.)

Mother: Dinner is ready. Where's your father?
Kino: Coming. I ran up the terraces. I'm starving.
Mother: Call Setsu. She is playing outside.
Kino *(turning his head):* Setsu!
Father: Here she is. *(He comes in, holding by the hand a small playful girl.)* Getting so big! I can't lift her any more. *(But he does lift her so high that she touches the low rafters.)*
Setsu: Don't put me down. I want to eat my supper up here.
Father: And fall into the soup?
Kino: How that would taste!
Setsu *(willfully):* It would taste nice.
Mother: Come, come . . .

(They sit on the floor around the table. Mother *serves from a bucket of rice, a bowl of soup, a bowl of fish. She serves* Father *first, then* Kino, *then* Setsu, *and herself.)*

Father: Kino, don't eat so fast.
Kino: I have promised Jiya to swim in the sea with him.
Mother: Obey your father.
Father *(smiling):* Let him eat fast. *(He puts a bit of fish in* Setsu's *bowl.)* There—that's a good bit.
Kino: Father, why is it that Jiya's father's house has no window to the sea?

- kimono   (kuh MOH noh) **a robe with wide sleeves and a sash, worn by Japanese men and women**

Father: No fisherman wants windows to the sea.

Mother: The sea is their enemy.

Kino: Mother, how can you say so? Jiya's father catches fish from the sea and that is how their family lives.

Father: Do not argue with your mother. Ask Jiya your question. See what he says.

Kino: Then may I go?

Father: Go.

(Dissolve to: A sandy strip of seashore at the foot of the mountain. A few cottages stand there.

Dissolve to: A tall slender boy, Jiya. He stands at the edge of the sea, looking up the mountain.)

Jiya *(calling through his hands):* Kino!

Kino: Coming!

(He is running and catches Jiya's outstretched hand, so that they nearly fall down. They laugh and throw off their jackets.)

Kino: Wait—I am out of breath. I ate too much.

Jiya *(looking up the mountain):* There's Old Gentleman standing at the gate of his castle.

Kino: He is watching to see whether we are going into the sea.

Jiya: He's always looking at the sea—at dawn, at sunset.

(Dissolve to: Old Gentleman, standing on a rock, in front of his castle, halfway up the mountain. The wind is blowing his beard. Withdraw the cameras to the beach.)

Jiya: He is afraid of the sea—always watching!

Kino: Have you ever been in his castle?

Jiya: Only once. Such beautiful gardens—like a dream in a fairy tale. The old pines are bent with the wind, and under them the moss is deep and green and so smooth. Every day men sweep the moss with brooms.

Kino: Why does he keep looking at the sea?

Jiya: He is afraid of it, I tell you.

Kino: Why?

Jiya: The sea is our enemy. We all know it.

Kino: Oh, how can you say it? When we have so much fun—

Jiya: It is our enemy. . . .

Kino: Not mine—let's swim to the island!

Jiya: No. I must find clams for my mother.

Kino: Then let's swim to the sand bar. There are millions of clams there!

Jiya: But the tide is ready to turn. . . .

Kino: It's slow—we'll have time.

(They plunge into the sea and swim to the sand bar. Jiya has a small, short-handled hoe hanging from his waist. He digs into the sand. Kino kneels to help him. But Jiya digs only for a moment; then he pauses to look over the sea.)

Kino: What are you looking for?

Jiya: To see if the sea is angry with us.

Kino *(laughing):* Silly—the sea can't be angry with people!

Jiya: Down there, a mile down, the old sea god lives. When he is angry he heaves and rolls, and the waves rush back and forth. Then he gets up and stamps his feet, and earth shakes at the bottom of the sea. . . . I wish I were a farmer's son.

Kino: And I wish I were a fisherman's son. It is stupid to plow and plant and harvest when I could just sit in a boat and reap fish from the sea!

Jiya: The earth is safe.

Kino: When the volcano is angry the earth shakes, too.

Jiya: The angry earth helps the angry sea.

Kino: They work together.

Jiya: But fire comes out of the volcano.

(Meanwhile, the tide is coming in and swirls about their feet.)

Jiya *(noticing):* Oh—we have not half-enough clams. . . .

(They fall to digging frantically.
Dissolve to: The empty seashore and the tide rushing in. A man paces at the water's edge. He wears shorts and a fisherman's jacket, open over his bare breast. It is Jiya's Father. He calls, his hands cupped at his mouth.)

Jiya's Father: Ji—ya!

(There is only the sound of the surf. He wades into the water, still calling. Suddenly he sees the boys, their heads out of water, swimming, and he beckons fiercely. They come in, and he pulls them out of the surf.)

Jiya's Father: Jiya! You have never been so late before!

Jiya: Father, we were on the sand bar, digging clams. We had to leave them.

Jiya's Father *(shaking his shoulder):* Never be so late!

Kino *(wondering):* You are afraid of the sea, too.

Jiya's Father: Go home, farmer's son! Your mother is calling you.

(In the distance a woman's voice is calling Kino's name. He hears and runs toward the mountain.)

Jiya: Father, I have made you angry.

Jiya's Father: I am not angry.

• reap (REEP) **gather in (as a farmer gathers wheat)**

Jiya: Then why do you seem angry?

Jiya's Father: Old Gentleman sent down word that a storm is rising behind the horizon. He sees the cloud through his telescope.

Jiya: Father, why do you let Old Gentleman make you afraid? Just because he is rich and lives in a castle, everybody listens to him.

Jiya's Father: Not because he is rich—not because he lives in the castle, but because he is old and wise and he knows the sea. He doesn't want anybody to die. *(He looks over the sea, and he mutters as though to himself.)* Though all must die . . .

Jiya: Why must all die, Father?

Jiya's Father: Who knows? Simply, it is so.

(They stand, looking over the sea.)

Act Two

Open on: The Japanese scene of sea and mountainside, with Fuji in the distance, as in Act One.

Narrator: Yet there was much in life to enjoy. Kino had a good time every day. In the winter he went to school in the fishing village, and he and Jiya shared a bench and a writing table. But in summer Kino had to work hard on the farm. On those days he could not run down the mountainside to find Jiya.

There were days when Jiya, too, could not play. He and his father sailed their boats out to sea to cast their nets at dawn. If they were lucky, their nets came up so heavy with fish that it took all their strength to haul them in.

Sometimes, if it were not seedtime or harvest, Kino went with Jiya and his father. It was exciting to get up in the night and put on his warm jacket. Down the stone steps of the mountain path, Kino ran straight to the narrow dock where the fishing boats bobbed up and down with the tide. Jiya and his father were already there, and in a few minutes their boat was nosing its way past the sand bar toward the open sea. Kino crouched down in the bow, and his heart rose with joy and excitement. It was like flying into the sky. The winds were so mild, the sea lay so calm and blue, that it was hard to believe it could be cruel and angry. Actually it was the earth that brought the big wave.

371

One day, as Kino helped his father plant turnips, a cloud came over the sun.

(Dissolve to: A field, and Kino and his Father. The volcano is in the background.)

Kino: Look, Father, the volcano is burning again!

Father *(straightens and gazes anxiously at the sky):* It looks very angry. I shall not sleep tonight. We must hurry home.

Kino: Why should the volcano be angry, Father?

Father: Who knows? Simply, the inner fire burns. Come—make haste.

(They gather their tools.

Dissolve to: Night, outside the farmhouse. Kino's Father sits on a bench outside the door. He gazes at the red sky above the volcano. The Mother comes to the door.)

Mother: Can you put out the volcano fire by not sleeping?

Father: Look at the fishing village! Every house is lit. And the lamps are lit in the castle. Shall I sleep like a fool?

Mother *(silent, troubled, watching him):* I have taken the dishes from the shelves and put away our good clothes in boxes.

Father *(gazing at the village):* If only I knew whether it would be earth or sea! Both work evil. The fires rage under the sea, the rocks boil. The volcano is the vent unless the sea bottom breaks.

Kino *(coming to the door):* Shall we have an earthquake, Father?

Father: I cannot tell.

Mother: How still it is! There's no wind. The sea is purple.

Kino: Why is the sea such a color?

Father: Sea mirrors sky. Sea and earth and sky—if they work against man, who can live?

Kino *(coming to his Father's side):* Do the gods forget us?

Father: There are times when the gods leave men alone. They test us to see how able we are to save ourselves.

Kino: What if we are not able?

Father: We must be able. Fear makes us weak. If you are afraid, your hands tremble, your feet falter. Brain cannot tell hands what to do.

Setsu *(her voice calling from inside the house):* Mother, I'm afraid!

Mother: I am coming! *(She goes away.)*

Father: The sky is growing black. Go into the house, Kino.

Kino: Let me stay with you.

Father: The red flag is flying over the castle. Twice I've seen that red flag go up, both times before you were born. Old Gentleman wants everybody to be ready.

Kino *(frightened):* Ready for what?

Father: For whatever must be.

(A deep-toned bell tolls over the mountainside.)

Kino: What is that bell? I've never heard it before.

Father: It rang twice before you were born. It is the bell inside Old Gentleman's temple. He is calling to the people to come up out of the village and find shelter within his walls.

Kino: Will they come?

Father: Not all of them. Parents will try to make their children go, but the children will not want to leave their parents. Mothers will not want to leave fathers, and the fathers will stay by the boats. But some will want to be sure of life.

(The bell continues to ring. Soon from the village comes a straggling line of people, nearly all of them children.)

Kino *(gazing at them):* I wish Jiya would come. *(He takes off his white cloth girdle and waves it.)*

(Dissolve to: Jiya and his Father *by their house. Sea in the background, roaring.)*

Jiya's Father: Jiya, you must go to the castle.

Jiya: I won't leave you . . . and Mother.

Jiya's Father. We must divide ourselves. If we die, you must live after us.

Jiya: I don't want to live alone.

Jiya's Father: It's your duty to obey me, as a good Japanese son.

Jiya: Let me go to Kino's House.

Jiya's Father: Only go . . . go quickly.

(Jiya and his Father *embrace fiercely, and Jiya runs away, crying, to leap up the mountainside.*

Dissolve to: Terrace and farmhouse, and center on Kino *and his* Father, *who put out their hands to help Jiya up the last terrace. Suddenly Kino screams.)*

Kino: Look . . . look at the sea!
Father: May the gods save us.

(The bell begins to toll, deep, pleading, incessant.)

Jiya *(shrieking):* I must go back. . . . I must tell my father.
Father *(holding him):* It is too late. . . .

(Dissolve to: The sea rushes up in a terrible wave and swallows the shore. The water roars about the foot of the mountain. Jiya, held by Kino *and his* Father, *stares and then sinks unconscious to the ground. The bell tolls on.)*

• **incessant** (in SES unt) without interruption

Act Three

Narrator: So the big wave came, swelling out of the sea. It lifted the horizon while the people watched. The air was filled with its roar and shout. It rushed over the flat, still waters of the sea; it reached the village and covered it fathoms deep in swirling, wild water—green, laced with fierce white foam. The wave ran up the mountainside until the knoll upon which the castle stood was an island. All who were still climbing the path were swept away in the wicked waters. Then with a great sigh, the wave ebbed into the sea, dragging everything with it—trees, rocks, houses, people.

Upon the beach, where the village had stood, not a house remained. All that had been was now no more.

(Dissolve to: Inside the farmhouse. The farm family is gathered about the mattress on which Jiya lies. Kino cannot stop crying, though silently.)

Setsu *(coming to stare at Jiya):* Is Jiya dead?
Father: No, Jiya is living.
Setsu: Why doesn't he open his eyes?
Father: Soon he will open his eyes.
Kino: What will we say to Jiya when he wakes? How can we tell him?
Father: We will not talk. We will give warm food and let him rest. We will help him to feel he is a home.
Kino: Here?
Father: Here. As soon as he knows his home, we must help him to understand what has happened. Ah, here is Mother, with your hot rice soup. Eat it, my son. Food for the body is food, too, for the heart, sometimes.

(Kino takes the bowl from his Mother with both hands and drinks. Setsu leans her head against her Mother.
Dissolve to: Evening. The same room, the same scene except that Mother and Setsu are not there. Father sits beside Jiya's bed. Kino is at the open door.)

Kino: The sky is golden, Father, and the sea is smooth. How cruel—
Father: No, it is wonderful that after the storm the sea grows calm again, and the sky is clear. It was not the sea or the sky that made the evil storm.

375

Kino *(not turning his head):* Who made it?

Father: Ah, no one knows who makes evil storms. We only know that they come. When they come we must live through them as bravely as we can, and after they are gone we must feel again how wonderful is life. Every day of life is more valuable now than it was before the storm.

Kino: But Jiya's father and mother . . . and the other fisherfolk . . . so good and kind . . . all of them . . . lost. *(He cannot go on.)*

Father: We must think of Jiya—who lives. *(He stops. Jiya has begun to sob softly.)* Quick, Kino—call your mother and Setsu. He will open his eyes at any moment, and we must all be here— you his brother, I his father, and the mother, the sister. . . .

(Kino runs out. Father kneels beside Jiya, who stirs, still sobbing. Kino comes back with Mother and Setsu. They kneel on the floor beside the bed. Jiya's eyelids flutter. He opens his eyes and looks from one face to the other. He stares at the beams of the roof, the walls of the room, the bed, his own hands. All are quiet except Setsu, who cannot keep from laughing. She claps her hands.)

Setsu: Oh, Jiya has come back. Jiya, did you have a good dream?

Jiya *(faintly):* My father, my mother . . .

Mother *(taking his hand in both hers):* I will be your mother now, dear Jiya.

Father: I will be your father.

Kino: I am your brother now, Jiya. *(He falters.)*

Setsu *(joyfully):* Oh, Jiya, you will live with us.

(Jiya gets up slowly. He walks to the door, goes out, and looks down the hillside.

Dissolve to: The peaceful empty beach. Then back to the farmhouse and Jiya, standing outside and looking at the sea. Setsu comes to him.)

Setsu: I will give you my pet duck. He'll make you laugh.

Mother *(leaving the room):* We ought all to eat something, I have a fine chicken for dinner.

376

Act Four

Narrator: The body heals first, and the body heals the mind and the soul. Jiya ate food, he got out of bed sometimes, but he did not want to think or remember. He only wanted to sleep.

All through these days Kino did not play about as once he had. He was no longer a child. He worked hard beside his father in the fields. They did not talk much, and neither of them wanted to look at the sea. It was enough to look at the earth, dark and rich beneath their feet.

One evening Kino climbed the mountain behind the house and looked up at the volcano. The heavy cloud of smoke had gone away, and the sky was clear. He was glad that the volcano was no longer angry, and he went down again to the house. On the threshold his father was smoking his usual evening pipe. In the house his mother was giving Setsu her evening bath.

Kino: Is Jiya asleep again?

Father: Yes, and it is a good thing for him. When he sleeps enough, he will wake and remember.

Kino: But should he remember?

Father: Only when he dares to remember his parents will he be happy again.

(A silence.)

Kino: Father, are we not very unfortunate people to live in Japan?

Father: Why do you think so?

Kino: The volcano is behind our house, and the sea is in front. When they work together to make earthquake and big wave, we are helpless. Always, many of us are lost.

Father: To live in the presence of death makes us brave and strong. That is why our people never fear death. We see it too often, and we do not fear it. To die a little sooner or a little later does not matter. But to live bravely, to love life, to see how beautiful the trees are and the mountains—yes, and even the sea—to enjoy work because it produces food—in these we are fortunate people. We love life because we live in danger. We do not fear death, for we understand that death and life are necessary to each other.

• threshold (THRESH ohld) **entrance to a house or building**

377

Kino: What is death?

Father: Death is the great gateway.

Kino: The gateway . . . where?

Father: Can you remember when you were born?

Kino: I was too small.

Father *(smiling):* I remember very well. Oh, how hard you thought it was to be born. You cried and you screamed.

Kino *(much interested):* Didn't I want to be born?

Father: You did not. You wanted to stay just where you were, in the warm dark house of the unborn. But the time came to be born, and the gate of life opened.

Kino: Did I know it was the gate of life?

Father: You did not know anything about it, and so you were afraid. But see how foolish you were! Here we were waiting for you, your parents, already loving you and eager to welcome you. And you have been very happy, haven't you?

Kino: Until the big wave came. Now I am afraid again because of the death the big wave brought.

Father: You are only afraid because you don't know anything about death. But someday you will wonder why you were afraid, even as today you wonder why you once feared to be born.

Kino: I think I understand. . . . I begin to understand. . . .

Father: Do not hurry yourself. You have plenty of time. *(He rises to his feet.)* Now what do I see? A lantern coming up the hill.

Kino *(running to the edge of the threshold):* Who can be coming now? It is almost night.

Father: A visitor . . . ah, why, it's Old Gentleman!

(Old Gentleman is climbing the hill. He is somewhat breathless in spite of his long staff. His servant carries the lantern and, when they arrive, steps to one side.)

Old Gentleman *(to* servant*):* Is this the house of Uchiyama, the farmer?

Servant: It is—and this is the farmer himself and his son.

Father *(bowing):* Please, Honored Sir, what can I do for you?

Old Gentleman: Do you have a lad here by the name of Jiya?

Father: He lies sleeping in my house.

Old Gentleman: I wish to see him.

Father: Sir, he suffered the loss of his parents when the big wave came. Now sleep heals him.

Old Gentleman: I will not wake him. I only wish to look at him.

Father: Please come in.

(Dissolve to: Jiya *asleep. The* servant *holds the lantern so that the light does not fall on Jiya's face directly.* Old Gentleman *looks at him carefully.)*

Old Gentleman: Tall and strong for his age—intelligent—handsome. Hmm . . . yes. *(He motions to the* servant *to lead him away, and the scene returns to the dooryard. To* Father*)* It is my habit, when the big wave comes, to care for those who are orphaned by it. Thrice in my lifetime I have searched out the orphans, and I have fed them and sheltered them. But I have heard of this boy Jiya and wish to do more for him. If he is as good as he is handsome, I will take him for my own son.

Kino: But Jiya is ours!

Father *(sternly):* Hush. We are only poor people. If Old Gentleman wants Jiya, we cannot say we will not give him up.

Old Gentleman: Exactly. I will give him fine clothes and send him to a school, and he may become a great man and an honor to our whole province and even to the nation.

Kino: But if he lives in the castle we can't be brothers!

Father: We must think of Jiya's good. *(He turns to* Old Gentleman.*)* Sir, it is very kind of you to propose this for Jiya. I had planned to take him for my own son, now that he has lost his birth parents; but I am only a poor farmer, and I cannot pretend that my house is as good as yours or that I can afford to send Jiya to a fine school. Tomorrow when he wakes I will tell him of your kind offer. He will decide.

Old Gentleman: Very well. But let him come and tell me himself.

Father *(proudly):* Certainly. Jiya must speak for himself.

*(Old Gentleman bows *and prepares to depart.* Father *bows and taps* Kino *on the head to make him bow.* Old Gentleman *and his* servant *return down the mountain.)*

Kino: If Jiya goes away, I shall never have a brother.

Father: Kino, don't be selfish. You must allow Jiya to make his own choice. It would be wrong to persuade him. I forbid you to speak to him of this matter. When he wakes, I will tell him myself.

(Dissolve to: Kino working in the terrace, weeding. It is evident that he has worked for some time. He looks hot and dusty, and he has quite a pile of weeds. He stops to look up at the farmhouse, but he sees no one and resigns himself again to his task. Suddenly his name is called.)

Father: Kino!

Kino: Shall I come?

Father: No, I am coming—with Jiya.

(Kino stands, waiting. Father and Jiya come down the terraces. Jiya is very sad. When he sees Kino, he tries not to cry.)

Father *(putting his arm about Jiya's shoulder):* Jiya, you must not mind that you cry easily. Until now you couldn't cry because you weren't fully alive. You had been hurt too much. But today you are beginning to live, and so your tears flow. It is good for you. Let your tears come—don't stop them. *(He turns to Kino.)* I have told Jiya that he must not decide where he will live until he has seen the inside of the castle. He must see all that Old Gentleman can give him. Jiya, you know how our house is—four small rooms, and the kitchen, this farm, upon which we have to work hard for our food. We have only what our hands earn for us. *(He holds out his two workworn hands.)* If you live in the castle, you need never have hands like these.

Jiya: I don't want to live in the castle.

Father: You don't know whether you do or not; you have never seen the castle inside. *(He turns to Kino.)* Kino, you are to go with Jiya, and when you reach the castle you must persuade him to stay there for his own sake.

(Kino and Jiya go, reluctantly, and Father watches them.
Dissolve to: The mountainside and the two boys nearing the gate of the castle. The gate is open, and inside an old Gardener is sweeping moss under pine trees. He sees them.)

Gardener: What do you want, boys?

Kino: My father sent us to see the honored Old Gentleman.

Gardener: Are you the Uchiyama boy?

Kino: Yes, please, and this is Jiya, whom Old Gentleman wishes to come and live here.

Gardener *(bowing to Jiya):* Follow me, young sir.

(They follow over a pebbled path under the leaning pine trees. In the distance the sun falls upon a flowering garden and a pool with a waterfall.)

Kino *(sadly):* How beautiful it is—of course you will want to live here. Who could blame you?

(Jiya does not answer. He walks with his head held high. They come to a great door, where a servant bids them take off their shoes. The Gardener leaves them.)

Servant: Follow me.

(They follow through passageways into a great room decorated in the finest Japanese fashion. In the distance at the end of the room, they see Old Gentleman sitting beside a small table. Behind him the open panels reveal the garden. Old Gentleman is writing. He is carefully painting letters on a scroll, his silver-rimmed glasses sliding down his nose. When the two boys approach, the servant announces them.)

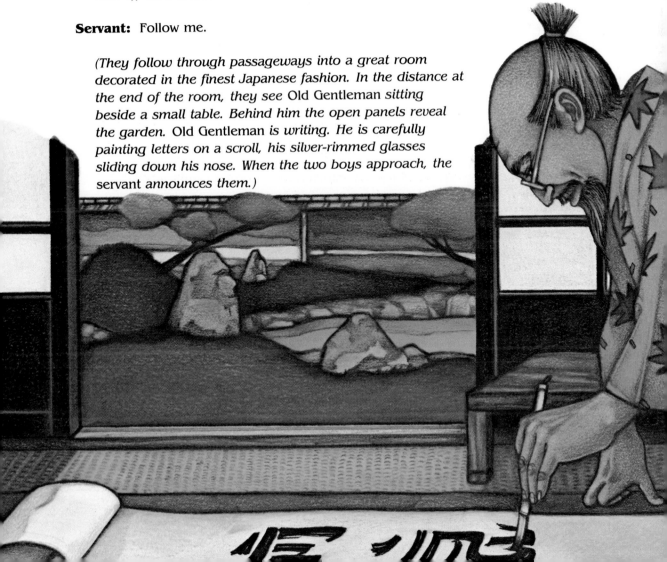

Servant: Master, the two boys are here.

Old Gentleman *(to boys):* Would you two like to know what I have been writing?

(Jiya looks at Kino, *who is too awed to speak.)*

Jiya: Yes, Honored Sir, if you please.

Old Gentleman *(taking up the scroll):* It is not my own poem. It is the saying of a wise man of India, but I like it so much that I have painted it on this scroll to hang there in the alcove where I can see it every day. *(He reads clearly and slowly.)*

> "The children of God are much revered,
> But rather weird—
> Very nice, but very narrow."

(He looks up over his spectacles.) What do you think of it?

Jiya *(looking at* Kino, *who is too shy to speak):* We do not understand it, sir.

Old Gentleman *(shaking his head and laughing softly):* Ah, we are all children of God! *(He takes off his spectacles and looks hard at* Jiya.) Well? Will you be my son?

(Jiya, too embarrassed to speak, looks away.)

Old Gentleman: Say yes or no. Either word is not hard to speak.

Jiya: I will say . . . no. *(He feels this is too harsh, and he smiles apologetically.)* I thank you, sir, but I have a home . . . on a farm.

Kino *(trying to repress his joy and speaking very solemnly as a consequence):* Jiya, remember how poor we are.

Old Gentleman: *(smiling, half sad):* They are certainly very poor and here, you know, you would have everything. You can even invite this farm boy to come and play, sometimes, if you like. And I am quite willing for you to give the family some money. It would be suitable as my son for you to help the poor.

Jiya *(suddenly, as though he had not heard):* Where are the others who were saved from the big wave?

• **alcove** (AL kohv) small room opening out of a larger room

Old Gentleman: Some wanted to go away, and the ones who wanted to stay are out in the backyard with my servants.

Jiya: Why do you not invite them to come into this castle and be your sons and daughters?

Old Gentleman *(somewhat outraged by this):* Because I don't want them for my sons and daughters. You are a bright, handsome boy. They told me you were the best boy in the village.

Jiya: I am not better than the others. My father was a fisherman.

Old Gentleman *(taking up his spectacles and his brush):* Very well— I will do without a son.

(The servant motions to the boys to come away, and they follow.)

Servant *(to Jiya):* How foolish you are! Our Old Gentleman is very kind. You would have everything here.

Jiya: Not everything . . .

Kino: Let's hurry home—let's hurry—hurry . . .

(They run down the mountain and up the hill to the farmhouse. Setsu sees them and comes flying to meet them, the sleeves of her bright kimono like wings, and her feet clattering in their wooden sandals.)

Setsu: Jiya has come home—Jiya, Jiya . . .

(Jiya sees her happy face and opens his arms and gives her a great hug.)

Act Five

Narrator: Now happiness began to live in Jiya, though secretly and hidden inside him, in ways he did not understand. The good food warmed him, and the love of the four people who received him glowed like a warm and welcoming fire upon his heart.

Time passed. Eight years. Jiya grew up in the farmhouse to be a tall young man, and Kino grew at his side, solid and strong. Setsu grew, too, from a mischievous, laughing child into a will-ful, pretty girl.

In all these years no one returned to live on the empty beach. The tides rose and fell, sweeping the sands clear every day. Storms came and went, but there was never such a wave as the big one. At last people began to think that never again would there be such a big wave. The few fishermen who had listened to the tolling bell from the castle, and were saved with their wives and children, went to other shores to fish. Then, as time passed, they told themselves that no beach was quite as good as the old one. There, they said, the water was deep and great fish came close to the shore.

Jiya and Kino had not often gone to the beach, either. When they went to swim in the sea, they walked across the farm and over another fold of the mountains to the shore. The big wave had changed Jiya forever. He did not laugh easily or speak carelessly. In school he had earnestly learned all he could, and now he worked hard on the farm. Now, as a man, he valued deeply everything that was good. Since the big wave had been so cruel, he was never cruel, and he grew kind and gentle. Sometimes, in the morning, he went to the door of the farmhouse and looked at the empty beach below, searching as though something might one day come back. One day he did see something. . . .

Jiya: Kino, come here! *(Kino comes out, his shoes in his hand.)* Look—is someone building a house on the beach?

Kino: Two men—pounding posts into the sand—

Jiya: And a woman . . . yes, and even a child.

Kino: They can't be building a house.

Jiya: Let's go and see.

(Dissolve to: The beach. The two Men, Jiya and Kino, Woman and Child.)

Jiya *(out of breath):* Are you building a house?

First Man *(wiping sweat from his face):* Our father used to live here, and we with him. We are two brothers. During these years we have lived in the houses of the castle, and we have fished from other shores. Now we are tired of having no homes of our own. Besides, this is still the best beach for fishing.

Kino: What if the big wave comes again?

Second Man *(shrugging his shoulders):* There was a big wave, too, in our great-grandfather's time. All the houses were swept away. But our grandfather came back. In our father's time there was again the big wave. Now we return.

Kino *(soberly):* What of your children?

384

First Man: The big wave may never come back.

(The Men begin to dig agian. The Woman takes the Child into her arms and gazes out to sea. Suddenly there is a sound of a voice calling. All look up the mountain.)

First Man: Here comes our Old Gentleman.
Second Man: He's very angry or he wouldn't have left the castle.

(Both throw down their shovels and stand waiting. The Woman sinks to a kneeling position on the sand, still holding the Child. Old Gentleman shouts as he comes near, his voice high and thin. He is very old now, and is supported by two servants. His beard flies in the wind.)

Old Gentleman: You foolish children! You leave the safety of my walls and come back to this dangerous shore, as your father did before you! The big wave will return and sweep you into the sea.
First Man: It may not, Ancient Sir.
Old Gentleman: It will come. I have spent my whole life trying to save foolish people from the big wave. But you will not be saved.
Jiya *(stepping forward):* Sir, here is our home. Dangerous as it is, threatened by the volcano and sea, it is here we were born.
Old Gentleman *(looking at him):* Don't I know you?
Jiya: Sir, I was once in your castle.
Old Gentleman *(nodding):* I remember you. I wanted you for my son. Ah, you made a great mistake, young man. You could have lived safely in my castle all your life, and your children would have been safe there. The big wave never reaches me.
Kino: Sir, your castle is not safe, either. If the earth shakes hard enough, even your castle will crumble. There is no refuge for us who live on these islands. We are brave because we must be.
Second Man: Ha—you are right.

(The two Men return to their building.)

Old Gentleman *(rolling his eyes and wagging his beard):* Don't ask me to save you the next time the big wave comes!
Jiya *(gently):* But you will save us, because you are so good.
Old Gentleman *(looking at him and then smiling sadly):* What a pity you would not be my son! *(He turns and, leaning on his servants, climbs the mountain.)*

(Dissolve to: The field, where Father *and* Jiya *and* Kino *are working.)*

Father *(to Jiya):* Did you soak the seeds for the rice?
Jiya *(aghast):* I forgot.
Kino: I did it.
Jiya *(throwing down his*   I forget everything these days.
Father: I know you are t   d a son to be forgetful on purpose.
     Tell me what is on y   l.
Jiya: I want a boat. I w   back to fishing.

*(*Father *does not paus   s hoeing; but* Kino *flings down his hoe.)*

Kino: You, too, are foolish!
Jiya *(stubbornly):* When I have a boat, I shall build my house on the beach.
Kino: Oh, fool, fool!
Father: Be quiet! Jiya is a man. You are both men. I shall pay you wages from this day.
Jiya: Wages! *(He falls to   g vigorously.)*

(Dissolve to: The bea   e Kino *and* Jiya *are inspecting a boat.)*

Jiya: I knew all the time   I had to come back to the sea.
Kino: With this boat, you'll soon earn enough to build a house. But I'm glad I live on the mountain.

(They continue inspecting the boat, fitting the oars, etc., as they talk.)

Jiya *(abruptly):* Do you think Setsu would be afraid to live on the beach?
Kino *(surprised):* Why would Setsu live on the beach?
Jiya *(embarrassed but determined):* Because when I have my house built, I want Setsu to be my wife.
Kino *(astonished):* Setsu? You would be foolish to marry her.
Jiya *(smiling):* I don't agree with you.
Kino *(seriously):* But why . . . why do you want her?
Jiya: Because she makes me laugh. It is she who made me forget the big wave. For me, she is life.

Kino: But she is not a good cook. Think how she burns the rice when she runs outside to look at something.

Jiya: I don't mind burned rice, and I will run out with her to see what she sees.

Kino *(with gestures of astonishment):* I can't understand. . . .

(Dissolve to: The farmhouse, and Father, *who is looking over his seeds.)*

Kino *(coming in stealthily):* Do you know that Jiya wants to marry Setsu?

Father: I have seen some looks pass between them.

Kino: But Jiya is too good for Setsu.

Father: Setsu is very pretty.

Kino: With that silly nose?

Father *(calmly):* I believe that Jiya admires her nose.

Kino: Besides, she is such a tease.

Father: What makes you miserable will make him happy.

Kino: I don't understand that, either.

Father *(laughing):* Someday you will understand.

(Dissolve to: Narrator.*)*

Narrator: One day, one early summer, Jiya and Setsu were married. Kino still did not understand, for up to the last, Setsu was naughty and mischievous. Indeed on the very day of her wedding she hid Kino's hairbrush under his bed. "You are too silly to be married," Kino said, when he had found it. "I feel sorry for Jiya," he said. Setsu's big brown eyes laughed at him. "I shall always be nice to Jiya," she said.

But when the wedding was over and the family had taken the newly married pair down the hill to the new house on the beach, Kino felt sad. The farmhouse was very quiet without Setsu. Every day he could go to see Jiya, and many times he would go fishing with him. But Setsu would not be in the farmhouse or in the garden. He would miss even her teasing. And then he grew very grave. What if the big wave came again?

(Dissolve to: The new house. Kino, Jiya, Father, Mother, *and* Setsu *are standing outside.* Kino *turns to Jiya.)*

387

Kino: Jiya, it is all very pretty—very nice. But, Setsu—what if the big wave comes again?

Jiya: I have prepared for that. Come—all of you. *(He calls the family in.)* This is where we will sleep at night, and where we will live by day. But look—

(The family watches as Jiya pushes back a long panel in the wall. Before their eyes is the sea, swelling and stirring under the evening wind. The sun is sinking into the water.)

Jiya: I have opened my house to the sea. If ever the big wave comes back, I shall be ready. I face it, night and day. I am not afraid.

Kino: Tomorrow I'll go fishing with you, Jiya—shall I?

Jiya *(laughing):* Not tomorrow, brother!

Father: Come—come! *(Setsu comes to his side and leans against him, and he puts his arm around her.)* Yes, life is stronger than death. *(He turns to his family.)* Come, let us go home.

(Father and Mother and Kino bow and leave. Jiya and Setsu stand looking out to sea.)

Jiya: Life is stronger than death—do you hear that, Setsu?

Setsu: Yes, I hear.

ALL THINGS CONSIDERED ────────────────

1. On one side of the farm is the sea, and on the other side is a (a) town. (b) volcano. (c) desert.
2. The fishing people have no window looking out to the sea because (a) the sea breeze is cold. (b) the morning sun is bright. (c) the sea is their enemy.
3. The Old Gentleman lives high up in order to (a) look over the sea. (b) be alone. (c) be near the volcano.
4. When the volcano starts burning, the sea looks (a) dangerous. (b) peaceful. (c) small.
5. The castle bell rings so the people can (a) go out to sea. (b) run from the volcano. (c) come up to the safety of the castle.
6. The big wave swallows the (a) village. (b) farm. (c) castle.
7. Kino's father says that living in the presence of death makes people (a) happy and carefree. (b) afraid and sad. (c) brave and strong.
8. The Old Gentleman wants to (a) help Kino's father. (b) start a farm. (c) adopt Jiya.
9. After the big wave, the people (a) never work again. (b) never return to the sea. (c) slowly return to the sea.
10. Jiya (a) loves farming. (b) marries Setsu. (c) fights with Kino.
11. In their new home, Jiya and Setsu have a window facing (a) the sea. (b) the volcano. (c) the town.
12. At the end of the play, Jiya says that life is (a) good even when it is sad. (b) stronger than death. (c) fun only for children.

THINKING IT THROUGH ────────────────

1. Who is the main character in this play? Why? What conflict does this character face?
2. Why do the people return to the fishing life when they could have lived safely up on the mountain slopes? Do you think this shows that the people are foolish or brave? Why?
3. In what ways are the people threatened by the land and the sea? How does this give the play its meaning? How would you state the theme of the play? Does such a threat affect any of the people of the world today? Explain.

Oral Interpretation: Review —————

Reading Dialogue

As you know, oral interpretation is reading aloud in a way that best expresses the meaning of a story, poem, or play. Plays are especially good to use for oral interpretation because they contain dialogue, the exact words spoken by a character.

Work with a group of classmates to present "The Big Wave". Each member of the group should read the lines of one character in the play. One person can read the narrator's part. Another person can read the stage directions. Before beginning, discuss what each character is like. After each member of the group understands what his or her character is thinking and feeling, begin reading the play.

Practice: Practice several times until all members of the group are satisfied with their performances. Now, perform the play for the rest of the class.

Composition —————

Follow your teacher's instructions before completing *one* of these writing assignments.

1. Choose a story in this book. Rewrite the story in the form of a play. To do this, you must write dialogue, or conversation, for each of the characters.
2. Write two paragraphs describing one of the characters in "The Big Wave." In your first paragraph, describe how the character looks. In the second paragraph, tell how this character behaves.

UNIT REVIEW

I. What do you think is the greatest "great idea" in this unit? Take time to review the selections in this unit, then write two paragraphs about this great idea. Use the following plan.

Paragraph 1: Tell which selection has the greatest idea. What is this great idea and how does the author express it? Does the author explain it, or does the author express it through the actions of a character, as Julius Lester does in "The Man Who Was a Horse"?

Paragraph 2: Tell why the idea appeals to you. Is it useful? Will it mean a lot to you as you go through school? Is it perhaps just a very interesting idea that may not offer much practical help? Be sure to give one or two examples to support your opinion.

II. Write a report on a story in this unit. Use the following plan.

Paragraph 1: After you have given the title and author, tell what you thought of the selection. Be sure to explain how it relates to the theme "great ideas."

Paragraph 2: If your selection is fiction, describe the plot in one or two sentences. That is, tell what problem is faced by the main character(s) and how the problem is resolved.

Paragraph 3: Explain whether or not other people would benefit from reading this selection? Do you think it would be more interesting to young people or to older people? Do you think people would remember it for the rest of their lives?

Paragraph 4: If the selection is nonfiction, tell the author's topic and what the author wants to say about the topic. That is, present the author's main idea. Then tell the author's purpose. Is the selection simply meant to be entertaining? Is it meant to explain something? Is it meant to convince you of an idea?

Paragraph 5: Does the author succeed in his or her purpose? Tell why or why not.

SPEAKING UP

Here are quotations from two great men and one great woman. Each expresses a great idea. Read each quotation and take time to think about its meaning. Choose one of the quotations and relate its meaning to the theme of one of the stories you have read in this unit.

Now, it is your turn to speak up.

1. Recite the quotation.
2. Tell what the quotation means.
3. Tell which selection you think is related to the quotation.

"Never can custom conquer nature; for she is ever unconquered."
Cicero

"It takes courage to be wise."
Horace

"Falsehood is so easy, truth is so difficult."
George Eliot

WRITING YOUR OWN PLOT

Pictures spark ideas. What ideas does this picture spark in your mind? What do you think is happening or is about to happen?

1. **Prewriting:** Look closely at the picture. List as many ideas as you can think of to answer the following questions. (1) Who are the characters in this picture? (2) What was happening when the photographer snapped the picture? (3) What happened immediately after the picture was taken? Be sure to include details about character, setting, and plot.

2. **Writing:** Write a story that develops each one of these questions into a paragraph. Look back at the notes you wrote in the prewriting stage, and decide which details to include in each paragraph.

3. **Revising:** Read your story. Is it interesting? Have you developed a single idea in each paragraph? Do your paragraphs make sense together? Have you used correct spelling, punctuation, and grammar? Make corrections and rewrite your paragraphs.

Glossary of Terms

This glossary defines terms that you have studied. The page references shown with the terms indicate where the terms are defined and discussed. Turn to those pages if you need to review the lessons.

Author's Purpose p. 254 Every author has a *purpose,* or reason, for writing. Often an author's purpose is to teach, to entertain, or to convince.

Autobiography p. 22 An *autobiography* is a true story of a person's life, written by that person. (See also *Biography.*)

Biography p. 22 A *biography* is a story about the life of a real person. The person who is the *subject* of a biography may be alive or dead. A biography may tell about a single event in a person's life, or it may tell an entire life story. (See also *Autobiography.*)

Cause and Effect p. 200 A *cause* is an event or idea that leads to a certain result, called an *effect.* A cause-and-effect statement often contains a clue word or phrase such as *because, so, since,* or *for that reason.* Understanding cause and effect helps the reader follow the events in a story.

Characters pp. 7, 15, 31 *Characters* are the people, animals, or creatures in a story who do things and have things happen to them.

Character Growth p. 294 *Character growth* refers to the ways a character changes from the beginning of a story to the end.

Choral Reading pp. 128, 204 *Choral* (KOR ul) *reading* is reading aloud in a group. It is like a chorus of voices speaking rather than singing.

Climax p. 136 The *climax* is the turning point in a story. The actions that the characters take to resolve the conflict in a story lead to the climax. (See also *Conflict* and *Conclusion.*)

Comparison p. 136 A *comparison* is a way of showing how two or more things are alike. (See also *Contrast.*)

Conclusion pp. 113, 136 Every story has a beginning, a middle, and an end. The ending of a story is called the *conclusion.* It is the part of a story in which the conflict is resolved. (See also *Climax* and *Conflict.*)

Conflict pp. 95, 104, 113, 136 A *conflict* is a problem that a character must overcome. In every story, the main character is faced with a conflict. The three basic kinds of conflicts are: conflict between persons, conflict between a person and a thing, and conflict within a person. (See also *Climax* and *Conclusion.*)

Context Clues p. 219 *Context clues* are the words surrounding an unfamiliar word. Context clues can help the reader discover the meaning of an unfamiliar word. They can also help the reader decide the correct meaning or pronunciation of a word with several meanings or pronunciations.

Contrast p. 136 A *contrast* points out the difference between two or more things. (See also *Comparison.*)

Dialogue p. 303 *Dialogue* is the conversation between two or more characters. Quotation marks indicate the beginning and end of a character's exact words. "Be careful," said Grandpa. "You haven't had hardly any experience thinking like a wolf."

Exaggeration p. 42 *Exaggeration* is a statement in which something is made to seem bigger or more important than it really is. Exaggeration is often found in humorous writing.

Fact p. 283 A *fact* is a statement you can check and prove to be false or true. (See also *Opinion.*)

Fiction p. 95 Literature that tells about imaginary characters and events is called *fiction.* (See also *Nonfiction.*)

Five W's p. 65 The *five w's* are question words that begin with a W. They are *who, what, when, where,* and *why.* These words ask the basic questions a reader must have answered in order to understand a story.

Foreshadowing p. 104 An author will sometimes hint about what is going to happen later on in the development of a story. Giving such a hint is called *foreshadowing.*

Idiom p. 145 An *idiom* is an expression whose meaning cannot be understood from the ordinary meaning of each word it contains.

Inference p. 213 An *inference* is a reader's guess about something that is not directly stated in a story. The reader uses details in the story and general knowledge to make an inference.

Legend p. 34 *Legends* are stories that have been told over the years. Although legends are based on the lives of real people, unreal events are often added as the story is passed along. Over the years, the extra details grow in number, and the events of the story become larger than life.

Narrative p. 303 A *narrative* is a writing selection that tells a story.

Nonfiction p. 95 Literature that tells about real characters and events is called *nonfiction.* (See also *Fiction.*)

Opinion p. 283 An *opinion* is a person's belief about something or someone. It cannot be proved true or false. (See also *Fact.*)

Oral Interpretation p. 19 *Oral interpretation* is reading aloud with expression. Through oral interpretation, a reader presents a selection in a way that can be understood and enjoyed by listeners.

Paraphrase pp. 122, 267 To *paraphrase* is to retell a story in your own words. A paraphrase should give the main idea and most important details of a story or passage.

Plot pp. 7, 95, 104 *Plot* is *what happens* in a story. It is the series of events or actions that take place. (See also *Climax, Conflict, Conclusion,* and *Rising Action.*)

Rising Action p. 136 The increasing tension in a story caused by conflicts and other events is called *rising action.* The rising action leads to the story's climax, or turning point. (See also *Climax.*)

Setting pp. 7, 187 *Setting* tells *where* and *when* a story takes place. A story may have one or more settings.

Supporting Details p. 275 *Supporting details* are statements that support the main idea of a paragraph. (See also *Topic Sentence.*)

Synonyms pp. 50, 174 Words that have the same or almost the same meaning are called *synonyms.* Writers use synonyms to add variety and interest to their writing.

Theme pp. 7, 259, 294 The *theme* is the basic idea of a piece of writing. It is the message—the meaning—that the writer hopes to give the reader. (See also *Topic.*)

Time Order p. 194 *Time order* is the order of events in a story. It tells which events happen first, second, and last. Clue words such as *first, next, then, later,* and *finally* help signal the order of events.

Topic pp. 259, 294 The *topic* is what a piece of writing is about. It should not be confused with *theme.* The topic can usually be expressed in a word or just a few words. The topic of "The Big Wave" is surviving a natural disaster.

Topic Sentence p. 275 A *topic sentence* states the most important idea of a paragraph. (See also *Supporting Details.*)

Turning Point p. 136 The *turning point* is the high point in the action of a story. (See also *Climax.*)

Visualizing pp. 56, 228 Forming a picture in your mind is called *visualizing.* Writers often use descriptive words and details to give the reader a clear mental picture of the characters, setting, and events in a story.

Glossary

ab so lute (AB suh loot) *adj.* complete; final; perfect

ac cu sa tion (ak yoo ZAY shun) *n.* a charge of wrongdoing

ac knowl edge (ak NOL ij) *v.* admit that something is true

ac quaint ance (uh KWAYN tuns) *n.* person you know, but not very well

ac tiv i ties (ak TIV uh teez) *n.* doings; movements

ad van tage (ad VAN tij) *n.* something that gives a person a better chance; something that is in one's favor

ag o nized (AG uh nyzd) *adj.* suffering greatly; in great pain

an tag o nize (an TAG uh nyz) *v.* make an enemy of someone; annoy someone

ap pli cant (AP luh kent) *n.* person who asks for something; one who applies

arc (ARK) *n.* any part of a circle

ar chi tect (AR ki tekt) *n.* a person who designs large constructions such as buildings

as cend (uh SEND) *v.* go up; rise

at om (AT um) *n.* tiny bit

au di tion (aw DISH un) *n.* a test for a part in a play or other performance; a tryout *v.* try out for a part in a performance

bail (BAIL) *v.* dip water out of

be grudge (bi GRUJ) *v.* feel angry at something another person has done; feel angry at someone else's good fortune

be wil der (bee WIL dur) *v.* puzzle; confuse

bi ol o gy (by OL uh jee) *n.* the study of living things

blob (BLOB) *n.* small lump or shapeless object

bluff (BLUF) *n.* cliff; high, steep land

bond age (BON dij) *n.* slavery

brace (BRAYS) *v.* make steady; hold firm

cen sor (SEN sur) *v.* refuse to allow something to be printed

cher ish (CHER ish) *v.* treat with love and tenderness

co in ci dence (koh IN si duns) *n.* two or more things that happen at the same time, by accident

com pete (kum PEET) *v.* enter a contest and try to win

com pet i tive ness (kum PET i tiv nis) *n.* trying hard to win against others

con flict (KON flikt) *n.* lack of agreement; struggle

con gre gate (KON gruh gayt) *v.* gather together; meet

con stant ly (KON stunt lee) *adv.* all the time; without change

cor dial (KOR jul) *adj.* friendly and warm

cor re spond (kor ih SPOND) *v.* agree; match

coun sel (KOUN sul) *n.* advice

crit i cal (KRIT uh kul) *adj.* at an important moment

cum ber some (KUM bur sum) *adj.* clumsy; difficult to manage

de hu man ize (dee HYOO mun yz) *v.* treat in a cruel manner

de spair (di SPAIR) *n.* loss of hope

de ter mine (di TUR min) *v.* decide; make up one's mind

de vour (di VOUR) *v.* eat up quickly

din gy (DIN jee) *adj.* very dirty-looking; not clean

dis a bil i ty (dis uh BIL uh tee) *n.* a handicap

dis cord (dis KORD) *n.* lack of harmony

dis pute (dis PYOOT) *v.* argue *n.* disagreement

dis sect (di SEKT) *v.* cut open and examine

dis tinc tion (dis TING shun) *n.* special quality

ec stat ic (ek STAT ik) *adj.* full of joy

en chant ed (en CHAN tid) *adj.* under a spell; charmed

en deav or (en DEV ur) *v.* try; make an effort

en dow (en DOU) *v.* enrich

en dur ance (en DOOR uns) *n.* ability to keep going

fal ter (FAWL tur) *v.* speak in an unsure way; seem unsteady

far-sight ed (FAHR SY tid) *adj.* smart enough to see what will be needed later on

flinch (FLINCH) *v.* draw back from something painful or dangerous

fod der (FOD ur) *n.* food for cattle

gen teel (jen TEEL) *adj.* polite; well-mannered

ges ture (JES chur) *n.* motion; hand signal

ghast ly (GAST lee) *adj.* horrible; frightful

glare (GLAIR) *n.* angry look

gon er (GAW nur) *n.* someone who appears to be impossible to save

head long (HED lawng) *adv.* very fast; with great speed and force

heart felt (HAHRT felt) *adj.* sincere; honest

heart i ly (HAHRT uh lee) *adv.* with spirit; with enthusiasm

hes i ta tion (hez uh TAY shun) *n.* failure to act promptly

hov er (HUV ur) *v.* hang in the air

hu man i ty (hyoo MAN i tee) *n.* all people

in com pat i ble (in kum PAT uh bul) *adj.* not in agreement; unable to live or work together peaceably

in con ven ient (in kun VEEN yunt) *adj.* troublesome; not easy to do

in ju ri ous (in JOOR ee us) *adj.* harmful

in scrip tion (in SKRIP shun) *n.* something written or engraved, often for a special occasion

in spired (in SPY urd) *adj.* having the idea or spirit to do something

ir re spon si ble (ir ree SPONS uh bul) *adj.* not responsible; unreliable

lay off *v.* put someone out of work for a while, often because there is not enough work to be done

leg end ar y (LEJ un deh ree) *adj.* found in legends

lik a ble (LY kuh bul) *adj.* pleasant and easy to like

lime light (LYM lyt) *n.* center of attention and interest

lure (LOOR) *n.* attraction

mag is trate (MAJ i strayt) *n.* judge

min gle (MING gul) *v.* mix together

mite (MYT) *n.* a little bit

mod es ty (MAHD us tee) *n.* lack of conceit

mop ing (MOHP ing) *v.* being in a silent or sad mood

mo ti vate (MOH tuh VAYT) *v.* cause to act

mourn ing (MORN ing) *n.* showing and feeling sorrow after someone's death

neg a tive (NEG uh tiv) *adj.* not helpful

ob vi ous (OB vee us) *adj.* easily seen; clear

op po si tion (op uh ZISH un) *n.* action against; resistance

pam pered (PAM purd) *adj.* spoiled; allowed too many privileges

parched (PAHRCHD) *adj.* dried out

per pen dic u lar (pur pen DIK yuh lur) *adj.* straight up; in an upright position

per plex ing (pur PLEKS ing) *adj.* puzzling; bewildering

plague (PLAYG) *v.* pester; cause trouble for *n.* something that causes trouble; a widespread disease

pos i tive (POZ uh tiv) *adj.* helpful

po ten tial (puh TEN shul) *n.* ability that is not yet used

pre vail (pri VAIL) *v.* win out

proph e cy (PROF i see) *n.* statement telling what will happen in the future

pu ny (PYOO nee) *adj.* small and weak

pur sue (pur SOO) *v.* chase; follow after

quip (KWIP) *v.* make a witty remark *n.* witty remark

ran sack (RAN sak) *v.* search thoroughly through; rob

raz zle-daz zle (RAZ ul DAZ ul) *n.* glamour

rec om mend (rek uh MEND) *v.* suggest someone who would be good for a job

re gard (ri GARD) *v.* think about; consider

re pro duce (ree proh DOOS) *v.* copy

rep u ta tion (rep yuh TAY shun) *n.* idea that most people have of a person's character

re sent (ri ZENT) *v.* show anger because of hurt feelings

re solve (ree ZOLV) *v.* determine; decide

re treat (ree TREET) *n.* a quiet place for rest

rup tured (RUP churd) *adj.* torn or broken apart

scant y (SKAN tee) *adj.* not enough; less of

scorn (SKORN) *v.* have a low opinion of

scram ble (SKRAM bul) *v.* climb quickly up or down, often on one's hands and knees

sen ti ments (SEN tuh munts) *n.* feelings; emotions

ser pent (SUR punt) *n.* snake

sheep ish ly (SHEEP ish lee) *adv.* in an embarrassed way

shin ny (SHIN ee) *v.* climb by holding tight with one's arms and legs and drawing oneself up

shrill (SHRIL) *adj.* high and sharp in sound

shud der (SHUD ur) *v.* tremble; shake

sole (SOHL) *adj.* only

sol emn (SOL um) *adj.* very serious; not cheerful

spe cial ty (SPESH ul tee) *n.* something a person does well

steed (STEED) *n.* fine horse

steep (STEEP) *adj.* very expensive; costly

strain (STRAYN) *v.* cause to work as hard as possible

strat e gy (STRAT uh jee) *n.* skillful planning

strode (STROHD) *v.* walked; past tense of **stride**

sub stance (SUB stuns) *n.* the important part; the real part

sulk (SULK) *v.* be silent and bad-tempered

sus pend (sus PEND) *v.* hang by attachment to something above

swin dle (SWIN dul) *v.* cheat

sym bol ize (SIM bul YZ) *v.* be a sign or symbol of

teem ing (TEEM ing) *adj.* crowded and moving

the o ry (THEE uh ree) *n.* idea that is used to explain an event

tim id (TIM ud) *adj.* shy

ven ture (VEN chur) *v.* express with caution

vir tue (VUR choo) *n.* goodness

wheel (HWEEL) *v.* turn quickly

wings (WINGZ) *n.* areas to the right and left side of a stage

wit (WIT) *n.* understanding and intelligence

wretch ed (RECH id) *adj.* very unhappy; miserable

Index of Authors and Titles

Page numbers in **bold-faced** type indicate profiles (short biographies).

399

ACKNOWLEDGMENTS

We thank the following authors, agents, and publishers for their permission to reprint copyrighted material:

AMERICAN BROADCASTING COMPANIES—for permission to adapt "Blind Sunday" by Arthur Barron and Fred Pressburger. Copyright © 1976 by American Broadcasting Companies, Inc. Reprinted by permission of American Broadcasting Companies, Inc.

AMÉRICAS—for "Lather and Nothing Else" by Hernando Téllez. Reprinted from *Américas,* bimonthly magazine published in English and Spanish by the General Secretariat of the Organization of American States.

BANTAM BOOKS—for "Runaways," reprinted from *Runaways* by Elizabeth Swados. Copyright © 1979 Swados Enterprises, Inc. Reprinted by permission of Bantam Books, Inc. All rights reserved.

BRANDT & BRANDT LITERARY AGENTS, INC.—for "Western Wagons" by Rosemary and Stephen Vincent Benet, from *A Book of Americans.* Copyright 1933 by Rosemary and Stephen Vincent Benet. Copyright renewed © 1961 by Rosemary Carr Benet. Reprinted by permission of Brandt & Brandt Literary Agents, Inc.

CHAPPELL & CO., INC.—for "The House I Live In" by Earl Robinson and Lewis Allan. Copyright © 1942 by Chappell & Co., Inc. Copyright renewed. International copyright secured. All rights reserved. Used by permission.

DELACORTE PRESS—for excerpt from *Ingrid Bergman: My Story* by Ingrid Bergman and Alan Burgess. Copyright © 1980 by Ingrid Bergman and Alan Burgess. Reprinted by permission of Delacorte Press.

DODD, MEAD & COMPANY, INC.—for "The Finish of Patsy Barnes," from *The Strength of Gideon and Other Stories* by Paul Laurence Dunbar. Reprinted by permission of Dodd, Mead & Company, Inc.—for "Harriet Tubman, Liberator," adapted from *Famous Negro Heroes of America* by Langston Hughes. Copyright © 1958 by Langston Hughes. Reprinted by permission of Dodd, Mead & Company, Inc.

DOUBLEDAY & COMPANY, INC.—for "The Bat" by Theodore Roethke from *The Collected Poems of Theodore Roethke* by Theodore Roethke. Reprinted by permission of Doubleday & Company, Inc.

EDUCATION DEVELOPMENT CENTER, INC.—for "A Lesson in Sharing," from *Songs and Stories of the Netsilik Eskimos,* translated by Edward Field from text collected by Knud Rasmussen. Reprinted courtesy of Education Development Center, Inc., Newton, Massachusetts.

FABER AND FABER LTD.—for Canadian rights to "The Naming of Cats" by T. A. Eliot. Reprinted by permission of Faber and Faber Ltd. from *Old Possum's Book of Practical Cats* by T. S. Eliot.

ROBERT FROMAN—for "Puzzle," poem and illustration by Robert Froman, from *Street Poems.* Copyright © 1971. Originally published by The McCall Publishing Company.

GLOBE/MODERN CURRICULUM PRESS—for "The Ten-Armed Monster of Newfoundland" by Elma Schemenauer from *Yesterstories 2 (The Lost Lemon Mine).* Copyright © 1979. Adapted and reprinted by permission of Globe/Modern Curriculum Press.

ROBERT GRAVES—for "The Penny Fiddle" by Robert Graves, from *The Poor Boy Who Followed His Star.* Reprinted by permission of the author and A. P. Watt Ltd., Literary Agents.

HARCOURT BRACE JOVANOVICH, INC.—for "Fueled," from *Serve Me A Slice of Moon,* copyright © 1965 by Marcie Hans.—for "maggie and milly and molly and may" by e. e. cummings. Copyright 1956 by e. e. cummings. Reprinted from his volume *Complete Poems 1913–1963.*—for "Mama and Papa," adapted from *Mama's Bank Account,* copyright 1943 by Kathryn Forbes. Renewed 1971 by Richard E. McLean and Robert M. McLean.—for U.S. rights to "The Naming of Cats" from *Old Possum's Book of Practical Cats* by T. S. Eliot, copyright 1939 by T. S. Eliot; renewed 1967 by Esme Valerie Eliot. All selections reprinted by permission of Harcourt Brace Jovanovich, Inc.

HARPER & ROW, PUBLISHERS, INC.—for "Harriet Tubman" and "Things" (text only), from *Honey, I Love and Other Love Poems* by Eloise Greenfield (Thomas Y. Crowell). Copyright © 1978 by Eloise Greenfield.—for "Prairie Fire," adapted from *Little House on the Prairie* by Laura Ingalls Wilder. Copyright 1935 by Laura Ingalls Wilder; renewed 1963 by Roger L. MacBride.—for "Shoes for Hector," adapted from *El Bronx Remembered* by Nicholasa Mohr. Copyright © 1975 by Nicholasa Mohr.—for "The Unknown Color," page 12, from *Copper Sun* by Countee Cullen. Copyright 1927 by Harper & Row, Publishers, Inc. Renewed 1955 by Ida M. Cullen. All selections reprinted by permission of Harper & Row, Publishers, Inc.

HARVARD UNIVERSITY PRESS—for "Success is Counted Sweetest" by Emily Dickinson. Reprinted by permission of the publishers and the Trustees of Amherst College from *The Poems of Emily Dickinson,* edited by Thomas H. Johnson, Cambridge, Massachusetts: The Belknap Press of Harvard University Press, Copyright 1951, © 1955, 1979, 1983 by the President and Fellows of Harvard College.

HOLT, RINEHART AND WINSTON, PUBLISHERS—for "The Runaway" by Robert Frost, from *The Poetry of Robert Frost,* edited by Edward Connery Lathem. Copyright 1923, © 1969 by Holt, Rinehart and Winston. Copyright 1951 by Robert Frost.—for "The Secret Sits" by Robert Frost, from *The Poetry of Robert Frost,* edited by Edward Connery Lathem. Copyright 1916, © 1969 by Holt, Rinehart and Winston. Copyright 1942, 1944 by Robert Frost. Copyright © 1970 by Lesley Frost Ballantine.—for "The Great Sock Mystery," from *There's Nothing That I Wouldn't Do if You Would Be My Posslq* by Charles Osgood. Copyright © 1981 by CBS, Inc. All selections reprinted by permission of Holt, Rinehart and Winston, Publishers.

JAMES A. HOUSTON—for "Let Our Children Live and Be Happy," from *Songs of the Dream People,* edited and illustrated by James A. Houston. Published by Atheneum Publishers. (a Margaret K. McElderry Book) New York, 1972. Adapted by permission of the author.

JULIUS LESTER—for "The Man Who Was a Horse" by Julius Lester. Adapted and reprinted by permission of the author.

ROSE K. LIEBERMAN—for "I Am an American" by Elias Lieberman. Reprinted by permission of Rose K. Lieberman, Executrix of the estate of Elias Lieberman.

LITTLE, BROWN AND COMPANY—for "Dear Lovey Hart, I Am Desperate," adapted from the first two chapters of *Dear Lovey Hart, I Am Desperate* by Ellen Conford. Copyright © 1975 by Ellen Conford. Reprinted by permission of Little, Brown and Company.

MACMILLAN LONDON LTD—for Canadian rights to "Down by the Salley Gardens" from *Collected Poems of W. B. Yeats.* Reprinted by permission of Michael B. Yeats and the publisher.

MACMILLAN PUBLISHING COMPANY—for "Who Has Seen the Wind?" from *Sing-Song* by Christina G. Rossetti (New York: Macmillan, 1924)—for U.S. rights to "Down by the Salley Gardens" from *Collected Poems of W. B. Yeats,* (New York, Macmillan, 1956). Reprinted by permission of Macmillan Publishing Company.

ZOLTAN MALOCSAY—for "My Hero" by Zoltan Malocsay, from *Boy's Life,* June 1976. Adapted and reprinted by permission of the author.

ELLEN C. MASTERS—for "Hamilton Greene," from *Spoon River Anthology* by Edgar Lee Masters. Reprinted by permission of Ellen C. Masters.

MCINTOSH AND OTIS, INC.—for "The Case of the Blackmailer," from *Two-Minute Mysteries* by Donald J. Sobol. Copyright © 1967 by Donald J. Sobol. Published by Scholastic Book Services, a division of Scholastic Magazine, Inc. Reprinted by permission of McIntosh and Otis, Inc.

SCOTT MEREDITH LITERARY AGENCY, INC.—for "Ooka and the Stolen Smell," from *The Case of the Marble Monster* by I. G. Edmonds. Copyright © 1961 by I. G. Edmonds.—for permission to adapt "Prone" by Mack Reynold. Both stories reprinted by permission of the authors and the author's agent, Scott Meredith Literary Agency, Inc., 845 Third Avenue, New York, New York 10022.

HAROLD OBER ASSOCIATES, INC.—for the T.V. script of "The Big Wave" by Pearl S. Buck. Copyright 1947 by The Curtis Publishing Company. Copyright 1948 by Pearl S. Buck. Renewed. Copyright © 1958 by Pearl S. Buck.—for "Thicker Than Water" by Paul Gallico. Copyright 1944 by Crowell Collier Publishing Company. Copyright renewed 1972 by Paul Gallico. Both stories adapted and reprinted by permission of Harold Ober Associates, Inc.

PRENTICE-HALL, INC.—for "The Black Box," adapted from *The Black Box* by Albert B. Carr. Copyright © 1969 by Albert B. Carr and William Brooks. Published by Prentice-Hall, Inc., Englewood Cliffs, N. J. 07632. Reprinted by permission of Prentice-Hall, Inc.

QUARTERLY REVIEW OF LITERATURE—

for "A Campfire and Ants" by Alexander Solzhenitsyn from *Quarterly Review of Literature,* XVII, #1/2. Adapted and reprinted by permission of the *Quarterly Review of Literature.*

SHELDON PRESS—for "The Parable of the Eagle" by James Aggrey, from *Aggrey Said,* compiled by C. Kingsley Williams. Adapted by permission of Sheldon Press, London.

SIMON & SCHUSTER, INC.—for "The Butterfly and the Caterpillar" by Joseph Lauren. Copyright © 1957 by Pocket Books, Inc. Reprinted by permission of Pocket Books, a division of Simon & Schuster, Inc.—for "Lame Deer Remembers His Childhood," adapted from *Lame Deer, Seeker of Visions* by John Fire/Lame Deer and Richard Erdoes. Copyright © 1972 by John Fire/Lame Deer and Richard Erdoes. Reprinted by permission of Simon & Schuster, Inc.

ST. MARTIN'S PRESS, INC.—for "The First Day," from *Anything Can Happen* by George and Helen Papashvily. Copyright © 1945, 1973 by George and Helen Papashvily. Adapted by permission of St. Martin's Press, Inc., New York.

LARRY STERNIG LITERARY AGENCY—for "The Wolf of Thunder Mountain" by Dion Henderson. Copyright 1959 by the Boy Scouts of America. Adapted and reprinted by permission of Larry Sternig Literary Agency.

THE JESSE STUART FOUNDATION—for "Split Cherry Tree," from *The Best-Loved Short Stories of Jesse Stuart,* published by McGraw Hill, New York, 1982. Reprinted with the permission of The Jesse Stuart Foundation, Judy B. Dailey, Chair, P. O. Box 391, Ashland, Kentucky, 41114.

LINDA SCHECHET TUCKER—for "Amelia's Bloomers" by Linda Schechet Tucker. Adapted and reprinted by permission of the author.

VIKING PENGUIN INC.—for "Frontier Fighter," adapted from *American Tall Tales* by Adrien Stoutenberg. Copyright © 1966 by Adrien Stoutenberg.—for "The Open Window," from *The Complete Short Stories of Saki (H. H. Munro).* Copyright 1930, 1958 by The Viking Press, Inc. Both stories adapted by permission of Viking Penguin Inc.

HARVEY UNNA & STEPHEN DURBRIDGE LTD—for "Christmas Meeting" by Rosemary Timperley.

WALKER & COMPANY—for "The Kick," from *Fly Like an Eagle* by Elizabeth Van Steenwyk. Copyright © 1978. Adapted by permission of the publisher, Walker & Company.

YOUNG MISS—for "The Confidence Game," adapted from "The Confidence Game" by Pat Carr with permission of *Young Miss* Magazine. Copyright © 1977, Gruner & Jahr USA Publishing.

Every effort has been made to locate David Wadsworth Cannon, Jr. to obtain permission to reprint his poem "Western Town"; the heirs of Knud Rasmussen to obtain permission to reprint "A Lesson in Sharing" outside the U.S.; Leslie Jill Sokolow to obtain permission to adapt her story "Aqui se Habla Español." If any of these authors or their heirs are located subsequent to publication, they are hereby entitled to due compensation.

The following selections are from the public domain. Some have been adapted for the modern reader by Globe Book Company: Aesop, "The Substance and the Shadow"; Ambrose Bierce, "Staley Fleming's Hallucination"; Emily Dickinson, "Hope is the Thing With Feathers"; John Donne, "No Man Is an Island"; Frederick Douglass, "The Pathway from Slavery to Freedom," from *Narrative of the Life of Frederick Douglass, An American Slave;* Chief Joseph, "Chief Joseph's Surrender Speech"; Emma Lazarus, excerpt from "The New Colossus"; O. Henry, "The Kind of Man She Could Love," from the story "Lost on Dress Parade," from *The Four Million;* William Shakespeare, excerpt from *Othello;* Walt Whitman, "What Am I After All?" and excerpt from "Song of the Open Road," both from *Leaves of Grass.*

403

Acknowledgments

Photo Acknowledgments

Paul Conklin/ Monkmeyer: xii; The Schomberg Collection/ New York Public Library: 23; The Granger Collection: 26; Culver Pictures: 51, 84, 124; AP/Wide World Photos: 146; Int'l Stock Photo/Robin Schwartz 1982: 179; Photo Fest: 180; Culver Pictures: 202; Historical Pictures Service, Chicago: 206; Culver Pictures: 214 (above); The Schomberg Collection/ New York Public Library: 214(below); Frederick Lewis/George Chung: 245; Spencer Grant/Photo Researchers: 246; Westlight: 249, 251; Culver Pictures: 261; Historical Pictures Service, Chicago: 264; H. Armstrong Roberts: 269; Hamrick/The Image Bank: 272; Int'l Stock Photo: 317; Mark Antman/The Image Works: 318; Culver Pictures: 349, 365; Frost Publishing Group: 393.

Illustrators

Bill Angresano: 52, 53, 58, 326, 329, 331, 333; Virginia Arnold: 321, 322; Michael Bryant: 337, 338, 339; Ted Burwell: 67, 69, 75, 21, 223, 225, 286, 288, 289, 291; Bert Dodson: 3, 5; Alan Eitzen: 107, 109, 111; Julie Evans: 139, 141, 143; Jeff Fischer: 183, 185; Joseph Forte: 36, 37, 38, 297, 299, 300, 301, 316; Ken Hamilton: 46, 47, 117, 119; Eileen McKeating: 149, 150, 155, 157, 163, 166, 167, 171; Neal McPheeters: 209, 210, 211, 277, 279, 281; Linda Miyamoto: 367, 369, 373, 374, 381, 385, 388; Joanne Pappas: 354; Don Schlegel: 8, 9 ,13, 22, 96, 99, 100, 101, 102, 131, 134, 188, 190, 192, 306, 307, 310, 311; Clare Sieffert: 233, 235, 239, 240; Gerald Smith: 34, 256, 257, 340; Matthew Snow: 114, 115; Cindy Spenser: 89, 91, 93, 197,198, 358, 360; Jean and Mou-Sien Tseng: 346, 349; Kimanne Uhler: 60, 61, 63; Kevin Walter: 22.

404